First published in Great Britain in 2018 by
Carcanet Press Limited
Alliance House, 30 Cross Street,
Manchester, M2 7AQ
www.carcanet.co.uk

A CIP catalogue record for this book is
available from the British Library,
ISBN 978 1 78410 436 8

The publisher acknowledges financial assistance from Arts Council England.

Typeset in Great Britain by XL Publishing Services, Exmouth, Devon
Printed in Great Britain by SRP Ltd., Exeter, Devon

Against the Stream

Personal Terms VII

FREDERIC RAPHAEL was born in Chicago in 1931 and educated at Charterhouse and St John's College, Cambridge. His novels include *The Glittering Prizes* (1976), *A Double Life* (1993), *Coast to Coast* (1998) and *Fame and Fortune* (2007); he has also written short stories and biographies of Somerset Maugham and Byron. Frederic Raphael is a leading screenwriter, whose work includes the Academy Award-winning *Darling* (1965), *Two for the Road* (1967), *Far from the Madding Crowd* (1967), and the screenplay for Stanley Kubrick's last film, *Eyes Wide Shut* (1999). The first volume of *Personal Terms* was published by Carcanet in 2001, with subsequent volumes in 2004, 2006, 2008, 2011 and 2013. The *Times Literary Supplement* said, 'Aphoristic, lapidary and sumptuously reflective by turns, *Personal Terms* is a joy to read both for Raphael's prose and mental powers. It is a work of iridescent intelligence, seductive charm, urbane temper and unflagging delight…'

Also by Frederic Raphael from Carcanet

Frederic Raphael

AGAINST THE STREAM

Personal Terms 7

CARCANET

Contents

For Beetle, then, now, always.

Introduction

Kingsley Amis considered writers who had recourse to notebooks to be somewhat suspect. The implication was that writing secretly and solely for the author's own eyes smacked of, yes, playing with oneself. Philip Roth, whose best-known work, often as he may seek to rise above it, is *Portnoy's Complaint*, told me that he once tried to keep a notebook. He was unable to continue because he didn't know who his audience was. Unsurprisingly, his novels are often cast in the rhetorical, stand-up mode of a woeful comedian: they tend to be laments, accusations and confessions, in whatever variety of voices. Without an audience to play to, such a performer becomes self-conscious, then mute.

My notebooks have been compiled with no audience in mind. Until some twenty years ago, when Michael Schmidt became my Maecenas, it had never occurred to me to type out (some of) the always handwritten pages of these *carnets*. Their only intended purpose had been, and remains, to serve as a repository of specimens caught alive and, like Nabokov's lepidoptera, pinned on the page for later inspection. I have not reproduced in print my manuscript dreads and regrets. Unless comic or lyrical, like that expressed by Catullus in his verses, self-pity is nobody's business or pleasure. If the volumes in *Personal Terms* furnish an involuntary autobiography, they do so by depicting the world from my point of view: I am shaped – who is not? – by choice and chance. What I write may be inescapably 'me', not least when false, jejune or pretentious, but my subject is not myself.

A number of the characters described and plots outlined have served as the source of fiction, sometimes almost at once, quite often years later. Not a few of the people and events have lapsed entirely from my memory: Denys Gueroult, for instance, is among those whom I would swear I had never met, were they not penned in my private zoo. It may be that the tone which I imagined to be dispassionate will strike some people as unduly caustic. If so, so be it: I am not a camera, but – as these *carnets* prove – I am a pen. The moving finger writes differently from the clicking keys. Manuscript has a small affinity with drawing: the hand seems to think, and shape sentences, as well as the brain. When writers abandon handwriting, they lose something of their signature.

Our daughter Sarah was invited, as a very young artist, to paint the portrait of the retiring Master of Jesus College, Cambridge. From the very beginning, when she needed the money and the kudos, she disliked commissioned work; but she agreed to go to Cambridge and meet her proposed subject. After an exchange of courtesies, she suggested that it might be best if she first did a drawing of the sitter. 'To find out whether or not you can get a likeness, you mean?' 'No,' Sarah said, 'so you can see what you look like.' Had Graham Sutherland adopted the same procedure in portraying Winston Churchill, he might have been spared the trouble of completing the portrait, which was so true, at least from the artist's point of view, that Winston had it destroyed before it could become iconic.

Sarah compared portrait-painting with being an ant crawling with searching ubiquity all over the face of the sitter. Like Goya, what she saw she drew or painted, never mind whether the sitter liked it. *Mutatis mutandis*, I write on the same principle. What is *not* on show in these pages, in the way of protracted *états d'âme*, has been excised at the terse suggestion of my wife, the best in-house editor a man ever had. I make no apology for the tactlessness of my reportage. I have never regarded writing as a diplomatic career (or any kind of a career at all). It is too bad if anyone finds my sketches caricatural or 'unfair'; as Pontius Pilate said, '*Ho gegrapha gegrapha*': what I have written I have written.

Against the Stream

30.7.81. Maggie Jones began in the BBC as a copy-typist; now, producer of *Talking Heads*, she convokes celebrities by their first names. When, under her aegis, I was on the air with Denis (Healey) and Malcolm (Muggeridge), she told me that she and her 'feller' were going to be in the Dordogne during the summer, in a cottage close to Lagardelle. She called on Sunday and proposed coming for an early evening drink with Gerry Davis, an Old Carthusian, and his twenty-one-year-old son, Danny. Davis drove an off-white Cortina of the kind that companies allot to employees who can take it or leave. Shortish and muscular, in a red Adidas shirt, he was at Cambridge between 1950 and 1953, but remembered me from school; *moi non plus*. He rowed at Cambridge and swam at Charterhouse. Since they had been doing building work all afternoon, I was prompt to offer them the pool. Gerry said he preferred to get to know me first. 'Ambitious programme,' I said.

Maggie was carefully edited: hair low and regular, teeth white, oran-gey-red dress over a bathing suit she never revealed. Danny wore bovver boots, shapeless grey-brown trousers, khaki shirt he lowered, appre-hensively, over his sun-scorched back; cropped head, putty face with jutting, colourless lips, boxer's malleable nose. Neither Maggie nor his father addressed anything to him. Davis was a Bodeite; he said that he once shared a study with Brian Glanville.* Maggie gave an unassuming account of her career and interests: hot-air ballooning is her gas-filled bag. Danny said he was a mechanic and jazz guitarist. He took one of the bronze knights from Michael Ayrton's chess set and examined it with such close appreciation that I suspected he might pocket it.

Davis is a solicitor for Readicrete, one of a team of five resident lawyers at their Hindhead offices. He had towed one of their electric cement mixers down to the Périgord in order to add a car-port to his cottage. Danny went to test the pool, but returned dry; its kidney form inhibited him from doing lengths, so he chose not to take the plunge. He drank beers (posting his cigarette stub in an empty) and told Beetle, 'Bring the matches,' when we moved from the patio to the house. She did not hear him, she told me, or she would not have done so.

---

* Brian Glanville has no memory of sharing a study with him.

M.'s interest in ballooning arose from living in Bristol, a centre for it. She relishes going up with those making their maiden flight. There is something voyeuristic about women who revel, like brothel madams, in the initiation of others. I was reminded of John Cheever's story 'Torch Song', about a female angel of death. Ballooning is not very dangerous, she says; the pilots' greatest difficulty is landing in a wind. The basket may be bumped along the ground or the passengers spilled out. M. was dragged, on one occasion, through chicken wire. You have to watch out for electric cables; risk from aircraft is negligible; there are, she promised, no mechanical failures.

I suspected stored danger in G.D. and his son; Maggie just might be there to see the eruption. G. has the cocky chagrin of the separated man. He may not love M., but he has her. He is content to explain small things – cement does not dry, it *hardens* – as if expert jargon elevated a drab career. Never have visitors shown less interest in the place. The ascended copy-typist played the happy star of our small stage; Gerry appeared content that nothing violent or embarrassing should happen.*

2.8.81. A meaty little friar of the classics, Sullivan might as well wear a cassock, though his rope belt would sport no chastity knots. Apart from an old aunt in Liverpool and brother Denis in Australia, he has no family; without children, his line lacks a future. He assumes that people are like-able and that they like him. With little notion that there is anything risible about him, unless he relies on it, he has always presumed Scouse pawkiness to be endearing; 'if you don't mind' a characteristic civility. His feminism declares itself in the claim that the female superior position (common in Ovid's Rome) implies male deference; it allows the woman to 'control the action'. He favours louche company and drops the same names – Patrick Dromgoole and Xaviera Hollander – again and again. Sporting an honorary colonelcy in the ranks of Amazonia, he goes out of his way to attend feminist conferences. At one, he was reproached – 'Sir, you are taking up too much room' – for dancing expansively on a floor where, among fifty couples, he was the only man. His mother, he declares, was very fond of him.

Born in Texas, Judy spent her childhood in rural Kansas. She runs a kindergarten in Santa Barbara. She neither likes the parents nor enjoys the children. Now in her late thirties, she was first married when she

* I later read a story by John Updike in which a couple go to see the friend of one of them so that he may witness their happiness, however transitory. Maggie's romance did not endure: her chap's lady returned to him, as he may have planned.

was twenty-one. She calls Sullivan 'Johnpat'; you can hear the inverted commas. She has tan skin and wears cotton overall-type outfits. The glasses are rimless polygonic. No statement of opinion by anyone else passes unchallenged; even her agreement can be prefaced by denial. The nose is neat but prehensile; she is a sniffer out, not least of ungranted favours. J. is about to go to Oxford, as a fellow of Wolfson, to write his Martial book. With much research in prospect, he intends to go alone. At a loose end for three months, Judy proposes, *more Americano*, to spend them with friends. She asked why we lived so far from stations or airports. Beetle told her that it avoided uncalled-for visitors.

I was hoping to hear that, after a lacuna since the breach with Tony, Anne B. had consoled herself with some willowy William from the Foreign Office, or indeed the milkman, or anyone at all. She remains inconsolable; or at least unconsoled. The Sullivans refuse to take sides; indifference is all their kindness. Judy's failure to arrive on time at Bordeaux (her train was nine hours late from Portugal) did excite some conjugal anxiety – John called to ask '*sapete alcuna cosa di* Judy?' – but their *modus vivendi* is void of sentimental niceties. Judy so dislikes domesticity that they play a hand of poker to determine who will do the washing up. Every two weeks a gang of men arrives to 'deep-clean' the house.

Do scholars regularly make reference to ancillary texts which they have not fully scanned? Is the composition of fibliographies a common practice? When I informed G. Steiner that I could Xerox and send him the Greek text of Ritsos' *Ismene*, of which he could find no translation, he preferred that I synopsise its 'argument'.

J.P.S. told us that Kenneth Dover, in his original introduction to *Greek Homosexuality* (1978), referred to having been buggered by Maurice Bowra. Harvard U.P. was scandalised and insisted that the confession be deleted.

John's friend Brad, a huge ex-football star, dropped some LSD and took a walk. He was held up by two muggers who demanded 'all your money, NOW!' Dwelling on the demand for immediate delivery of *all* his money, he itemised the difficulties in the way of instant compliance: most of his cash was in the bank; he would have to go get his chequebook; his house was jointly owned with someone who was out of the country; it would take a while to put it up for sale and realise the money; his belongings would need some time to sell, etcetera. The protracted literal-mindedness unnerved his attackers. 'I don't know what the guy is on,' one said to the other, 'but he's sure higher than high on something.' And off they went.

Life and Loves. Having assisted in the rescue of a man off Noah's Long Island home, Jason and his brother have a feeling of renewed and justified conceit. Jason and Susie and their children are visiting the older Noah and Miriam. The saved man comes to the house with the brothers. When his alarmed mistress arrives, she is indignant at finding him in relaxed good spirits. She has been so worried that the pair come to blows. We cut to Jason and Susie driving back to the big city, seemingly reconciled by their amusement. Then, in Voice Over, as the car moves away from us, onto the bridge into Manhattan, we mix to the quarrel which will precede her leaving him.

J.P.S. refers, with regret, to our old tutor Renford Bambrough having become 'right-wing'. John remains cautiously loyal, the caution partly sentimental, partly politic. Renford will always be the man who taught him Greek prose composition. Judy holds that R. is a 'closet roué'. If so, it is probably in a closet for one.

Life and Loves. Jason is revealed not to be the son of the father whom he goes to see in the Retirement Compound; that he is no more than Noah's half-brother is both relief and divorce. His mother Gertrude's insistence on living her own life comes home to him in his alarm at Susie's appetite for independence. This declares itself in an attack on his mother's 'extortionate' black lover. When he tells Gertrude that she shares the latter's favours with someone else, she says 'We all share people with other people, don't we?' Knowledge of his true paternity prompts Jason's affectionate return to the bedside of his dying nominal father. Sympathy is readier when it can be a performance.

John says that he first went to the US because it was the quickest way to secure a divorce from Mary. He still sees his pretty, dark-haired second wife ('Judy Sullivan'). Married to a realtor, she lives in Buffalo. While bruised by her defection, he makes light of it, as he does of most things; and wishes that others would. He has since been in a lot of beds. He insists that Irish blood explains his capacity to absorb alcohol without impairing his wits; but a weary undertone, when he boasts of his workload, suggests that his brain is paying pickled taxes.

12.8.81. Patrick, Jilly and Emma Sergeant have just left. The contrast with our other summer visitors, Tony Smith and Shirley Williams, lends charm to the Sergeants. Shirley, a wife without a husband, fearful of the flesh, but not short of it, punishes herself with a self-denying diet and runs about in bursts of energetic pointlessness. Smith is the director of the British Film Institute; a grey man, just into his forties, he has been a Fellow of St Anthony's. On the fringes of smartness without being smart, he has some sort of an important job without marked importance. His publications, on communication theory, supply him with credentials, never fame. He wore rather elegant, or elegantly intended, new clothes; they might have looked elegant on someone.

According to a recent poll, Shirley's portmanteau party is still holding forty-three percent of the votes. Roy Jenkins' resounding victory at Warrington suggests that he will probably be Prime Minister, should the 'swing to the centre' be maintained. Shirley has the unflinching tolerance of a woman who will give you the time of day so long as she never has to alter her clock. When the deputy High Mistress of St Paul's begged her, almost tearfully, not to destroy the Grammar Schools, it served only to hold her to her guns: enemies are to be appeased, friends denied. The levelled world they claim to want is one in which they would never live without a measure of dissidence.

Shirley invited herself to Lagardelle. We were assumed to be flattered. She has the 'lumping in' style of the good (and persistent) guest. She brought carefully weighted gifts: English biscuits, marmalade for Stee. One morning she even made his bed. If she winced at luxuries – why did we need two swimming pools? – it was because she feared what others might think if she were found to have wallowed uncritically in them. She was willing, in her calculating heart, to put us down rather than compromise herself in the eyes of those in whose houses she would never seek to be a guest.

Politicians of the Left frown at what comforts them and are wary of those with whom they are most at ease. Advocating a society in which they are likely to be less comfortable than at present, their pleasure is to moralise rather than to live.

13.8. 81. I fell out with Shirley over the integrity of the IBA Board. She and Master Smith claimed to know what could have happened better than I knew what actually did. Reiteration of the facts was necessary, with specific detail, before their prejudice – identical with their pride – could be dented. Crusty with the lichen of office, Shirley challenged my account of the part played by Lord Thomson on the old Tory grounds that she had 'known him for thirty years' during which he had repulsed countless opportunities to enrich himself. Did it follow that he was incapable of the intimidation of which I observed him to be guilty? Dislike of losing, or being crossed, need not have anything to do with money. Glorying in being privy to the machinery of appointments, Shirlet and Smith were disinclined to conceive of unworthy motives *chez le gratin*. Her benevolence is without remorse; I should not care to be at her monitorial mercy.

The egotist does only what is best for him; he spares us the prig's confidence that she knows what is best for others.

Patrick and Jilly had been kind to Sarah; Patrick has often played host to me, after tennis in Highgate; we felt an obligation. Four days seemed a long time to talk to strangers. The morning of their scheduled arrival, *il tombait des cordes*. The house was lachrymose with leaks, the guest flat awash after an uncured deluge from the roof of the little pool. We faced the prospect of an indoor life with outdoor people: the tennis court was the only place where we had expected easy conversation. As they arrived, the weather cleared. They proved excellent guests, as generous in taking as in giving. How mature Tony and Shirley had been and how superficial Patrick was by comparison; yet how much more alive he and Jilly were, and how very much more amusing!

P. has now abandoned Maggie Thatcher in whose company, he was peacock-pleased to declare, he had spent a candid hour on the previous Thursday. I recall that he jettisoned Jim Slater with similar abruptness. Thatcher has not succeeded and he will not pretend otherwise. The fun of being a journalist was to be of help to one's friends; who can help those incapable of helping themselves? Patrick thinks of sixty thousand pounds a year as no more than a decent screw for his 'young men'. He travels first-class, even to Bordeaux, and likes to be recognised. He was not pleased to be called 'Mr Patrick' (his bag being labelled Sergeant, Patrick) in the VIP lounge.

Jilly has money of her own and a tongue – made tarter by the South African accent – which Sarah has incited her to use. Jilly has no plans for her own escape from the Highgate doll's house, but she has subsidised Emma's. Drink is a happy feature of their diet; Jilly claims to need the sugar to power her forehand; she proves that she has conquered her dependence by limiting it to white wine; it's the ice, she says, that makes her tipsy. Patrick takes whisky and soda in a beer mug. He was warned by his fond and faithful wife against becoming 'as fat as an old eunuch'.

15.8.81. Patrick had a Jewish mother who converted to Catholicism. Since, at the time, both the girls had Jewish boyfriends, they were thrilled to learn of the Semitic skeleton in the family cupboard. Shaped more by war service in the navy than by ancestral connection, P. was pleased to tell an old story, about the American aviator brought down by British fire, which ended with the tag 'You shouldn't have joined, mate, if you can't take a joke!' His father, well over eighty and blind, is contemplating a third marriage. His last wife was thirty years younger than he. On the Monday she seemed in excellent health; on the Friday she was dead; her husband blind. He lost his sight at the shock of her death, though there were medical reasons for it (diabetes?) which could have been diagnosed. Patrick goes for a check-up every six months, an alternative to abstemiousness. His father's latest lady is a Jehovah's Witness. He has consented to conversion, even though he is known to say, 'Every woman is delightful and different and every wife is always a terror and the same'.

17.8.81. Peter Nichols called, just as we were sitting down to lunch with the departing Rubinsteins: could they drop in on their way north? They have not yet sold their place near Ribérac. Thelma has been an art teacher; a shortish, plump, dark woman with large eyes, she notices more than she chooses to declare. P. does the talking; she does the thinking. With Ken McLeish's inclination to believe that working-class origins warrant a ticket to sympathy, Peter hurries to display social stigmata. They have been to stay with Hal Prince on Mallorca. They were there for a fortnight ('We soon learned to say "two weeks"'). Last year they had a lot more fun. This time they were swamped by the New York rat-a-tat of Adolph Green and Betty Comden and Harry Grossman, the composer, who were working with Hal P. on a musical based on what happened to Norah after she walked out of the Doll's House; women's lib and sugar.

Hal has in common with Alan Pakula the fastidiousness which abandons specific identity in favour of dandyism. He has become rich as a result of the unlikely theatrical success of *Evita*. Despite his staging genius, he shows little aptitude for film; Ken Russell is to direct the screen version. Hal is married to a girl/woman called Judy, née Chaplin, California-raised daughter of Sol Chaplin, a musician. She knew everybody from way back. Peter conjured her up with an explosion of black hair and ebullient smartness. He sees her as wasted in the hermetic luxury of the gilded ghetto in which successful New Yorkers are content to live. P. is intrigued by their sophisticated emptiness. He says that after the wisecracking smartness of their opening sallies, such people reduce everything to snappy formulae.

Nichols and Thelma had stayed overnight in Nice where they bumped into Bryan Forbes and Maggie Smith and who all else at the Hyatt Regency on the *Promenade des Anglais*. B.F. is directing a movie called *Ménage à Trois*, with David Niven. People are afraid no one will understand the title. P.N. did not know Bryan, but introduced himself, brazen with the confidence of his successes, *Passion Play* the latest. He harbours grievances, especially vis-à-vis the BBC. Mark Shivas commissioned a mini-series which was abruptly terminated when Jim Cellan Jones took over. I remembered (and did not say) that Mark had found the scripts disappointing. Peter had taken routine acknowledgement of the episodes as they were delivered as an earnest of enthusiasm. He attaches inflated significance to the decorum of a class to which he claims to be glad not to belong.

He has little time for the Social Democratic Party; a more 'radical' solution is needed for England's malaise, though he cannot articulate what it might be. He made play with the need to shoot a few people when a left-wing government achieves power. Yet he had small confidence that such executions would procure either happiness or justice. Without specifying who the scapegoats should be, he was happy to contemplate their fate. Demanding to be told why the violence of the Left was so much more deprecated than that of the Right, he was close to arguing that the Bennites would establish their credibility only by claiming a few, or several, victims to balance those (of what date?) already sacrificed by the Tories.

Dismissive of the intelligence of actors, P. himself is a performer more likely to hold your attention while impersonating others than *in propria persona*. In repose, he takes on a lugubrious aspect, more the condemned man than someone apt to lobby celebrities in grand hotels. Thelma asked Beetle how old I was, because P. looked so much older. He is fifty-four, an about-to-be-pot-bellied, high-shouldered, busy man with slim shanks and a cropped grey head. Prognathous, with village graveyard teeth, he is at once entertaining and unappealing. He is married to a lively woman who almost identifies herself with his work. She supplies communiqués with enthusiastic uneasiness. He is writing a pantomime for the Royal Shakespeare Company, about the Opium Wars, in which Dick Whittington's great-grandson plays some part. I can wait.

P. and T. were once the Frayns' best friends. They used to visit frequently. Michael, the eager host, always on the balls of his feet, believed in domestic democracy: protracted debate preceded commonplace decisions, such as whether to go for a walk. Reason served in the office of impersonal authority. Though Frayn was courteous and articulate, many things were not said between them. He looks like a 'strained corpse', P. says; he should know. Something disturbed their friendship before M.'s break with normality. The Frayns once called P. and T. from Biarritz, wanting to come and stay at Ribérac for a few days. The Nicholses responded that the house was full, although it was not. Peter envies Michael's worldliness; he assumed it to be a Cambridge habit to solicit addresses and introductions from one's friends.

P. and T. were happy to take whatever was available in the way of dinner and a bed, quite as if it were the beginning of a warm relationship. I do not expect to get to know them well; no closeness is likely between P. and me. There is pain beneath the jokey mimicry: he was good as Christopher Morahan, whom they had introduced to his present wife, thinking she might be suitable for C.'s oldest son. P.'s work is founded on sorry experience. He re-opens cupboards like a housewife with a dwindling larder who is afraid she may never get to the shops. Determined to extract every possible laugh from its painful preservation, he hoards his potted past. Yet he scarcely controls his laughter at Thelma's Welsh father, who refers to the Champs Elysées as 'the shambles easy'. P. thinks of going to America because of the largeness he sees there; Broadway opportunities cannot banish doubts about whether he could become American, 'though millions have'. Fretted by the grieving chain stamped Made in England, he is a kennelled talent. As he sniffs the far horizon, his glum larkiness mantles incurable parochialism.

Life and Loves. Jason goes alone to dinner with the young couple with whom he has become friendly and whose marriage he has idealised. He tells them of his fantasy of advertising for a woman who will be his mistress, solely for sex and with a view (unlike those matter-of-fact sentimentalists in the *New York Review of Books*) to nothing but fucking. A few days later, the 'innocent' Maria calls and offers to perform that role. She must have appeared to be bright and sensitive, pretty and of a quasi-virginal fastidiousness.

19.8.81. To insist on other people being happy is a form of selfishness; when they have nothing to complain about, they will have no excuse for not listening to me.

How unnerving the angry bombs in everyone's luggage! We hear the tick and stand away from the suspect traveller, clutching our own undisclosed tragedies and grievances like contraband treasures.

20.8.81. As we veer towards death, solitude settles on us like grave clothes, never to be changed or doffed.

Deprived of the 'h' on my typewriter, I am like a runner with a small, sharp pebble in his shoe.

Helge Rubinstein upholds the institution of marriage by sedulous service as a counsellor. She confesses to wondering, sometimes, whether she would ever have started a family had the pill been available in her day. She takes instruction from Hilary, quite as if she had once been his secretary, but there is a small rebellion in her resolve to learn how to play tennis properly: coaching revives her body even as Hilary's declines. They asked us – it was a kind of election – whether we would consider going walking with them in January in the mountains of Nepal. Beetle thinks Hilary doesn't like her and is pretty sure that she doesn't like him. Recalling V.G.'s office, she has H. down for a bully, though he is always cordial with us.

I prefer to play the host. It required effort to allow Patrick to take us to lunch at Domme. I made sure to be lavish with the flow of wine at other meals. I never cared about money until I began to have some. During days of unworthy work, I am driven to accumulate more and more, the better to penalise myself by lavishing it on others.

24.8.81. On Friday evening, when I was expecting California, Zara Steiner called. Ken (she called him 'McLeish') had collapsed in Greece and been taken to hospital in Athens. The English telephone people were unable to give her the number; no one could read Greek script. I obtained it, with small difficulty, from the French. The Athenian hospital officials were kind and articulate: *bebaios* I could to speak to Ken. Sedated if scarcely sedate, he said there was a brain surgeon at hand. He had fantasies of impending surgery, even though the doctor to whom I spoke assured me that there was *tipote* wrong with his *kardia* or his *kephali*.

Ken had been at Delphi where he and George Steiner had found each other congenial. G.'s imminent lecture made him so nervous that the two of them had a bibulous lunch in the heat. G.'s performance was literally stunning: at its climax, Ken keeled over. Steiner's vatic delivery seemed to have laid him out. Tests discovered his condition to have its source in a car accident in Mallorca twenty-two years ago. Ken's spinal column had been forced upwards by the thumping shock. The impact created a small pocket at the base of the skull, which filled with fluid. Delphic heat caused the fluid to expand, putting pressure on the brain, from which the other symptoms derived. Might it be that the anguish which K. has suffered 'from his nerves' has a physiological source? It is typical of the insular notion that 'character' determines conduct that no NHS medic has proposed a thorough physical examination. All K.'s doctors had prescribed drugs to treat a 'psychological' condition susceptible of practical remedy. He is scheduled to travel to London with a medical dossier prepared by the Greeks, on which the NHS may be persuaded to act. He never delivered his lecture on tragedy, but he has been wheeled out as a pundit by the left-wing Greek press: they declare it a scandal that, when a *savant* was taken ill at Delphi, there was no machinery for treating him (or anyone else) nearer than the capital.

After Ken passed out, at the end of George's *tour de force*, he was asked whether he had not had too much sun. His whispered response: 'No. Too much Steiner'. He was semi-unconscious for two hours. They thought he had had a heart attack. George names Geoffrey Kirk the calm hero of the hour. There was no ambulance in Delphi and no cardiogram at Livadia, where Ken had been taken in a private car. Kirk showed officer-like qualities in commanding a helicopter to lift the distinguished Hellenist to Athens.

On Ken's account, he and Steiner had had a rare meeting of minds; but this evening G. was scathing. Due to excess traffic on the M4, Ken had missed the plane that carried the other symposiasts to Athens. He was out of his depth, socially, from the moment he arrived in Delphi. When not 'behaving childishly', he was intellectually 'lightweight'. Taken ill, he panicked, cried like a baby, refused the simplest treatment. Does Ken merit so spiteful and premature an obituary? G.'s gleeful recital had a brutality which I was powerless to negate, not having been there. Like many academics and pedagogues, Ken is no stranger to bluff, but he has a rare breadth of reading and synthetic culture; his musical knowledge and Hellenic proficiency certainly trump George's.

Ken and P. Nichols carry their 'working-class' origins (hardly proletarian) as if at once a garland and a cross; gaucherie is their certificate of being in the right. A Jew or an American will be quick to change accent, posture and attitudes as he achieves wealth or fame or status. Nichols is forever amassing reparations for his deprived past. After proposing themselves for dinner, and having been quick to stay the night, neither has had the routine politeness – so middle-class! – to drop us a card of thanks. As they left, Thelma said, 'Perhaps we shall see you at Beaumont'.* It might have been civil to suggest, if never to mean, that we take tea with them at their house. P.'s grievances are an insurance against having to honour social graces. It suits him, as it does Ken, to play the class inferior: it allows for there being courtesies he need not observe.

27.8.81. Ken has returned to England unable to sit or stand without falling over. His brother-in-law to be, who had never seen him before, says that the symptoms could be those of a stroke, despite the absence of aphasia or paralysis. This morning, Stanley Baron called and mentioned that K. had written to say that he and I were ready to proceed with the Greek book. I never endorsed any such *démarche*. K. must need to bank whatever commissions he can procure; his present condition is made doubly fragile on account of the cash he had to find, and will continue to need, as a result of the move from Lincoln because his children were bullied at school. He now has double-vision and will be unable to work for at least ten days. He has acquired a taste for junkets and talks of going to a classical conference in Oslo in October.

Robin Jordan came to the Queen Elizabeth Hall just before my Byron show with Alan Bates and asked for my autograph like a stranger, sly fellow. Having fallen into his trap, I recovered wryly. He offered me the kisses of his new Argentinian Jewish wife who, he said, volunteered them to wish me luck. She was about thirty, sharp-featured but pretty, with brownish-red hair and a complaisance which seems to R.'s taste. Now lean and without precise nationality, he survives in the gutter like a rat who is also a dandy. They live in Florida.†

28.8.81. Shirley discerned a tragic figure in Sir Keith Joseph, a man who has reasoned himself into isolation and despair. She liked and respected him when he was Minister of Health. He believed in public service, cared nothing for self-advancement. He had the brains, if never the wit, to

---

* We first met them, a few years earlier, when he walked over to our table at Popaul's restaurant at the Hôtel des Voyageurs in Beaumont and came up with the winning line 'Didn't you use to be Frederic Raphael?' His flattering friendliness soon proved to be purposeful: he wanted to quiz me about how to deal with Mark Shivas.

† I was in the same house at Charterhouse with Jordan, J.F.R. He was awarded a 'closed' scholarship to Christchurch College, Oxford, for which I was barred from competing by the Charterhouse headmaster on account of my unChristian conduct in abusing a visiting preacher for vilifying Jews. I never saw or heard from Robin again.

make himself liked and respected. By pure cerebration, he moved from the concerned left to the ideological right of the Tory spectrum. He came to believe that he would better serve party and country by abandoning compromise. Convinced that monetarism and honesty were synonyms, unsmiling determination made him the ally, even the evil genius, in certain eyes, of Mrs Thatcher. He had been married for many years to a hard, capable woman who left him during the first days of the Thatcher government.

Donning the hairiest shirts as earnest of his earnestness, he became a zealot. He addressed meetings all over the country, having announced the titles of talks calculated to aggravate students and infuriate Trades Unionists. As Secretary for Trade and Industry, a kind and intelligent man has turned himself into a paragon of intransigence. He believes his position to be logically impregnable and that he is the only sane man in the asylum. Yet he has been cozened into funding British Leyland almost to the exclusion of any other industry. The rigour of his discourse has won him neither the applause of his party nor the gratitude of the BL workforce. He is accused of tightfistedness when, in terms of actual cash dispensed, he has given away no less than his spendthrift predecessor. He has made himself the scapegoat for a policy in which he may well believe but lacks the two-facedness to implement.

29.8.81. Burt Weissbord reports that John Schlesinger's *Honkytonk Freeway* has opened in sixty cities and took an average of $1,500 over the holiday weekend. No more than twenty people are likely to have attended any performance. J. spent twenty million dollars of Universal's money on a confection which did not even have any pretensions. Blaming 'the Americans' for a failure which they alone had the funds and foolhardiness to sponsor, he has sworn never to make another film in the US. Paramount, his old friends, have been the first to dump him. Were I the tycoon *du jour*, I should make him an offer, however modest, he would have difficulty refusing. A flop from such a talent can be a good sign for those who have not invested in it: John can only go up from here.

I idealise females because I never went to school with any of them.

Arnold Wesker's lamentations are again *à la une* in the *Sunday Times*. Did the RSC actors have no right to dismay when offered unperformable parts in *The Journalists*? A.'s complacency is revealed not so much by his sentiments as by the clichés in which they are voiced. He boasts of 'twenty-five years of being a playwright' rather as shops in Beverly Hills announce that they have been there since the day before yesterday.

On the Contrary. The necessity of Prometheus: ruling circles have to be subverted. For even a divine society to be articulate, it had better allow room for what disconcerts it.

3.9.81. John Schlesinger asked that we send *A New Wife* to Paramount because of his close friendship with Barry Diller. Rejecting the package, Paramount let it be known that they would be glad to see anything I wanted to do next. John is so mortified that he will not agree to the script going anywhere else with his name attached. We have become reconciled at the one moment in the last fifteen years in which he has no cachet whatever: inverted opportunism. What kind of a rat swims towards a sinking ship?

5.9.81. Only gods speak safely in the future tense.

The representation of Oedipus as a *tyrannos* brought low by an inadvertent 'sin' is of a man not entitled to privacy, the theatrical paradigm. The drama-king, Dionysos enacts his personal *agon*; the god motoring his own machine.

Sartre made 'good faith' dependent on conscious choice, itself a performance, hence inauthentic.

8.9.81. In Cahors. A woman in a wrap-around skirt walking in the hot street towards the post office was caught by a gust of wind. It blew the skirt up from white and shapely legs; unspoiled flesh against the used face above the clothes. I nearly said '*jolies jambes*', just to give her pleasure; then I heard that English voice and its freight of joylessness.

13.10.81. Paros, Mykonos, Ios. The wave of tourism, like tepid lava, has carried plastic and cheap glass to previously secret corners. A plastic lavatory seat was the submarine treasure on the public beach at Mykonos where we once bathed alongside the Steinbecks (not that he ever swam). The new charm of Ios at sea level lies in the pretty girls who spread themselves naked in the sun. Lack of shame baffles furtive curiosity: who can spy on what is blatantly offered? Naked males dangle their egos with unlovely obstinacy. A trio of Germans took too much sun on their first day and were scorched like unbasted joints. Burnt here, blanched there, they veiled their afflicted – never their sexual – parts with bits of silly clothing: socks, a little hat, a pair of shorts.

On the last morning, on the way to the Olympeion, I went into a small antique shop selling the kind of copper and brass Byron might have seen. The bearded proprietor looked at me and said, 'You have translated the great tragedies? Aeschylus rather than Sophocles?' That intuitive sense of a stranger's personality used to be common *chez* the Greeks; it is rare in a Hellas full of money and of regret, almost, for what it has cost.

Waiting on the quay for the Naias on Mykonos, a pretty girl, no more than nineteen, with her baby. She was with a couple, the man grey-curled, the woman well-preserved; perhaps the child's grandparents. The absence of an obvious father for the child recalled an old idea of mine about a couple who kill their unwanted or sick infant, on an island in a foreign country. They are obliged forever to wander from one place to another. If they settle, and have to establish their identity, there may be inquiries about what happened to the infant. As long as they keep moving, no one will do anything but take their money; a father and his daughter, it might be, who live in fugitive isolation.

16.10.81. Schlesinger wants to pursue an idea I suggested over a year ago, about the Lucan affair. His Lordship was said by Aspinall to be a born 'leader of men'; did he ever lead anyone further than the bar or do anything more noble than be born? Dandified coteries who take exception to social change, and are bonded by corrupt chivalry, recur in societies in which wealth is no longer increasing in the wallets of those cradled in its expectation. Resentment and snobbery are common neighbours, as Maurice Cowling's sour candour concedes. How about the juxtaposition of a Lucan and a Kagan, both lords, both on the run, obliged to disguise themselves as a homosexual duo, two men who both need and despise each other; a murderer and a finagler who has disgraced the ermine he never deserved? Imagine Lucan obliged to circumcision in order to qualify for asylum in Israel. Can it be worth it to an anti-Semitic prig to stay immune at the price of being a Jew?

The second anniversary of my father's death. The most memorable thing he ever said to me was 'It doesn't much matter who you marry'. He seemed dedicated to the beautiful woman he had been bold enough to capture; yet he could deliver himself of that cold remark. With his post-war bowler and brolly, he appeared so English that I tended to forget how much he liked America and all that 1930s jazz. Back in England, fidelity – to Irene and to Shell – seemed, like Adamson's pin-stripes, to suit him perfectly. His gambling was as restrained as it was habitual. He always termed it 'investment'. Had some millionaire (his uncle Jessel for instance) left him a fortune, he would not have reflected for a second on the justice of inheritance or the putative claims of others. He was a fortune-hunter with no fortune. Because I was his only son,* I had the idea that I must be important to him.

18.10.81. On her way home to England towards the end of the war, travelling on a Portuguese ship, S. and her friend were pursued by sailors who intended to rape them. They 'had their trousers down' when somehow the girls managed to get away and were chased around the deck. Eventually, they hid in the men's lavatories, the one place no one expected to find them, and crawled out when it was dark. They then concealed themselves under the tarpaulin of a lifeboat. When they reached Lisbon, they were interned, for days or weeks, by the Portuguese authorities. S. was terrified of men for some time thereafter. She particularly feared being alone with her father; she always wanted her mother to come and say goodnight to her at the same time. I believe that her brother, who later rather wasted his life, was also on the ship.

At the end of my BUPA check-up, I had a reassuring meeting with a Dr Isaacs, a bald Welsh physician with goggle eyes. Qualified since the age of twenty-one, he cheerfully laments never having had anything but responsibilities. He feels cheated of his life. Integrity makes us wish for duplicity. His son is a double First and a brilliant lawyer. He seemed surprised when, having been asked about my children, I told him that they were wonderful.

A cousin of his was murdered about a month ago, in Swansea. He was walking to *shul* on a Saturday morning, a clever and nice man, with his three children, when they were rammed by a man in a car. Dr Isaacs' cousin's legs were broken. While he lay in the street, the driver got out and stabbed him seventeen times, under the eyes of his children. He died on the way to hospital. A taxi-driver saw what had happened and followed the killer, radioing for assistance as he went. When caught, the murderer proved to be a German called Neumann.

Isaacs said that he had never been bothered by the sight of blood since the days when he took chickens to the kosher slaughterers and stayed behind, as if for a treat, to see the sheep killed. He mentioned with clinical clarity that his cousin had a severed aorta. He was forty-one. Isaacs' gleaming good humour was all but unchanged by the story he told. He

---

* My manuscript has 'child' where I have substituted 'son', since my father did indeed have another child, the illegitimate daughter, Sheila. The discovery of her existence and her arrival in London did nothing but embarrass him.

accepts the absurdity of life. Less interested in reasons than remedies, he congratulated me on my physique, as if I had kept a second-hand car in sound running order.

After the Byron film was transmitted, another Isaacs got in touch with me, Tony, of the BBC *World About Us* team, which he captains. He wanted me to front a clutch of programmes about South America which he is having prepared. I was tempted, as so often, because I was asked. Why reject the chance to have access to the 'best' people in six such countries? (I am not that easily had: I turned down four films during my fortnight in London.) Asked whether I spoke Spanish, I answered, with evasive honesty, that I had no Portuguese.

I drove up to Cambridge for dinner with the Steiners. I had hired a Ford Fiesta at Heathrow. I parked it all day in rainy London. When I went back to it, I failed to notice that the driver's seat was wet from leaks in the roof. By the time I arrived in Cambridge, my trousers were soaked. I was spared the comedy of sporting George's spare pants (my father would have said 'bags') by the loan of a sumptuous cowled robe which Zara had bought in California. We had a poor, generous meal, and watched the slow second episode of *Brideshead Revisited*. As the end titles rolled, I said, 'Let me know when it starts'.

The western powers are more powerful than they care to acknowledge; to admit their superiority might oblige them to exercise it.

Wandering through the familiar and unfamiliar streets of Cambridge, I was filled less with nostalgia than with the apprehensions which G. had installed. A coward without a visible enemy, I had no appetite for books or goods. I might have been a ghost; the city walked through me. I left late, reluctant to arrive too soon at the McLeishes, hoping for some consolatory encounter. Valerie had sent directions, but no indication of the distance between one landmark and the next. I drove and drove across the flat landscape. Farmers' harrows had scored the only marked distinctions. Autumn was a flat dish, brimmed with light. The grey exclamation mark of a church spire or the low excavation of a rivulet, fat with sun-hammered water, as if somewhere a flood was giving notice, provided the only punctuation. Villages were indicated, left and right, rarely traversed. The road bent and then straightened, often for a league or more. It was surprising to see how many people inhabited this undecked barge of peat sitting on a buried ocean. There is no bottom to many of the fens. Tractors can sink and sink to unplumbed depths and never be recovered.

The drive to Holbeach St John took an hour and a half. I had to cross a wide ditch, on a concrete slab of a bridge, before I found myself in a cluster of new houses, a quasi-suburban Close in the breadth of the country. The McL. house was on the left, where the buildings were less new. It is their first detached residence, bigger than their place in Hewson Road, Lincoln, but with fewer rooms; they plan to build an annex. Green sleeves of land trail behind the house and girdle it with apparent largeness. The long garden, with its elevated lily-pond, is richly loamed; the spinach was fat, as if engorged with green blood. A neighbour keeps his pony in the paddock at the far end. Its manure is thrown, smelly bonus, onto adjacent gardens, tipping the blackish earth with fertile pungency. Almost anything will grow here. K. and V. do not know what will come up next and wonder if they will have the knowledge to cultivate it.

The neighbours are friendly. When K. was in hospital, one of them, seeing V. putting up curtains whose ends failed to meet, offered to lend her money. Another, said to be very nice, is a Pole with – why did Ken tell me? – overt anti-Semitic credentials. The house was white-plastered; it might have belonged to a jobbing builder. The furniture sat about like conscripts waiting for assignment. The books on the shelves were still in bales. There was a folded ladder in the upstairs loo. I took them a Wok as a housewarming present.

3.11.81. K. was large, fattened on his back, a measure of apology in his careful shyness. We were new acquaintances on that account. He moved easily enough about the little house (there was always something near enough to lean on), but took a stick when we went into the garden. Reprieved, he is still under sentence, for life. V. gave us an excellent lunch, including purée of swedes, homemade and colourful. She has lost weight and gained confidence. It is hard to believe that she is younger than I am; she has the middle-aged resignation of the provincial school-teacher, obliged both to endurance and to insecurity. K. is now able to do most things, but not for long. He cannot put one foot directly in front of the other, as if on a tight rope, without falling over. It might not be difficult to get through life without indulging in such a manoeuvre, but something is fused in his brain and unlikely to be mended. He can work for no more than an hour a day and cannot read at all; a poor look-out for a journeyman of limited fame whose main weapon has been speed of performance. He never commanded big fees, but he could always hope for regular work. Having no capital, he must generate income through the accumulation of pages.

George labels him my 'evil genius'. K. is neither evil nor, I fear, a genius. G. claims that he behaves like a parody of me; he is inclined to frivolity or playfulness beyond his means. Steiner makes a system of his own ambition: because grandiloquent and domineering, it has to be adult and worthwhile. He despises K.'s gentleness. Physical self-pity may disgust him; he is scarcely proof against it morally. Uncourted by the *Sunday Times*, he is determined to see writing on the wall for the whole literate world. He could not abide a metaphysic that was not incomprehensible; simple ideas are necessarily false. As a friend he is false too; he must wound if he is to achieve intimacy.

George's heart attack in Paris may have been agonising; it did not impede his loquacious appearance on *Apostrophes*. Publicity and mission are one with him; he craves an ovation, yet preaches like an intellectual Meursault, as if ardent, like Camus' anti-hero, for outraged howls. While longing to break the code of eternity and talk to God in the second person singular, he is consumed by the present world; appalled and excited by its brutalities and its rewards, he would not be anywhere else: heaven can wait. He takes sensual pleasure in things of the mind, as only the misshapen can. His bluff, mantled in trilingual erudition, calls for an intellectual pathologist too subtle for easy availability. He boasts that, in a tight spot, he can always invent passages from Hegel which no one will ever have the patience to expose. Keeping his intellectual records in inaccessible quarters, he leapfrogs the local taxes to which monoglots are subject. He presumes himself involved in so complex a geopolitical congeries that he may well not know which safe house contains real secrets, which bumph. Exalted on an *auto-da-fé* of his own heaping, the faggots are the texts to which his polysyllabic verbiage must allude, though the world longs to torch them.

The self-portrait can be the most pitiless of pictures; it should have the accuracy of those who need not even look up to achieve a likeness.

Inverted Antaeus, I have only to have England beneath my feet to feel weakened.

4.11.81. Albert Speer could never abandon the idea of his own importance. Hallmarked by Hitler's favour, he survived as the whitened sepulchre of the Third Reich. Its last beneficiary, he made a show of donating tithes from his many interviews to charity. So long as he could parade his guilt, he was free to imply his innocence. Confident that he had done all he could to achieve her victory, he accepted no blame for Germany's defeat. His most recent book suggests that allied private enterprise was more efficient, inventive and flexible than the machinery insinuated into the tissue of German industry by the greedy ineptitude of the SS. Did it occur to him that a healthy society would never have embraced the Nazis in the first place? Why was Hitler's Germany fighting except to justify the savage methods Speer came to declare unrewarding? Appealing to civilised norms which the Nazis found contemptible, he implies that there might have been a decent way of achieving indecent ends. The justification of ideology relies on a distinction between the right and wrong way of wrong-doing.

Having served his time in Spandau, Speer became an ex-convict too exemplary not to have a car sent for him, a room reserved, a bottle iced. The Allies had a vested interest in preserving, in the aspic of publicity, a German of the inner circle who could appear civilised and intelligent and yet had behaved more disgracefully than anyone on the winning side. Speer's acknowledgement of the effectiveness of allied bombing raids (discounted by some military historians) assuages consciences troubled by the Dresden and Hamburg fire storms. How can we verify his claim that Czech workers were 'not unfriendly' when he visited them on the eve of the Nazi defeat? Must we take his word for it that the Reich Minister was exempt from the odium felt for other Nazi leaders or that Germans in general were popular in a country which they had dismembered?*

What is more revealing than Speer's partiality for the 'sincerity' of Nazi thinkers, notably Otto Ohlendorf, by whose callous intelligence he was once seduced? Imagine a mass-killer capable of articles that you might find in *The Economist*! The murderous Otto's execution, after the Nuremberg trials, served to lend martyred authority to his essays. Speer, the technocrat with publicly washed hands, proved *récupérable*, unlike the anti-hero of Sartre's *Les Mains Sales*. He endured as a greying scape-goat, hung with garlands and royalties and promised that he might safely graze, next to the dodo, in the retirement section of Animal Farm.

I dreaded going to speak at the Cambridge Union. Had the president not been Irish, should I have been so easily seduced? When told that Melvyn Bragg was to be my partner, I made intimidated noises: how should I second so smooth an article? As it turned out, I was *épaulé* by Humphrey Burton, who seems still to be Head of Music and Arts at the BBC. Teddy Taylor M.P., our heaviest opponent, had the rounded shine of an absconding pawn from the great chess game of state. Can such a

---

* Had Speer ever read Hašek's *The Good Soldier Schweik*? Did he have any ear for irony or alertness to prudent deception? Early 1945 was no time for Czechs to make waves.

man have real prospects of being in the Cabinet (or even of refusing to be in it)? When he took his place at the despatch box, or whatever Unionists call it, I had to admire the seriousness of his address. Entering into the straight-faced levity of the occasion, he was eminently patient when interrupted: 'Of course', he said, as he gave way to me on a point of detail.

The first two speakers, undergraduates, raised not a single laugh; they were very earnest. I had mentioned to Claire Tomalin that I was going to speak at the Union and recalled how intimidated I had been by the performances of our contemporaries. When I was polite about Nick's eloquence, C. denied that he had been a good speaker and confessed, unless she insisted, that she had always been embarrassed to hear him. H. Burton told Giles Kavanagh what a brilliant public speaker I was. When I challenged this, he recalled an evening at Joan Bakewell's dinner table where, he insisted, I had entertained the guests 'without using a note'. Can there be people who do use them on such occasions?

Burton is the very instance of the higher apparatchik; no surprise that he has been empanelled on the Arts Council. He wore a ruffled evening shirt and pranced to the lectern where he read a dull and canting speech. I had written mine out, but delivered it as if the pages before me, at which I scarcely glanced, were on quite another topic. Prudence led me to sit down when on the crest of a firm wave of laughter, although it meant omitting three or four good jokes. A phobia was purged; in an elderly maiden speech, I had held the audience like some Disraeli of the sticks.

It is amusing to cleave to the formal rectitude which even the educated have abandoned. Grammatical niceties are a form of nostalgia.

Ken Tynan died with a dandy's gallant flippancy. Breathless with emphysema, he gasped and stammered, but scarcely stopped talking. If he could not easily get a word out, who could get one in? Snob among levellers, red among blues, he could provoke any regime, yet accommodate himself to it. Refuting Descartes, he was a parasite whose distinction lay in rising higher than his host.

Robin Jordan: as a schoolboy, he was sensitive and seemingly refined, gentle yet attracted to muscle. The change from the chaste, Hippolytan style to that of the cosmopolitan sensualist is almost too pretty to be true.

The crassness of Anthony Burgess's W.S. Maugham figure in *Earthly Powers*. Not hesitating to deal at basement level with Great Issues, B. seems unaware that they have been broached with more wit and subtlety by a host of previous pens. He treats homosexuality with a coarseness that makes cardboard out of flesh. To create characters, he lists characteristics. Flippant and industrious, gluttonous and gross, he is a slapdash cook in a fancy restaurant, doling cream and spices onto re-heated meat.

My exiled artist should resemble a composite of Michael Ayrton and David Garnett. Like M., he has become literally shorter, the result of his warped backbone. Like D.G., red-faced eccentricity is all that remains of his narcissism. Having married a much younger woman, he watches her take a lover with serenity which contrasts with his rage at critics who fail to appreciate him. When young, he was famous; in old age, he can imagine being cut dead even by obituarists. The last twist of the knife comes when his mistress, a plain, devoted girl like Rachel D., telephones London with a false report of his death. She imagines that if she can have the newspapers print his obituary before he dies, it will prove how misguided his paranoia has been. She discovers that today's press is as vindictive *de mortuis* as about the living. She finds the cuttings under his body when she next goes to visit him. An old friend has been quick to send him the bad news. Her ruse to keep him alive has killed him. Imagine the horror; then the pride. How pretty the unspoiled *potager* is! And how full of beans she feels! She leans to savour some of his raspberries as he lies there, face down.

Why did Michael volunteer to be the eyes of the waning Wyndham Lewis? Because he so much admired the other's draughtsmanship? Or because of some deferential vindictiveness in the face of a *fascisant* genius who, now weak, might have used his strength, when he had it, to crush the man on whom he has come to depend?

6.11.81. The *Brideshead* cult proves how regularly the British look forward to nostalgia. They never blame themselves for their actions, or inactions, because they presume that they are always too dutiful to be free to do what they would like; but that *is* what they like. The impertinence of desperate refugees seeking entry to Palestine nettled them, not least because it drew attention to the presumption of the mandated authority in being there at all. Having purchased Arab support, Whitehall concocted a morality out of a geography rigged by victorious gerrymandering.

The invention of 'War Crimes' had the effect of branding the mostly dead Nazis with sole guilt for what the German people voted for and many did. After the Great War, the British and French were willing, even eager, to maintain the 'fiction' of national identities, hence German 'war-guilt'.

After World War II, fears about the direction in which Germany might incline made it prudent for allegation of national guilt or even complicity to be ruled out of court.

9.11.81. The President of the Union was reddish-haired and browed, smallish eyes in a big, turnip-shaped head. He controlled the debate without the *ex cathedra* facetiae of Percy Cradock, whose white and officious hand was quick to ting the presidential bell. One prancing, velvety fellow aped the manner and manners of the *années cinquante*, camp with frayed edginess. The reason why Kavanagh had been elected was no more evident than the ambition which usually fuels ascent to petty princedom. Although he is doing research, he thought that he might become an actor. He brought a girl back to have coffee and drinks. There was no sentiment between them. It was surprising how many undergraduates came out in the wet; life must be duller, or the mildly famous more attractive, than our assumptions of juvenile cynicism allowed.

A girl who had not been at the debate (sorry, but she had been rehearsing an unsingable work at CUMS, Cambridge's music society) asked to be introduced. She stood there, a pretty child, babbling of this and that. Impersonal desire blazed on her cheeks. Reputation was the seducer. Craving only proximity, she glowed in the light of her own appetite. She went away satisfied, unless kindled, by a heat she alone had generated.

The politically ambitious are wise to look for a style to imitate rather than for a principle to honour.

After the War. Having had a safe education in wartime and 1940s England, Aaron has become, through academic success, the simulacrum of a well-brought up gentleman. He is involved with a virginal but not cold Catholic girl, also bright; they have what they like to think a 'mature' relationship. Although they do not make love, he is pleased, if not satisfied, by their paired affections; Gillian is someone to be proud of. Previously he had an adolescent passion for a Jewish girl who resisted his less subtle advances, for fear of becoming a slice from a cut cake. Maybe she had already been caught in compromising circumstances by her mother while lending a hand to a less scrupulous lover than our hero, whose Englishness is confirmed (and desire moderated) by the rosiness of his clever lady.

Another early thread: the isolation of the clever boy by the 'pogrom' which teaches him to distrust the male sex. He is a man alone, looking for reliable maturity, which he thinks he has found in Gillian, not least because she is trapped in a metaphysic apparently as inescapable as Jewishness. He could not endure, or risk, a 'free' woman's freedom: he needs the bondage of others. Much though he advertises his wish to liberate G., he is drawn to her because he can at once respect and despise her virtue. All this is background to his trip to Paris when he meets the girl whose story is the crux of the novel. The play of the two women's calls on his desire; the confusion of motives tells of his compromised condition. He falls in love with the French girl (after an episode with a prostitute whom he seeks, absurdly, to 'acquire') and realises that he, in his turn, wishes to become her gaoler and her torturer, echoing the characteristics of the 'nice' doctor in whose house she spent the dangerous last years of the war. When he again sees G., he realises that her desire is equally double: he answers her prayers because, in her eyes, he is (by Catholic definition) dirty and corrupt as well as being, as it happens, brilliant and eligible. Aware that he hates and loves her, he agrees to marry her, knowing that he will 'always' love the other.

11.11.81. Language, André Neher implies, diminishes the creation. Man has become a talking animal nostalgic for the silence of the womb.

We are the hostages of what we discount. Comedy begins with confident prediction.

Paradise was rural until Plato rigged the ideal city into a blueprint for the just society.

If God spoke, we should be unable to understand Him; if we understood what was being said, it could not be God who was saying it.

After the War. Pierrette kills her doctor lover, if only by withholding his medication, after he threatens to break off the relationship she has resumed with him, quite as if she has missed his wartime exploitation of her defencelessness. Accused of causing his death, she tells the court of how, as a young girl, she was raped and abused. Aaron alone guesses that she relished what the doctor did to her: it allowed her to feel no guilt at having survived where others died.

Aaron is too clever, too dashing; he has failed, through want of tact, to get a Cambridge fellowship. His brother, Bernard, a historian of European politics, is devilling in Parisian archives. Fat and bearded, he has orthodox loyalties, never beliefs. He is prepared, not least by his physique, to be marginal. His historiography is painstakingly accurate;

Aaron's prose pains-fakingly brilliant. Researching German and Italian funding of pre-war Rightist and anti-Semitic groups in France and England, B. has the stamina to scrutinise stacks of old newspapers and pamphlets. He seems to thrive on antique print. Aaron is surprised to discover that his brother has a pretty, richly endowed mistress. He can endure being trumped by Bern's dull industry, but Heidi comes as an affront. Aaron's flirtatiousness conceals a desire to fuck his brother; deception alone makes him nice.

Aaron's English wife realises, at some point, that he wants her because it is safe to hurt her, as he cannot hurt his enemies. Perhaps he confesses as much; perhaps it makes her love him more. It allows her to know herself. Blessed, or cursed, with precocious confidence, A. does nothing authentic except surreptitiously. Everything for which he has been praised and rewarded is an imitation. Secrecy and callousness, denial and shame are all parts of his neatly knotted parcel.

The willingness of 'ordinary' German soldiers to participate in mass murder implies their need, once embarked on killing, to make sure that no survivor could crawl to the witness box to testify against them.* Killing becomes a prophylactic against conscience: what men do becomes why they do it.

The ideological divide between Soviets and Americans has narrowed since the end of the war; affectations of mutual detestation have intensified. It is less the 'ideas' of both sides which have increased the tension than their material arsenals. Only a posture of absolute antagonism can remove the absurdity of being equipped for nothing less than mutual extinction. How can either side concede that their differences are petty when the only means for settling them are annihilatory?

18.11.81. The palindromic date recalls Nabokov; he was childishly beguiled by the charms of *vice versa*, vices and verses. Polymorphous literary perversity was all his pleasure. The rage with which John Osborne writes about him in Ken's *Anti-book List* is consistent with O.'s sullen

---

* The cult of Holocaust denial, which was little practised when these notes were made, is of a piece with the wish to deny that any crime ever took place and so to disparage anyone who claims to have survived it. The convenient tradition of making a Jew an automatically untrustworthy witness marries with earlier practice to fortify the 'logic' of denial. Christopher R. Browning's *Ordinary Men*, describing how unexceptional citizens were recruited to become murderers, was published in 1992.

distaste for sexual funny business. The nice comedy is that V.N. led a conjugal life of conspicuous devotion; Osborne, straight as he may be, has conducted his affairs with callous egotism of which N., for all his self-preening, can scarcely be accused. O. is a linguistic puritan and a practical wanton; decorous in life, V.N.'s hedonism found furtive fun in paronomasia (e.g., in *Ada*, incest and nicest).

I sent Ken a new electric typewriter to help him over the practical difficulty of writing. He has always used a manual machine. He would plough with a horse if he could. When he phoned to thank me last night, I heard desperation in his cheerful tone. The paralysis of his left side continues to wing him. He lacks energy for a return to the hectic rhythms of work he once considered normal. Mortified by the reception of our *Oresteia*, he has fantasies of vengeful litigation.

19.11.81. Ritual congratulations from California, at last with telephone calls from Burt and Ron (who did not get the title straight but loved the script). I cannot repress a flutter of excitement and relief, even though the likelihood of a production is small. Yesterday afternoon Leslie Linder called with 'good news': his friends in San Francisco want to make *Roses, Roses...* and plan to start in September. I have little confidence that anything will actually happen. Ron has been stung into circulating the script again. He seems more eager to eliminate Leslie, whom he may see as a rival, than to make use of the funds to which he claims access.

My dreams are prodigious with fantasy. One was of a plastic palace, a luxury hotel from which I could find no exit, though I kept walking through doors that were so labelled. Outside the luxury, I found myself once more enclosed within it. In another dream, I hailed a Rolls-Royce in which Churchill was travelling. The 'commentary' declared that it was the only car equipped with a champagne gauge on the dashboard, so that the driver could be sure that the bottle was at the correct temperature when required.

Imagine Catullus envying the slaves at Sirmio for the freedom of overheard ribaldries about the coming of 'Baldy' Julius for whom the Catulli are making lavish provision.

26.11.81. Sartre was the grandest fifth wheel ever hitched to the bandwagon of the future. Was his devotion to the *damnés de la terre* excited by their indifference to his work? His post-war advice to the Jews, recommending them to embrace martyrdom, to agree to be defined by the objurgation of the mob, consigned one single category of mankind to be 'essentialised' by the votes of those who wished them no good. Might it be that a certain envy impelled him to such counsel? What could supply a more salutary hallmark than rejection by all those who proclaimed themselves to be on the (supposed) Right? The howl of the crowd becomes a certificate of worthiness. Is there a link between the fate embraced by Camus' Meursault and Poulou's masochistic dream, in *Huis Clos*, of martyrdom (*'douze balles dans la peau'*)? Sartre's advice to the Jews was composed, in 1947, by a man who had arrived, by climbing the left face, at the peak of the post-war Parisian literary world. In 1940, he had gained academic preferment after his path was racially cleansed by the removal of Jewish *profs.**

27.11.81. Shirley has won Crosby. The SDP spokesman on the radio said that she probably gained no more than four percent of the vote on the strength of her personal qualities. The swing from the two major parties was in line with Warrington and Croydon. The drift to the centre has become tidal. How can the waters gather in so unlikely a place and how will they be contained there? What will a centrist government actually manage or want to do? The danger is that such an alliance will be short of experienced ministers. Can its leader have the decisive competence to turn victory into success? How often is moderation rewarded with allegiance? If it succeeds, the electorate becomes partial to the pleasures of rougher trade. Bored with the decorous, it is liable to flirt with flashier suitors. The SDP is playing the nice card in a society where adultery, corner-cutting, benefit fraud and violence are activities of choice for the adventurous.

30.11.81. In October, a young *soi-disant restaurateur* called at Lagardelle and asked, in my absence, whether I would translate something into English for him. Madame Carcenac, Stee's recent, inept *prof d'anglais*, had given him my name, probably to get out of doing the work herself. Beetle assumed that the text would be brief: 'The Management requests... etc.' In the event, a plump pamphlet was delivered. It concerned the sun-worshippers of the pre-Christian Périgord. Excavation undertaken by the newly arrived *restaurateurs* showed that Belvès had been an important centre of the cult. Later, it was claimed, Belvès – where the Knights Templar established a treasury – was a staging post on the way to St Jean

* In 1941, Sartre had little hesitation, it seems, in assuming a senior teaching post, in a fashionable Parisian lycée, vacated by the eviction of a Jewish professor.

de Compostelle. The old town was honeycombed with secret passages and dark with secrets.

The young man, who said that he was a dentist, or at least a dental assistant, seemed clean and plausible. The opposition to the proposed installation in Belvès was, he said, the result of peasant prejudice and rumours to which *Sud-Ouest* had added its ignorant mite. The newcomers proposed to use the site of the old Lycée (now removed to a nearby hilltop) as 'scientific laboratories'. They could not enjoy the *primes* for bringing new sources of employment to the region unless they got going more quickly than could be done with a laboratory, hence the restaurant. Was there something slightly cracked in the young man's solemnity? Why would he lie? What might he be concealing? The brochure was intended to bring *gourmets* or *savants* to Belvès. Entry to the grotto of the Templars would be restricted to patrons of the restaurant. The fanciful prose hardly made the journey seem alluring for either category. He returned two days ago with grateful champagne and more odd publications.

NATHALIE WOOD flashed on the headlines of the news last night. So loud was the intro music that we could not catch why she had been featured. Stee thought that he had heard '*Elle avait quarante-trois ans*', an obituary tense. We waited through the whole news before she was mentioned again, after the result of the *tiercé*. As everyone now knows, she had been drowned. Her eulogy was spoken by the Antenne 2 showbiz lady, a flowery, big-eyed blonde in colourful cozzie and modish *gilet*. She took the opportunity to flirt with Patrick Poivre d'Arvor, who is never wholly unwilling, or willing. Then came a snappy resumé of Natalie's career, a clip from *West Side Story* and that was that.

This morning the BBC mentioned how happy she and R.J. had been and how much money they had. She was drowned after going out alone in the motor dinghy (some reports mention an 'inflatable canoe') belonging to their 'luxury' yacht. The odd fact, casually attached, was that her sortie took place at one in the morning, after returning from a party on Catalina. Natalie was said always to have been terrified of water. In *Splendour in the Grass* (described in France as a film about a young girl abducted by Red Indians*), she had had to pretend to be drowned in a river. Her double turned out to be a non-swimmer. Kazan then promised just one take, but she had to do four. At least she had actually to drown only once. How soon did R.J. raise the alarm? Quite quickly, it seems; this hardly suggests that N. had had a placid nocturnal impulse to rendezvous with the stars.

* A confusion with *The Searchers*.

I spoke to Natalie in June, when she and R.J. were in Cannes. She wanted me to do a script about Zelda Fitzgerald. They were thinking of coming to see me at Lagardelle, which they took to be just up the road from the Hôtel du Cap. 'Eight hours up,' I said. So that was that. My only solo meeting with her was in 1968, while Richard Gregson was negotiating with Dick Zanuck and David Brown for the biggest deal I ever made. She was waiting to lunch with us at the Connaught; twenty-nine years old, very pretty. Her mini-skirt disclosed smooth, naked, glossy legs. Born in the business and famous long enough for her modesty to be tailor-made, unspoilt by being spoiled, she had the grace to enjoy her looks and her success.

Stony-faced and monosyllabic, R.J.'s looks are preserved by a paucity of expressions. He could do very little as an actor, but he did it frequently and very rewardingly. For the rest, he played a nice game of Frisbee and never made trouble for anyone, unless he was mad, and then through a lawyer. He was married for a few years to Stanley Donen's first wife, Marion, a considerable lady, they say, whom we have never met.

Natalie and R.J. belonged to the top class of Hollywood society; if never at the top of it. They came to Gareth Wigan's dismal Christmas bake-out on Yuma Beach, quite as if it mattered to them. They never had anything better to do than what they were doing. Natalie lay on the beach, gazing at her image in the mirror from her pocketbook. It was as if she hoped that, as long as she looked at herself, she would not change.

Asked what she wanted for Christmas, she said, 'Yesterday'.

While N. was married to R.G., she came to London and lived in his often-burgled Pimlico house. Smaller than her guest-house in Beverly Hills, it may have been a comedown (even if we did begin with a bucket of Beluga when we went to dinner), but she acted as if happy with it. The desire she excited made N. seem the artefact that Harry Gordon declared her, during his brief, opinionated tenure as *Town* magazine's film critic. She had the constructed glamour which professionally attractive women parade to embellish the moment when men make their move.

Which was the more fabricated, Natalie or Audrey? Audrey too affected conjugal normality and sustained it for a long period, although Mel Ferrer was a bore of a pretentiousness to make Euphues break wind. Audrey's talents were more unusual; her elegance, however sticky, was a class above Natalie's neatness. She provoked desire which transcended the erotic, though that may not have been what she most wanted.

In John O'Hara's short story 'Natica Jackson', an ordinary man is seduced from his wife and children by a film star. The abandoned woman avenges herself by taking her two small children for a ride in a power-boat. Out at sea, she throws the kids into the water and drowns them. I am pretty sure it took place in California; the dénouement may well have been off Catalina. Had Natalie ever read the O'Hara story? Did Zelda's apparent suicide kindle some dark fuse? Natalie had always dreaded Death By Drowning; she rendezvoused with a killer who long harboured in her shadows.

1.12.81. The word now is that Natalie had been drinking, though the coroner said that she was not drunk. R.J. and Christopher Walken, their guest on the boat, are said to have had a quarrel. N. took to the dinghy to avoid the metaphorical waves. Alcohol rendered her a poor sailor and she fell into the sea, either as she got into the boat or as she sought to control it. R.J. raised the alarm soon after she had stormed off, but she was not found for several hours.

2.12.81. Most of my day went on an act of folly, the denunciation, in a letter to the editor, of Noel Annan for his supercilious article, in Karl Miller's *London Review of Books*, on Tom Bower's book about the de-Nazification process, immediately after the war, when Annan was a Poobah in the British Zone of Occupation.* He has since had a golden career and is a determining force on the yellow-brick road to academic preferment. I have hardly taken a dangerous step, though undoubtedly an imprudent one, in attacking such an eminence. Why bother? I have suddenly – *somewhat* suddenly – recovered a passionate rage over all that.

Pierre Vidal-Naquet's *Les Juifs, la Mémoire et le Présent*. V.-N.'s father was deported, like his mother, in 1943 and died/was murdered in 1944, an *enraciné* of exactly my father's age and, if more intellectually artic-ulate, of similar temperament. In his analysis of the use of Masada as

---

*   Annan was reviewing a book by Tom Bower about the sloth with which the British pursued Nazi 'war criminals'. Annan's disdain for Bower's journalistic enthusiasm led me to denounce the whole tone of his article. After my letter failed to appear in the journal for several weeks, I wrote to Karl Miller affecting surprise. He became very dignified at the suggestion that he was blocking criti-cism of his ennobled contributor. When, at last, he did indeed publish my letter, it was subjoined by Annan's response to it, for which Miller had, no doubt, been waiting. Annan affected to back away, saying that he did not wish to compete with someone of my rare eloquence, and then delivered a parting slap or two. Tom Bower and I have been friends ever since.

an Israeli foundation myth, V.-N. declines to see Flavius Josephus as a kind of quisling. The Jews who elected to kill themselves rather than surrender at Masada (leaving only a craven female to tell the brave tale) were never the elite of some homogeneous national resistance. A sect of sicariot outlaws, with no appetite for a central and cohesive Jewish state, committed themselves to a suicidal last stand. Death was scarcely a brave option, or if brave, no option: the Masadans can never have expected to prevail, or survive; the embodiment of futile intransigence, their example was adapted for patriotic purposes by Yigael Yadin. Taken seriously, the myth is the text for a dismal prophecy: the Masadans were so uncompromising that they could never hope for a mundane settlement. Israeli inflexibility may lead to another Masada; never another Munich.*

Pierre V.-N. regards Israel as a fixture; at the same time, he wishes that Begin had not been put into power or that, once there, he had responded with pronounced generosity to Sadat's heroic gesture. There is something poignant in the latter's isolation. As long as he was known principally for his early flirtation with Hitler, which led him to be imprisoned by the British, Sadat was respected as an authentic hard case. His decision to do what no Arab leader (since King Abdullah) had ever proposed – to live and let live with the Israelis – embarrassed those who had not been noticeably dismayed by his youthful support for the Third Reich. Once the Rais was revealed to have a measure of humanity, his assassination was little deplored. The denigration of the dead Rais plunged *Realpolitik* to a new basement. What Europeans most resented was his disinclination to invite them to prance in and mediate. Their mooted interposition in the Sinai will never preserve the peace. If Egypt changes her politico-military strategy (unlikely without a revolution, which is not itself unlikely), she will have the right to demand that the European 'peace-keepers' quit the country. In the only circumstances under which neutrals might serve to avoid bloodshed, they will be embargoed from doing so.

Sadat was the sole Arab leader to wish to spare his people a war they could not win. The canard so glibly spread about his taste for ostentation and his impatience with critics may be both justified and unjust; self-denial is hardly the mark of other Arab tyrants. Egypt is a poor country. Renouncing war could never of itself procure an economic miracle. Hence Sadat's *volte-face*, after the 1973 war gave him the kudos to risk it, had disappointing internal consequences. The continuation of a war economy

* More than thirty years later, Pierre Vidal-Naquet's study of Flavius Josephus inspired me to write *Jew Among the Romans*.

would clearly have been worse. The Egyptians – though unlikely to be difficult to recruit to 'the Arab cause', if the money is right – seem largely to have welcomed détente with Israel. The collapse of the Fez summit, however, suggests that the notion of a once-and-for-all settlement of the Arab/Israeli conflict is fatuous. The fantasy of a single 'Arab nation' mirrors the Zionist (and Nazi) fantasy of a single Jewish people, with a single purpose. Since Israel is beleaguered and most Jews associate themselves, to whatever degree, with its survival, the unity of 'the Jews' is more practical than that of the Arabs.

Whether Israel is accommodating or intransigent, does she truly occupy the key position in the region? Her destruction cannot cure Arab resentments and rivalries, internal or external; her existence muffles them.

The winter trees wearing spats of fog.

Money teaches the young how to age.

In every marriage is there one who has played safe and another who has taken a chance? The question is, which is which?

What cruelty lacks a happy witness?

The man with a beautiful wife waits for her to age so that he may have the liberty to tell her exactly what he thinks of her.

The origin of the first-personal narrator in fiction can be discerned in the tragic messenger, that apparently impartial bearer of inescapable news.

A ventriloquist whose lips never move, God delegates language, choice and the divisiveness of logic to man. Human speech is possible only in the dark light of divine silence.

The opinions of the gods are never interesting; they are merely decisive.

The aesthetic always omits something. The beautiful and the true have no necessary community. Art and falsehood are close cousins; life and happiness distant.

The woman in the Post Office, weighing the letter, lifted her upper lip, short-sighted, as she squinted at the scales.

Peter Green was, it seems, rejected by UCLA, after the trial run to which we were brief witnesses. Yet he is of much larger intelligence and originality than John Patrick S., whom UC offered the choice between LA and Santa Barbara. Geoffrey Kirk seems neither to be much liked nor much admired. He has brought dullness into areas of the Classics which never before seemed dull, myth in particular. Jane Harrison declared that she was nauseated by the primitive religions in which she was constrained to interest herself, but she never made their details anything but illuminating and significant. Kirk touches nothing that he does not dim.

After the War. Aaron and the girl in Paris: his alarmed realisation that he wants to make her suffer. He craves the centrality in her life which fear alone can procure and maintain.

Fair's Fair. A man in love with his mistress cannot bring himself to break with his wife. The mistress acquiesces, but requires him to tell her whenever he makes love to his wife. On each occasion, she reciprocates by finding another man. She then recounts the details to her lover. He makes love to his wife more and more frequently; and so does his mistress seek more lovers to tell him about. One day she is murdered by one of her casual pick-ups. The husband loses interest in his wife. 'I know,' she says, 'you don't have to tell me: there's somebody else.'

In the *Sunday Times* office. John Carey was reading what Christopher Ricks had to say about his (excellent) Donne in *The London Review of Books*. Carey is said to be a karate expert. He once reduced a threatening and powerful (undergraduate?) attacker to helplessness. Ricks, on being introduced to Judy Sullivan, said 'Is your name really Judith? Why do you call yourself Judy? How will it sound when you're fifty?'

That little boarding house in Provincetown, run by a genial, matronly middle-aged landlord. Our bedroom was chintzily charming. For breakfast, you went down steep stairs (mind your head) and saw the early birds sitting in the narrow lobby, on chairs and sofas, with neat plastic trays on their laps. We chose to go into the warming garden and waited a long time until a handsome black boy brought us generous, overcooked ham and eggs. The place was so full of adorable touches that it was a guilty pleasure to get away. At the orange-juice bar by the sea-wall, the young blond boy wanted to speak French. He had spent several months on the Loire and was afraid of forgetting what he had learnt.

The establishment of Truth leads always to lies; the institution of Justice to injustice. All revelation is a blind; all finished states flawed.

Blood blurting from a picked scab.

The Editor's Compliments. Two men who have been at university together, with adjacent tastes and ambitions, have always regarded each other with suspicious fraternity. The wife of one does reviews for a quality newspaper on which the other man is the literary editor. He treats her with attractive familiarity. The wife cannot bring herself to betray her husband by being amiable to his 'enemy'; nor does the editor feel comfortable with the idea of desiring a woman who seems happy with so disagreeable a husband. One day the two men coincide, by different paths, at a cultural event in a foreign city. They discover that their mutual suspicions are fugitive and ridiculous. They should have been friends long before; they can now make a comedy of obsolete animosities. On their return, the literary editor finds that the other man's wife has heard of their rapprochement. She can now show interest in a man from whom she has been embargoed by conjugal solidarity. He is soon able to begin an affair with her.

At the Caballo Blanco. The plaited reminiscences of a husband and wife recalling the same occasion – her lover coming to collect her – from the point of view of remembered pleasure and remembered anguish. Whose is which?

Forgiving and Forgetting. A man leaves his wife for no reason that she or anyone else can guess. It lies in an entry he has encircled in the obituary column of the newspaper: his wife's lover of many years before has died in a distant town. He has no further call to remain with her and protract the show of happiness designed to gall the dead man.

Often divorced or recoupled, Toby C. tends to fall back on a couple of steady, familiar friends when his love life goes through a painful or empty phase. One summer, he parts from his current wife in inglorious circumstances and descends, *en catastrophe*, on Bryan and Annette, who have rented a Riviera villa bigger than they need. They cosset and comfort him, though they have scant sympathy for his scandalous misfortune. One day, on the beach, Toby picks up with a girl whose accent and affectations appal his patient hosts. Her sexual allure enraptures and soon repairs his self-esteem. When topless Jackie moves into the villa, B. and A. make polite efforts to tolerate her scorn for their proper domesticity. The philanderer tells them that he has never known such joy as the aitchless girl gives him. The long week comes to an end and they all depart on their separate ways. Soon afterwards, B. and A. hear that their old friend is about to be re-married. They are not invited to the ceremony. He is marrying someone with whom he fell in love on his return to London. He is embarrassed to have them present, since they knew 'the wrong girl'. *Sleeps Six.*

The celluloid tripes of life hanging on cutting room hooks.

9.12.81. After reading Vidal-Naquet's intelligent and uneven text, I was struck by the coincidence that our fathers were born in the same year and wrote him a letter. By way of a visiting card, I enclosed a copy of *The Serpent Son.* Last night, there was a telephone call and it was the savant himself, a rather hesitant voice that I took at first for an international operator. He spoke good English, gentleness in his tone but no timidity. He gave me his private address and telephone number, as if it were an unusual gift, as it may well be. I asked if he were ever in the Périgord and there was a small metropolitan shudder in his denial. He lives in the *rue* Cherche-Midi in the *sixième.* When I mentioned the address to Beetle, it fostered remembered and simple pleasures. The temptation to live in Paris revived with sudden charm, though I am sure we shall resist it. Stee wants to stay in the French system, but in London.

Is it true (and, if so, is it important?) that, as Keith Williams* told me, Harold Pinter now wants to direct plays and films because, as he was quoted to have said, he has nothing more to say? What has he said? Proving how enigmatic sterility can be, he has rendered Jewish tailoring adaptable to the dandyism which makes nothing seem so natural as the unnatural. Where D.H.L. postulated blood, Pinter affixes mottos and clichés, relics of moral and personal notations, menacing tags, shredded intelligence, to compose a collage of inhuman, *appliqué* absurdity. The mortician of feeling, attracted only to what is in decline (are there any children in his work?), P. has no use for the quick. Making the separation of art from life into aesthetic finesse, he pastes *coupures* of the 'real' world on cut-out characters. As *Accident* proves, there is something provisional, even trite, in his verbal riffs from a *milieu* to which he has had no first-hand access.† The Oxonian dialogue derived either from Nicholas Mosley's stiff novel or from a poorly furnished imagination. The lack of clever volubility on the part of any member of the donnish cast was as implausible as it was convenient for a writer with small experience

---

* BBC TV's Head of Plays at the time.

† Dirk Bogarde told me that, during the making of *The Servant,* he asked Harold why his posh characters invariably dined off lobster Thermidor. According to Dirk, Harold asked what else they ever ate.

of academic loquaciousness. H. is most at home with spates of chat from the (usually male) fantasist, the manic and the bully. Any call for educated conversation discomfits him. His academics' dialogue dresses tailored dummies.

10.12.81. Richard Gregson has been in LA for Natalie's funeral. R.J., he told us, has been 'wiped out' by her death. It seems that N. had a big bruise on the side of her head. The presumption is that she slipped while getting into the dinghy, for whatever reason, at one in the morning. How did the mooring rope come to be untied if she was not yet aboard? Since she was used to the dinghy, did she find it easier to untie it and then push herself off from the yacht as she went aboard? Was she distressed by an evening gone sour? The guy at the place where they dined said it had been a happy party.

Philippe Labro (quite the Hollywood specialist) wrote a slick article in *Paris-Match* telling of N.'s inability to tolerate solitude and of the succession of psychiatrists required to reconcile her to herself. The break-through came, he says, when she was able to fly unaccompanied from LA to NYC. Polite and nervous in her stardom, her beauty rode piggyback on a small person always afraid that it would slip off. That slip between the yacht – symbolising Californian success and social elevation – and the little dinghy, into which she could not quite fit her fugitive self, is as sweetly apposite as any creative writing professor could ask chance to make it.

R.G. was uncertain how he would be received at Natalie's funeral. R.J. proved 'a perfect gentleman'. He is going back to work this week, the children to school. In that small, privileged world, accustomed to drama and marital peripeties, R.J. is sustained by the solidarity which indiffer-ence supplies. He is taking the children to Gstaad for Christmas; they are going to stay with Richard and Julia over the New Year. Money cannot buy everything, but it can make up for a good deal.

Two men bereaved by the loss of the same woman. To what degree can she be the same person to both, and to what extent are they aspects of that single figure, The Husband, always inadequate, always necessary? Was N. the star who, whenever possible, wore a bracelet in her movies to hide the scars on her wrists? She always insisted on the contractual right to keep the jewellery her character sported.

N.'s dependence on secretaries and hired help suggests a scene in which a friend commiserates with her over her husband's infidelity. She sighs and says, 'Oh I can always get another husband, but where do I find a secretary like Mary-Ellen?'

Poland is under martial law. Worldwide, fifteen million children a year die of malnutrition. Peter Ustinov, speaking from Switzerland, says that the world spends as much on armaments every hour and a half as it gives in a whole year for the relief of guiltless suffering among the destitute. He preaches movingly, but who moves? I care more about writing a good book than about the Poles. Is it because of their anti-Semitism or their Catholicism? Of course, as we always say, they have little or nothing to lose, except their rations and their lives. The loud impotence of the West is as conspicuous as it was twenty-five years ago, when we watched the brutal abortion of Hungary's freedom. Yet menacing voices in England, speaking for Militant Tendency, declare in the nasal accents of the uncompromising, that there is no future for the mixed economy. In the brief brackets between his interviewers' 'impartial' questions, their spokesman promises measures to turn England into an intoler-able paradise. No previous example can enlighten or deter our village Robespierres. How will an unmixed, unadventurous economy earn the revenue its guardians propose to spend? A flat, grey, impoverished society is the commissars' vision of fairness. This aspect of England needs to be looked at in *Heaven and Earth*.

Uxorious, not sexy, Gideon is a natural guardian of lame ducks. Tom's persecution can be raised, in a general form, at a Labour Party meeting. G. has the compromising, suspect sensibility of the bourgeois, without the wealth to protect it. He has been to university, but has no comfortable provenance. His long-time bridge partner, Norman Horowitz, might be selected to play in an England trial, without Gideon. N. plays bridge in London, perhaps in a team which has a good run in the Gold Cup. He can be called in when someone else's regular partner dies or is ill. Gideon has a sense of the unreliability of everything. He has an innocent, secret correspondence with little Brenda Smith, a literary librarian from South London. Like Sean, the bully, she might be black; or she could be some-thing quite different: the kept woman of a man who is both jealous and violent. The latter's menace breaks Gideon and drives him home again. This, rather than any moral impulse, occasions his return.

Pamela. She has been a nurse and first meets Norman as the result of an accident that requires stitches. He introduces her to Gideon. He seems unaware that P. is attracted to him and of her disappointment that he is already engaged to Jane, or whatever her name is. She is never ready to be friendly with N.'s wife and refuses to learn to play bridge, thus aborting any rendezvous à quatre. P. is polite to N. on the telephone; the touchiest part of the story lies in her phantom relationship with him. The Shands move to the same district (the Stour estuary) as the Horowitzes, having found 'heaven' in a little cottage with derelict charm. Only then does N. reveal that his marriage is breaking apart. P. is excited by the possibility of N. being 'free'. When Gideon walks out, she hopes that N. will replace him. Finding that he has another woman, she accuses him of encouraging G. to leave her and of being 'an evil man'. She sees him in her dreams as a devil with two penises. Images of his ravishment of her are at the erotic centre of her religious fantasies: she watches herself screaming with enjoyment when subjected to all the things she 'could never do'. She writes accusing letters, threatening to denounce him as a tax-evader, pederast, liar, foreigner, crook. This will play only if her sensible personality is calmly established in the Chaworth chapters, when she can be a social worker or a marriage-guidance counsellor. 'Your wife,' people tell Gideon, 'is an angel.'

The Catholic priest, Father Burgess, concerned with the rise of 'witch-craft' in the Stour region, might come to exorcise the cottage (he can have been in the habit of comforting the old biddy who lived there). Rowan Simmonds' South African background; he has never got over being acquitted in the treason trial and has a Judas complex.

Norman is a UCL man who should have been an Oxonian; he makes up for it by presumptuous stylishness. He works hard at the Bar and has the florid address of a man who prefers a more rhetorical manner than is commonly practised. Opinionated, but without specific commitments, when he appears on *Any Questions*, his sardonic insolence is weighted to provoke more laughter than outrage. In truth, he believes himself to be very English. Short and bespectacled, he has a tall, clear-sighted accent. Gideon is square-jawed, brown-haired and quite athletic, but lacks Norman's attack. He had hoped to be a don, but broke down while writing his PhD thesis. He met Pamela at that time. Her sexual fantasies come out after N. seems to have been left by his wife and G. has followed her example. N.'s wife pops up to assist the devil in his outrages; she may later be accompanied by the Other Woman, who bears the initial 'A'.

Piers Rougier asks Miranda to allow him to take 'artistic' photographs of her. There is a market in the town for paedophile studies. Can policemen be committee members of political parties? If so, one such could be on the track of a child molester, the 'martyred' Rowan Simmonds perhaps.

He treats Cora badly and patronises her as a domestic slave. At the end of the book, G. and Pamela ask Father B. how they can enter the Catholic Church. Together, if not happy, G. and P. crave insulation between them and the cold sky. Candidates for bliss no longer need Latin.

5.1.82. On New Year's Day we went to the Rubinsteins' luncheon. We had toasted the New Year in with port, after playing charades at the Wick. It mixed badly with the champagne we had at supper. I had very little, but woke with a headache. The threat of travel increased the tension. I hired a Ford Fiesta to take us to town and on to the airport the following day. By the time we were in London I had an irreversible migraine. I had to ask for sanctuary upstairs. I took two paracetamol, but it was not enough. I had looked forward to the party far more than Beetle, who gallantly went on in alone. I lay under a cheap eiderdown on a single bed, listening to 'Lovely to see you' from below. I was due to do *Any Questions* that same night. Uwe Kitzinger, alerted to my malaise, was quickly into the breach, before it had been opened. A third tablet began to put me right. I went downstairs after two o'clock, but ate nothing. Martin Gilbert, plumper and plummier, greeted me, after I had greeted him, with urbane amiability. I had made his Christmas by choosing his Auschwitz number among my Books of the Year. A telephone call left me marooned with Will Wyatt, a BBC potentate whom I failed to recognise. He has, it appears, written a praised book. He was sympathetic over the Byron affair; he had heard of my distress (which I deprecated) from Eddie Mirzoeff, whose self-importance provoked much of the ill-feeling.

Sarah saw a bumper sticker in NYC. 'The paranoids are after me'.

Karl Miller has neither printed nor even acknowledged the long polemic against Noel Annan which I sent him well before Christmas. I suspect he dare not risk giving offence to his patron.

I reported to B.H. at 4.30 in order to catch the car to Reading for the broadcast. We left so early because we had to pick up an incoming member of the team, John Palmer of the *Guardian*, at 5.45. I had to spend forty-five minutes having tea, and an egg sandwich, with a Mr Herbert Tate, who is in charge of continuity for Radio 4. It falls to him to 'warm up' the audience. In his pin-striped suit over a fleshy, spread body, he looked like a cashiered limo-driver, docked of his peak cap. He had been with the BBC ever since coming out of the army; he was now too old to leave, though not to wish that he had, despite his claim to be happy where he was. I should have preferred to read a book, but I sat there interviewing him as my life trickled away. He told me that when, on a *Desert Island Discs*-type programme on R2, someone chose a classical record, the producer declined to play it. Whoever it was refused to continue with the programme.

Palmer was quite tall, slimmish, with a cropped beard like a chin-and-jaw glove. Keen and articulate, he issued decided opinions from a well-ordered index. He confessed to pleasure that he and Peter Carrington were on first name terms. He lives in Brussels, covering EEC and NATO affairs. He has worked for the *Guardian* for seventeen years and has a French wife, from Picardy.

Our driver, David, had difficulty finding the Caversham Estate in the back streets of Reading (it seemed to be all back streets). The *Petit Village* restaurant eventually shone like a good deed on a dark night. We had a poor meal on which David Jacobs poured the watery gravy of his admiration. There was David; there was Maggie and there was Mrs Woodhouse. We had seen her on the box doing a programme about the pets of Beverly Hills. I sympathised with her for having to spend so much time with the B-set. She was not amused. She imagined, it seemed, that people should be brought to heel as easily as animals. Forbes Taylor later assured me that he had known her twenty years before, when she was supposed to supply a trained dog for an episode of *Robin Hood*. She had promised a beast that would do anything they wanted. It did not.

Oh the banality of the discussion and the urge to cadge applause! At first, it seemed odd that the Tory MP, a jolly overweight called Patten, should be seconded by Mrs W. (whose popularity, Beetle suggested, was bolstered by her nominal proximity to Mrs Whitehouse), but 'balanced' by Palmer and myself. By the end of the programme, I had been converted to parlour pinkness by the Home Counties' bark of the complacent, strident lady to whom, at dinner, I had been determinedly polite. It must be comfortable to swim in cant as roundly as a goldfish in a bowl.

David Jacobs' father-in-law sports a Monty Wooley beard, spectacles and the pride of men whose daughters share famous beds. A keen walker, he often dodges over to Dieppe to go for a trek. Torn between a sense of life's seriousness and the knowledge that voice and intellect qualify him only for superficialities, Jacobs is the kosher Richard Baker, part shrewd observer and music lover, part pander, like all the BBC brass, eager for tin. He agreed that the 'Celebrities Guild' is an embarrassing affair, but it is a charity, he says, and does good work.

David has polite renown, but lacks the provincial brashness which has allowed Michael Parkinson to overtake him in the surge to fame. He masks his origins by the careful modulation of his voice. Shining with smoothed-away pain, wariness behind his accessible geniality, he has had good luck and he has endured publicised anguish.* Enlivened by deadlines and by the need to honour a series of engagements, he must never miss assuming the chair lest another be deputed to take it. Not false, never wholly true, he handles his broadcasts with unobtrusive clarity, the public with tact and affectations of concern (putting a prompt question to a questioner when it seems humane); yet there is always over him the dread of being attacked, denounced, abused. He is decent but never considerable; if cheap, never nasty. The cheapness lies in his lack of spontaneity; between him and the BBC driver, natty, uncomplaining, ready-when-you-are, there is a very narrow gulf. I like him and I despise him, as I do my own willingness to take part in so muddle-browed a programme, for all the opportunities it affords to slide a red word in edgeways.

6.1.82. At the *Sunday Times*, the sly, ambitious Julian Barnes is disappearing, only to yield place to a saturnine, spade-jawed John Ryle, nephew or great-nephew of Gilbert, a word-child with no more warmth than a snowman. He signalled his arrival with a toadying piece about the *London Review of Books*. An insert photograph of Karl Miller proved that he is still twenty-five. Alan Brien, bloated and pink as a skinned rabbit, came in and played pasha in the space vacated by James Fenton, whose self-esteem depended on preening himself in the mirror of other people's apprehension.

7.1.82. In the car coming back from Reading, I was conscious of the futility of attempting to educate the public by *petits pas* and, at the same time, of the need not to leave the common arena to those who use it only for partisan purposes. I wished I had never been to the dismal place in which the local committee took deserved pride, a complex built by subscription and hard work. Oh the selflessness of those jostling to serve on the pingpong sub-committee! The process of thinking about others, and stopping them from smashing the Space Invaders, is also the process of rendering them banal. Those who love their neighbours seldom have a high opinion of them. I can hardly wait to look up flights even as I salute

---

* David Jacobs' and Richard Marsh's wives were killed in a car crash in Marbella which both husbands survived uninjured.

the decency of those who take time off from their stamp collections in order to take an avuncular interest in model trains.

The SDP craves a world proof against excessive ambition, full of playgrounds where people go carefully, sanctuaries both from evil and from excellence. It dreads anything that cannot be taken care of by condescension. The vegetarian rush to synthesis, the composition of the peace treaty ahead of the crunch of opposites, asks society to accept a suburban ethos instead of the strut which once rendered England both too big for its boots and stylish enough to command attention. Shirley's bustling humanity yokes her need to burn off self-doubt to allegiance to Catholicism, with its sadomasochistic amalgam of self-righteousness and *pour mieux sauter* abasement.

I said to Palmer that I thought that the age of ideologies was past. He replied that the number of fundamentalist doctrinaires was increasing. I meant less that men can no longer be recruited to superstitious faiths than that it was impossible for intelligent people to believe that there could be a one-size-fits-all solution for the world's ills. The collapse of Marxism means that the last social card has been played; no class of persons can now be expected, through a monopoly of power, to cure the endemic stasis of mankind. The end of alienation is a fantasy; man cannot be encased in some new unity suit of language. It remains likely that the stupid and the vindictive will, in the name of creeds without the smallest intellectual foundation, succeed in destroying mankind. What is clear, but can never be proved, is that no design is necessary to human existence; it is itself in no way necessary. Language cannot do what philosophers and preachers have wished: The Word can never be the ladder to another world.

The glamorisation of space attempts to make heaven a refuge to which technology, rather than virtue, may secure entry.

Benign clubs, like the Pugwash fraternity, which unite savants from each side of the ideological divide, offer occasions for mutual admiration (and deception). Their existence symbolises the common interest of notables, their impatience with the usual channels and the alpha-boys' appetite for a separate peace.

11.1.82. Pierre Lavelle, who was born in Lagardelle, arrived as I was pruning the plane trees in the courtyard so that they spread but do not rise (as on the terrace of the Hôtel des Trois Couronnes at Vevey, where

H. James set the opening of *Daisy Miller*). Plane tree leaves are almost unique in being useless for compost, but rapid growth renders them suitable to create summer shade. Lavelle was driving a rackety white Peugeot 204 which his *garagiste* had lent him while he waited for a new Renault. He came, ostensibly, to collect some sunglasses he left here a couple of years ago. Yvette and the boys were with her family in La Chapelle Péchaud.

He has become thicker rather than fatter. With the flattened, broad face of a fighter, his expression is more glowering than aggressive. Wanting in female attributes, he lacks that enlivening touch of coquetry without which a man becomes a bore. Intelligent, energetic, well-informed, nothing he says is personal. He is good-natured in his way, but without humour or antennae for anyone else's distress. Pierre continues to fly; the boys have no interest in it. They did judo for three years but have abandoned it to go separate ways. P. has a very rich brother-in-law who runs a big firm in Bordeaux. They paint and face buildings all over Europe and in the Middle East. The boss fought in Indo-China and then became a decorator with a small company. He learnt the job for two years and then set up on his own.

In twenty years he has expanded from a two-man operation to an international company with four hundred employees. He drives a Rolls-Royce and his wife a Porsche. They have an estate with its own hunting grounds. The weekends are heaven, the week – Pierre promises – hell. The *patron* used to know all his employees by name; now men work for him for months and he never even sees them. I said, *'Réussir, c'est toujours perdre quelque chose'*. P. smiled, as if at a keen student. He is glad to have a rich man in the family, on whom to pin the hope of favours, but with whom, he swears, he would not care to change places. He is determined to be satisfied with what he has, so long as he need never criticise himself. He may not be a dictator, but he will not take dictation. Although his position as a functionary obliges him to defer to unseen bureaucratic masters, society in St Nexans is more open than it was in Grives. Since the busy periods are seasonal, *viticulteurs* are not permanently obsessed with their farms.

Before Christmas I went to California. I now have small expectations that my scripts will be filmed, but I fly first-class, am met by a limo and stay at the Beverly Wilshire (where once, in 1969, I was labelled on the booking register as 'writer-director'). Yet even as I seek to be base, the standard is falling. The 'independence' of Spielberg, de Palma, Lucas and others embraces no ambition to give their work substance. The comic book is their literature. Immune from intrusive influence, they should be able to re-imagine cinema; but innovation is a danger to success at the box-office; and success at the box-office is what success is.

13.1.82. The birth of Benjamin (they have started their tribe at the end) has promoted the Weissbords in Burt's parents' eyes and released substantial funds. He and Kathie have moved into a large house on Bentley Circle, off Sunset on the way to the San Diego freeway. It looks modest from the garage on the steep roadway. Once past the guard-fence, you are into a large garden, with a pool close to the street, but screened from it. Steps go down, under umbrageous trees, to the long, low house, mostly wood; there is a guest-house lower down. The living room has a blockwood floor, a screened fireplace ensconced in the right-hand wall; the low, beamed ceiling is painted white. Glass doors give onto a broad terrace overlooking West LA. There is another terrace on the roof of the sitting room. The place was occupied by the same people for over forty years. It retains the dated dignity of the rich and unfashionable.

Living modestly in immodest circumstances, the Weissbords appear unpretentious, not least because they are irredeemably plain. Burt has learnt a little generosity, perhaps because his company is in business with two movies, one – *Ghost Story* – a purported hit. The house is provisionally furnished, but the lines have been drawn for the usual commissioned chic; Merle Mardigian will do her decorative stuff once the builders are through with remodelling the west wing. It is a house in which a rich young couple can become a richer old couple without having to move.

I spent quite a lot of money around Beverly Hills, most of it on Christmas presents which I brought in through the Green Channel without being questioned. The immigration man was civil to me, but called after a black man who had gone past his desk to collect a package 'Oy, what do you think you're doing?' The black man had been hailed by another immigration officer who intervened just as my man was about to send him to where he had come from. Empurpled with self-importance, my chap told me that the black was 'not very polite'. My passport had already been stamped, so I ventured: 'I thought you were tolerably aggressive yourself.' The bully consented to be chided, in the right accent, and there I was, back in the UK.

Paul met me and we collected my mother from Putney and set off on the long drive to Colchester, which Pab managed, despite the freezing conditions and an underpowered car, with grousing good humour. Irene had one of her chesty conditions. She confessed to Beetle that she thought it psychosomatic. She was exasperated by the builders who have been haunting Balliol House for months. The workmen upstairs went off one weekend leaving the water running in a disjointed pipe and she was flooded. Her insurance company treated her with the benign partiality which, more than anything else, gives her satisfaction. She loves to be pampered by those whom she scarcely knows.

We saw an *insalata mista* of an Italian movie the other night. It included a sketch in which a callous Alberto Sordi, brilliant in three different segments, left his old mother in a wretched old people's home which he tried to persuade her was '*un palazzo*'. We were reminded of my father being dumped in the miserable *Royal Hospital and Home for Incurables* with its reeking, functional coldness. It was impossible to chide Irene at the time; it smacks of unkind premeditation to think that there will come a moment when she will expect the attentions she failed to offer. Cedric lost his claim on her when he could neither withhold favours nor bestow them: she had charge of what money there was, and there would be no more. The main lines of their relationship were scored by fear. She dreaded penury; he desertion or betrayal. In my youth, they appeared devoted. Such is the cunning with which the middle class used to conceal whatever was genuine, in the way of passion or hatred, that the young had little chance of perceiving the essence of any matter, especially intimacy.

In Chicago and New York, Cedric had had to excuse himself for being a Limey. In London, Irene could not relax, because she was never certain that she had proved herself nor even quite what she was hoping to prove. Because she was a woman, and beautiful, she could expect indulgence. Her probation looked like freedom, but even her beauty could not be too freely enjoyed, lest it arouse the jealousy of the suburban women with whom she was sentenced, if only by her own timidity, to pass her time. From the moment we landed in England, she scarcely saw a man independently. Yet Cedric never abated his jealousy; it ate him in his sequestered old age. To live in dread replaces courage with endurance, life with longevity.

15.1.82. It looked as though Mrs Thatcher was about to be put to the cruellest of public tests; having to live through the loss of her son. The most partisan opponent might have been moved. Anxiety humanised her; tragedy might have made her popular. Now it seems that Mark was never in danger; we have been gulled into unwarranted anxiety. It may have been hoped, in the newsroom, that tragedy was looming; comedy was, in truth, always prevalent. Because he was the son of a public figure, a dull, acne-marked young man of twenty-eight, indulging in a sport which called for endurance and nerve but is scarcely a challenge to the imagination or the intelligence, had lavished upon him all the expensive energies of government agencies and the ostentatious assistance of adjacent powers. In the circumstances of a motor rally in the desert, were hazards not to be expected? Extravagant measures were taken to retrieve a playboy involved in no very noble activity and treasure extracted from the public purse to reassure his mother. Has she herself ever been concerned by the ill-fortune of other young persons in distressing conditions? The clan of the famous and powerful can depend on the goodwill of its adherents. In a pinch, all successful people are the friends of others; all conspire to prove success the supreme good. Never in danger, Mark Thatcher and his *co-équipiers* could have been returned to civilisation without the costly show which proved how important his mother was. Now he is being pressed to abstain from rallying, rather as if he were some Franz-Ferdinand to be deterred from going to Sarajevo.

From the inconclusiveness of language comes the necessity (as in inevitability) of fiction.

Reasons why are less important than evidence that; yet man cannot endure a merely natural world. *Deus sive natura* implies the difference between the alternatives.

God contains all possibilities, all things are possible in Him, provided He makes no pronouncement. As soon as a god speaks, He may be challenged; He has come down.

When man loses faith in the afterlife, he becomes a fugitive from death.

Faith allows liberation from tenses: it unlatches the brackets of time and allows the credulous to slip between them.

God as mathematician is immune to the reproach of having done or not done anything; He has, of necessity, no intentions.

24.1.82. The scatter of corn on the new village hall, traces of the *quine* from the previous Saturday.

4.2.82. In his ill-tempered and interesting *The Impact of Labour*, Maurice Cowling attempts to make historian's use of the analysis of cant and rhetoric, passages of speech and print which statesmen and hacks produce under the pressure of ambition or moral salesmanship. Ignoring their sincerity, which will always elude definitive measure, Cowling notices only that such and such sentiments were expressed or programmes mooted. His unspoken theme is what he depicts elsewhere as the retreat of Conservatism from a battle with the Left which might have halted the rise of socialistic influences. He writes with vigorous ineptitude; resentment embargoes any lapse into elegance or irony. Pronouncedly lacking in respect for his own origins, Cowling is the very type of man who picks up his aitches: he would like nothing better than not to be what he was born. Sartre said that shame could be a revolutionary emotion; it can as easily be counter-revolutionary. The alarm excited by a man so inimical to compromise should not obscure the originality of his enterprise.

What kind of vanity drives Shirley and David Owen to challenge Jenkins, clearly the most experienced and capable potential PM in the SDP ranks, for the leadership of a 'movement' which has more dignity than direction? Rather than mock the SDP for its want of specific policies, it might be revealing to place, not judge, its extreme centrism. The British seem to respect the Gang of Four as people of integrity rather than of unballasted ambition, even though Bill Rodgers does little to charm and a good deal to aggravate the public; tactlessness too can ape sincerity. There is much talk of courage, none of ratting. It seems that all radical solutions are disagreeable to the voters, even as they chide their leaders for failing to produce them. The secession of the Four is regarded as an act of moral distinction, less because it presages a new political initiative than because it appears apolitical. They may support parliamentary democracy against extremists who are impatient with the formalities and decorous delays of the House; but unless parliament is seen, in rosy light, as a good thing in itself, the Four can be held, in objective terms, to prefer the form to the substance. Even the call for proportional representation smacks of dismantling the antagonisms that provoke articulate dialogue.

What today's politicians can do is so limited that they have become, like entertainers, less criticised than reviewed. Bernard Levin, as Taper, was the first to read parliament for a kind of national theatre. His cap-and-*belles-lettres* mockery pandered to the gallery of his *Spectator* readers. Levin was to 1950s politics what Tynan was to the theatre. Both employed a tone of condescending asperity. Ken began seriously; he wanted a new theatre and persuaded himself that only a new society could supply it. Levin imagined that he wanted a new society; in truth he too wanted only a new theatre.

Without any investment in propriety, no stake in preserving appearances, Ken had the classic lineaments of the bastard. Yet he was not a deprived child; if his titled father was not married to his mother, he never maltreated her. K. grew up a Peacock in all but name; his early outspokenness on taboo subjects carried a presumption of privilege; lack of restraint in sexual matters has always been the mark of the swell. Alienation trumped belonging: as Sartre declared in *Genet, Saint et Martyre*, victimisation is the beginning of liberty. When the outcast embraces his exotic status, he can build an authentic identity which does not work against him.

The disproportionate survival rate, in the camps, of Communists and religious fundamentalists underlines the importance of decision, never mind what is decided; those who hesitated were lost. The undivided self does not connive at its own destruction; it refuses to accommodate its enemies by conceding anything to their logic.*

The bastard is a singular rebel. To look at, he excites no hostility; he belongs to no discrete race or caste. He is a natural only child, closer to reality, to the earth, to an a-social world, than those born into the soft cradle of a familiar social order.

Had Tynan been required to swear loyalty to Beaverbrook, he would have been embarrassed; recruited by Max to supply punctual insolence, he could swagger into the stronghold of everything he had previously held contemptible. The solicited mercenary has none of the docility of the conscript or the altruism of the volunteer. Luring them onto wealthy rocks, the Beaver hailed smart henchmen to his lair with the prospect of profitable piracy. He himself had been gulled, then embittered, by elevation to the Lords: the Establishment excluded the upstart Canadian from real power by gagging him with ermine.

As for K.T., the blanched beanstalk became a Jack who never gave another stage performance, yet remained a player. Ken transcended his time by guessing ahead; his precocious leap into the future was also the thing which aged him. If he never guessed how much money would be available in show business, where new identities could be acquired and where fraudulence, carried off with assurance, trumped the real thing, he foresaw that to be in at the foundation of a National Theatre would give him pivotal clout.

---

* This note illustrates the dangers of moral schematics. Communists survived in the camps more because they were well-organised and looked after their own and had the callous means to send others to their deaths than because of the spiritual quality of their faith.

At Oxford, he had charged his contemporaries a pound a head to attend a party for Orson Welles. The money stocked the buffet; the fun lay in selling the guest of honour's favours. Ken seemed sophisticated, not because he had done more but because he had read more, in transatlantic places, than others of his generation. He had the alert impudence to recognise that Orson, if still young, was old enough to be disappointed. Like so many fomenters of sedition, K.T. was a snob. Who entertains more subtle schemes of rebellion than someone half in love with what he plans to betray?

Orson, the darling of pre-war New York, had become the most pampered outsider in the West. He too had attacked the establishment, the better to establish himself; by assaulting an unforgiving manipulator,[*] he immolated himself in sensational flames. The dilettante Daniel, gloriously scorched from the fiery furnace, emerged a lion. Ken could imitate, never overtake, his model. He lacked the magic trickiness that had made O.W., both briefly and forever, the smartest rabbit in Hollywood's hat. Ken was a fan in search of a dancer, a moth in a flutter for a flame. Yet – such is the tragi-comedy of the critic – he could do nothing more practical with his prize, once he had found him, than to cash him.

By the end of the fifties, having proclaimed himself in England, what could Ken do but decamp to America? First, he found another father figure on whom to do the dirt: Mick Balcon employed him at Ealing for a well-paid season. Ken's receipt took the form of an article denouncing English films and declaring 'I owe you £4,000, Sir Michael'; a debt which, depend upon it, remained outstanding. Ken lived above his means, as others do above the store; he worked hard, earned fattish sums and was always on the game. He had an unsentimental sympathy with tarts. He was grateful for their existence and tutelage, just as he read the pornographer as a liberator, pornography as an art-form.

He announced himself a socialist, but what he enjoyed was exciting alarm. The arresting of the clock makes the game of master and mistress, governess and ward, deliciously sexy. Ken told me[†] that nothing would make him physically brave. I suggested that in an emergency we public schoolboys were conditioned to behave like British officers. Ken would not allow that anyone could cure his eminent cowardice.

Yet (and hence?) he loved bullfights. The *torero* is another kind of dandy. He dons a fancy costume and renders himself sparklingly vulnerable before going out to confront naked force. The bull knows no subtlety;

[*] William Randolph Hurst, on whom the character of Charles Foster Kane was blatantly based.

[†] Over Steak Tartare at Overton's, paid for by the BBC.

the bullfighter nothing else. By turning in a tighter circle than his brute adversary, his horny mate, he outwits and dances him to a standstill. K.T. did not deny the cruelty of the *corrida*; he was addicted to it. The bullfighter excited the fearful fan: the slim, androgynous man did what his admirer would never dare to do. Ken wished, with the coward's fervent appetite, that he could impersonate the *torero*'s lone mastery of himself, the bull, and the crowd, a triple balancing act which could be fouled by a single nervous gesture.

However much he might be corrupted by money and by the degeneracy of shaven bulls, the *torero* was still the man who transcended the mercenary by selling his life not only dearly but also artistically. Who but a bullfighter combines showbiz and mortal defiance? Motives irrelevant, performance is all. Imagine K.T. being attracted by a woman who sides passionately with the doomed beast; he would smell her humanity like musk, her scruples would leaven desire. Ken, being no beauty, a celery-stick, needed a logic, a ruled game, to prime and merit his passion. Naturalness could never cover his bets. He was the very instance of what my *Sunday Express* editor, John Gordon, found abominable. There was nothing he was happier to deliver than a blow below the belt.

Tycoons deplore the uxorious: what boss cherishes a man who would just as soon go home?

At Biron. The landscape alight from a spring sun, the sky cyclorama-clear. The *château* was officially shut. I summoned the *châtelaine* by pulling a rope attached to a jangling bell bracketed high on the adjacent tower. We were treated to a personal tour. The long, thick dining table had shallow craters and runnels scooped out of the dark oak. Communal soup could be poured from one end. On the tomb of the builder of the chapel, smiling skulls grin at the prospect of the resurrection depicted above their heads in a sequence of Romanesque panels, carved in local sandstone by rude masons.

Killing It. The girl prolongs her contact with the 'celebrity' not because he is famous, as he likes to think, but because he was a witness to her brief, happy passion. She is drawn to the house where she paraded her lover. The celebrity imagines that she really wants him rather than the memory which he frames. By some clumsy gesture, paraded as candour, he defiles what she treasures by telling her what a nobody her lover was.

15.3.83. A panicky letter from Steiner foresees the closing of *The Portage* in the face of a campaign conducted by Martin Gilbert, who refrains from abuse and sports no irony. He shows only that George's arguments are inaccurate, his whitewash of the wrong hue. Steiner has set a real monster among fictional characters who lack the rhetorical resource to confute him. Gilbert denounces an aesthetic category mistake: what is no more than provocative on the page becomes obnoxious on the stage.

Christopher Hampton wanted credit for a 'new play', but consented to reblock it from G.S.'s old hat. Hitler's velveteen monologue is enough to entice a great actor; the lack of imaginative freedom in the other characters is an affront not only to Martin Gilbert's notion of historical rectitude but also to the drama itself. Hitler becomes the vessel for authorial paradox, as if his actual personality and history were now as unreal and irrelevant as King Lear's. Can one imagine the tragedy of Lear being criticised on the grounds that his reign had not been as beneficial as Shakespeare is free to suggest? The transformation of historical figures into fiction is now so common on the TV screen that it would not be surprising if schoolchildren refused to accept archive pictures of Churchill and others on the grounds that they do not resemble Hardy or Eric Porter. In the grave dressing of Steiner's presumptuous prose, Hitler fails to be sufficiently remote; the paradox-monger succeeds only in composing a travesty of the truth.

G. telephoned yesterday in such affectionate tones that I could not bring myself to be in the least unkind. In cases of serious illness, we are all prone to mimic M. de Guermantes when advised of Swann's fatal affliction. G. will, I assured him, outlive us all. I have often suspected him of wilfully degrading me by alerting me to my enemies' opinions, however woeful his recital. Yesterday, he told me eagerly of the squib in Godfrey Smith's column, putting me among the three best stylists in the language. George must need my support. He was amused, perhaps relieved, to say that Claire had called him, the day after calling me, to offer him the Kissinger memoirs, at any length he pleased, this a week after my letter to J. Whitley deploring G.'s *licenciement*. It seems that I wagged the dog. There was no question, J.W. assured me, of G. being struck off.

The Chastillon has changed proprietors since last year. The food was excellent then; now... What can one say of *soupe de moules* without *moules* or of *osso buco grillé*? The head waiter, embarrassing in his gaunt incompetence, could find no rationale for the latter dish. *En bons pensionnaires*, we endured lunch and dinner with exasperated amusement. The service was slow, the portions so small that the plates, embellished with huge doilies, resembled the pudding faces of Flemish burghers encircled by copious ruffs. Gérard, our *moniteur*, took me, Stee and Sarah up to the peak on Monday. Although it was cloudy, there had been snow on the Saturday night and there was promise of an easy, powdery descent. When we arrived at the summit of the long *téléski*, we found that wind had scoured all the snow from the crest. Flagged as a *descente rouge*, it was now all ice. Once up, we had to go down. Gérard, for all his calm dismay, took the lead. I am not sure how or why I fell at first. It seemed no more than a lurch. He was below me, protectively, and I tripped my skis over his. It seemed that I might right myself at once. I had time to apologise, avoid him and then trip. I began to roll down the glassy dome of the mountain. It was steep and lacked the dips and bosses which might have slowed me. I rolled over and over, faster and faster. Gérard shouted '*skis devant*'. As I accelerated downwards, I speculated on what this slogan meant exactly. Often nervous on the slopes, though perhaps not often enough, I was not frightened. I was certainly dismayed. I expected to stop, but I did not. The ice was hard. I felt its fenders crashing into me.

5.4.82. Had I known what was likely to happen next, I should have been more apprehensive. Launched on my head-over-heels way, I had the insouciance of a falling child. I knew myself to be beyond aid; with no clear idea of how to arrest my tumbling, I accepted the indignity with surprising humour. Finally, getting my skis ahead of me (as if it had taken a long time to translate Gérard's shouted command into action), I managed to brake in a patch of shock-absorbent snow. I had hurt my shoulder, but I had a clear, unbruised head. A few yards further on, there was precipice, rocks beneath. I have torn the ligaments in my shoulder and will not serve overarm for a while.

A young policeman recently paralysed by a gunman acknowledged, seemingly without anguish, that he would never make love again. Even in appalling cases, there seems to be a human capacity for anaesthetising the intolerable. Is it part of the machinery by which we digest mortality? If we were fully aware of what we are losing, daily, it would not need the wrecking of our physical faculties to induce despair. The fact that irretrievable yesterday was once tomorrow, that every achievement of our lives is the result of expending our tally of time, would be enough to generate catatonic terror at the passage of a single second. The scandal of mortality is endured, even relished, as I did my fall. His sense of absurdity makes man the laughing animal whose distinction, in that regard, from other creatures was first noticed by Aristotle.

Laughter admits that language has its limits; whereof we cannot speak, thereof we can make a joke. Jugurtha, thrust into the pit from which he would be taken only to appear in Marius's triumph, after which he would be executed, remarked 'How cold this bath of yours is!' It is hard not to hear frantic laughter in his pitiful utterance.

The respect once given to the old depended on their carrying the history of the race. Their store of experience a treasured resource, they were valued like maps. The rise of the library primed the decline of the rhapsodes. It became unnecessary to entertain actual bards, or to book their presence, in order to have access to their words. Capacity to file information eliminated the need for live testimony. Deference to age persisted only as long as it was easier to consult a *gerousia* than to check in the stacks and the stats. Orderly files are the enemy of old people; shelved wisdom evicts the grave *signor*. The machine dehumanises knowledge; it defines it as whatever the machine itself can tabulate.

When a speaker in the Falklands debate says that he wants to hear no more about the cost of the operation, he concedes that money dominates modern calculations, not because man has become more mercenary, but because he has smarter accountants. Whatever the lure of the brand of Islam endorsed by Khomeini, he seems to all intelligent people, unless Michel Foucault is intelligent, to be reactionary; he holds that man can be saved without technology. The technologically-dominated West cannot but ridicule him. Vestiges of nineteenth-century confidence in progress suggest that, while it is inconvenient for Khomeini to be unreasonable, he is bound to be unsuccessful; history – our history – is on the side of reason and its side-effect, material advancement.

The homogenisation of the world is, we choose to insist, inevitable. Dreaming of the universal currency of the pre-Babel tongue, Western man sees particularism as an impediment to harmonious organisation. Must we yearn for the happy beige of uniformity? The winnowing of distinctions will leave mankind living in a burrow of Babel; its Esperanto will lack words for the poetry of higher things. Since hope of heaven has been the main cause of the creation of hells on earth, there are worse prospects than that of bungalow billets in a world without distinctions. The catch is that man cannot, by the nature of the flesh, be lodged for very long in rigorous equanimity. Eliminate the neuroses which baulk and spice his happiness and he will revert to savagery or tumble into unreasoning panic. The killing machines alone will be happy.

Pascal presumed that a punter's throw could pass for spiritual allegiance; his notion of faith turns St Peter into an immigration officer. The terms of Pascal's wager cannot be pronounced out loud without becoming ignoble. The wisdom of risking a flutter on salvation may be *lived*; it can find no dignified statement. What can be lived rightly cannot always be rightly argued: words are The Fall. Speech interrupts G–d, according to mystic fundamentalists such as André Neher. As soon as man propounds a doctrine for human salvation, he cannot be saved by it. What is currently fashionable can never appeal to leaders of fashion.

All methods of teaching art serve notice to artists that they must find other forms of expression.

Michel Pic: *L'avenir promis aux masses, quelle salut sinon la migration au passé?*

Steiner's 'Difficulty' seeks to make obscurity a distinguished way of preserving a secret while confessing, or even boasting, that there is indeed something arcane to be disclosed. The concluding paragraphs of Wittgenstein's *Tractatus* ask readers to put themselves in the author's lonely place. Had he been capable of Pascal's modest vulgarity, or high-minded immodesty (two sides, same coin), W. would have come out clearly with his doctrine. The Talmudic slant of his vision enabled, required or prejudiced him to embody doctrine in practice, not theory, hints not declarations. If he enunciated his truth, it could no longer be wholly true.

W. did not fall into the error Gödel attributed to Russell and Whitehead. He avoided the Epicurean crux by refusing to define the world or its ramparts. The remark about the limits of language draws attention less to the dominion of speech than to its limitations. The key is the personal possessive which Wittgenstein attached to both 'language' and 'world'. W.'s vision of language as mundane is evidence less of positivistic narrowness than of a piety which falls silent in the face of what cannot be said: the literally unpronounceable name of G–d.

Refusal to articulate is both moral and aesthetic: words cannot encompass the unspeakable. Every time an inexpressible truth is paraphrased, it is debased, hence ceases to be wholly true. Who can take seriously a religion which procures recruits on the grounds of its celestial rewards? By spelling out the dividends of religious conformity, Pascal hoped, and failed, to lend dignity to Christianity's prospectus.

The writer-as-artist would always sooner have something new than something good to say. Lying is choice when the truth is already out.

During the last twenty-five years, I have wondered, rarely but now and again, what became of Bryce Cottrell. Of all the Carthusians of my vintage likely to succeed, he was the paragon. If he had small charm, he had insistent powers of ingratiation; not particularly intelligent, he was indefatigably studious. Clumsy in movement, gauche in address, he was not athletic; yet he managed by persistence and application to secure places in the second XI cricket and the third XI soccer (which entitled him to bag his large behind in blue 'cuts'). Having won a classical scholarship to Corpus Christi, Oxford, when he was sixteen, he stayed on to become Head of the School. What could prevent him from gaining a place in the Cabinet? Black-haired, hunch-shouldered, loud-voiced, spotty, had he been a Jew, what a Jew he would have been! The motor of his ambition carried no silencer. A blaring paragon of conformity, Bryce did nothing wrong and never looked right. He clambered up the ladder with unstoppable gracelessness. Unappetising without being unpleasant, he could not be loved but never deserved to be disliked. He laughed at other people's jokes as a politician must, lest he lose their votes; he made none himself. His energetic place-seeking never quite gained him a seat alongside those whose eminence he sought to emulate. I am pretty sure that he got a First in Greats and I heard that he had married Nurse Monk, from the Charterhouse 'San'.

I knew nothing more until last night. What had become of Bryce since he gave us all the slip? How nice if some *coup de théâtre* could now be sprung! He is a stock exchange analyst, working for somebody and Drew. He was on TV, commenting on the effect of the Falkland Islands drama on share prices. Well-spoken, slightly plummy, he offered sensible, forgettable views: in times of uncertainty, panic was traditional; things go down and things rise again. It was hard to guess why he had been chosen, among all the available mouths, but he performed competently.

The mediocrity of Charterhouse declares itself in the lustreless glow of its brightest products. Set to scramble up ladders which lean against blank walls, they scale the heights and seldom get anywhere that matters. The only Carthusians who ever make names for themselves are the misfits, to whom ladders were not offered. The right-minded will say that making a name is a counterfeit ambition, but the great public schools, of which C'house claims to be one, affect to shape their pupils for leadership. Carthusians may do well; they seldom do better. The outstanding instances of my time are William Rees-Mogg and James Prior. Even in a reduced country, it is no small thing to become a cabinet minister or the editor of a once great newspaper; yet neither man makes a convincing show of greatness. Prior's red, hot bluster suggests that he has taken dietary hints from Ted Heath, under whose tutelage he was promoted and for whom he would, I suspect, still prefer to be devilling. Simon Raven has parodied both Jim P. and the Mogg in *Alms for Oblivion*; caricature is a Carthusian tradition. Peter Morrison (Prior's fictional surrogate) is graced with virile handsomeness and an obsolete, if not complacent, sense of decency. Simon flatters but he is undeceived; the Prior character has standing without *auctoritas*, the mark of the second-rate.* Should he ever become the leader of the party, it will be because he is the kind of king whom kingmakers enthrone, confident of being the power behind him. The Carthusian who merits promotion earns it by showy deference; rather than impose himself, he waits to be selected. The school is a factory for your obedient servants.

The empire rewarded its management with praise and titles; the books of flattery need never balance. No deliberate scheme had to be devised; to deceive others, it is neat first to deceive oneself. The ease with which swindlers can be swindled is equalled only by the outrage with which they greet those who trick them. Who relies more on the moral scruples of others than those who have none? The arbiters of Charterhouse were but the meanest of provincial ushers and, no doubt, subject to the illusion of a British mission to redeem and serve the heathen. The public schools' self-winding moral apparatus had no conscious purpose, no calculated trickery. The ability of, for instance, Burgess and Maclean to pass undetected, despite their eccentric behaviour, is explained, at least in part, by the fact that they were bluffers in a school of bluff; everyone was trying to seem more extraordinary than he really was, if only because it could be assumed that they were all, at heart, much of a not-too-muchness.

When an enterprise goes bankrupt, its deceptions come to shrill light; as soon as wheels cease to turn, cracks become evident. The Poulson case is a paradigm. It needed small wit to guess that there was a great deal of corruption in local government long before T. Dan Smith and his peculations were exposed; Ronnie Geary's experiences with the ruling junta in Colchester were clue enough. How often does anyone stop to examine what seems to be working and, more particularly, paying off? Only Poulson's amateurishness (and addled generosity) rendered him vulnerable.

---

* Prior's unsubtle revenge was aimed at Simon's middle stump: he labelled *Alms for Oblivion* 'James Bond for poofs'.

8.4.82. George told me, with glee, that Saul Friedlander was writing a response to A.H. In the event, S.F. has not limited himself to *The Portage*. His quarrel is with the whole revisionist literature of the last ten years or so. Since Faurisson and the other deliberate falsifiers merit no subtle refutation, F.'s targets are Fess, Fassbinder, Syberberg and G.S. He makes play with the hoary term '*kitsch*' to describe imagery used to turn myth into confectionery. The *kitschlich* treatment of Hitler is devised to make him assimilable: the Führer is rendered part of the process whereby man digests unpalatable history and can cease to be made colicky by it. What would a better method be? The accumulation of facts, in an unfanciful manner, seems properly dignified: amass enough evidence and a due verdict will result. Will it? It is precisely the 'personal touches', like the reminiscences of Adolf's valet (to whom he was a hero), that have been deployed to sweeten the figure of the lonely, dedicated dictator who can be made to look as much like Hulot as Chaplin.

Every attempt to explain or represent Hitler in known modes, of irony or historiography, appears to leave something out. The sense that H. has somehow escaped conclusive portraiture leads to increasingly *méchant* efforts to re/collect him. It would be nice to believe that Steiner's bringing him back to life is less an exercise in scandal than an attempt to make sure that he does not get away again. In damning homage, G. loads his Other with a degree of self-knowledge which, had the actual A.H. been capable of it, might have cured his paranoia. Given the last word at his own court martial, G.'s Adolf does not say how sorry he is, or isn't; considering the effect of his actions in quasi-rational terms, he looks only at what followed from his behaviour, as though such a reckoning determined his standing. He is not a romantic monster complacent in his genius and authenticating his actions because they are his. The impudence of his retrospective self-assessment is ruefully ironic: if he is to have a permanent, unchallengeable place in the consciousness of any people, he realises, it cannot be that of post-war Germans, who seek by all means to dissociate themselves from him, but in that of the Jews, who cannot suffer anyone to be ignorant of his unique significance. The state of Israel proves the necessity of its existence by reference to the indigestible fact of the Holocaust. If A.H. did not exist, Zionism would have had to invent him: he is essential to its mythology. Israel alone has a vested interest in maintaining Hitler's unique monstrosity.

There is a trace of frivolity at the heart of all creative activity; the cult of surprise is implicit even in scholarship. How often learned articles take the form of detective stories, with a list of suspects, a tense search for the unexpected solution and a triumphant unmasking, at the end, of the why-didn't-I-see-it solution!

Kitsch is a way of allowing you to have your cake and ice it too; Midas the confectioner renders edible whatever he can touch. The essence of *kitsch* lies in the fact that it is, above all, not unique. All carbon and no top copy, its efficacy depends on repetition; commanding the public scene, it seems inescapable, like the ten thousand flags of the Nazi rally. A single swastika could never have the effect of blanketing the vision of the faithful; what made Nazism seem irresistible was a visual no less than a broadcast lie, repetition as argument. Art is as weak against *kitsch* as reason against rant; it cannot make itself seen in the exaggerated glare of what, like Speer's pillars of light at Nurnberg, is not substantial at all, just as no reasonable objection can be raised against the bellicose voice of the orator at a meeting serviced by Stormtroopers.

Jack Yeats' refusal to have his paintings reproduced is in direct contrast with the propagandist's use of posters which are, it seems, without an 'original'. Since the poster depends on proliferation, the artist makes singularity the trademark of quality. Posters have a price, not a value. *Kitsch* may find an eventual market at auction, just as instruments of torture find a place in museums, but its essence is that, like journalism, it is forever ephemeral.

Even Hitler's methods of warfare were theatrical; the Stuka dive-bomber delivered a rhetorical shriek; it ranted its way to intimidate its victims. Once steady hands had ceased to regard it as an undeniable banshee, it became so easy to shoot down that it was taken out of service. The *panzer* attack was not only a brilliant use of technological material, it was also a parade, an exercise in theatrical display. The blitz appealed to Hitler, whose element was fire, not because it was militarily effective but because it brought his show into the West End. Had the Luftwaffe confined its attacks to England's airfields, the island would have become defenceless, but such cool strategy lacked dramatic allure. Explanations never fully explain anything; Ockham makes sufficient what cannot be exhaustive. Might it be said that the extermination of the Jews remained, until the end, on the Nazi agenda because disappearing Jewry was the only act of magic still feasible?

Lechery too can be an aspect of alienation.

12.4.82. When death is the only terrible thing, we wish it on others the better to escape it ourselves. The morals of pass-the-parcel are brought to the issue of nuclear war. The less we have reason to take the Russians or ourselves seriously, the easier it becomes to see how war could come about, if only because nothing can count as a valid reason for preventing it. The reliance of great powers on great weapons leads to the conclusion that nuclear weapons are the only decisive machinery. We have become content to live in a playground surrounded by an electrified fence so powerful that no enemy dares to pierce it and we have no means to escape from it. Our luxurious fun has been procured in such a way that we dare not face those excluded from it. We watch them through the loopholes in our defences, knowing that if we reach to touch them we shall be fried. Luxury, like deprivation, is a form of not having things.

9.5.82. Mark Rydell has had a great success with *On Golden Pond*, which poor Tony Harvey should have directed but could not because the dates didn't fit. I went to see M. in his little house on Bobolink Place where we worked together on *Roses, Roses*. He sits complacently on his newly-laid nest egg. When I last visited him, his agent Stan Kamen was not returning his calls. Now Rydell speaks of a $150m gross for his old people's picture. If you cannot discover a new young star, disinter two old ones. The logic of the biz credits Mark, as director, with the achievements of his aged duo and the Merlin role in having made their magic flower again. He is thinking of selling his house, which is entirely suited to his purposes, and moving to the beach, which will be inconvenient. Prices are around a million nine, two million one. Many scripts are now soliciting his nod; the telephone rings a lot. A pretty girl was arriving as I left. He has a new Mercedes 450. Success has watered him into new green confidence. I had made inquiries about *The White Hotel* and found that he had acquired the rights. He cannot, I am sure, deliver anything but a cheap revision of what is no more than an allusively shaped meringue. The artfulness of D.M. Thomas demands a film-maker of the order of Munk. Ambition, curiosity and disdain take one to odd destinations.

We were conveyed to LA by Frank Price of Columbia. I spent the first days communing with Burt about the idea which we were to audition on the Friday. We had good sessions in his beige offices on Gayley Boulevard, at the west end of Westwood. How could we fail to proceed with a project to which, I was promised, Columbia had already responded favourably? Why would they spend fifteen thousand dollars on bringing us into harbour if they were not prepared to give us a prime berth? Their investment was small enough to encourage them to take a chance and too big for there to be reason to change their minds. Yet they did. From the beginning of the meeting, the response was muted. I spoke at length, not unconvincingly, while the company simply sat there. Price is a small, thin-lipped man with a reputation for wanting to give the public only what he is sure they want. In navy blue suit, white shirt, no tie, he looks like a cop with the mob in his pocket, and vice versa. His young assistant wore a red floral dress and no make-up, which established her youth and her business-like purposes. She congratulated me on my career when, after an hour in a mental sauna, we left without sweat or deal.

We had been preceded by two ladies, neither young, who came out giggling dryly together. When Burt, dazed by our noncommittal reception, was trying to work out where things had gone wrong, I suggested that perhaps the previous meeting accounted for our unhappy reception. I may have been partly right: Ron told me later that Columbia were trying to persuade Fay Kanin, the president of the Academy and one of the two ladies who giggled, to script *Tickets*, a book Columbia owned. If she did not accept the job (and it seems she would not), the rumour was that they would be approaching me. This political subtlety made comforting sense: they were rejecting Burt, not me.

Tony Harvey has had a serious road accident and is in hospital in San Diego. His rented car stalled in the fast lane of the San Diego Freeway and the traffic that ran into him broke most of his bones. One thing is certain: two women will not be having a love affair over his dead body.*
His life is said not to be in danger; his career seems beyond recovery. But then I once thought the same of Rydell.

Success has no smell.

We did the usual things in LA; little else was available. Our best evenings were with the Donens, who took us to *Valentino*, and with the Mardigians who gave us a delicious lobster dinner in their patio. Ron bought the green lobsters on his way home, one huge Maine specimen each. The walrus and the carpenter never had a better time. I suppose the bill was paid by William Morris, but I was touched by the effort made by two people who had been working all day and to whom, for all our

---

* Tony Harvey had directed the film of my novel *Richard's Things*, in which a man's wife and his mistress meet and fall in love after he is killed in an accident.

affectations of intimacy, we remain strangers. The middle-aged become adept at facsimiles of closeness. What made the evening memorable was the lack of communication and the courtesies it provoked. How much can quasi-strangers say to each other, or want to reveal, when face to face? In a glass darkly may be the most agreeable mode. There would be no call to see Ron and Merl if mundane prosperity, ours and theirs, did not depend on it. How touching the efforts that people take to make the best of a mediocre job and to be gracious in the process!

There is odd courage in the willingness of the film community to spend month after month, year after year, in cushioned anguish, waiting for a favourable turn of the wheel. LA parades a society wedded to putting a good face on its face. Unenviably enviable, its denizens scan the horizon for a relieving column of easy money. The video market and electronic games are expected to recapitalise the movies; but will the accountants be willing to allow the new revenue to cover losses from traditional movie-making? The growth of the automobile industry did nothing to bale out the livery stables. Something explosive is happening in the entertainment business. It is unlikely to have many consolations to offer the thoughtful spirits in the business, if any.

I may be about to jet back to LA on the track of more ignominious money. Hal Ashby wants me to script a remake of *An Affair to Remember*. Bludgeoned by the disappointment of more original hopes, I may embrace a soft option for once and so fund our return to London. We shall have to find a flat in June, and the money to pay for it. At present, Lagardelle could hardly be more beautiful; spring and summer seem confounded. Even my little apricot tree, which seemed doomed to eternal barrenness, sports seven tenacious nodules, fuzzy promises; the plum trees carry as many green buttons as some Victorian ball gown. Everything has flourished since we sacked the gardeners. Everywhere the shrubs climb the sky where once they were cut to the quick, and slowed. The *boules de neige* explode in snowy bursts.

On such days we can only wait for the disaster which will mock our Arcadian privileges. The Argentine drama threatens to supply the fuse. Britain's spasm of nostalgic righteousness has less galvanised than embarrassed the world. It is as if a respectable pensioner had suddenly taken offence and sprinted after a mugger brandishing his double-barrelled umbrella. Carrington's complacency led him to misread Argentinian purposes and, worse, to send signals to Buenos Aires indicating the passivity of the British. Harold Nicolson's prescription for diplomacy – to be very precise – was never honoured. All the effort spent on rationalising the armed forces now reveals their slimness to be the consequence less of a healthy diet than of malnutrition. Few elements of the fleet have up-to-date defensive systems.

20.5.82. The rise in Thatcher's popularity, as the public is faced with an issue dated enough to understand, has made military action a near certainty. The government has surged in popularity by behaving irrationally and angrily. Since the Junta, in a different world, finds itself in a hardly different case, by at last having some claim to represent the almost united wishes of Argentinians, there are negligible prospects for a sane, cynical settlement. It seems longer than a month since we assembled at Peterborough for that session of *Any Questions* when we liked, some of us, to think that the Argentinians might quail at the sight of so much Britannic energy so loudly displayed. In fact, the government has been resentful and uncertain for so long that it rendered it easy for Buenos Aires to miscalculate Britannic resolve and competence.

Strong for the principle of Finest Hour solidarity, Mrs T. was furious against whoever hesitated to support the war effort, though war has yet to be declared. It is a contest unlike any since the Great War: a confrontation without enmity. Might a world war be kindled by the pettiest of fuses? In the short term, Britain is likely to be changed more signally than the world. If the invasion is successful and the casualty lists do not include too many names of Anglo-Saxon provenance, the Conservatives, having mishandled both the diplomatic and the strategic preliminaries, will be confirmed in power. It does not require a coherent policy in order to conduct a small, distant military campaign. The bill will be paid with better, gallant grace than any increase in nurses' wages. Having arrived at a way of damaging the country's economic prospects in a patriotic fashion, the Tories will procure the votes of those whom they can continue to victimise. This may be unfair, even if true; it could be argued that the Tories have been in charge without being actively responsible for what has happened. This confirms their view of history: since nothing can be accurately or scientifically predicted, only 'natural leaders' can cope with it.

Certain Things Must Not Be Allowed To Pay; and certain people will have to pay for them. It is generally agreed that there will now be a battle and rarely disputed that, once victory is achieved, negotiations will be resumed and the future of the islands arranged so that the British are not served with a bill they cannot afford. Honour will be satisfied; nothing else. Mrs Thatcher will be captive to success just as she would be the first victim of failure. The Socialists cannot win in either event: victory will silence them, taking advantage of defeat would make them the profiteers of humiliation.

The only time that the Labour Party ever drew a dividend from an issue of foreign policy was in 1945, when it could be suggested that they had stood firm where Neville Chamberlain ratted. Michael Foot's 1940 *Guilty Men* gave the plausible impression that the Tories alone had been weaklings and sell-out men; no mention was made of the sedulous pacificism and timidity of the Left.

13.6.82. The eclipse of the Social Democrats has been sudden and may be irreversible. The new party has made a virtue of parochial modesty at exactly the moment when Britain's pride has revived. The party of reason risks foundering on an uncharted rock which, a few months ago, no one imagined to be capable of making a hole in a major vessel. Owing to the ineptitude of two of the great departments of state, the Prime Minister finds herself in an impregnable position. What policy could never contrive, accident has secured. The Falklands Affair is a minor matter concerning minor powers. The Junta is now denounced as a vile conspiracy of criminal louts, but the British government did not hesitate to sell them some of the weapons which are now turned against it. If the islands are judicially British, it remains true that every sly opportunity was being taken to cede them, slowly and furtively, to Argentina. British diplomacy was ensnared by its own imprecision, a strategy of casual tokenism which seemed to connive at a polite Argentinian invasion. The last time the British were faced with solemn and incontestable duties over the fate of an island, the Labour government – guarantors of Cypriot independence and integrity – abandoned northern Cyprus to the Turks without even invoking sanctions against them. Had the Chinese revoked the lease of Hong Kong, ahead of the legal calendar, would muscle have been added to indignation?

The belief that some general law against violence has been upheld by the British action in the south Atlantic is humbug. However keenly we cheer the Task Force, at the supporters' club level, the actions of Mrs Thatcher, in patriotic defence of her own importance, is a symptom of the collapse of international morality, not its endorsement. It proves only that governments will, where they can, procure their own advantage by spilling blood. If London itself had been within range of Argentina's (French) weapons, there would have been much more talking. With great relief, and suitable background music, the British have emigrated from the present to the eighteenth century.

Driven on by a bellicose parliament bored with finicky practicalities, Mrs Thatcher has abdicated from cant and had recourse to jingoism. 'I am their leader, I must follow them' has been her slogan as she scampers to keep up with the militants who have, in other matters, been her least reliable allies. Having fumbled a pretty opportunity to divest herself of the unprofitable encumbrance of the islands, she has committed herself to an unlimited investment of men and money. How could she have done otherwise? By proving to the world that a power with the means to evict an intruder by force had the dignity and maturity to rely on diplomatic machinery. It is possible that suitably prolonged, nicely baited, negotiations might eventually have lured the Argentinians into a compromise or even a withdrawal. At worst, Britain would have lost what she never very much wanted to keep and would have set an inexpensive example of rectitude. No one would have had to die.

To speak of self-defence, when the self in question is incorporeal and eight thousand miles away from the body politic of which it is suddenly said to be a vital component seems far-fetched. If the Argentinians had been persuaded to concede the right of the Foreign Office to supervise the welfare of British passport-holders, there would have been no need for the islanders to lose the protective mantle of Whitehall, whatever that was worth. An offer of, say, £100,000 for everyone who wanted to quit a place where the Spanish language was about to be forced upon them could have cleared up a lot of trouble at reduced cost. The islanders are largely hired hands and might welcome a generous incentive to abate their love of the place, if indeed they are moved by it. Transfers, under an expensive tariff, are part of the modern game. If the Falklands represent a vital asset, the government should fall for having so grievously undervalued it. What likelihood is there that reason will ever prevail among the nations if, in cases like this, when any outcome would be acceptable, a supposedly *rusé* power like Great Britain cannot suffer the matter to be resolved by diplomacy? In flexing never very powerful muscles over a marginal matter, the government has missed an opportunity for the salutary hypocrisy which might have set a better example to the world than lethal pyrotechnics initiated to gain the applause of the media.

15.7.82. Radiant with malice, George tells the story of the seduction of Hugh Lloyd-Jones, whose collected papers I had been inspecting at the *Sunday Times*. The Regius Professor had become a virtual recluse. Taking refuge from his wife, he settled for a hermetic existence in his college rooms. He first declined to be intrigued by the petition of an American academic lady who begged permission for an interview after, she promised him, having flown the Atlantic expressly in that hope. He then agreed to give her three minutes. Mary L.'s pitch was simple and direct: she wanted to collate all his ephemeral work, reviews, casual articles, speeches and what not all in a single volume. She was soliciting no more than access to his *scripta minora* and his assent to her editorship.

She had the dignity and credentials to convert suspicion into provisional acquiescence. Not outstaying her stipulated sliver of time, she flew on to Jerusalem, where she had an academic assignment, having promised to get in touch when the Master had had time to reflect.

L.-J. arrived in Jerusalem soon after the lady and offered not only his intellectual capital but also his hand in marriage. It was a hand that was temporarily tied, but which he proposed to shake free. The lady's situation was rather different: she was both a mother and, it seems, a contented wife. Her suitor would take no refusal; what she had initiated with such boldness he was determined to conclude with equal audacity. Whatever had seduced the *professoressa*'s admiration in the abstract beauty of his scholarship had so strong a hold on her that when he deployed the full force of his personality, she was unable to deny him.

The couple are now married. Their academic lives have been less easily united. He is a professor at Oxford, she at Wellesley. If he had the will to impose himself emotionally, she knew better than to put herself entirely in his power by abandoning her tenure. Too much in love to endure long separation, he is forced to commute across the Atlantic. The Regius Professor of Greek is not required to teach undergraduates, but he is expected to give so many lectures per year. True to the terms of his office, if contrary to its spirit, he is now delivering a batch of lectures in the course of a few days before flying once again to the arms of his new wife.

Small Print. G. and I had lunch in a pub near Barrow Road. Zara was in Leeds, examining; partly for the money but more, I suspect, because she admires the professor. Perhaps she is not averse to being absent from the house while G. is there; it pays him out, in small change, for the weeks when he is absent in Geneva. Zara has risen high enough in her profession, despite a modest style and lack of native connections, to be chosen to write the next volume of the *Oxford English History*. G. denies none of her qualities, but cannot help disclosing a certain dismay which is also an obsession: his wife is undoubtedly his best friend and there is, he says, no one with whom he is more at ease when discussing his work and his hopes. Zara is the perfect sounding board, although she lacks the languages which would enable her to follow him in the obscure reaches of his elaborations. She covers diplomatic history; he takes care of the rest. Their intellectual alliance is strong and, apparently, enduring. If their children have felt the consequences, they had little choice but to seek to join the folks at the top table.

All set to insert himself in a distinguished pillory, George offered me the great subject for a novel which, he says, has never been explored: a marriage of true minds so spiritual that it banishes desire. There can, he insists, be too much understanding; eros cannot abide an excess of mutual esteem. He cannot invite me to love his wife, but he can solicit an assault from outside on something he dare not rupture from within. 'A subject to suit your genius,' he said.

The author of *Antigones* seems blind to the possibility that it is from his own daughter, on whom his pride has loaded such suffocating burdens of resentment and emulation, that the true twist in the story can be expected. He wants, he thinks, to see her happy as well as laurelled, but he has himself blocked her from the light in which he believes he hopes to see her. How apt then his greedily apprehensive reading, when he and Z. stayed with us a few years ago, of a very bad novel by Piers Paul Read, *The Professor's Daughter*! It concerned the scandalous behaviour of the daughter of an Ivy League faculty member. A lame piece whose author never put a foot right, G. found it irresistible.

G.'s physical flaws lend energy to his mental agility. A verbal magician, he bewitches his students into forgetting his lopsidedness. They are intrigued by a charismatic teacher who, unlike H. L.-J., has time for them. If he knows how to beguile an audience with a loud mixture of flattery and intimidation, he is limited by his own defective ear. Gleeful at the number of Cambridge colleagues, contemporaries and rivals, who have opted for Early Retirement, he presses the title upon me for a novel about the local scene. The unwillingness of the English professoriate to rage, or even to murmur, against the dimming of the light strikes him as deliciously supine. He himself is in line for further continental dignities, while observing the Cambridge potentates who evicted him fall back on the thin cushions available to those who agree to renounce their chairs.

16.7.82. We went again to Glyndebourne, mecca of the cultivated bourgeoisie. This time at least we managed not to burst into smoke. I also took the precaution of wearing a shirt which could not lose its studs, since it did not require them. We left Langham in good time and stopped for tea in Lewes, near Shelley's Hotel. The shoppe looked tasteful enough, but we had scones cut from the white cliffs and sat at a table shingled with crumbs. A trombonist due to play in the 'show' gave us directions. It was hard to understand how we could ever have got lost on the previous occasion, unless it was because we had such complicated instructions.

The first person we met was Eddie Mirzoeff,* at whom Beetle darted a glare of disdain. Later we were in the tea queue, with John and Deirdre, when whom should we see but the Lamberts. Jack seemed largely

---

* A small BBC TV producer with whom I fell out over the production of my Byron film.

recovered from the multiple afflictions which put him in danger a year or so ago. He looked like a Gainsborough after unhappy restoration, the jaundiced varnish removed to leave a pinkish-grey, thin-skinned undercoat. Catharine was flowing all around us in no time. You cannot help liking her, unless you get to know her. Jack greeted the news of our return to London with the scarcely veiled hope that it did not mean (i.e. that it did mean) that we were having to sell our Dordogne house. He endured the word that we were doing no such thing without overt signs of disappointment and allowed me to buy them iced coffee.

The influence of Puvis de Chavannes strained through P. Hall's idea of daring lay, like classical draperies on the nudes of Lord Leighton, over the vulgarity of his vision and the tedium of the piece. Where would the current generation of National Theatre directors be if it weren't for smoke guns? To spice the show, we were treated to one bare breast on either side of the stage and several, of a droopy order, in the divine frieze which descended from the flies, like some Olympic charter flight, at the climax of the redemption. Hall himself, in a white dinner jacket, fat as a jacket potato, came on at the end to kiss the hand of his leading ladies and, one did not doubt, would have done the same for his own arse, had it been within range.

The most pleasant encounter of the evening was with the dance critic David Cairns. He has the informed gentleness and good humour which suggest a man worth knowing. John Whitley, whose manner is, in general, uncontentious, stood out against the dinner jacket rule, if rule it is: he wore a sat-in light blue suit and linkless shirt. Deirdre has the air of a beauty queen in exile, obliged to suffer behaviour which would never have been acceptable had she been on her throne. They are kind and uncritical, effusive in their gratitude for the use of Lagardelle. John seems marginal to the arts, a man who has been lucky but does not call it luck. He hints, not infrequently, that he has been in trouble with his masters, but he has proceeded from assistant literary editor to Arts Editor, despite the convulsions which have riven the paper since his arrival. He has the soft-spoken persistence of those who never raise their voices but regularly make themselves heard. I imagined him to be a Harry Evans man, but he told me that he had not commiserated with our once popular leader when Rupert M. chose to drop the pilot (some spell him Pilate, it seems).

I was invited to visit *The Times* during my few days in London. A brace of young men, led by Nicholas Wapshott, took me to beer and regaled me with opportunities to appear on the leader page, a treat which would once have flattered me into voluble polemics but which now seems obsolete.

20.7.82. The state of England in this mid-summer is increasingly farcical; only Aristophanes could handle its diverse absurdity. From the Falklands to the Queen's bedroom is a long haul and a short step; in both cases an absurd invasion has led to calls for Strong Action and the resignations of those deemed unworthy of High Office and Responsibility. Perhaps the logical step would be for Rear-Admiral Sandy Woodward* to be posted outside Her Majesty's bedroom door.

One of those oddities of English pronunciation, beyond the comprehension even of the most *rusé* foreigner, came on the BBC news disclosing the scandal over the conduct of the Queen's long-serving bodyguard, Commander Trestrail. The announcer deputed to blow the gaff declared that the Commander, for whom Her Majesty is said to have had affectionate feelings, had had a 'home-oh-sexual' relationship with a male prostitute. There was denunciatory force, without etymological pedigree, in those two long ohs. Churchill's wartime way of saying 'Nazi' and 'Gestapo' (Jest-a-po) refused those terms the intimidating weight which pronunciatory orthodoxy might have conferred.

29.7.82. News that the Greek government has become more or less openly anti-Semitic does not come as a great shock. That strain has always been immanent in the Greek Church and was prominent in the '*Ellas Ellenôn Christianôn*' peddled by the colonels. Greek politics are of a savage subtlety. For fear of the Russians, the history of Greece since 1945 has been manipulated by the British and then by the Americans. It could be said that the hostility of Athens towards Israel is displaced rage against Washington. Andreas Papandreou was elected not least on account of his American-educated promise to face down Uncle Sam's recurrent intrusions. He will continue the pro-Arab stance of the previous government because it helps to isolate the Turks and offers other Muslims no cause to side with Ankara against Athens. Will Greece be drawn into a practical alliance against Israel? Such a move offers no tangible rewards. Despite Andreas' loud opposition to the EEC and NATO, Greece will remain in both. Whatever the *hubris* of the US, the Greeks dare not alienate Washington too decisively lest the Turks take licence from their isolation. Anti-Semitism is now being visited on an indigenous Jewish population so small that not even paranoid Hellenes can truly believe themselves threatened by its presence. The only time that I recall Jews

---

* The commanding officer of the victorious Falklands operation.

being mentioned in Greek conversation was on Mykonos in 1962 at the Hotel Leto (where we were unable to get a room last October). The manageress was exaggeratedly pro-Semitic, in the style of Alan Barnsley (aka Gabriel Fielding) the following year in Cheltenham;* her condescension was not pleasing. Since Sarah is a name never used in Greek families, we had at once been recognised as Jews.

In his study of the Peloponnesian war, Ste. Croix seconds Thucydides in arguing that there must always be a distinction between the internal and the external behaviour of the state. Is that why Plato ignores foreign policy in his 'ideal', landlocked polity? Louise Purslow argues that the Chomsky position is indistinguishable from isolationism, but it could be said that such a posture is the best for states to adopt. Is there not a case for hawking the Foreign Office to private ownership? As it is, we have Mrs Thatcher retrieving her domestic prospects by an overseas adventure provoked by the ineptitude of her own ministers. She has persuaded the public that a moral lesson has been dispensed to the rest of the world. In fact, the Falklands War has been an expensive and unrewarding exercise; had the same money and as many lives been lost on a commercial venture, it would have ruined its sponsors.

The Sicilian expedition may have lamed Athens, but success would have brought substantial material benefits. Victory would not have made the armada a whit more moral, but it would certainly have rendered it profitable. Mrs T.'s task force responded to the national vanity, as the Vietnam war did to that of the US, until it didn't. The Americans calculated that their area of influence could be extended and secured by crushing a small country. Britain's commercial prospects have been damaged and no profit engendered by an eight-thousand-mile sortie. The Venezuelans offer immediate proof; others will follow. If Sweden or Switzerland or, God help us, West Germany had reacted with armed indignation to a similar affront, should we not have supposed that these states had relapsed into anachronistic folly? What is odd is how willing the country has been to go along with such a Quixotic expedition, especially by comparison with its reaction to the Suez affair, a quarter of a century ago, when real interests seemed to be at stake. In sorry practice, Eden's policy had small chance of success, even if successful; what Britain had not been able to afford in 1947, when she renounced hegemony in the Middle East, was unlikely to be sustainable a decade later. The last throw of an imperial power on the wane is always liable to leave her flat on her back. Britain

* 'I love Jews,' he threatened me.

was also stabbed in the latter quarter, since the US could scarcely replace her in the Gulf before the previous overseer was beyond redemption.

The electorate suffered no lasting trauma from the Suez episode; the British chose domestic luxury rather than endure the austerity required to arm a waning empire. If, however, the UK had pursued a policy of military intransigence, despite Macmillan's feared collapse of the pound, London could have played the independent card with more advantage than was gained by capitulation to Washington's economic diktat. The Israelis have chosen the harder option because they have none of the Foreign Office's illusions about 'ultimate solidarity'. The more tactlessly the US is treated by its clients, the more its allegiance, however surly, is likely to be secured. In 1956, the British, by coming to heel, promised Eisenhower that they lacked the nerve for defiant dissent. The diplomatic rule is that a great power's least acquiescent underling gets the biggest subsidies to keep it on side.

Menachem Begin acts as though what matters is the way in which his decisions are reported, the (Woodrow) Wilsonian fallacy. In the *TLS*, C.M. Woodhouse writes of the effect of W.W.'s moralising excursion into foreign affairs. He could not have done anything more likely to muddy the waters of the world than to declare the right of self-determination, which few 'peoples' have ever enjoyed and which can never, as Byron saw, be granted, only fought for.

30.7.82. George told me, with small sympathy, what a disappointed man Renford was. I should have guessed as much from the speed with which the latter denied it. R. and Maurice Cowling are now political buddies. M.C., it seems, was in hospital and found himself the fellow-patient of a man called Robinson, a multi-millionaire who, perhaps chastened by illness, announced the desire to bestow a benefaction on his home town's university (he himself had gone out to work an early age). During his convalescence, M.C. and Renford had several meetings with their mark and persuaded him that he should think in terms not of a mere building or library but of a whole college. Renford began, G. promises, to have the ambition to be its first Master. Robinson did indeed come up with the cash, as proved by his college's prospectus and name. Renford's hopes were not realised; a scientist was appointed in the place for which he had been angling. He remains President and heir apparent to the mastership of St John's, but Harry Hinsley, the recently elected incumbent, need not retire for many years. Renford's chances cannot have been enhanced by his abortive attempt at secession; in any case, the front runner (cf. Jago in *The Masters*) is often the likeliest to be nobbled. Renford was very friendly when I saw him at Easter, but he has neither answered my long letter about his small, but excellent, philosophical tome nor passed comment on the Catullus I sent him. Even when we did write to each other, he had a way of bunching all the material of his brief, sloping letters into the upper half of the college paper which he always used. His body is locked in an awkward angle; he proceeds like an Anglican Groucho stuck for a cigar. His little pursed mouth and the faint words issued from it suggest sour fastidiousness. He seldom speaks ill of anyone, yet one senses a cache of malevolence. His tone so soft that he might be whispering in your ear, his eyes fixed on some distant target on which he lacks a sufficient arsenal to mount a loud assault. When did he last shout and what at?

4.8.82. Not having been to Ramatuelle for several years, we took a detour through the cork forests. We passed under Gassin or Grimaud or whatever the last crowded hilltop place was, and took the coast road past our innocent youth. The road seemed to have been moved; the traffic was choking. We passed a barracks from which the jeep may have come that first lifted us to the walled village where Madame Isnard housed us for five hundred francs (*anciens*) a night and 120 more for the kitchen and the Butagaz.

Today's Ramatuelle is a turban of ramparts around a carpark and a café. Publicity has breached its secret; too many people, greedy for the seclusion their presence denies each other, have tramped on each other's dreams. There are still elements of what we remember: the crutched lime tree in the square, the vine-covered terrace of the café where smarties from St Trop asked us whatever we found to do in a place like this. We walked along to Mme Isnard's door, expecting her to be long gone. 'Isnard' was painted on the door.

We went in to find a little souvenir store selling lilac sachets of Herbes de Provence. I asked the woman behind the counter if old Madame I. was still alive. 'She was here a minute ago,' she said. 'And what about her daughter, Marcelle?' '*C'est moi*,' she said, pulling her hair from her face, smiling at our surprise. She had, it seems, spent the last thirty years in which we have done whatever we have done living the same life, by her mother's side. Polite but not welcoming, she did not expect her mother, who just gone upstairs to make lunch, to be pleased to see us. The old lady was, it seemed, too much pestered by casual callers. We were sentimental enough (she had indeed remembered us on the previous occasion) to think that, had we insisted, she might have been touched by our return.

We drove to Escalet, recalling the hot path through the pine forest to a beach dominated by a burnt out villa. It is now a resort, surrounded by villas. Overheated tourists sported beside a sea fouled with pollution, its hem buttoned with jellyfish. We retreated to the Mas d'Artiguy, the only hotel near St Paul de Vence with a pool. We spent one night in a very expensive concrete cave without the advertised *climatisation*. When we looked through the huge glass doors at the starred restaurant, it was so unappetising that we turned away. The place stretched cavernously in all directions. The staff lacked the grace or pride, the guests the ward-robe or the manners, to live up to the opulence of the décor. We passed the morning by the very large, chilly pool, listening to the intrusive tria-logue of what sounded like three trainee girl agents from the N.Y. branch of the William Morris Agency. Young and unattractive, they did not display their breasts to the expensive sun. Other women, one very fat, another very thin, did so, lending the pile of concrete a pinch of genteel naughtiness.

At the *Ermitage du Rion*. The headwaiter admired his English and was very matey with it. When Beetle failed to finish her *salade Niçoise*, he asked if there was anything wrong with it. She said 'No', politely; where-upon he said, 'Then finish it up!'

Tom and Malou Wiseman have just bought an old mill in Cabris, not far from the rented place near Grasse where they have lived for ten years. At the bottom of a steep lane off a side road, the mill is a broad, white-washed seventeenth-century building; handmade doors to all the rooms and cupboards. There are olive trees and – two terraces down from the well barred house – a tiled swimming pool. The property of a rich French family, it has been well maintained, never modernised. There is not yet much in it, except for beds, boxes of paper and a desk for Tom's type-writer, an instrument ponderous enough for a pronunciamento. Dirk Bogarde's friend Tony tipped them off about the place being for sale for only two million francs.

The enthusiasm which Warner Brothers once had for Tom's J.R. Oppenheim novel has not survived its poor sales or his first draft screen-play. He sat on the threshold of his lovely new house, on the sagging white wicker furniture left by the outgoing owners, and could afford, just, to be philosophical about his rewarding disappointment. He was a feared movie critic and showbiz columnist and cannot quite under-stand how little those activities have qualified him for screenwriting. He now regards himself primarily as a novelist, although he has only the heaviest gifts – solemn cogitation, earnest attention to important issues – and none of the zestful language which brings a novel to life, life to a novel. He evaluates the market, collating the ingredients necessary to its exploitation, even to the point of living in America for a year in order to familiarise himself with the going ambience; yet he lacks the flair to transform shopped knowledge into original work. His ideal audience is, or was, Arthur Koestler, another man of intelligence and journalistic energy for whom the caressing of details was never as attractive as the articulation of the general. Both are liable to confuse the Big Book with the big topic. In K.'s case, he achieved one masterpiece, *Darkness at Noon*, which proves the rule that no rule lacks an exception (Gödel's law has an aesthetic cousin).

When Tom sent me his Oppenheim book, I assumed that he was pattern-bombing potential puff-writers. In fact, I was possibly the only, certainly the first, person to whom he posted a copy. There was some intelligence, much research and little taste in the text. Teller and J.R.O. were grossly enlarged. O.'s wife, Helen, who supplies an object of lust for the Teller character, is depicted as a handsome American woman with a welcoming cunt; an insatiable collaborator in her own debauch. No doubt such ladies exist and behave as T. was at such pleasurable pains to describe, but her lack of personality made it seem that one was reading a juicy manual, not a specific story. The combination of a calculated treat for the reader and a rending of history's knickers did not amount to a recension of *The Magic Mountain*. I told Tom exactly, though not unkindly, what I thought. If he took my comments to heart, he has the quality not to resent them. Once I realised how much more important to him my views were than I had presumed, I did my best to apply balm to the bruises. He responded with generosity to my efforts to be generous. Having renounced journalism, he remains a journalist.

John Schlesinger was shocked when I told him that I had seen Dirk travelling on the same plane as myself and had not even said hullo. My aloofness, if that is what it is, seemed to him unsociable and – worse! – unprofessional. Imagine preferring to read a book to making a mark! I cannot now remember the reasons for my breach with John. Even when the rift seemed irreparable, I dreamed, literally, of its repair. Had *FFTMC* been a success in the US, or had I had a hand, as I was asked, in *Midnight Cowboy*, for which I was unsuited, we might have maintained our, as J. put it, 'association'.

In the early sixties, the cinema seemed to offer chances to participate in a public art in which adventure, gold and fame might all be found, quickly. I was amused to dazzle or bamboozle John (his usual response to an unusual idea was 'How do we do it, dear?'). If he came from a cultivated background, he lacked any thorough culture, especially when it came to books. The homosexuality which he did not conceal, though he belonged to a generation that sometimes flaunted, but was more frequently cautious about its public display. It also seemed like a certificate of sophistication, as it had at Cambridge, when we often played at being camp, to escape being our suburban selves. John and I had an easy rapport; Jewishness gave us a common reference, never common obligations, still less beliefs. When war came, in 1967, we made gestures of solidarity: John went on a sponsored trip to Israel, where he made a perfunctory documentary under the aegis of Wolf Mankowitz. The latter's opportunism was cited last week as an excuse for the listless consequence of their expedition. After the war had been won, Wolf showed himself the more pragmatic Jew; it was better for Israel to have deals made for film production than for patronising 'artists' to play the vegetarian vulture over the spoils of its victory.

12.8.82. John has been with Michael Childers 'on and off' for fourteen years. I met M. first in John's house in Beverly Hills, at the reconciliation after our long *froideur*. Neat and not markedly feminine, polite but not deferential, independent not distant, he made a little conversation and was gone. J. and I sat by the pretty pool and then went down the hill to Hamburger Hamlet, where I was made so sick that I have not eaten a commercial hamburger since. In the intervening years, Michael has grown plumper and more lady-like. Recently he had a serious lung operation (in Dallas); still convalescent, his diet seems calculated to break all sensible limits. They talk of caution and practise excess. John gave us recipes at every possible cue. As visitors, he and Michael were happy to share a double bed in the flat; but their main pleasures are now at the table. They talked of Maisons-Laffite more than once; they had been sumptuously spoiled because Someone Who Knew Someone had been their host.

Michael has the tact of those used to being less welcome than their lovers, and the impatience behind public civility. A good guest, he would not be surprised or sorry if he never saw us again. When they took us out to dinner, he enjoyed conspiring against his lover to order a second bottle of Château Grillet, not expensive by Californian standards at two hundred francs a bottle, but no bargain. He judges very accurately how severely J. can be taxed. He wore nice soft clothes; Beetle envied him his Dior shirt. Sometimes he sported towelling trousers, ample enough for thick thighs and wide hips.

He has had the good sense to make his own career; photographing Sylvie Vartan his principal meal-ticket. He claims to have taken every picture of her ever printed. He did a lot of pics of John Travolta, who is now not as big as he was (only bigger). I heard that M. disliked England, but he now knows a lot of famous people, on what Julian Jebb called 'the buggers' circuit'. George Cukor figures frequently on his and J.'s lips. J. now has the appearance, in long shot, of a cross between Sidney Greenstreet and Father Christmas, benign and sinister *à la fois*. It was not conceit that made me realise that he needs me more than I need him; it was the realisation that I do not need him at all.

John cares for little but recognition. He is, however, devoted to his parents. His mother was recently declared to be on her deathbed, but rose from it because she had to go and make her marmalade. Bernard had cancer twenty-five years ago and 'beat it'. He has become shameless and self-indulgent: at his age, why refuse himself brandy or cigars? J. salutes his hedonism, but drew the line when the old boy took a leak in the herb garden (and denied he had done so). J. likes to be in England because he knows that his parents' time is limited. He is much possessed by death and sickness.

David Peel died about a year ago. He had been Michael Grimwade's lover, then his closest friend. I once visited his discreet showroom, opposite the Connaught. He specialised in Roman antiquities. I was taken with a gold signet ring with an inset seal. He wanted four hundred pounds for it, in the mid-1960s. A shiny man, with a schooled walk and cultured voice, he had been an actor and had a prelate's presence. He died after a long and very painful illness. Michael G. became a little strange once it was over. He wanted to have a memorial service in the actors' church, though D.P. had long ceased to appear on the boards (he pre-dated the box). Recently Michael canvassed the idea of some annual ceremony, which Schles considered excessive. Peel had, I think, been a Catholic. He left most of his fortune to M. who was, perhaps, seeking to honour his benefactor with a secular requiem.

We spoke to M. last week. He is supposed to be decorating our new flat. He sounded perky but was going into hospital this week, something sudden. He had said previously he would be working through August. I was considerate enough, unless it was inconsiderate, to ask what the matter was. He replied, with a sort of chuckle, that he had an internal lump they wanted to remove. Since this is the week of the COHSE [Confederation of Health Service Employees] strike and the waiting lists are long and lengthening, it must be that the doctors take a serious view. How bravely some people face the loneliness ahead of them! Their relationships are febrile; their happiness without the children to hold it together. Their cruel kindness is partly generous, partly acquisitive; patient with each other's foibles, they relish each other's discomfiture. Those who live for pleasure have a penchant for pain.

John and Geoffrey Sharpe have known each other since they were nine years old; aging friends, they now share a house, with a number of acres, in Kent. They bought Strawberry Hole Oast not least on account of the name which has had – 'as you can imagine, dear!' – several glosses put on it. The restaurant pays substantially for the upkeep; the property's produce is sent to Covent Garden and served at *The Grange*, now a poor table. G. lives much of the time in France (he has a place near Eze, a flat in Paris) and does not want to work any more. They keep *The Grange* going largely because Dominique has been such a loyal servant and they cannot give him his *congé* at his age, not that he is signally ancient*. If he had run the place as he should, he would no longer be dependent on the favours of his masters; he could have betrayed them long since. J. and G. have joint ownership of Strawberry Hole and have willed it to each other; the survivor takes all. There are occasional rows. During *Yanks* (John dates the world by his productions, as we once did by royal reigns), he took a hamper of goodies down for the weekend without informing G. The fridge was full of 'ten pounds' worth of provisions' which G. had 'specially' brought in. There was a quarrel in which it was yelled that separate arrangements had better be made thenceforth when it came to entertaining.

Sacha Guitry once advised a young man to get used to giving expensive presents to his women; in that way, he would never notice when generosity had to yield to necessity. I suspect that J. has always followed that advice, whether or not he was aware of its source. He has provided the bed in expectation of a shared breakfast. If Michael has a measure of independence, he also depends. John has made frequent use of the hustler services available in LA to suit all tastes and pockets. He saw a lot of Natalie and R.J. They sometimes lent or chartered him the fatal yacht. John's unlikely taste for sailing was developed during a cruise of the Turko-Greek islands after shooting *Yanks*. It cost two thousand dollars a day, worth every cent. The straight rumour about N. is that she was having an affair with Walken. If J. cannot quite believe the unlikely story, it amuses John to repeat it. Why did I greet him with such courtesy and spend a week trying to breathe life into a manifest stiff? The prodigal *tante* had returned and was soliciting my help. I am a sucker for reconciliations. Were it not for this blasted move to London, I should have

---

* Dominique, a handsome young man, played the male whore in the scene in *Darling* in which Diana and Larry Harvey go with a party of swingers to watch an exhibition in a brothel.

turned down both the films which I am so lucky to have been offered and so frail as to undertake.

The solid Edwardian flat my keen-eyed mother has found for us in Stanhope Gardens is convenient for the Lycée and we shall not be obliged to stay longer than three years. We shall see Paul and Sarah and my mother will be glad to see us, at least to have me within reach. Now that Irene is working regularly for Paul and Charlie at *Genius Loci*, she has renounced old resentments and displays even older qualities: wit, energy and enthusiasm. She should have worked all her life; she would by now have become a very successful businesswoman, a decided ex-New Yorker, transplanted but fruitful.

I see Greece becoming the *poubelle* of Europe. My fantasy of a simple life on Ios will founder before I have time to be disillusioned. Ritsos provides me with daily flights to his imaginary Hellas. Only the fairly happy few can still hear the songs the Sirens sing. We are lashed to *temps perdu* as Odysseus to the mast. All that beguiles us is slipping astern. We have taught ourselves the knots that hold us to the machinery of caution and yesterday's calendar. Coming to London, at once desirable and 'essential' to Stee's education, will take us from this isolation, protracted and fraught with idiotic 'problems' (I have just come back from shouting at the loo for running too freely), back to a life we lived fifteen years ago. London may provide new friends; it will certainly procure new enemies.

Was any monster ever more thoroughly domesticated? My only jewellery is the ring in my nose.

14.8.82. J. told me, again, how he decided to be a director, the controller, so far as possible, of his own destiny. He joined the army in 1944, when things were still serious. His father had done distinguished service in the Great War and expected J. to become an officer. He had been hopeless at games at Uppingham,* but he accepted that he must try to prove himself manly. He was drafted into the usual basic training, complete with night exercises and endurance tests. On one of them, he had to wear wet clothes for several days and caught rheumatic fever. It was assumed at first that he was skiving; only when he was too weak to reach the lavatory was the doctor called. He was taken to hospital and took two weeks to recover, whereupon he was returned to the OCTU [Officer Cadet

---

* John's public school was, in fact, Sherborne. 'Uppingham' is too sweet a Freudian lapse to be excised.

Training Unit]. On an assault course, he mistimed his leap onto a rope and fell heavily. The sergeant-major shouted 'On your feet, sapper!'

'I can't fucking move.'

He had broken his ankle and never became an officer. In that moment of agony and rage, he decided that he would, if he survived, seek to become the master of his fate. Having been excused commissioned ambition, he became an entertainments wallah. He soon had the shouting sergeant-major in drag. He went to the local music halls and stole jokes and routines from touring comics. With busy inertia, he imposed himself on an environment which yielded to him only when he had proved himself useless. The commitments of masculinity were beyond him: war, women, physical excellence. He became an orchestrator of what he could never live. Judged a failure by reality, he became a successful manipulator of its counterfeit. Sent to Singapore, he became a khaki impresario. Peter Nichols told us how he went to join the notorious company and was met by J.R.S., to whom he said, 'Aren't there supposed to be a lot of homosexuals in the unit?' 'Yes, dear,' said J., with an imitable leer.

16.8.82. Tom Maschler telephoned on Friday. Before he was put through, I tried to imagine what good news he could possibly want to tell me. Had he made a paperback deal for my stories? Did he want a piece about the new novel for his spring catalogue? He was coming to our region on Wednesday. He and his family had rented a house near Avignon. He began by asking whether we would drive over and see them. I doubt if he had any real wish for us to do so. The truth, in a diaphanous veil, was that – like so many of those who do us a favour by announcing their advent – he was hoping for another dish of cadgeree.

He makes himself the advertisement for his famous authors, a service he has yet to render me. In twenty-five years I have rarely had an interesting conversation with him. Paul asks why I know him if I like him so little. My answer was not the whole truth, but it was true: I feel an affinity with him. I am also easily possessed by strangers. Afraid of giving offence, I seldom reject an overture without the dread of driving its author into the ranks of my enemies. Hence I find it difficult to refuse anybody anything; in T.'s case, however, I am willing to make an exception. So memorable are his gaffes that, when he is absent, they seem quite endearing. When he first came to Lagardelle, he walked onto the terrace outside the sitting room and said, 'This is the best thing about the house.'

18.8.82. The comedy of Ibsen lies in the Victorian dress in which tragedy is enacted. As soon as we hear that a man has been seventeen years in an upstairs room, we may be sure that he will be down shortly.

13.9.82. Our new flat is around the corner from where my grandparents had a flat, at 71, Cromwell Road, when I first came to England, as a baby. Next month I am to go to Liverpool to address, God help me, the Granada Literary luncheon, at the Holiday Inn not a few yards from where I first landed in this country. Perhaps we have been exiles long enough; one may worry about the condition of the swimming pool and fear for the sanity of the cat, but there is something seductive in the life of a great city, however lamentable its decline. Our flat rumbles with the subterranean proximity of the District and Piccadilly lines; in the kitchen you seem to hear the wheels, in the dining room the rush and in the bedroom only the grumbling of the trains, louder when destined for Wimbledon, deeper when heading to Piccadilly or Hammersmith.

We went with George and Zara to Michael Ayrton's show, of early work, at a gallery so far down the Fulham Road that we were almost in Putney. G. was gleefully doleful about the unfashionable locale. M. would hardly have relished such an *éloignement* from the West End which, when he was twenty, seemed his manifest destiny. Elisabeth was walled in chintzed flesh; she tilts her head back and only the eyes, laden with purple make-up, announce the same woman. We greeted her and the brood with more effusiveness than enthusiasm. We liked her; we loved him. Both G. and I suspect that Elizabeth valued us more as potential purchasers than as intimates. She was keen to make others pay for whatever of Michael they took away from her. Macmillan's want me to be M's biographer. I am lunching with them this week. George suspected (probably with malicious justice) that Tom Rosenthal has abandoned plans for a *hommage* because such a book would be too expensive and lack a public. R. volunteered his help with all the speed of an ally relieved not to be summoned to the front.

53, Stanhope Gardens was built when my grandparents were young. Its solid mass declares the confidence which Edwardian speculators had in the endurance of the respectable middle class. However profit-minded the landlords, there was no evident corner-cutting. A varnished mahogany rack in the lobby disclosed, by the slide of a handy paddle, whether tenants were IN or OUT. Servants were human burglar alarms: as far as society was concerned, their presence left the flat empty. A slot beside each name is labelled 'cards'. When was the last one inserted? Bernard Sheridan's old friend, Louis Hayman, lived here before he became chairman of Leopold Joseph, the banking firm whose original partners played bridge, for modest stakes, at Crockford's when I used to go there. They had the quiet address of Jews who had done well enough to wish to stay inconspicuous. Such self-effacement carries an element of amusement, as if at a discreet deception.

Lunch with Peter May and George Greenfield. Modesty is the recognition of superiority, or it would not be modest. P.B.H.M. so lacked any critical awareness of other people that he seemed without the slightest 'side'. He had no reason to disparage others because they never disposed him to self-doubt. Yet his early retirement suggests that he was riven by all kinds of stresses. As a source of saleable dirt about other players he proved an unproductive void.

Bernard Sheridan was more annoyed by the promptness of the BBC's condemnation of Israeli officers who 'did nothing'* than outraged by the massacre itself. He has the callousness of his profession: he cannot spend time in sorry brooding over people whom his arguments have failed to save from condemnation or even from the gallows. He had Rhodesian black clients whom Smith hanged. He does not lead a 'Jewish' life; his partisanship is less that of a Zionist than of a man alert to prejudice. His dignity is not particularly well-dressed, his competence neither well-organised nor assertive; like the bed-bug, he gets there just the same. He takes the strain not only of his clients' anxieties but also of a Down Syndrome daughter to whom Bernard devotes regular and patient affection. Neither stimulating nor impressive, he is a good man.

28.9.82. George Steiner took me to lunch at the Savile Club. If I am elected, I shall have to verify how many ells it carries. I put on my suit for the occasion. He wore his little foreign camel-hair coat and showed me round the nicely numbered 69 Brook Street. It was, he said, once the home of a famous *horizontale* and has an Edwardian afflatus about it. There was the usual supply of decrepit elderly members, refusing to go gentle by taking the stairs rather than the tight lift. I have no confidence that I shall be elected, although G. says it will be an honour for them to have me. I remember lunching there with Jack Lambert, at the same round table as Hugh Trevor-Roper, who could not refrain from being uncivil about A.J.P. Taylor. G. makes much of the fact that he is also a member of the Athenaeum, yet lacks confidence in his welcome at the Savile.

---

* If that is true, they did more or less precisely what British officers did in 1941 during the pogrom in Baghdad, when the city's Arabs were left to massacre its Jewish population.

Frank Muir spotted us in the dining room and came over, full of pink affability. He has made it fashionable to be witty without being cruel. He and Denis Norden are the two best after-dinner speakers I have ever heard. We recalled the days when they were partners in a talent agency run by Kevin Kavanagh where Leslie Bricusse and I were made generously welcome. I asked whatever happened to K.K. Frank, straight-faced for a moment, almost whispered that he had committed suicide. K.K., an overweight, apparently bluff man of urgent energy, was the son of Ted K., the scriptwriter of *ITMA*.

G. was so pleased by Frank's affability that he asked him to be the proposer of my membership. Is there still an element of anti-Semitism in London clubs? It's always nice to have something against one's fellow members. Bob Robinson, hardly less cordial though certainly less likeable than Frank, promised to subjoin his name. Only Richard Baker, who was being lunched by Christopher Martin of *Omnibus*, looked at me with baleful mien. He is ceasing to be a newsreader and has, I suspect, a much less affable character than his honest air on camera is calculated to convey. He greeted me with wary chumminess. Is he being courted as the next anchor man for *Omnibus* and does he fear that my presence might suggest another name to Martin? Baker's music programmes are well received; his middlebrow fluency licenses him to be the Huw Weldon of the future, if the future needs one.

11.10.82. I took the 08.50 from Euston to Liverpool. The long green landscape was unfamiliar and uninteresting. I have no Proustian fascination with the glamour of place-names. Under a grey sky, the autumn greenery undulated between fewer towns than I expected. Milton Keynes came up first. There was a huge rectangular glass and steel building next to the station, an apron of brown mud before it. Crewe, once a busy junction, has an air of rusty provincial desolation. I shared a breakfast table with a neat young man in his twenties who announced himself a perfectionist and a reader of the *Daily Express*. He worked for Lloyd's Insurance and was going to see a client in Liverpool. With his well-washed confidence, sitting there in First Class, he had already been aged, or promoted, into respectability.

He was nostalgic for the *bon vieux temps* when a man's word was his bond. Today's City was full of people you could not trust. He considered Mrs Thatcher a woman of resolute principle. He would certainly vote for her at the next election. He had been at a Poly in Lewes, but left without finishing the course as soon as he was offered a good job. He had no regrets, he said, regretfully. His life had proceeded with a complete lack of surprises; everything in his cottage garden was rosy enough, but a life which looks exactly like the picture on the packet clearly had something missing. I quizzed him with some thoroughness, this young Tory vaguely conscious that he might have a soul, and then returned to my place to read about the effect of American foreign policy on Guatemala.

Liverpool station was grand and grey. The first thing I did was to check the return train. With luck, I should be there only for four and a half hours. Philip Oakes was waiting for a taxi, which turned out to have been booked in my name. Philip is not in much of a hurry to put his hand in his pocket any more than I was to extend mine: he wrote disobligingly about *Richard's Things*. He is fifty-four, a journalist, tart but never stylish. Maybe a poet, scarcely a writer, he has produced some slim volumes. Like many people with little worth remembering, he has a capacity for total recall. He is eager to tell stories about Alan Brien, and they are always ones you have heard before. He offered the one about A.B. digging up plantain at Stour, the home of Randolph Churchill, and also about A.B. abusing Evelyn Waugh at White's, after which E.W. accused Randolph of hiring a Jew to blackguard him. Was A.B. a Jew? Oakes said, 'A quarter, I think.' 'Ah yes,' I said, 'like all those people who will be quick to disclaim all connection with the Chosen if there was ever any trouble again.' I elected to speak in a clipped, Old Carthusian way. Oakes' involvement had been the reason why I nearly refused to make the journey.

The city was grand and deserted. The hotel was localised by ships' lanterns, brown panelling and transatlantic nomenclature for the public rooms. We were to lunch in the New York room. I sat in an adjacent banqueting hall and rehearsed the speech I gave at the Union. It had hardly seemed worth the trouble to break open a new pack of jokes. Nervous without being anxious, I hated my weakness in coming at all. I went for a walk in order to be spared my hosts and fellow-guests for as long as possible. Ocean liners no longer put in at the Alfred docks, but the marbled mountain of the Cunard building still dominates the estuary. I saw its grandiose dome and high white shoulders on the first day I landed in England after crossing the Atlantic, in ten days, on the old *Scythia*. The docks are now a petty tourist attraction; the maritime museum contains some rowing boats and a steamship tender. MAURE- TANIA is emblazoned on one of its brick walls. Liverpool's mercantile past has left huge edifices, lost confidence set in stone. There is room for many lanes of traffic, few cars to fill them. When, on leaving, my driver took a wrong turning and headed for the Mersey tunnel, she turned round in the one-way street and went back without incurring a hoot of protest.

The lunch was of tasteless lamb, tinned corn and peas, a lump of cheese. Libby Purves, who has a clear, professional style on the radio, turned out to be a bastion of flesh, as grey as the Cunard building, seven months pregnant. I sat next to a woman called Rohde; she has some anchor-person's job in Manchester TV and went to the same dentist as Penelope Mortimer. She had the sad availability of the divorced women who rave about the pleasures of liberation. Philip Oakes, who knows everything about trivial potentates and is as provincial as kippers, said that she was important in the North-West.

My jokes were well enough received, but my unselfish pitch for the subsidy of the arts by the public purse was not welcomed by a Liverpudlian 'doctor' even larger than Libby Purves. He harangued me afterwards on the beauties of some local black dance company; they had so excited him that he was tempted to join them on stage. He was a Marxist circus-tent of a man. Swaddled in flesh, bespectacled and umbrellaed, he denounced ballet and opera as forms of conspicuous bourgeois consumption. He had the hard-headedness of the ideologues who uphold the virtues of the marketplace with the same credulity as the meanest capitalist. Unless art can find its own unsubsidised audience, both argue, it does not deserve public money; and if it can, it doesn't need it. He was the kind of believer in free speech whose garrulity will never allow anyone else to speak freely. He went away, a pin-striped pudding, pursued by whispers that he was a gate-crasher.

Gerry Durrell, with his young wife, Lee, had an air of corpulent smug-ness and the vocabulary of a clubman. He has much the same delivery as his brother Larry, the calculated discretion of a sensualist before an audience of prudes. Very practised, in his red-faced ginny way, he spoke fluently from handwritten notes. He spent his childhood in Corfu; presumably Larry was there too, which makes the latter's flight to the Med. and his discovery of Prospero's Cell less romantic. I am somewhat sorry that Larry didn't win the Booker Prize. He will probably not have another chance and it seems odd to give the thing to a novelist who has not, this time, written a novel.*

23.10.83. After any meeting dedicated to the socialising of literature, the strongest feeling is that one has wasted the day. Yesterday I spent an amiable three-and-a-half hours with the judges of the *Fiction Magazine* short story competition. Judy Cooke is a nice, creased little lady who lives in a tiny house (once a doctor's) in Jeffreys Street, NW1. We had been in Camden two days before when I parked in the same row of meters before

* *Schindler's Ark* by Thomas Keneally.

going to see *Fitzcarraldo* on P. Oakes' recommendation. He has been a film critic for fifteen years, but I affected not to know it. Redeemed only by the thunderous menace of the tropical locations, the movie was dull and protracted, without characters of any but perfunctory individuality. The story of Lopez of Paraguay would have been much more dramatic.

I do not intend to read any more books which contain statistical tables or symbols.

Eric Paice has recently retired as Chairman of the *Writers' Guild*. Depressed by the erosion of drama slots on the networks, he proposes to emigrate to the novel. Many are doing the same, it seems; we shall, no doubt, be treated to a series of books about TV writers in their middle years looking back in nostalgic dismay at lives devoted to composing programmes such as *The Avengers*, as P.'s has been. Elongated in the mackintosh exacted by the wettest October on record, he looked like a pipe-smoker who had decided, too late, to kick the habit: splay-toothed, yellow-faced, his eyes looked out from a wince of narrowed lids. He had lived in TV as 1950s Fleet Street hands did in print, selling themselves with perky shamelessness, imagining that prostitution gave them a tragic destiny. Unlike the *pute de métier*, however, they lacked the shameless-ness to strut the *trottoir*. The Philip Oakeses tout their slim volumes as an alibi for their bellied lives.

Cambridge. I parked in Alpha Road, slightly above my station. Helen Lee had made cucumber sandwiches in, Guy thought, unsuitable brown bread; there were little biscuits, delicate and crisp. Helen is a bright, desiccated woman, self-assured in speech, doubtful in femininity: there will never be any kissing her. Guy has taken Early Retirement, though he remains Librarian of John's. Scarcely evicted without honour, he has come out in a mysterious rash. The lady doctor told him that they were 'nummary', which he was quick to translate as coin-shaped. She did not know the etymology. Guy left the surgery having taught more than he had learned. He is sure that he is not afraid of death and cannot think why he should be so. Was it less the fear of death than the obligation of choice of what to do next – since he was now without full professional remuneration – that had brought him out in nervous coins? The unpretentious malice of the classicist makes Guy a jolly, shrewd observer. He knows what is what and is not afraid to throw at least the second stone. He thought that Kirk should not have been made Regius Professor, since he is not really a Greek scholar at all, but a 'philosopher'. It seems they are not going to fill the vacancy yet. He doubts whether Pat Easterling

will get it, even when she is a year older. Helen lamented the gracelessness of the eulogy spoken over the seven retiring lecturers at the annual
meeting of the classical faculty. Guy was surprised that I had contributed
to the Appeal.

2.11.82. Ken and Valerie came to tea before we went to the party, in
Lamb's Conduit Street, for the launch of the *bouquin*, published by Ion
Trewin, consisting of Lists of Hates. It is a remake of a volume of which
I.T. professed ignorance, called *Red Rags*, 'hymns of hate' from pre-war
Oxford, edited by the young Quintin Hogg. Though capable of walking
short distances, Ken uses a wheelchair these days. Valerie has lost weight
and gained confidence. She told us about this friend whom they have
known since before his marriage. He and K. have been joint tutors at
summer schools at which Michael directs a play performed by the pupils.
This year there was a Jewish boy of eleven to whom another tutor, an
Oxford don, took such a liking that he began to plan his whole education. Since the boy's mother telephoned frequently to make sure that the
goyim (whose term?) were taking proper care of him, the don was able to
make his admiration known to the lady.

Bryan and Edna, a couple who teach at Summer School meet up with
an old friend who has become increasingly morose. He had married
a woman of assertive personality who resented the couple's previous
acquaintance with Trevor and was nettled by any reference to it. This
year Trevor comes alone and they are amazed to find him 'the old Trev':
energetic, inventive, amusing. They have a splendid two days before the
wife arrives, with another man who she makes it clear is her lover. She
is forever sending him on errands. Trevor reacts without evident jealousy or resentment. Is it something new that the woman had a lover?
Edna recalls that Trev's wife had once come upon the three of them
(Bryan, Edna and Trevor) laughing together and said to Edna., 'I see, I
see, I didn't realise before that you two had an affair before I came on the
scene'. The story would work best if Trevor had been suddenly liberated
by his wife's infidelity. When her husband ceases to be mortified, she
punishes the lover by ordering him about. This gives the three others
something to laugh at. Their amusement impels the wife to return to her
husband, seriously. *The Old Trev.*

K. left his wheelchair and played the celebrity author for longer than his
stamina well allowed. I sought to get him, sweat standing on his chalky
brow, out of the hot narrow gallery where Mel Calman's drawings were
on sale. The wine of small fame had gone to K.'s head. He pitched into

the street so out of control that I feared he would fall slap on the Portland stones; somehow he righted himself.

11.11.82. Lunch with Hilary at the Garrick. He had recovered from the toothache which inflamed him for several weeks and presented a professionally amiable countenance. He takes pride in the fact that there is a five-year waiting list for the club. When I told of my election to the Savile, he said that he had resigned from it some time ago. Kingsley is said to be writing a novel unofficially known as 'Howard's End' in which he is to tell all about E.J.H.'s sexual tastes. It is foolish to expect discretion from writers, especially those who have done little except hang around, but there is something contemptible in such prompt vengeance on his own credulity. Kingsley, I ventured to say, is not a very nice or admirable figure; and Maud agreed. No more is John Gross, recently summoned to be George Weidenfeld's heir and now, apparently, given the air instead. Since he has no marked character, he could persuade himself that he had exemplary taste; he had published one book and supposed that it made him a man of parts. Hilary thought for a moment and then looked rather indignant. 'I think,' he said, 'you're being far too kind.'

As we were finishing lunch, I recognised Richard Rougier at a side table. When he was on his way to the door, he came over and saluted me. I always had the impression that he did not like me. I was surprised by the middle-aged lawyer's affability and the sentimentality with which he looked back on our youthful bridge games at the O. and C. and Crockford's. He now plays at the Portland. Certain people inhabit middle age as if elected in advance of the waiting list. I suppose that R.R. (the son of Georgette Heyer) is younger than I am. He went away blessing my literary endeavours like a pontiff.

We happened on Claire Tomalin and Michael Frayn at the Hampstead Theatre on Wednesday night. The indifferent play seemed greatly to recommend itself to the parochial audience. F. looks like a scarecrow who has gone up in the world. The glasses still make him the gig-lamped owl of the Remove. He offered wine, like the gaffer, during the interval, but turned proprietary after we declared the play to be poor stuff. He said that it was well-constructed and that he would have been proud to have written it. He seeks to confirm his own stature by determining that of others. Success leads some people to put on weight; Frayn has put on height.

Claire says Michael is uncomfortable with theatre people and distributes kisses with difficulty. Or is it that, uneasy with himself, he cannot quite credit the applause he elicits? He made a lot of money from *Noises*

Off. Does anyone with better things to do stay for the third act? His plays are not so much the greatest thing since Kleenex as Kleenex itself: clean, comforting, disposable. The thinness of the man has nothing healthy about it; skin drawn tight over bony face, he is a kind of airmail envelope, kept as light as possible, to reduce the charges. He now thinks himself important and, as a benefactor of the Hampstead Theatre, took any criticism of it as critical of himself.

I visited the *ST* a couple of days later and had a spat while trying to be sociable with John Ryle. I told him about John Moss telling some officious customs man merely to present the bill and save his moralising reproaches. The young Ryle riled me by saying that my tale reflected little credit on either participant; we owed deference to the representatives of society. I suggested that he pay closer attention to the text; he then doubted whether verbals were 'text'. When, later, I referred to Nancy Cunard's mouth as 'a slit trench in the sex war', he wanted to know whether I had originated the phrase. *Qu'il s'encule.* Fenton breezed over, a man for whom self-importance and modesty are synonyms. He wanted to know which Evelyn Waugh story involved the old woman giving a ball, but forgetting to issue invitations. Claire said it was an O. Wilde story. Was it? Fenton was reviewing the stage version of *A Handful of Dust.* I said that there were too many adaptations. He said, 'Look who's talking!' I said, 'I have never adapted anything for television.' He shivered blackly. Later I recalled *Image of a Society* in 1961.

René Lefèvre: 'What would happen if we could no longer have confidence in our traitors?'

18.11.82. I spent the weekend in Manchester, my first time in the city. I drove up on a clear, dry autumn morning and returned the next evening on a winter road, slick with rain and sleet. Burgess remembered me from a party in 1964. He also remembered a line – 'if that convenes' – from a TV play of mine (*A Well-Dressed Man*) he could neither have seen again nor read, since it was transmitted in the early 1960s. The son of a pit pianist and a dancer, he went to a Jesuit school and had the hell beaten out of him. He regards the Jesuit fraternity with the mixture of gratitude and revulsion evoked by his cruelly effective *paideia*. He believes that he is a great novelist but has few other pretensions. A busker who can do everything available to genius except create something unforgettable, his range of knowledge and quotation was impressive, but he missed two sitting targets planted to flatter him: Joyce extracts in an unJoycean style.

Susan Hill alluded frequently to her husband Stanley, a fellow of Balliol and editor of the Oxford Shakespeare, as though the fact that she was married to so great a celebrity should be bruited *urbi et orbi*. Having renounced novels, Hill has taken up radio plays which makes broadcast drama the most important thing in the world, apart from her husband, Stanley. She wore pretty pretty clothes, including a little Mexican *nombre* set with oval mirrors, perfect costume for a diminutive narcissist. Parading affectations of equality with ladies such as Judi Dench and Peggy Ashcroft, she knew everybody only because they all wanted to know her. She did not dine with us on Saturday night because she had friends to stay with. She took herself off with the air of summer departing from the year.

After leaving Mr Williamson (another Stanley!) P. lived for a year with a man but that didn't work; she is now alone. She has offers but rarely takes them up. She was less reluctant with an American lawyer during a recent trip. When they got into bed, he said, 'I want to please you,' in such a solemn, courtly voice that she burst out laughing. She says that she was embarrassed; but what is established by such laughter is that there was, in her mind, a third person in the room. That kind of laughter has to do with fear of appearing ridiculous in the eyes of someone who would never talk like that. Is she still aching for the man she divorced? Her maturity did not make her feel at all responsible for the feelings of the lawyer, whom she humiliated to entertain an absentee. It did not, it seems, occur to her to want to please him.

1959. Christmas in Torreroja. The stealing of the Christmas tree; the Nazi in the villa; the Israeli ship in Malaga harbour. Anna and Charlie, her beauty, his affair with the ugly cornpone wife of the hairless/bearded writer who cannot write. The lapsed Catholic: 'I don't even know what day Christmas is'. Hans and Juliana and their 'little boy'. Hans let it be known that he was 'in the Resistance' in Holland. Larry Potter said 'What it means is he stole coal.'

For my fourth radio talk. Secrecy and the cult of spying, especially institutionalised, which has followed the rise of the OSS, the CIA and the Cheka. Need there be all this furtive apparatus at all? *'J'adore la clandestinité.'* Plots and plots: Forster's oh yes the novel tells a story... But: we can never know the whole story. The necessity of concealment, the claims of openness. The countervalent virtues and vices of democracy: CIA and the Freedom of Information Act. The consequence of separating Church from State: religion has morals without power, the state power without morals. UN and the destruction of ideals. Can states be moral? Cf. Thucydides. Language always comes one size too big, unless it's too small.

A large not quite stout youngish woman, without make-up came to the studio 'for the experience'. She was at Reading University, reading linguistics and regretted not getting a First. Having detected a flaw in one aspect of the teaching, she was invited to stay on for a PhD. She went to Colombia to learn Spanish and lived for three months in a remote *pueblo*. One night, she was attacked by six men with machetes who clearly intended to rape and then kill her. She 'talked them down' by reminding them of their mothers and sisters. She said that she made them laugh, at or with her. She was able to postpone her fate and death and, somehow, to run into the road in front of a jeep which picked her up. In Bogota, she took an overnight bus which drove for eighteen rough hours, an experience almost worse, she told me, than what preceded it. She still has nightmares and the build of a military policeman. *Lingua franca.*

19.11.82. At tennis in Highgate this morning, a rather beefy man in glasses was walking behind the netting in his kit. I heard 'Freddie' and, following my blank look, 'Rob Knights!' 'Rob!' I had not seen him since he directed three episodes of *The Glittering Prizes*. We played on adjacent courts. His opponent was a cumbrous man with a pale Polish moustache. When I was leaving, R. and I exchanged phone numbers. I imagined that he had some project in mind, but he wanted to know if I would be interested in 'some rather competitive men's doubles'. I had, it seems, passed my audition. He said he had set up a film, based on a property of his own, with Olivier. He is welcome.

Roy Yglesias took me back after tennis to his flat in Frognal for coffee and a bath. He has made a good living as a publisher (Longman's) and text-book writer. His flat is unmodernised; it has a geyser for the bath. You cannot run hot and cold at the same time. Roy used my hot bath after I had finished with it. Schooled in Real Tennis, now in his mid-sixties, Roy plays a clever, economical game, relying on his excellent eye to use the volley from the solar plexus of the service court. He went to Lancing and was in all the teams. He always sports an MCC sweater on the tennis court. He and his wife, Bids, have a house in Sussex, which she prefers.

The Real Thing, the new Stoppard play, sent Beetle to sleep before the interval. Stoppard avoids all naivetés except the assumption that cynicism is proof of maturity. He defies the critics without embarrassing them; when he sends his message on a blank form, they take it as the saltiest kind of code.

5.12.82. We are at the Beverly Wilshire for the who-knows-how-manyth time. We left England just over a week ago, but the lotus tastes so delicious and so much the same that we dream of staying for longer, if not forever. The flight to NYC was a doddle. Before we left London, I returned from buying the stand-by tickets, of which, in these hard times, there is a plethora, and could not find my passport. I ran round the block (having been out to the deli for tongue) and then I ran round it again. My suede jacket had a hole in the pocket. I called the embassy; they were unreproving and helpful. With only an hour and a half before check-in, we called a cab and set off in precisely the mood we would least have wished. Mr Goldschmidt at the embassy was ready and quite quick; sixty dollars was enough to secure a paper for whom it might concern and we were at LHR in good time. The flight was as dull as the movie (one of those over-accessorised Agatha Christies) and, after a couple of hours at JFK we were on a quarter-full plane to New Orleans. A kamikaze black lady taxi driver drove us to the Marriott House as if we were late for an emergency operation.

We stayed two nights, the length of a rainy day. The rain stopped and started without changing the grey atmosphere of the flat, remote city, full of wider and thicker people than one is likely to see in Europe. We took a trolley ride along the last functioning route, St Charles's Avenue, with its colonnaded houses. The greying exfoliate capitals and bird-limed crenellations on the white and yellow mansions suggest that there is not quite as much money as there was, but still plenty. An act of will on the part of its founding fathers, New Orleans may founder on the facts of nature: the river is threatening to burst out of the levees and take a new course down the centre of Louisiana. Millions are being spent to keep it in its present place. If the catastrophe occurred, a new inland lake would be formed, today's Morgan City within its compass. New Orleans would become a back-to-front metropolis, the docks no longer where the water was deepest.

Louisiana blacks are a bright, often weighty race for whom no politicians, except those of the region, are likely to have a thought. Even the whites, with their sprawling accents, their monotone provincialism, consider themselves ignored, as ignorant, by central government. Jimmy Carter went to the White House on the crest of a wave that did not endure, but did not lack volume. His mission to Washington aborted by events alien to the issues on which he campaigned, he was brought down by a tripwire which did not cross his original path. Had there been no Iranian crisis, or had he dealt with it better, Carter might have been a decent successor to the vulgarity of Nixon or the crassness of Ford, just as the Social Democrats might have been nicely placed, had the Falklands episode not given Mrs Thatcher the charm which her domestic policies could never have procured. She has made herself taller by digging a ditch to isolate her own position. What now serves to elevate may later undermine her. Meanwhile, she has disposed of any member of her government with tendencies to generosity or a foot on the middle ground.

Charlie's mother: 'Looking at it with hindsight, I wish I'd spent more time on my back.'

Does Shelley's 'puff-foot the tyrant' owe something to the domination of Byron over its author?

A woman in blue trousers outside the lighting shop, made into a 1914 poilu by a red stripe of light reflected from a standard lamp.

Jim Whitehead and Miller Williams, from the Arkansas faculty, were among poets invited to go to Plains, Ga., to read to Carter after his defeat. Who can imagine H. Wilson or Ted Heath choosing to salve their wounds with poetic salt? What current English power-figure, except for the lame Foot, might seek solace in a literary evening?

We drove along the coast towards Baton Rouge to visit San Francisco, an *ante-bellum* mansion remote enough for me to stop and ask directions from a black boy of about thirteen, standing on the gravel outside a store. He leapt back as I pulled up. That slim skip of alarm found its long explanation two or three hundred miles away when, in a diner in Mississippi, I sought directions to Little Rock from a seated group of two state troopers and three national guardsmen. Large, sour-visaged, in their thick thirties, they had had no instruction in xenophilia. My arrival was an intrusion, my accent an affront. A badged national guardsman was cosmopolitan enough to have been as far as Tallulah, where the interstate forked north to Arkansas. I could ask again once we got there. In truth, I had no need of the advice; a legitimate excuse to seek conversation in the deep South was irresistible.

The cotton fields, black sticks tufted with white, were like burnt stubble dubbed with detergent. By the roadside, caged farm equipment was snagged with flakes of unthawed cotton. Metal slaves of a declining economy, the rusting machinery had the obsolete menace of abandoned weaponry. The townships were sets for Faulkner; the poor people's houses were grey clapboard, with wired chicken-runs, decrepit porches. The most modern businesses were Funeral Homes.

We pulled up at a pecan farm. Duckboards led to a shack where they sold bagged, semi-shelled nuts. The trees were bare and grand, branching from quite low in the trunk, spreading wide into gothic colonnades whose arches did not quite make junction at the top. Pecans are harvested in the fall. The man who served us had a stainless steel hand. He had a machine which crushed the shells without damaging the kernels. The reddish inner husk has to be detached by hand.

Having stopped at Wendy's Hamburger for supper, we arrived at the year-old Fayetteville Hilton just in time to have the Coffee Shop close in our faces, politely. The hotel has the four-square bulk of a colonial fortress. The staff was mostly of college students making a buck. The education budget of the state of Arkansas is the smallest in the Union. The university is well-endowed, on account of its football team, the Razorbacks. To raise money for the new library, facing the Students' Union, they recruited their most successful ex-football coach to head up the appeals committee. The university also sports a very popular basketball team, which was playing on the same night that I gave a public reading. I doubt if I should have been as well-attended anywhere in England or that an English audience would have been equally responsive.

Our waiter at Mr B.'s Bistrot had been in England during the summer. He had succeeded in shaking Princess Di's hand at morning service near Windsor.

13.12.82. Bill Harrison, my screenwriting professorial host, told me that a man called Taft had been on the line from LA. The message came only twenty-four hours after I handed the script of *An Affair to Remember* to Gene's courier at JFK. Quick news is nearly always good news. Gene's response was indeed ecstatic. I had got away with murder, or at least larceny. G.T. had come with dubious references; Ron had had to take him to the Writers' Guild before he received payment for another client. He is, he says, the same age as Warren. It is as if they had approached the rendezvous from different sides: Warren retains the accoutrements of youth; G. seems already to have an acquaintance with age. Not fat, but puffy, his throat is engorged and mottled with blanched scar-tissue. Yellow-grey in complexion, he wears untailored yet expensive-looking clothes; anything sharper would accentuate his physical asymmetry. He has a domed head, with sparse greying longish hair. He presides over what he calls 'The Taft Organisation'. Its *siège social*, at 185 N. Rexford, is an adobe bungalow; at $1,300 a month, it's cheaper than a suite of offices and less cramped.

Gene has a long history (or at least geography) in Hollywood: at twenty-three, he was working for J.L., Jack Warner. He is, he says, a trained lawyer with the ability to remember inessential details with paginated precision. He despises executives with the venom of someone with lofty credentials. Yet he confuses 'incredible' with 'incredulous' and takes 'gratuitous' to mean 'offensive'. He is the kind of man that no one would choose to have anything to do with except for money; and he doesn't have it. He must, at times, have been of use to some people. When we dined at La Scala, Bob Evans made a point of coming by, and stayed to eat, with his lady, a Russian called Nina, of handsome, if never pin-up, appearance; her quick humour brought salt to the table. Evans was affable, effusive, and dirty. His skin looked rough and less tanned than stained. One expected him to smell, if only of something expensive. He can outrun Sammy Glick, but he also knows how to laugh at himself. He recalled having persuaded Mr Williams of Turnbull and Asser to have his shirts ready for a fitting within four days, instead of four weeks, after he had admired a collar designed for Candy Bergen and sought replicas. R.E. told the adamantine Englishman that he was making *The Great Gatsby*, during which Robert Redford was to take delivery of, or have in his possession, boxes marked T. and A. The scene could be shot in two ways: showing R.R. in close-up or, on a reverse, revealing the named boxes in full. The shirts previously denied for prompt fitting became prudently available.

Bob described coming on some promotional literature about Paramount which omitted his own decade-long part in the company's growth. Lesser men, with shorter tenure, had mounted self-congratulatory pictures on the pages. He had been lunching in the commissary opposite a girl guileless enough to introduce herself as the editor of the house magazine. He went for her 'without the gloves'.

On the day before we were to leave, Gene insisted on driving me, badly, out to Paramount for a further huddle with Bob. Although he is no longer an officer of the company, Evans's name was emblazoned across the solid door of his offices. He seems willing to be recruited to G.'s production. He kept saying that our picture was sure to be made, either because he wanted to cheer Gene up (he has recently been 'stiffed' for cheques worth $150,000) or to impress me with his predictive clout. Evans is about to go into production with *Cotton Club*, an expensive number about the famous 1930s night spot in Harlem where my parents would go occasionally. Since it was run by the mob, blacks were barred, except as performers.

I remembered Bob from a party in London more than ten years ago. André Previn was still married to Mia Farrow and took a script of mine to her. Evans seemed thin and furtive, black eyes never still. He now wears glasses, low on a nose that runs from coke and has recently been broken on the invisible glass of the new door on the William Morris Agency. He had just written a hand-scripted note to Charlie Bludhorn protesting at his deletion from the credits in Paramount's self-celebratory magazine. Sylvester Stallone backed out of *Cotton Club* a few hours before his participation was to be announced. Bob showed me a Xerox of his letter to 'Sly'. It accused him of being 'most unique' and warned of the slenderness of his reputation outside the golden jail of his *Rocky* success. He would be well advised not to seek his fortune elsewhere if he was incapable of keeping his word. The tone was surprisingly head-magisterial. Bob imitated Stallone's bruised voice on the telephone, saying 'No one ever spoke to me like that before, *never*!'

Gene told me that Bob contrived the success of *Love Story* by buying up the whole first printing. The book went straight to the top of the Best Seller list.* G.T. offers to do the same for me, if it indeed it is an offer, and indeed for me. He has invested all his treasure in the project. I suspect that he has in mind to extract a considerable proportion of revenue from the 'novel' he wants me to concoct. We could have done without his company for dinner on our arrival, but he had sent a huge limousine to LAX to meet us. He provided an even bigger one to return us to it. His comments on the script were intelligent and succinct. He did everything right, but remains a wrong number. I was in his office only on Saturday morning, with his plump little secretary, and the defeated Jerry Gershwin, now Mike Medavoy's leg-man. Gene used to have a male helper. He fired him when he had nothing but praise for my script. Stiffed for $150,000, who employs a dog that fails to snarl?

At our meeting at Century City on the Monday, Gene took a dislike to Patricia Boyle, the lawyer whom Medavoy has installed as Head

---

* This trick was first pulled by Joseph Kennedy after JFK wrote *Profiles of Courage*, which was thus promoted into meriting the Pulitzer Prize. The classical scholar Erich Segal wrote the script and novel of *Love Story*. As a result he could afford to buy himself a copy of the great Pauly-Wissowa classical encyclopaedia which would have been beyond his means as an academic.

of Production. Her notes on the script were largely irrelevant, but G. antagonised her where flattery might have been politic. Although insignificant, she could do the harm which G. seems almost to court. Hasty and over-confident, he dreams of millions and spends ingratiating money: eight $35 ounces of caviar at *La Scala*. His own 'date' Judy Quine is worth millions, which she did not bring with her.

While waiting for me in his rented Ford outside 'Madonna Man', he was impelled to go in and buy a leather jacket. 'Nine hundred dollars.' 'Don't worry, Gene,' I said, 'it doesn't look it.' On another occasion, his silver fox jacket gave him the appearance of an escapee from the Disneyland wildlife section. He seeks to recruit me to a project to replace Jagger with Baryshnikov or whatever he is called who was in Herb Ross's *The Turning Point*. Medavoy would like me to rewrite the script. G. asked would I read it? He seemed almost hurt, certainly resigned, when I said that I would read it gladly, but was unlikely to take the job. He imagines that he has earned my loyalty, which has been done by less sedulous but more seductive people in the past. G. will never be the subject of anecdotes like those that make Jo Janni folkloric.*

Back in Essex, I used Jo's 'I should take him home, sir, if I were you' story at the prize-giving at the Colne High School on Friday night. They all said that it was the best speech they had had at the school. They can never have had a very good one. I encouraged the young not to be docile in the face of life and not to suppose that they had to be egregiously deferential. The headmaster, ten years younger than I, was grateful and a little miffed: he said that he did not altogether agree with everything I had said. I made bold to say, with a smile, 'That's exactly why I said it.'

We were treated to a scraped Mozart violin duet, a number on the piano accordion, three unaccompanied carols and some words from the chairman of the governors. Afterwards there was a sale of my work which I neither expected nor welcomed, but went very well. I signed a score of books and a number of the kids' programmes. The cookery class had made excellent sausage rolls. The pretty head-girl brought me coffee. I drove off as if I had done them a favour, holding a white envelope pressed upon me by the assistant headmaster. I was embarrassed to find that it contained a book token for ten pounds.

17.12.82. Victor Arwas has opened a gallery in LA. Things have been moving slowly, despite a gaudy opening, magnificent with flowers. The next day, a lady stood looking into the window, where a splendid

---

* I had no idea that Gene Taft was dying, without complaint, of AIDS.

Bonnard was on show, among other classy items. Having hovered and hovered, she went inside, pointed back, and asked, 'How much is it?' They quoted the price of the Bonnard. She blenched. 'For a flower arrangement, isn't that a little steep?' She had been captivated by one of the floral embellishments. LA socialites assumed that the gallery's contents were all reproductions. In fact, the art was real; the customers were reproductions.

The *Fiction Magazine* party, at 68A Lancaster Street, off the Portobello Road. The front door was open on a cluttered hall. You could have stolen a bicycle. The party was upstairs in a room decorated with a painted cast-iron image of the Madonna looking down at a baby couched near some lilies; white-painted, enamel angels hovered against a blue background. The thing was said to have come from Florence, quite a parcel. Paul's Bedalian friend Davina Black was cropped, amused and amusing, but less glamorous than when threatening suicide. Now chucklesome and tolerant, she is a researcher for Labour MPs. Her Bedales friend Morna, who went to teach in Spain, became part of a Chilean exile group. She has returned to Mexico where she ministers to refugees who have been evicted and often tortured by Pinochet. I said that I thought her father was CIA, but Davina was certain he was not. She is, however, convinced that Tim Slack is in MI6. He has the credulous loyalty and schoolboy team-spirit to qualify for that self-parodying organisation. Davina met him at the House when the Geoffrey Prime scandal was breaking and imitated his constant nervous ticking with scornful humour. Might he have been disconcerted to be talking to someone whom he had transported, all but dying, to intensive care? She smiled as if I had mentioned an old acquaintance.

Morna was kind to Paul when he felt unwanted; she stayed with Davina throughout the period of her darkest darkness. Like the heroine of *Torch Song*, Morna seems disinclined to spend time with the healed. In a variation of Cheever's story, the hero realises that he is cured by the fact that his mistress has lost interest in him. She fancies a duck only so long as it is lame.

Antonia Byatt found it unfortunate that at the age when men most wanted women, there was always the risk of pregnancy; hence all the drama of whether or not to marry. When pregnancy was no longer an anxiety, and women eager for adventures, men no longer desired them. When I suggested the job of professor in Arkansas, she seemed not uninterested; but her six-year-old, a fair, up-tilted girl in a tartan dress, ankle-length, has a father who works in the City with whom her time has to be shared. Antonia is a friend of Louise Purslow. She said how tough Louise was and always made her rewrite things. I said, 'she doesn't do that with me, which can only prove how much more she expects from you than she does from me.'

La Byatt said that she liked Karl Miller more and more as she went along. I said that many people were in the same case; in view of the first impression he gives, it is almost inevitable if he again comes to mind, one should think better of him. To cover her embarrassment, I advanced the p. to q.4 view that Doris Lessing was a dull writer. A. did not wholly demur, except over *The Golden Notebook*, which I conceded was an important book. When it was first published, I wrote a fan letter to D.L. Doris responded by saying that I had behaved exactly like a film producer. This because I suggested lunch in order to discuss her writing a segment for a film about marriage which, for a short time, Jo Janni and I were supposed to produce. Nothing came of it; and just as well: Doris cannot write a line of dialogue which any living lips could care to pronounce.

Antonia was at the same Quaker school as J. Dench, A. Foulds and, of course, D. Foulds, whose *protégée* she was. Dudy still writes to her. A.B. agrees that Dudy has remarkable mordant, minimalist powers. Her brilliance doesn't mitigate the uneasiness her name and history elicit. A.B. is a better friend of Anne Diggle, as D.'s sister now is. A. always wanted to be a farmer; a man called Diggle was the answer to her maidenly prayer. Oddly wilful and decisive, the Foulds girls! When Dudy had finished at Cambridge, having been a star in every domain, she went to John Barton and asked what she should do to become a professional actress. He said, 'Get a new face.'

A.B. said that she had wanted to write a 'Proustian' novel. I asked whether she had read T. Kilmartin's new translation of *A la Recherche*. She replied that she had read it in French. She might have been mentioning the most arcane language in the world. I said that having read it in French had not stopped me reading it in both the English versions.* She was made uneasy by my unimpressed opinion of Dan Jacobson, who has become a 'reader' in her faculty. His students, she said, adored him. My experience is that students will adore just about anyone who has time for them. D.J. had, I said, written one excellent story, *A Dance in the Sun*, and that was about it. She had to agree but wished she did not.

---

* I was set to review T. Kilmartin's version by Claire Tomalin. I found several ineptitudes, one of them nicely buried in a very late page indeed, which proved my diligence. No one else found any fault with Kilmartin's superficial renovation of Scott-Moncrieff. K. happened to be the literary editor of the *Observer*.

20.12.82. Eva Neurath, widow of the founder of Thames and Hudson, has a house off Highgate Hill, set behind big black gates. You go down a latticed walkway through a secret garden. The place has the air of a private museum furnished with the ample stock of a man with the foresight to escape from Hitler's Europe in time to bring his sideboard with him. Mrs N. is a little old lady with a large old history; she has had husbands and lovers; even now, although blind in one eye, she knows very well what is going on. Her semi-blindness is due to the ineptitude of Trevor-Roper, the eye-man (as opposed to his brother Hugh, the I-man). He had confessed that he botched the operation and declared, gallantly, that he would not be sending a bill.

We shared a supper table with a dull, distinguished party, including Roy Strong's wife, the set-designer Carola Oman Trevelyan, or something triune of that order. If she were adapted for television, it would have to be in three parts. She had been working in Sweden and had not had a good time, though she was quick to advertise the importance of the commission. She reminded us that she had worked with J. Schlesinger on *The Tales of Hoffmann*. Her 'Trevelyan' was the tassel on an already well-feathered cap. Like many Cornish people, she seemed to think it an honour to come from Cornwall. Her grand opinion of herself billowed across the table like a breath of old air. Professor Robert Browning, probably a much more interesting man, listened greyly to her vanities. I wished we could bring the subject round to Byzantium rather than discuss the merits of Peter Hall, whose booed *Macbeth* proved, in madame's eyes, the stupidity of the New York audience. She said that she liked Peter and made it sound like quite a paradox. For me, he is a man of more words than he can keep.

I was getting some food from the buffet when a very tall, grey man with occluded eyes and transparent skin found the nervous authority to declare that he had recently been reviewing my Byron book for the *New Republic*. He talked literally above my head, this stranger, and in a tone of eloquent regret. He had, he said, discovered rather suddenly that he was extremely broke and was prepared to do anything for money. When a man's best means of raising cash is to review books for fancy New York publications, he has to be a remarkable failure of some kind; but I had no clue as to who this huge derelict might be. I quizzed him respectfully; had he been an academic? He had indeed, for a while. We talked of Byron. Having gained the impression that he had not written a wholly amiable review of my little number, I corrected a few of his glib *aperçus*. He listened with anxious attention. I was somewhat embarrassed by his towering humility. Not quite a bore, he seemed an old young man, isolated through an inexplicable shift in time and riven by bewilderment which others took for seniority. I escaped, after a prolonged bout of uneasy proximity. Who was he? I was informed that if he had a scar on his cheek, he had to be Stephen Spender.* I once wrote a rather brutal review of a volume of his essays on Anglo-American literature. His ingratiations, I had said, gave the impression that his motto was 'I'm Stephen, Fly Me!' Jack Lambert told me the publishers had secretly endorsed my pejorative view. Was Spender advising me that his moment had now come? He offered later to send me an offprint and seemed earnest for further contact. We agreed to use T&H as a 'drop'.

David Wilson, who had rooms on my landing in my first year at St John's, came beaming across to us. When young, he was an earnest Methodist and drank only lemonade. Cheerful, loud and lucky, he has capped an impressive career with being appointed Director of the British Museum; the least likely to succeed has had a great success. With the sunny aspect of someone who has exceeded his own expectations, he enjoys the tenancy of a five-storey town house. He never liked practical archaeology. Having the lucky sagacity to choose a then arcane topic, he researched the history of the Vikings (he had a Swedish wife to mount on the prow of his long boat) and achieved eminence without finding his course thronged with rivals. We had not seen each other for twenty-eight years. We met with exclamations of pleasure and promised not to allow a similar lapse before our next happy conversation. I shall not miss him, nor he me, if we do not speak again until we are eighty.

The temptation of a double life lies in the desire not to have missed the pleasures of deception. Who can fully relish the world if he has a clear conscience?

21.12.82. Lunch at the Savile with Bernard Sheridan as my guest. Sitting at the long common table, I was next to Victor Pritchett. He said he thought I didn't write short stories and was flustered to hear that I had recently published two volumes. He is sustained in perennial middle age by the acclaim gained by a neat talent and no tendency to scandalise. A long-serving *New Statesman* pundit, he perfectly suits the English taste. He resigned, seven years ago, when Bruce Page was made editor. As I collected my coat, Graham Benson told me that he has just got Ted

---

* Folklore promises that, at the outbreak of the Spanish Civil War, the secretary-general of the Communist Party of Great Britain, Harry Pollitt, incited the handsome young Stephen Spender to go and play Byron in the Spanish arena. They needed a martyr.

Kotcheff to direct a movie. 'And we've got Arnold Wesker to write the script!' 'Well,' I said, 'all you need now is someone to do the rewrites.'

Bernard has built up an excellent practice without being in the first class. Madame Scholly told him how she had been bilked by a travel company which owed her some three hundred pounds they had received from their clients, but failed to pass on. She was worried by the cost of litigation. Bernard sued without telling her, recovered costs and damages and delivered the money to her. She was touched and amazed, gave him an excellent meal and a bottle of vintage Armagnac.

22.12. 82. Mandy Redman told Beetle how jealous Liv Ullman had been at their first meeting at the White Elephant when we were about to make *Richard's Things*. It was Mandy's first substantial part. L. was so condescending during dinner that Mandy went to have a cry in the Ladies. When she came back, she found a folded note on her plate. It said that she had been spotted across the room and if she could get out of her commitment to *Richard's Things*, the writer would be glad to have her in his latest film. It was signed 'S. Spielberg'. For a moment, M. believed that her bigger chance had come; and then she sensed that something was not kosher (the note was addressed to 'Dear Ms Redman', which was implausible since S.S. could scarcely have known her name). She folded the paper, without visible reaction, and put it in her handbag. She looked up and saw Liv, leering: 'You guessed.' Mandy said that she had told Peter Wood about *Richard's Things*. He said, 'I'm not sure F.R. likes me very much.' Mandy says that the mere mention of my name makes people nervous. The director of the Bristol Old Vic could scarcely believe that she had actually spoken to me. He seemed to think that I was too clever for conversation with mortals. Does this nonsense account for the baulking of my directorial/theatrical ambitions?

Jo Janni, in hospital after a severe stroke, woke to see a priest administering the last rites to a patient in the room across the well from his own. He told John that he dreaded a visit from a similarly benign harbinger of The End. For his next visit, John put on a black sweater, contrived a dog-collar out of loo paper and made an ecclesiastical entrance, waving a benediction. Later, he dangled his limp forefinger and slowly erected it. 'Any advance?' Jo shook his head. Will they ever again be able to quarrel as they did in the old days? John says they had only one big row on *Yanks*, when Jo went incommunicado with his mistress on the day when they had an Equity strike over the casting of a non-member. John had been a great friend, and remains a great fan, of Vanessa, but he broke with her after she called at his house for a contribution to the Workers Revolutionary Party. He was in the middle of a production at Covent Garden in which the stage-hands were proving recalcitrant. 'Perhaps you haven't heard the full story,' she said. He gave her both barrels and has not heard from her since. In general, he takes care to keep all the lines open to those whom he has employed or might employ him. He winced at my indifference to diplomatic niceties. Olivier calls him 'Johnny dear'. When John travels, he packs a specially typed and updated 'postcard list' with four pages of forget-them-not obligations. He has an unaffectionate but enduring link with Peter Hall, who has encouraged him to stay on the board of the NT, despite the irregular success of John's productions and his frequent absences from the UK. Hall dares not leave his power and financial base. He is sure that if he were not the commander-in-chief he would have no post at all: *Aut Caesar aut* looking for work.

An underling who remains loyal when everyone else has proved fickle can expect to be junked as soon as the fallen idol has rallied enough of the king's men to put him together again.

In Manchester, talking to Burgess on the Sunday morning in the hotel lobby, I saw a familiar, all but unchanged face I had not seen in thirty years: Tony Church, Peter Hall's liegeman at the ADC Theatre in Cambridge, and ever after. He had never been young and was now not much older; gaunt and grey, a character actor with the furtive air of a villain who had never done anything wrong. I called out, 'Tony Church', and he turned as if he feared he had committed a misdemeanour. Now Chairman of the Arts Council Drama Panel, he had come to cast an auditioning eye on the Royal Exchange Theatre.

Bill Harrison was adopted soon before the war. By some means he discovered his actual name, unremarkable and, I think, monosyllabic. One day in NYC, a Texan was amazed by his similarity to a friend of his, who bore Bill's mother's name. On the verge of solving the problem of his origins, he was moved and excited; then something faltered in him. He says he 'lost interest' and never took the conclusive step to determine who he was or whether his mother was still alive. Merlee says that Bill is very 'needy'. Also a Texan, she feels that he does not offer her sufficient security. She has taken up nursing and makes much of anatomical studies: she went on and on about 'doing the penis'. One of Bill's doctor friends advised him to dissuade M. from becoming 'a waitress in a hospital', but M. has the persistence of those who suffer from a grudge.

Perhaps she has been inspired by Jim Whitehead's wife, 'Guin' (pronounced as in 'Guinea'). She bore him seven children (including triplets) and has been a nurse for some years, partly in revenge for Jim's *machismo*, partly in fulfilment of a childhood ambition baulked by her parents' Mississippi gentility: they did not approve of the promiscuity of hospital life. Guin and Jim were the prettiest things on the Jackson campus. He was about to be a famous footballer when he was injured and became a poet and philosopher. Now what-the-hell corpulent, he snacks on crackers and mayonnaise. She worries about him, but will not change her ways to modify his. She seems to love him; corpulent as he may be, he has the virility to retain the allegiance of the beautiful woman she still is. Jim said, 'They all say Mr Raphael is the smart one. But I know it's Mrs Raphael.'

Merlee neither is nor has been beautiful; there is a scratchiness in her voice, a needling contradictory habit which marks Bill as a man of patient endurance. She claims that he has hurt her in a way more humiliating than anything Jim ever did to Guin. Miller Williams is married *en deux-ièmes noces* to a girl called Jordan (did her parents admire the cheating *golfeuse* in *The Great Gatsby*?). He seemed a decided, stick-assisted cripple when we were last in Arkansas but he has been straightened out by a marriage which Merlee deplores. Rendered unhappy by another's happiness, M. believes that Bill has not long to live, though his high blood pressure scarcely explains her plans for a separate life.

Nikos Stangos, Stanley Baron's colleague at Thames and Hudson, is a neatly toiletted person in, I suppose, his mid-thirties; he may be older than he looks, unusual with Greeks. He lives with David Plante and is the first cousin of Asteris, now re-installed as a leading journalist in Athens. It seems that Asteris never retrieved the wife from whom, so he persuaded me and perhaps himself, the Colonels had malevolently separated him. Back in 1967, so he told me, the Colonels would allow her out only if she (and he) never returned to Greece. Nikos indicated that she had made no serious attempt to escape from Athens. Is it possible that the wife rather than the regime was Asteris' principal torturer? Nikos is a decidedly permanent exile. His mother still lives in Athens. She and her husband came from Constantinople in the Great Exchange of 1922. During the war, they sheltered a Jewish couple in their flat. It was assumed that after the Liberation the Jews would decamp, but they refused. Eventually Nikos's parents were obliged to move out.

29.12.82. John Schlesinger's 'cocktail'. The house was all lit up and promised Gatsbyish delights, but neither the advertised Oliviers nor any heaped goodies were on show. The attendant famous were, as usual, smaller than their reputations, except for Alexander Godunov, who was with Jackie Bisset. She has thin legs (in blue stockings), very curled black hair and a memory which would make a sieve seem retentive. Never was beauty more uninterestingly allotted. For a publicity moment, she passed for powerful: she and Candy Bergen were the posted producers of *Rich and Famous* which made them neither. She had all but forgotten *Two For The Road* and certainly Stanley's injunctions 'Brush your hair, Jackie!' Conceited and witless, she was more dependent on Alexander than he on her. Fair, blue-eyed, springy with unaggressive energy, he is destined to be saved by his qualities; she is being eroded by hers. About twenty-seven, Godunov was born in the extreme east of the USSR, went to Riga and became lead dancer with the Bolshoi. Dissatisfied with life in Russia before he had experienced anything but its privileges, he sought asylum from a society in which success depended on official endorsement. America's wealth of alternatives was more seductive than money or stardom. The wife whom he loved and who loved him joined him for a while; but she could not bear to leave either her mother or Russia. She became a patriotic heroine on her return. They are allowed to speak on the telephone. He has no principled dislike of the Soviet set-up and knows enough of the upper echelons to take a shrugging attitude. The politburo is by no means all-powerful: the military and the KGB also run the state. Andropov, he says, is of Jewish origin. Canard or tribute? I did not inquire. He asked whether I had ever read Baron Munchausen, a character he might be able to impersonate in a modern version. I remembered Rhonda Gomez coming all the way to St Laurent to propose an 'idea' to combine the talents of Rudolf Nureyev and Mick Jagger. Alexander speaks intelligible English; but will he ever be a fluent actor?

Another guest was Philip Roth. I recalled a silly contretemps on a Manhattan sidewalk, in 1967, in the interval of Jules Feiffer's *Small Murders*. Roth had insisted that we had met before; I knew that we had not. He soon found Alfred Kazin more congenial. From being a haywire prodigy he now plays the vertically lined professor, in Chekhovian spectacles. He is said to be happy with Claire Bloom; yesterday's darling is now middle-aged, but she still might embellish a dream or two. Roth's apprehension makes him stiff; a once funny writer who is not much fun, he elects to be clever rather than amusing. He said he almost wrote to me to applaud my *Listener* article dealing, in tangential fashion, with the Lebanon massacres.

Bill Harrison had been a student of Philip's at the University of Iowa. P. had nearly taken up a teaching post in Fayetteville at a time when desperate for a divorce, which was difficult to get in NYC, where adultery was still a minimum qualification. He was all set to go to the Ozarks for three years, but then panicked. He is writing a novel as usual and lives a Proserpinal life, six months here, six there. *Portnoy's Complaint* brought fame and taught him its price; notoriety and success pinned on the same lapel. His books still honour the connection between before and after the jackpot, through the unengaging character of Zuckerman, or whatever P. calls his altered ego.

Too honest to claim the maturity which his donnishness mimics, he expects to be attacked and is half-inclined to lead the charge. With the complacency of the bestselling prize-winner, he advises you not to go too far: leave that stuff to him. Twisted in the wind of publicity, fortune's pretzel has not allowed success to blow his mind. Unlike so many English authors, he neither snaps nor grovels. With enough money to furnish his privacy, he resembles Arthur Miller in having acquired a famous beauty. The star of David overprinted on Claire makes the pairing less remarkable.

30.12.82. The unsmiling intensity of Alexander's gaze: the dancer (or is it the Russian?) does not smile in cautious apology, in the Anglo-Saxon manner. A. did not flinch from the particularity of his feelings. He stayed close to me as we spoke, our eyes no more than a foot apart; his blue gaze could not be avoided. He wanted the emotion of conversation, not the babble. Lack of humour was also lack of resignation. To smile would be to yield ground. One can be excited by the unEnglish intensity of such men without caring to see them again.

31.12.82. Sarah and I drove from Langham for a late lunch with George MacBeth and his lavishly named wife, Lisa St Aubin de Terán about whose new novel I was reading when Sarah said she had been commissioned to paint her portrait. We drove through decembral Suffolk in search of The Old Rectory at, or of, Oby. We were heading for the village when I saw a large, grey, unkempt building behind grey hedges and guessed it to be 'the old rectum'; a rusty blue Mini on the gravel outside its heavy front door. The house seemed deserted. One of what looked like 'Georgian' windows was a black rectangle with a white painted frame. There was a brick wall between the drive and the garden, a hooped doorway in it. Although visitors in cars cannot have been frequent, we waited in vain for a spontaneous welcome. I pulled the rusty metal bell-button. It came out several inches; the ringing was prolonged. The dimness of the house and its air of neglect hardly suggested servants. My imagination sought to load the Shetlanded girl who finally gave us entrance with the allure of the glamorously christened lady whom Sarah had been invited to immortalise. She was, in truth, the *au pair*. She seemed rather thick, due perhaps to the quantity of clothing she was obliged to wear to avoid being congealed.

The house was old, damp, dark and very cold. A fire, slumped in the drawing room grate, scorched the legs but hardly dispelled the clamminess of the air. MacBeth is a tall, skeletal man, fairish-haired, bespectacled, humourlessly smiling. I have never read his verses nor did I know that he had been a BBC producer for twenty years. He retired in 1975, but has only just begun to receive his pension. The house contained a wealth of musical instruments; there were two Victorian pianos in the dining room; no music. G.'s uncle, or cousin, has imported his bagpipes, but had gone with G.'s nine-year-old daughter to Norwich. Offered a drink before lunch, I thought to be accommodating by asking for a glass of wine. 'There you have me,' MacBeth said. The size of the house, its remoteness and the seigneurial pretension of leaving the door to be opened by a servant made the emptiness of the cellar into an eccentricity. I was given a glass of sherry.

The lady of the house came in, silent, neither ugly nor as handsome as her catalogued appearance. She had a smallish auburn head, polished cheeks and a wedge of a nose. Her body seemed disproportionately large, with fleshy calves, wide hips, hunched shoulders. First married when she was sixteen, she still has the aura of a child-bride, and child-mother, as it turned out: the MacBeths have a baby, Alexander, nut-coloured, very masculine-faced. Lisa fed him medicine from a bottle handed to her by the thick girl. She tested its temperature against the back of her hand with unexpected competence. Lisa's origins are 'part Channel Island' and part South American. She told a few stories, under heavy polite questioning, but did not seem fully present. Perhaps she was shy; perhaps she felt ill; perhaps she was bored; she did, however, confess to liking the idea of being painted and, during the conversation, offered her profile, first one side, then the other, as if in audition.

There were no modern paintings of any kind in the dusty mansion. The walls held a freight of lithographs and drypoints of Victorian provenance, wilfully banal in quality and subject matter and decked with Christmas holly and fir. We might have been in an austere boarding house which had failed to observe twelfth night the previous year. 'Lunch is served' was declared by the Shetlanded lass. It consisted of a bowl of turkey and carrot soup and a plate of ham sandwiches which I mistook for the bread and butter to sop the soup. They were the main course. An ashen fire warmed the room so weakly that, seeing Sarah posted to the Arctic chair on the far side of the bleak table, I offered her my coat, an act which struck McB. as so Quixotic that he all but guffawed. There were lumps of cheddar and Edam and a pudding of pieces of tinned pineapple covered with pink phlegm. I had a fancy that G.M. received his pension in kind: leftovers from the BBC canteen delivered in monthly kegs.

Because of the unusual history of her early marriage, and the flight from it, I had assumed precociousness in Lisa. Less pitched into maturity than deprived of childhood, she had lived with her abductor husband in Venezuela, where they were rich. She had gambled a few times for very high stakes. On the first occasion, she joined in a game of dominoes, assuming it to be a diversion for adult nurseries. She discovered that she had accepted partnership in a high-risk enterprise, through which she was steered by a cool partner. Why had she not simply withdrawn? Her smile indicated that inability to get out of things was the motif of her life. She wears the self-mockery of the fatalist: to accept that what-ever happens is inescapable was her only escape. Why else was she in a decrepit rectory (once the residence of Wordsworth's brother) with a strange Scot twice her age, who had first sheltered her from an enraged husband, and then installed her as the youngest antique in his collection? The answer, she indicated, was that her life resembled the distant game of dominoes in which she had agreed to be snagged. Delicately beefy, living a frail female fate, she agreed to be the modern incarnation of a traditional, precious helplessness.

Their cobwebbed house a deliberately dated repository, the MacBeths spend much of their time at auction sales; there are weekly opportuni-ties in the vicinity of Acle. With a confessional ripple of thin lips, they admitted that their purchasing fetish has filled the twenty-one room house with Victorian beauty and litter. Old typewriters hang on the damp, dark walls. Whether a small baby will survive the polar condi-tions is another matter. Would the mother's fatalism endure Alexander Morton George's disappearance with peasant passivity?

The laird showed us round the manse. The library was lugubrious with black books opened at spidery engravings. There was a case of novels in the drawing room, a tall, narrow, black double-doored reliquary for Hugh Walpole and other job lots. The only quite new book in a stack in the flagged hall was a translation of Claudel by the unappetising Edward Lucie Smith. They had no TV, not even in the servants' hall. Lisa's nine-year-old daughter's bedroom had an unmade-up bed. G.M. said that normally she was very tidy. He had helped to conceal her from her Venezuelan sire when he came in pursuit.

I presumed that George himself favoured tidy habits until I saw the bedroom he shared with his child-bride (actually L. is almost thirty). It looked as if it had been shelled. There was a huge double *armoire*, chestnut drawers between tall doors. Clothes and other articles were strewn about the freezing room (dead fire in the grate) as if after a search by an unfriendly police force. Elsewhere in the rectory, the furniture was of some elegance; there were also dank, braided armchairs, with head-rests, that might have dignified the local Rotary Club in the 1880s. Floors were part-covered with auction-room drugget.

G.M. works on a Smith typewriter which may well date from before the Great War. He has a couple of the same brand in reserve in case he needs to cannibalise them for parts. A portable of the same vintage, in a clever little case, could be folded down over itself to allow a black lid to cover its shoulders. Can it really be that, as she told Sarah, Lisa considers writing to be an undemanding medium in which one need work only a couple of hours a week? G. writes detective stories, on the machine, as well as poetry. He finds it easy to devise plots, because poems too have to have schemes; characters are more difficult, since he has to invent people other than himself. He was at New College and read Greats, an exact contemporary of James Rennie,* whose bobbing head he remembered, but whose lame leg he never remarked. He recalled that James did not get a First in Greats (though he did in Mods). George, who evidently did get a First, became addicted to verses because of having had to write them in Latin and Greek.

The MacBeth clan was reportedly extirpated in Scotland in the twelfth century; fruit of a maverick that took surreptitious root elsewhere, he wheezes at his fugitive luck. A classicist with small interest in the subject, a philosopher with distinguished teachers (B. Williams, A. Quinton, Austin, Ryle, the whole *galère*), he claims to have been greatly drawn to it all, but displays no philosophical bent. At Oxford with Tom Wisdom, he had never heard of the latter's Cambridge professorial father. Scholarship has been banished in favour of antiquarianism. I saw no texts or publications on the Classics. When the conversation lagged, he drew out an anecdotal heirloom: he had once been pissed on by a tiger at the London zoo. 'And did you not wash for a week?' He simpered, as if the subject of washing were rather *osé*.

The place had a black bathroom, with a Victorian candle bracket at the shoulder of a bather who could freeze to death with a well-lit book in his hand. In the front hall, black cobwebbed wires from the bell-pull converge and run along cracked walls before rising to dangling bells big enough to serve as egg-cups for ostrich-eggs. The drawing room had

---

* James Rennie and I were together in the Classical Sixth at Charterhouse. After I met him a few years later, Beetle and I asked him to dinner. He told us that adulterers should be branded on the forehead. He became a parliamentary draughtsman. We never saw him again.

tall Victorian windows with built-in shutters; high curtains with turned endings, one of which they maintain has been stolen.

MacBeth responded rather warmly to my idea of making a film of *The Waste Land*. The widow Eliot was determined to honour Tom's last will, however, and would allow nothing but straight readings. How about a film which would match the measure and gloss the imagery without actually citing the text? He greeted this notion with such enthusiasm that I thought he might well appropriate it. They go to London only to attend parties, quite often. They also have people for the weekend, especially in the summer; she gardens, he watches.

Lisa said that once in Venezuela she had someone to lunch and he stayed two years. It was the custom to propose to guests that they stay a little longer, but this particular architect was especially durable. He sometimes went home for weekends, only to return with larger and larger drawing books. This evidently often-told story was another jewel dispensed from a narrow purse. The afternoon grew dark early; it seemed that we too had been there longer than expected. A cup of tea was not suggested; butterscotch was offered from a tin.

George Steiner had warned me that G.M. was 'very right-wing', into leather and altogether an unappetising character whose work was not worth reading. G. never fails to carry his puncture kit; most people's are to repair punctures, his vocation is to deliver them. MacB. did say that he enjoyed Simon Raven, perhaps to pander to the Carthusian connection. The sainted Lisa seems ambivalent, with her dependence on servants, her modest narcissism, the self-enveloping, anachronistic style of her young agedness. McB doesn't like the telephone and leaves it to ring; she follows suit. I asked whether they failed to respond even when their daughter was out of the house. This nudge of reality struck them awkwardly. Either no emergency could matter more than their pleasure or, more likely, they relied on someone else answering the thing, even if only 'Blodwyn'. The normal was absent, but not replaced with intensity. Straight-faced frivolity passed for poetic *sérieux*. They live as the rich would if they had no money.

Etre Narcisse, c'est toujours vouloir se noyer.

Orpheus deliberately turning round at the end of the ascent from hell.

Driving along Western Avenue, I came abreast of a motorcycle. On the stiff boot was taped WAFFEN SS.

5.1.83. In the summer we took Charlie to be destroyed; a harsh word, not a harsh act. She had been operated on for cancer a year earlier, aged thirteen, and she had begun to fall down, like Norman Panama's wife, unable to piss standing or squatting. We could not again leave her to the mercies of the Smiths. Becky seemed hardly to notice her mother's disappearance. Yesterday, after failing to recover from a hysterectomy, she too was taken to Colchester and did not come back. Never pretty or affectionate, she was adopted by the children not least because she was not favoured by nature. For the first time in twenty years, we have no dog. My mother said that Becky's air of dejection reminded her of my father during his last weeks. Her eyes became more dignified and watchful as appetite receded; the lids fell into a senatorial cast, her good nature resided in the thick tail. She suffered us to pump water into her, and belched like a boozer, open-mouthed and resonant; but she drank voluntarily only on the first couple of days and never ate a sausage, or any of the scraps, duck, pheasant, turkey which would once have had her springing at the table. She went to her death without fear, agony or, it seemed, presentiment. When I carried her into the vet's, she was inert; after the injection of purple death she fell asleep without a twitch, unlike Charlie who had been stronger and seemed to stretch her length against the numbness as it took her. I heard myself say to the vet, 'I think I'll just piss off, if that's OK.'

Zara Steiner had been invited to a bibulous dinner for ex-members of the 'intelligence community', including Michael Howard (the historian, not the politician). She was no drinker, the others drinkers indeed. All manner of remarkable and disreputable revelations were uncorked. The sober outsider was apprised of vintage secrets which had been racked in the darkest cellars. When she got home, she was all set to disclose to George the answer to the riddle of it all. But she has a poor memory for anecdotes; she was sure she had heard everything, but remembered little. Given unique access to a golden treasury, she could not salvage a single ingot. The next morning, Michael Howard called to say that he feared she had been honoured, or lumbered, with more than discretion recommended. If he was warning her to keep her mouth shut, her pen capped, he asked of her only what she could not fail, alas, to deliver: some scholar, no reporter, she can recall things only by taking immediate notes.

The old are the most tantalising of historians' archives, because the most perishable. Z. had been to see the ninety-three-year-old Sir K.(?) Scott, who had been in the FO before the Great War and whose memory went back to the 1880s. She had written about him as though he were dead before she found him living in the dower house of Boughton House, the English seat of the Duke of Buccleuch. Its thirty-one rooms are filled with a collection of English watercolours assembled by Sir K., through petty purchases, during the twenties and thirties. He talked for three hours while his second wife prepared an excellent meal on the Aga.

Only three of the wonderfully furnished rooms in the dower house were heated. In one there hung a Van Eyck for which Z. said she would have given all she had, which would have been nothing like enough. The old diplomat had retired in 1947 since when he devoted himself to his garden. The winter garden was in brilliant bloom. He consented to have a sleep after lunch only when his wife, who had been his nurse, said that she must show their visitor the fruit and flowers of his efforts.

Her ladyship was in her fifties, not a favourite with her sister-in-law, the duchess, to whom she insisted on introducing Z. The maid in the big house did her instructed best to deter them, but Lady S. was determined and, although Her Grace was about to leave for London, an entrance was effected. The Duchess was frosty at first, but her visitor was Alan Pryce-Jones, whose capacity for elegant sponging is symbolised by the size and chic of his luggage. Z. said, as indeed she could be sure, that A. P.-J. knew her husband. The ice melted.

Lady Scott told Zara that Sir K.'s family had assumed that she married Sir K. in the hope of a prompt and juicy inheritance. They found no fault in that. By making him happy, however, she sustained him beyond his expected span. If she hoped for gratitude, she little understood aristocratic priorities. The old man's longevity blocked the expectations of his heirs. A gold-digger might have been tolerated; a good wife was inexcusable.

George is convinced that the treacherous nexus in the Establishment goes back to Mountbatten and his circle. He would have it that Edwina's infidelities were deliberate in their recklessness; his passive lordship took masochistic pleasure in knowing of them. The combination laid them open to catastrophic blackmail. G. takes the fact that Le Carré places the meeting between Karla and Smiley in Delhi as a textual hint that the spies who betrayed 'our' secrets, out of other than financial motives, were mostly of upper-class origin. The most dangerous penetrations came from those above suspicion.

The FO did no vetting of diplomats until after 1945 and then only casually. The lower class consular service had never been spared investigation. George's boldest claim was that Mountbatten was a master of duplicity. As CIGS, immediately after his viceregency, he was also responsible for Intelligence. Sexual ambivalence prepared him to be adept at concealment. In a great drama (how keen G. is, *en bon hégélien*, to see the world as theatre!), the disgrace of the father could account for the two-facedness of the son. Louis of Battenberg was unjustly sacked in 1914 for fear that he was of unreliable patriotism. A fighting chief of questionable lineage was a plausible scapegoat for a family of German origin. The German roots of Sir Eyre Crowe on the other hand seem to have warranted the force of his anti-German sentiments; they certified inside knowledge. Crowe was asked only to write; Battenberg would have had to act. The latter's ejection proved that the British royals had moved beyond caste solidarity and were willing to sacrifice one of their own to bourgeois chauvinism.

Who knows when, or why, Mountbatten began, if he did, to flirt with, or bat for, the other side? No solemn treason was involved: he never chose the interests of the other. What cause was more important than his own? Was his circle easy for the Russians to infiltrate? He may well have preferred them, in theory, to Americans, though the US was probably irrelevant to his priggish desire to be the ace of trumpery.

It amused those like Guy Burgess to favour Russians because they weren't Yanks. Was Mountbatten immune to such giggles? Steiner suggests that when the Americans were beginning to win the battle of the Coral Sea and the British empire clearly slipping into the American sphere of influence, someone at the highest level might have argued that commerce with the Russians was a necessary evil if the hegemony of the world was not to be removed entirely from European hands. A less subtle view of the M. circle is that they were morally *pourris* and that their secrets then allowed the Russians to gull, blackmail and intimidate them.

G. gleamingly proposed that the Eumenides caught up with M. when he was blown up: what if some entirely different organisation blew up his yacht, for motives which had nothing to do with the IRA? The lack of security suggests complacent conceit. Did Mountbatten presume that he enjoyed some exceptional immunity? The Steiners now insist that of all the totems available, none is so sacred with current royals as that of Uncle Louis, nothing more unforgivable than to blacken his reputation. Are the Windsors protecting a tarnished hero and expiating the treason of one of their own? The abandonment of Battenberg (and later of the Romanovs) signified the passing of the age of royal cousins. Contempt for democracy and bourgeois life could find no slyer expression than in the veneration of Janus.

Beaverbrook got him right!

Steiner promises that, with the success of *Earthly Powers*, Burgess is a millionaire. The success comes from advances not sales. 'There is also going to be a film, they've already cast the Pope.' G. told me that Updike too is a millionaire. Convinced of the correlation between money and achievement, G. venerates quantity as only quality can. He is intensely curious about Burgess. Was he really as encyclopaedic as everyone says ('he reads dictionaries!') and as linguistically proficient? I had asked A.B. whether G. called him Anthony or Burgess; after thought, he said the latter. Alcohol puts a dome over him; brain and memory are bottled, levity destroyed. Prompt, but not quick, he embodies the laborious spontaneity of the Memory Man; he remembers because it is his trick, not his pleasure. It is difficult not to like him, not easy to warm to him.

9.1.83. As editor of the *TLS*, John Gross continued to employ Anthony Blunt after he had been exposed as a Soviet agent. Steiner is excited by such shamelessness; it borders on complicity, unless it's envy. How could Gross, usually so deferential to received opinion, have taken so bold a stance? The paradox dissolves before it is posed. How unlikely is it that such a conformist should be emulous of the duplicity of which Blunt is the most elegant contemporary case? The iconoclast of *The Rise and Fall of the Man of Letters* had the safe temerity to challenge totems which few influential persons continue to revere. He might as well as have ironised about the predictive powers of the Delphic oracle. He has bent so far backwards as to be canted forever in the posture of a star-gazer; never did servility adopt so high a falute. By continuing to employ Blunt, Gross was at once daring and bland. The surreptitious violence in his quietism blended Quixotry with as close as he dared to come to dissidence. He rubbed the straight noses of the British, who had appointed him the Noah of their literary ark, in the residue of their own humbug. Did they not always assume that an exceptional career in one of the great universities procured the right to pass for a gentile? The Apostles were a secular Pharisaic sodality, a neo-Etonian Pop whose members were recruited for life to a mental aristocracy to be judged only by its own members. For Gross, the retention of Blunt was an act of self-regard; it certified him to be at once sovereign and lackey.

The arrogance of Lennox's younger sons, in the Van Dyck double portrait; how superb the contrast between it and the fair-haired confidence, frayed by responsibility, of the heir, depicted alone on another canvas, less beautiful but graced, *tout seul*, by the fortune of primogeniture! Some are born great; others thrust their greatness upon you. The face of Van Dyck's

Strafford could be of some slightly sinister, very able, banker starched in the stiff fancy dress of his armour. Privileged access to a doomed generation gave Van Dyck the lineaments of an official portraitist who survived a *Titanic* full of illustrious models. He descried the vanity of those who thought it their right to be wrong, the smug poise of an aristocracy without the wit to be wary. The vivid faces, the perfunctory tailoring of the costumes presage how easily empty heads would come to be parted from their finery.

11.1.83. John Schlesinger was here to lunch. Now very fat, he scarcely gets to his feet without a tottering struggle. The grey beard gives him the aura of a gay Father Christmas. His parents cling to life. His father is, he says, a vegetable who needs only a cigar, a glass and a lavatory. His mother has broken her hip twice, but – at the age of eighty-five – has emerged once more from plaster and climbs the stairs. John always assumed that his rages were unique to him, but not long ago he saw his father fly into a passion and actually strike his beloved wife. His parents' solidarity has long sustained J.; their growing fragility weakens his assurance. The failure of *Honkytonk Freeway* continues to mortify him. He read me the draft of a letter responding to Alex Walker about his exaggeration of the budget. A.W. 'used to be a friend'. It seemed pitiful that a blow-dried opportunist's copy should cause so much grief.

J. asked anxiously if the BBC paid promptly. He has made a fortune, and spent it. He has staff and offices and cars; hence his willingness to regard the crappy Paramount project as something he wants to do. So bruised that he has become sentimental about England, J. has turned against 'the Americans' with the animosity of a spurned lover. His strongest feelings derive from aversion ('Hate them all, dear!'). With no appetite left for *méchanceté* or for anything 'big', in financial or artistic terms, he wants only to be a 'working director'. He has unreliable sweetness, an eye and an ear and a very small brain. I spent a pleasant few hours with him, but it was a relief when he set off, on foot, across the Sahara of the Gloucester Road to go home, before proceeding to Scotland to make his Guy Burgess number.

Can Alan Bates play a convincing Old Etonian? After seeing *Butley*, I wonder. John dotes on old acquaintance; he swears that Julie gives a very moving performance in the second of the Rattigan diptych. I should sooner believe him than see it. John says he would like to preside over a record programme on the radio, like the one Dickie Attenborough used to present. Can a man grow larger and shrivel at the same time? Once it was possible to believe that J.'s arrogance was the fruit of vanity; was it not always the public face of private fears? Affectations of engagement with serious issues have concealed little bear's wish to be picked up and cuddled.

13.1.83. At *the Sunday Times*. Claire Tomalin made endless fussy references to an imminent meeting of the Royal Literary Fund. She is due to make the opening statement and was nervous of the male chauvinists on the committee. It is hard to believe that she was all that anxious, but can it be that she is less smug than I choose to see? She admitted that she had never heard of Robert Escarpit, but later she said that perhaps she had heard of him. There was panic in the literary department when its attendant officers were requested by the Mag, at short notice, to produce considered judgments on the Best Twenty Young British Writers, as selected by some enterprising promotion. Most of their works were unknown to them. Claire was flicking through novels in order to have the last word on a matter already decided.

John Ryle, who can be no more than thirty, gloated over having been on a cruise which was worth, as they say on the backs of cereal packets, 'more than £900'. Is the main purpose of being in the literary department to qualify for freeloading? They all blame the editor, Frank Giles, for their own lack of wit and courage. He is afraid of Murdoch, who is rarely there, but omnipresent. If *The Times* is at greater risk, dread of impoverishment has affected both papers. A man brought his bicycle into the lift when I was going up; it would be stolen if he left it in the street. Claire's was shackled to the railings. She apologised for its obsolescence. Like many conceited people worried about tenure, she knows when to bend the knee, and the ear. She proposed lunch at a 'working man's caff'. Despite our misplaced accents, we ate the cheap grub without being jostled by cold shoulders. When the time came to pay, she confessed that she had no money with her. By way of thanks, she told me that Karl Miller spoke of me with great respect.

James Cameron, at the Odeon Leicester Square, waiting to see *Gandhi*, revealed that Michael Ayrton was quite disliked at the Savile. Contrary to the ethos of the place, he had a way of telling other members to 'bugger off', if they attempted to join a conversation. Cameron's Indian wife had found Michael patient and courteous. She was less impressed by 'Old Henry' Moore. His wife had boasted to her about how well the son of a coalminer could do.

Jim Cellan Jones says that all witnesses at courts-martial lie like, indeed, troopers. He recalls giving evidence at the trial of someone who had lifted a boat by a crane, employing the wrong knots. It had fallen from a height. As a supposed expert, he said he would have done it in exactly the same way. Prosecuting counsel produced a manual recommending a different procedure. Jim said, 'It must be out of date'.

15.1.83. I have been reading MacBeth's poems. How differently they colour that afternoon! What a bank of uncashed revelations! He makes melodrama out of the commonplace; he cannot take a step without putting the boot in. Can a retired BBC producer have led so violent a life? How did Lisa St A. de T. enter and alter it with her suppliant insistence? MacBeth fights savage psychic battles in peaceful Norfolk, digs trenches, fires heavy verbal artillery, spuds gouts of poetry from the placid ground. He seemed passive, revelling in what others could find only laughable, but only one laugh interested him, the last. The young woman, nailed by him into motherhood, stars in a drama of her own fashioning and makes of her acquiescence an enigma more winsome than integrity could contrive. All her qualities are accidental, the result of *tutti frutti* lineage. Having composed an Usher-like household for himself, G.M. lives in its cracked shell as if it were something gracious, settled and dignified. Flying piratical colours in a crumbling place bought at auction, he picks at secret wounds until they fester fruitfully. The blackshirted aesthete is a closet Sweeney Todd; he holds up a mirror for the customer's approval and sees him as sausages at the same time.

16.1.83. Mrs Thatcher was competent on the box. One wished her false; she was true, which may be worse. Her popularity is independent of her being liked, a condition with no parallel in Michael Foot. Fearing its dreams cannot be realised, the Left all but welcomes the postponement of taking power. The Right is less nervous of the future because it has fewer hopes.

18.1.83. My mother gave a dinner party for our anniversary. Pleasure was tainted by the presence of Margaret Piesse, now a severe, grey Tory lady. She takes any criticism of Thatcher to be critical of herself. She had recently served as a juror in a multiple rape case. The accused (and convicted) were black; so was their accuser. One of the other jurors was a respectable black man who, early in the trial, was heard to observe that he would not care to be in the accused men's shoes. Taking this to mean that he believed them guilty, Margaret was surprised when, during the jury's deliberations, he was in the small majority in favour of acquittal. His main argument was that the victim should not have gone out with the accused, even though at first she had been in a car with several other people, who had been dropped off. He held that she deserved what she got for consorting with such men. Then again, a unanimous verdict might have marked him for an Uncle Tom. Margaret said, with a snatch of youthful vitality, that she recognised the judge in her case as someone she had fancied, many years before, when he was staying with some Yorkshire neighbours.

She counts the value of her shares every day. Her Toryism is fanatical; she bridled at the suggestion that the police were racially biased. It was all I could do to keep the peace between her and Paul, to whom, despite her status as a guest, she displayed open antipathy. Though she has lost her looks, she retains the air of the pretty provincial girl of our weekly doubles games in the 1950s. She said she never really liked tennis; she preferred exercises, which she still does. Although solitary, she spends freely on clothes and her hair.

Jack used to call her 'tyko' and was pleased to have caught so pretty a prize. She seemed as perfect a second wife as a returning hero might hope to parade. Her girlishness, which lasted well, carried a flush of embarrassment; their relationship owed its flawlessness to the want of any demanding desire on either side. Jack had been humiliated by his Weybridge wife's infidelities when he was away in the army. Determined not to make that mistake again, he made a different one. He married a girl stunned by the death of her husband of six weeks and who never ovulated again.

19.1.83. We went to an Academy screening of an old-fashioned Sidney Lumet movie with Paul Newman. The best scene was at the end, in court. A young couple came into the Bijou as the film was reaching its climax. The girl began giggling and snorting behind us. Sarah asked me, as the credits rolled, 'Shall I throw this glass of orange juice over them?' I said, 'Yes'; and, as the lights went up, she did. They neither moved nor made any sound. The juice ran down the fringes of their pale leather *blousons*. As we walked out of the leather-armchaired screening room, Sarah said, 'Charlie Lederer!'* We came home and ate Beetle's excellent *osso buco* and drank a bottle of Nuits St Georges 1971.

* Charlie Lederer was a handsome Hollywood screenwriter and socialite. Stanley Donen told us how, during the war, he had been on a diplomatic mission to India. In Delhi, the wife of a resident British bigshot remarked on how the presence of Jews had lowered the social tone. Lederer, who was half-Jewish but did not, as they say, look it, was standing near a cabinet containing the lady's valuable collection of jade. 'Don't you like Jews?' he said, 'got a reason?' 'Not really.' Lederer pulled the cabinet down and smashed the precious contents on the marble floor. 'Now you've got a reason.'

Bulla, the 'Robin Hood' described by Dio Cassius, was captured and interrogated by the great jurist Papinian, then (in the third century C.E.) praetorian prefect. 'Why did you become a brigand?' 'Why are you prefect?' (quoted in Ste. Croix, *Class Struggle in the Ancient Greek World*).*

20.1.83. Warned that Steven Rose, professor of biology at the Open University, was very left-wing, I suggested we meet at the Ritz Bar. Just over medium height (though he holds himself tall), he had the corduroy and beard-fringed appearance of the eternal, seemingly continental, student. His eyes have a perky vigilance, but it seems as if the lids on one side have been transposed: the lower rides over the upper in the corner, with the permanent hint of a wink. He was very willing to help in my search for a plot and drank three Campari sodas in the process; they gave him 'the illusion of summer', he said. He agreed that big pharmaceutical interests regularly use the Third World (and convicts) as guinea pigs, with no clear notion of consequences. Genetic engineering is a big gamble, with huge profits in prospect if, for instance, it proves possible to prime diabetics to produce their own insulin by injecting appropriate genes. Insulin has been generated in culture but no one is sure that implantation will work.

The question 'What is life?' has become vexed: US labs have been applying to patent 'life' – living organisms – which they have created. The legal issue arises whether private interests should be allowed to sequester 'living entities' for their own profit. There is a sense in which this amounts to micro-slavery. Have scientists the right and has law the authority to deny access to new healing elements because a particular pioneer has got there first? A new Nunn May drama can unfold here, without the cold-war trimmings.

Rose holds that we are reaching the point where immense advantages will accrue to the rich. They will be able 'naturally' to control the world's health and, without conventional wars, regulate the global state. Command of technology will allow them to play God with a subject population without the need to monitor their activities. Laymen will have no means of distinguishing 'natural' from rigged epidemics. The proles will continue to believe that God is responsible for the plagues which rich nations, their agencies and corporations, may be at liberty to foist on them. The principal use of the poor will be to provide the

* Lemprière tells us that Papinian was ordered to write an oration to 'excuse or palliate' the murder of Geta by his brother Caracalla. When he refused he was 'brutally put to death by the tyrant' at the age of thirty-seven.

powerful with guinea-pigs just as once they supplied them with cannon fodder.

T. had his own showbiz column in the *Evening Standard* when he was twenty-two. He gloried in his making and breaking potency until one day, at the Cannes festival, he sent word to Yul Brynner that he wanted to see him. Brynner did not want to see him and said so. His indifference to T.'s venomous reputation made the boy-wonder wonder. He realised that he was less king than courtier. He abandoned flashy journalism and wrote a weekly arts column in the *Guardian*. Having renounced malice, he remains puzzled by the world which he seeks to understand by frowning. He says that he reads a lot, but evidently very slowly; he avoids newspapers because they take so long to get through. He seems devoid of regrets or resentment, though bad reviews hurt him as much as the next man. He neither noticed Sarah's paintings nor ate Beetle's apple amber. Having abandoned self-admiration, he has never learnt flattery or its prudent partner, discretion. He keeps a flat in London, in the same house as the Fowleses; he seems to like it here, but he is neither English nor American, although his awareness of the US market is vigilant. He was amazed when I told him that I have never in my life gone into a bar in a city and ordered a drink.

21.1.83. Did the same person play host to the two guests I entertained to lunch, today and yesterday, at the Savile? Yesterday, I arranged to meet John Leach, Gerry's brother, who works for Pfizer's, in order to quiz him about the pharmaceutical companies' skulduggery. I invited him for 12.45. I was still waiting in the lobby at 1.30. A white-haired stranger came down from the dining room to say that a number of members had seen me on my own and would like me to join them. His name was Tom Bairstow; he described himself as a hack, had been deputy to Paul Johnson at the *NS* and now wrote on the press for the *Guardian*. He had, he said, always admired my style and made a flattering distinction between a real writer and a scribbler like himself. I had no sooner been made welcome at the communal table, and invited to sip an excellent claret, than J.L. arrived, large, grey-haired, rubicund, neither apologetic nor brazen. We were obliged to decamp to the 'ballroom'.

Unembarrassed by the horological *malentendu*, he primed me with useful information. He confirmed that it is now feasible to poison the whole world without administering any manifest drug or causing any vile symptoms which could be traced to an extraneous agent. One of the key discoveries has been the isolation of 'one of the causes of happiness'. In this light, political problems can seem to have a 'chemical' solution. It has puzzled scientists why morphine has the effect it does; why the extract of poppies should provoke intense euphoria has been assumed to have a solution relating to the ingredients of the morphine/heroin process. Recently, they have found that what they have labelled 'endorphins' are responsible for the feeling of happiness in humans. They are generated in the brain and release sensations of pleasure. Scientists expected their chemical nature to have similarities to that of morphine; they found that their ingredients had nothing in common. What counted was not the content but the formal structure of the two agents. Chemically alien, morphine and endorphin had the same 'shape'. The exhilarating effect of morphine was not due to any mysterious substance. Its molecular structure deceives the brain as a comforter deceives the sucking infant.

The next stage in the genetic structuring process is to create a virus which generates endorphins in such a way that a tumour will generate 'happiness'. The virus could then infect the brain tissue and kill with kindness. An antidote can also be created which will vaccinate cells against the viral infection which will first generate 'happiness' and later kill from the effects of the tumour that does the happy work. On the other hand (there always is one), the endorphins might reduce insurgent proles to acquiescent inertia; death will then follow from the tumours which have been the factory for their temporary pacification. Do I get it?

Renford Bambrough was today's guest. We were both early. I had been playing tennis at the David Lloyd Club. Its three huge hangars are in waste land near Hounslow, off the M4. The sumptuousness of the clubhouse lends a zest of sin to the virtue of taking exercise. Patrick Sergeant had just flown in from Luxembourg. Eddie, the chauffeur, had brought Jilly from Highgate; our fourth was a Yank called Ellsworth; he had reached the third round of Wimbledon in 1948. He liked England so much that he went to work for a bank in the City. A cold-eyed Wasp, he played a decent game but lacked warmth or personality. After our four, I played a single with Patrick and beat him six–nil. As we sat in the Jacuzzi (if you value your membership, you take a shower first), he resembled a nudist emperor, robed in flesh.

Renford looks unexercised, egregiously bulky, correct as an undertaker. He told me that he was warned, as a tiro, that Wittgenstein did not like 'tourists'. He took this to mean any outsiders. Later, he realised that W. was vexed by 'persons from Tennessee' who spent a few days in his colloquies and went home to announce they had studied with him. Now fifty-six, Renford was a Fellow when he was twenty-four. He retains the aura of early eminence. He soon wanted to be a philosopher but was careful to pursue his classical studies until his fellowship was secure. He speaks in an articulate, wary undertone, eyes down, like a spymaster who will say this only once. There may be something that he believes or wants, passionately, but the caution of the ambitious provincial, when it comes to strong feelings, makes him furtive, not least when being candid. No more than J.P. Sullivan does he ever want to go back to where he came from: Sunderland, was it?

He takes himself to be welcome at the BBC, where his broadcasts have been numerous over the years; he says that he has a 'standing invitation'. Louise Purslow, a BBC producer with smart responses, rates him a bore. Do I? Why did I invite him to lunch? He is someone I used to know, and learn from, if never quite enough. He is loyal to Wisdom, in a somewhat step-filial fashion (one never hears of R.'s parents). All his hopes are now bent on the Mastership of St John's. The presidency, which he holds, is no longer a permanent appointment; he is almost at the end of a four-year term. The President is the leader of the Fellows; strictly speaking, the Master is not a Fellow at all; he is, for instance, a guest at Feasts. Renford acts as if to smile were weakness. When he laughs, pinkly, is the only time he looks at you, quickly, nervous of complicity.

24.1.83. Ian Bannen was at the screening of *The Verdict*. He greeted me with the provisional warmth of those with just one improbable thing in common: our chance meeting after Jim Ferman claimed to have written the script of *The Trouble with England*. Grown long-jawed and Josserish, Bannen had forgotten Jim's name; he remembered only that he was inclined to 'flip'. He had thought well enough of his directorial talent, but said that he became fiddly, ill-humoured and incapable of getting to the end of anything; a puzzle, if not an embarrassment. I recalled the 1960s when Bannen was with Samantha Eggar. He was Roman Catholic, Richard Gregson told me, and tormented by the sinfulness of such delectable venery. Quite the leading man in those days, he has since had neither success nor failure. His present companion is called Marilyn, a squattish blonde woman; she seemed nice and undemanding. He said, by way of ingratiation, that he still wished that I had written 'that play'.

25.1.83. At the screening of *An Officer and a Gentleman*, across the room was Bryan Forbes, watchful for famous button-holes. He hesitated, perhaps from myopia, perhaps attending hotter possibilities, and then came and did the friendlies. Small, grey, rather rumpled, he has been writing novels and has bought an IBM word-processor for which he promises he paid two thousand pounds more than the current asking price. Having been almost everything he ever wanted to be – writer, director, producer – he seems reconciled to industrious relegation. His new novel is called *The Rewrite Man* and concerns a hack who 'gets involved with all kinds of people you and I both know'. He still has his Virginia Water bookshop and promised to ask us down to lunch so that I could sign all my novels. He volunteered that *The Glittering Prizes* continues to sell well. He took my number and promised to call. *Voyons.*

The startled blush of litmus smacked by acid.

In the restaurant in Bordeaux, after the chorus girl with whom I had been chatting about Hollywood (she once knew Darryl) went off to work at a strip club, one of the men at our communal table said, '*Vous avez dû la suivre, monsieur; vous aviez des fortes chances.*'

How About It? A married man, alone overnight in a foreign city, happens to talk to an adjacent woman in a restaurant. She is a dancer who poses *seins nus* in a nightclub; why doesn't he come? The man sees no reason why he should not have an adventure for once. He goes to the club, has drinks with her afterwards, and spends the night with her. Not as young as she seemed, she is amiable and accommodating. He leaves her in the morning without shame or a backward glance. At the airport, he finds fog and the usual winter delay. In the bar, he gets into conversation with a young Englishwoman. He is driven, as if to warn her of male duplicity, to tell her of his adventure of the previous night. He sees himself die in her eyes, unless… he doesn't. Suppose she shows signs of being excited and suggests they find a hotel. It amuses her to see the mixture of alarm and conceit in his face.

Or: the man has told his wife that he is going abroad on business. In fact, he has a rendezvous with the love of his life. Her flight is delayed, then cancelled. He goes to the restaurant where he meets the dancer. Who will ever know that he has betrayed both his wife and his love, which now seems much less compelling? The next day he returns home. His wife has discovered the rendezvous and refuses to believe that he has not been with his lover. In a melodrama like real life, the wife might well leave him on account of what never happened.

28.1.83. Christopher L. asked us – Beetle, Stee, Sarah and me – to dinner in his basement flat in Earl's Court Square. Stee had a high fever and Beetle called to cancel. C. was so disappointed that I agreed to go with Sarah. Tinned chicken soup, cottage pie with (frozen) broad beans, were accompanied by chilled Spanish white wine (he insisted on opening two bottles), tinned guavas, then Nescafé. C. told us that he worked for

Sky High Tiles. Previously, as a freelance inventor, he had designed and patented a clip which allowed tiles to be mounted on rafters without using nails, which made for remarkably accelerated installation. He tested the clip in a wind tunnel at speeds up to 120 mph. SHT were eager to buy the patent. Wary of taking a lump sum, for tax reasons, he agreed to an arrangement whereby they would make him a marketing consultant, with a salary and a car. When the lawyer handling the patent papers rang to say that he was ready to complete the transaction, C. went to the company's offices to find that nothing had been drawn up concerning his remuneration. The lawyer assured him, as an impartial consultant, that there was no reason not to complete the business in hand. C. was paid a ritual pound and signed away his invention. He heard no more from the company. He called and sought a meeting with the managing director. He was given an appointment, but found no one in the office. He never heard from SHT again. He considered legal action, but was told that he could never afford to pursue the matter as far as it was likely to go. SHT were prepared to take it to the House of Lords. C. qualified as a barrister and has family connections in the law, but he flinched from protracted litigation and allowed himself to be robbed. SHT had made contact, at the outset, with their principal rivals, in order to make a cartel agreement, so that C. could not play them off against each other.

Can this story be true and why am I tempted to doubt it? Now divorced and, having renounced the law, C. works as a journalist. He is thirty or so, slim and of medium height, with an air of postponed dejection. His mother is Greek, a Vlastos, and he is proud of, if not dependent on, the vague aristocracy of his Chiot connections. He brought out a commissioned family history, in French, very flowery and flattering. Almost handsome, almost very charming, he may well resent Sarah's reluctance to yield to his advances; we probably saw him at his least assured. Although he vaunts himself on his Hellenic connections, he does not speak the language. He reads carefully (he even remembered phrases from *The Limits of Love*), but he seems neither educated nor classy. He told us of a tart in Warwick Avenue who, although short of clients, is obliged now and again to snub a masochist who solicits her lest he lose his appetite by being given easy access to her services.

31.1.83. Peter Woodthorpe was invited to Number 10 after the PM and her *époux* had been to see *Anyone for Denis?* It was before the Falklands episode. P.W. made bold to ask Madame what, in two words, was the main thing that worried her. She replied, with small hesitation, 'Council houses.' She considered that their tenants lacked the responsibilities of property owners and hence were potentially 'disloyal'. The slave-owners of the old South encouraged their darkies to form family ties, if never to own property, for similar reasons: the best shackles are homemade.

1.2.83. Sarah and I had lunch with Denys Gueroult. I fear that I lured her into something as distasteful as a second-hand glove. I parked near Carlyle's house. The restaurant Santa Croce is opposite the barges where Dotty Tutin lived in the 1950s; Leslie Bricusse and I once took her for a sandwich at an adjacent pub. She was nervous and a little supercilious. I feared she thought she was wasting her time with us; more likely she was pining for Larry Olivier, her lover in those days. His intermittent attention (and Vivien Leigh's shrill jealousy) robbed her of her health and almost of her sanity. It is odd how little I ever liked or desired Dotty, or she me, despite our common ambitions.

Denys G. resembles an elusive quotation: easily forgotten and not usefully remembered. He shares a house with a man whose business it is to arrange firework displays. The bills are often 'into six figures'; the pyro-technician lives well, but apprehensively, being more often burned by his clients than by his artifices. He is sometimes urged to do things at short notice, payment to follow. Gulf monarchs are quicker to hire and fire than to meet their obligations. It is futile to press; vizirs are liable to say that, since one cannot dun the sultan, one must consent to be done oneself.

The Radio 3 Magazine, which D.G. edits, began by selling fifty-nine thousand copies in November; its circulation is now half that number. Only five people staff it, however, so it may escape abrupt extinction. Its existence has coaxed a series of short stories I should not otherwise have written. I watch its struggles to survive with callous sympathy. Sarah brought her charm and some of her sketches. G. was polite, but he is an editor without egotism, hence without daring. Having been in and around the BBC for a long time, he has the fatalism of those of whom little has been asked, and to whom less has been given. Camp, but respectable, he knows a lot of people whose names are not quite weighty enough for dropping; they can only be floated.

Guerra Civil. I first met Sam Eskin at Selene Chapman's house in Churriana. The *finca Rosario* had ten bedrooms and serenadable wrought-iron balconies. The residence of the late 'Don Geraldo', otherwise Gerald Brenan, it stood among pendulous orange groves where, today, big jets reach their point of no return at Malaga international airport. The baro-nial hall, adjacent to a fifteenth-century cloister, had a cathedral ceiling with black oak beams. There were Arab horses in the stables, exercised by a tall, doleful groom who sat Quijote-countenanced in the saddle and had only one arm. His name was Federico. Four other servants supervised the place and its tenants. Selene, twenty-five years old, fair, pretty, short and bored, felt watched. Her husband, Carter, was a movie director who, she said, was often called to Madrid; we suspected that he went more frequently than he was called. He was about to make an *ave atque vale* spectacular about Hannibal. Rome could easily be built in a day, thanks to resources available under that Iberian Augustus Francisco Franco; but first Stephen 'Ben-Hur' Boyd had to commit.

Sam had driven trucks and shot men. A man of action and a manipulator of stock, he had been on the picket line and also a friend of Jimmy Hoffa. He drove a VW and carried a self-made stash. Veteran of the Abraham Lincoln Brigade, he had no tact or sentiment when it came to Spain and its labyrinth: he had been there before and here he was again. His life was a bunch of short stories, never a novel. In Andalucia to collect folksongs, he had small Spanish and less music; but he did have the equipment, the energy and the will. When we talked about the 'tragedy' of the Civil War, he remembered the liberty it had granted him rather than the democracies' betrayal of Spain's elected government. So what if the owner of the *Finca Rosario* was not a Swiss businessman but almost certainly a Nazi or someone who bankrolled Nazis?

He preferred the rough to the smooth. He hated Walt Disney and his cute image of the US. Children were not creatures to be cossetted but coaevals and co-evils; they should expect neither mercy nor favour. Asked to imitate a donkey, he imitated a *donkey*, not an imitation of a donkey: he became a rough barrel-bellied *burro* with a bellows-operated diapason of frustrated lust. If he had been able to extend a two-foot dong, black and gristly and ready for action, he would have. He was so loudly realistic that Paul burst into tears. Sam went right on to the dying sigh of his lusty impersonation.

10.2.83. *En route* to California, I Concorded to JFK. My neighbour was a young businessman called Phee. Having already been in the air for eighteen hours, from Kuala Lumpur, he talked continuously. Thirty-three years old, he was vice-president of a family Fire Extinguisher business that turns over thirty million dollars a year and will probably quadruple in the next five years. Big-chested, dark-haired, energetic and complacent, he had a taste for 'contact sports'. An 'A' tennis player, he had shied at rallying with Ivan Lendl one time and now regretted his timidity. Industrious and self-reliant, a member of the post-Vietnam generation, plump with new affluence, he believed that America had been ungratefully used by the rest of the world; it was time other people learned to stand on their own two feet. He had no notion that the activities of the richest and most powerful nation were anything but one hundred percent altruistic. Loving father (of three) and decent husband, he was about to celebrate his tenth wedding anniversary by taking his wife to NYC for a few days and buying her a fur coat. His father had been 'active in the Church'; his ample family was evidence of his piety. He said that he did not know any Catholic jokes.

He went to Boston University. I doubt if he has done much reading since. He had an unclouded conscience and a God-blessed belief in his future. He and his brothers would build up the business for a few more years and then sell it to a conglomerate and enjoy the millions for which his father had laid the foundations. *The Towering Inferno* had been the best commercial for his business that he could ever imagine. The water stored on the roof in order to furnish the climax of the movie would more plausibly have been distributed in tanks on several floors, but the scheme was generally sound. Phee talked largely about himself, less out of self-satisfaction, perhaps, than shyness.

His father died when he was sixty-two, a hard man with little time for sentiment. Phee's mother was 'Italian', although she no longer spoke the language. He had never been to Italy. His father was Chairman of the American Fire Prevention Association and had just laid down the gavel after their convention when he felt unwell; six months later, he was dead. He had taken few pleasures in life, but he had ensured the prosperity of his heirs, who collaborate with easy fraternity. They employ three hundred people, none unionised, and take very good care of them. After twenty-four hours travelling, Phee was due on the ice hockey arena the following day. *Ad Dei Majorem Gloriam.*

I was told that first class was full on the TWA plane from JFK to LAX. I gave the very pleasant clerk at the check-in the cigar which I had been given on Concorde, a very small tribute to his geniality. He went off and, by some secret means, found me a seat in the full compartment, next to a Mrs Hillman, a lady with the tenacious frailty of those who have abandoned hope, but still have their pocketbooks. She noticed that I was reading I-zay-ah Berlin just as I did that she was filling in a book of crossword puzzles with the dedication deserving of a worthier task. Each of the puzzles (she did them at quite a rate) had a nostalgic theme: she was back in the twenties and thirties. Her son had been at Trinity Hall, Cambridge, in the sixties. I asked what he read. I think the answer was 'Law'. She looked at me for a moment through her shrewd spectacles. 'He's dead now. He was killed.' The rest of our conversation was show-biz triviality: she knew David Jones and Sheila Allen. She told me that just as his career was beginning to revive, John van Eyssen had been hit by a taxi-cab and had both legs broken. 'Must've been an old friend driving it,' I said. She liked John. She was on her way to LA to have just one dinner, with an old old friend, a woman. When, with proper remorse, I asked her to give John van E. my good wishes, she said I should write my name down. She said, 'Oh! We tried to get you to write something for us one time!' It was a series about Lloyd's of London.

11.2.83. I saw two stars under the soggy Californian sky. After Burt and I had discussed the script all day, with a break for lunch at a Deli (I had stuffed cabbage, more stuff than cabbage), Richard Dreyfuss came in around five, prompt, neat, plain, small. He is at present on bail after a road accident that revealed a packet of cocaine in his car. He is said to have greeted his arrest with the view that God had decided to step in, presumably before his price dropped. Clean, tubby and middle-aged, with a cap of grey curls and thick spectacles, he looked like a little Jewish lawyer who had joined an athletic club, while no athlete. I felt that I knew him from another occasion, although there had never been one: he reminded me of Brian Marber. If B.M. had been American, might he have been a movie star? There is remarkable indifference in Hollywood to the physical beauty of male stars; only the second echelon have to be pretty.

Mind you, Warren is pretty enough. Tall, smooth and *rangy*, he has the eyes of a man who has seen it all, or all he cares to see. Gene Taft took me up to his house, somewhere above Mulholland Drive, on the Sunday afternoon. The Hollywood Hills were Irish with mist. The calendar seemed to have slipped back a decade or more; we might have been in Raymond Chandlerland. Gene was driving his sister's car and wore the nine-hundred-dollar fur coat, his sole badge of luxury. It was admired by the actress leaving Warren's warren. Surveyed by the Polyphemus eye of a camera, we had to pass thick white gates and drive along an alley of concrete panels to the front of a white place that seemed almost deserted, despite the cars. The modernism of the house ('I built this place,' Warren told us) was a flashback to the 1920s: the wide living room sported white sofas in an alcove by the unlit fire, a grand piano, few books, no pictures: a bachelor pad with little padding.

Warren may be intelligent, but either has little culture or takes care not to be caught going through customs with it. There is stiffness in his high shoulders; he is beginning to walk like an older man. He is forty-seven; time to lie about his age. The face is creased, the brows low; he frowns boyishly, but the crinkly show of good humour may double with myopia. There is something in him of the cracksman wary of leaving too many clues. He is amused to have made a Hollywood movie glorifying communists, though his own politics are probably soft-boiled. He remains boyish by daring his elders to send him to bed, his happiest playground. His charisma is a function of will: handsome enough, he decided that he was a movie star and the industry has gone along with that. He is said to have been offered five million dollars (on account of fifteen percent of the gross, from the first dollar) to do our re-make. He asked warily about Sarah, then went upstairs to find the water-colour she had given him and which, he said, he kept pinned up, among very few things, in his work-room. He is weary of directing and claims you cannot act and direct at the same time; there is too much to worry about. We went into the kitchen where he squeezed me a big glass of orange juice and sat down to carve himself diet-conscious slices of cold turkey from the refrigerator. He had been cool in the face of Gene's pitch, but the conversation between him and me came so quickly to a point of intimacy, or its facsimile, that he warmed to the idea of our collaboration. He said he no longer wanted to get involved with people he did not know because that made it impossible to tell them to fuck off without heavy hassles and subsequent apologies. He wants to do the picture with Schlesinger, with whom he has never worked but whom he feels he knows well because of John's long relationship with Julie. He said, with a rather touching lack of calculation (or caution), that he could sometimes scarcely distinguish their two faces and saw them imposed the one on the other. Freud smiled; Fred too.

I had heard too much about Warren's flirtatious temper to be over-excited by the amiable protestations with which I quit his house in order to take the long black limousine to the airport. Gene called last night and told Beetle that Warren had been about to propose that they get another writer, but he had liked me so much that he had now changed his mind. Warren retains the buoyancy of the boyish; he seems in great shape, though he rarely exercises (he has a tennis court, but doesn't play tennis) and he cannot meet anyone without seeming to do them a favour; evasiveness is only the subtlest aspect of his availability. Gene loves him with a possessive distrust that amounts to obsession. I doubt if G. feels much desire for anything except money; even money may be less impor-tant than the coup which secures it. He has no wish to 'cure cancer', as he says, frequently; he wants to be *rated* and to be proved right in resus-citating this frayed formula for turning shit into gold.*

---

* I never saw G.T. again. Warren continued to dither. After Gene died of AIDS, Warren did indeed star in a remake of *An Affair to Remember*, his co-star was his wife, Annette Bening. I do not know who received credit for the script nor who directed it. It went, as they used to say, straight to DVD.

21.2.83. Any Questions in Gloucester. The headmistress of Cheltenham Ladies College was the virgin on the panel. She was one of those ladies whose intelligence has never been leavened by any suspicion that she was attractive. She delivered her ideas like milk, with a self-deprecating little clatter. Edward de Bono, on the other hand, is practised on platforms; his blue overcoated, dark-haired chic serviced the rumour of his fame. The inventor, or at least the populariser, of 'lateral thinking', he went to Oxford and teaches medicine at Cambridge. An Odysseus whose Trojan horse trots in all directions and smart enough to have become renowned, even in Salt Lake City, de Bono lacks the wit to surpass his reputation. A Maltese who could as well be Canadian, he has made his own dull luck.

We drove down the long and cold road with Patricia Hewett, now a parliamentary candidate, of the Bennite persuasion, for Leicester. She is a rather pretty, at least personable, woman in her middle (i.e. late) thirties, has no children and contact lenses. Born in Canberra, she has no doubts about her right to pronounce on British affairs. She likes to be alone with strangers and relishes the pastoral aspect of politics. Opinionated but not predictable, partisan but not fanatical, she has made public-spiritedness into a benign form of parasitism; she sets out to counsel the deprived in order to deserve the attentions and emoluments of the well-placed.

I conned the Reith Lectures, 'The Arts Without Mystery', twice before going to discuss them with the author, Denis Donoghue, and Roy Strong on a live broadcast. It was clear that they were the work of a complacent and irritable mind, but I was not decidedly hostile when I boarded the honorary taxi for B.H. We were offered a dose of Moet et Chandon and smoked salmon sandwiches, quite as if we were attending a fund raiser. Roy Strong had better be cleverer than he appears; he is small, has a large moustache, like a pantomime broker's man, and wore a very long brown scarf. His hesitations may well be those of someone who knows exactly what he means to say.

Donoghue knew only what he had said before. Very tall and thin, in a fleshless rather than exercised fashion, he wore a tweed coat, of slatey complexion, grey flannels. With the provisional geniality of a priest on a mission to cannibals, he abandoned ecumenical affectations as soon as he failed to incur deference. He declared that he was weary of defending his position, but had no other ground he was willing to occupy or even to survey. Like a battery bird, sitting where he had always sat, he supposed that he was establishing his integrity rather than confirming his inflexible squat. Worse than a bigot, he was a bore. He attributed to Strong the use of the term 'transgression' in order to embark on a topic which neither of us had broached and which he then dismissed as unoriginal, quite as if originality was required for a review of well-worn ideas. After the broadcast, he said, 'I didn't know which to kick, the microphone or F.R.' I said, 'If you are still labouring under the same perplexity, I should strongly advise you to kick the microphone'. He laughed, just.

I have never been in England very long without feeling that I am being eaten alive by vegetarians. The English turn you into a turnip and then they make soup out of you. It would suit me to be done with everything that cannot be packed and evacuate forthwith. Oh to have half a million pounds and the tools of my trade *et praeterea nihil*! What less enviable than to be a demi-Midas, turning every other thing I touch to tin?

Last Thursday I went to play football in Holland Park. I once thought I was too old at thirty-five and yet there I was at fifty-one, an age at which some souls take early retirement, being rewarded with 'well in' when I successfully tackled those young enough to be my sons. In the mid-1960s, I played in Hyde Park twice a week and reached the stage of almost resenting not once being offered as much as a twelfth-man-and-linesman's place in Glanville's Chelsea Casuals. Brian was there this Thursday, presiding over proceedings which needed no president. He almost walked away because the goals (sloughed coats) had been made too wide; better to play, as usual, with no keeper and goals a mere chink in width. Kind and warm, he has the commanding good humour of those who never find themselves a joke, but always have one to tell you.

28.2.83. The Gollancz party for D.M. Thomas, an elderly person of my age. He was a lecturer in English at a college of further education until translated to fame by *The White Hotel*. He has not only false teeth but also, it seems, false lips; he looked dubbed. He resembles one of those jalopies composed of scraps from various sources. He says he lives 'near Wales' and is actually a Cornishman. Convinced that his success is entirely merited, he looks at you without a shade of interest or geniality.

I talked at length with Joan Bakewell, who is always pretty and lively and whose dyed hair seems nearly as natural as her smile. She is back on the box and writes short stories for *Punch*. Recently she spent three weeks in China and was, she said, very naughty in getting away from her guides. She takes pride in saying that Marghanita Laski is a great friend of hers. She told me that Ronald Hayman had been at Cocteau's deathbed. He travelled across Europe, immediately after Cambridge, and called everyone '*Maitre*' and they all invited him to their deathbeds. I remarked that he had written a rather good book about Nietzsche. She acknowledged that this was so, though she wished it were not.

Later I was talking to Michael Holroyd and a lady called Josephine Falk, from the Arts Council; she was so winsome over the powers she fancied she wielded that she was almost doubled over by their burden. Holroyd introduced a woman who said she wanted to meet me, Vicky Feaver. I asked if she was any relative of William (the translator). 'He's my husband and he left me four months ago.' She was a poet, dressed mainly in black, with pepper and salt hair, rather pretty. She has four children and proposes to write a book about Stevie Smith. Married for twenty years or so, not waving but drowning, she is in the same house where she lived with F. I had listened that very morning to pretty Anne Raeburn and gym-mistressy Irma Kurz talking about 'splitting up'; goodness how *practical* they were! You should never, they advised, leave someone *for* someone else; you should just leave. Men were accused of fear and cowardice and women were told that things had to be faced if they were to be borne. Their confidence that things would work out was at odds with the shattered truth that stood so nervously in front of me in Dover St. I said that I would talk about Stevie Smith to James MacGibbon, who owns her estate. Vicky F. told me that she was in the telephone book 'under Feaver, with an "a"'. Nice title.

2.3.83. Years ago, when I was an *habitué* at Crockford's, there was a member called Alan Fry, a sandy-haired, rumpled and leather-elbowed commercial photographer. Diffident as a Pigalle pimp, he had a south London accent and played golf at Wimbledon Park. Only just not as charming as he assumed, he was an indifferent bridge-player, but he played briskly and liked to give the impression that he had a system all of his own, 'Fracol'. It came down to playing the weak no-trump regardless of vulnerability. One day, soon after I had bought the ample sheepskin coat which I still wear, I took the one sheepskin left hanging in the front hall at Crockford's; buttoning it outside, I was dismayed to find that it was tight and of inferior quality. Its owner had to have taken mine. In the event, the thing was readily put right. What sticks with me is the detritus in those alien pockets: keys, change, scraps of paper, hinted at a life utterly different from my own. Those keys opened doors which I should never recognise; the pieces of paper, with their creased script or lists of purchases, were vacuously cryptic. Imagine if an address had been among his petty effects. The finder might go there and discover no one at home. He opens the door and is tempted to… do what? Take something, because he seems invisible, like Gyges? Then again, the key might be to a flat where the Fry character's surprisingly beautiful mistress lives. What could such a woman find to want in such a man?

Paul Tortelier in his dressing room, receiving the tributes of his votaries, seemed even more exalted than he had on the platform where he had the allure of a cheerful Don Quixote, gallantly *à cheval* on his chestnut cello. After playing the Richard Strauss he was still decked in Cervantes' aura. Large blue eyes under shaggy, articulate brows, after-glowing with the brilliance of his performance, he had all the *mondanité* of the self-aware celebrity. He gave Sarah a genial, artist-to-artist welcome; we discussed for some time the prospect of her painting his portrait. The problem was that he was never still. The next day he would be in Sweden; he was rarely in Paris, his home in the Midi. He had quick good manners, like a benedictory prelate. His right hand was a swollen claw from his efforts; he could neither shake hands nor sign autographs. There was anxious humour in his attitude to the vital implement that hung lamely from his cuff.

3.3.83. At the Queen Elizabeth Hall. We were having a drink before listening to Brendel. Harold Pinter and Antonia Fraser came towards the bar and I offered them a glass. They had the brazen air of people who have been acquitted of doing something they had clearly done. The death of Vivien Merchant is said to weigh heavily on Harold. He has always been civil to me, if only in the style of an actor who never knows when he may need work. Amiable, if scarcely forthcoming, he seems lopsided. His passion for Antonia is as understandable as all feelings for which there is no explanation. Fleshy and cow-eyed, a figure apt for epic rather than lyric celebration, she resembled a tug inflated into a ship of the line by having H. in tow.

They give the impression that they have contrived a mutually enhancing merger into a great love, as happy as that of Kingsley and Jane, when it was happy. Harold's almost friendly face stalls you at a distance. Like a brazen dentist with a sideline in stolen goods, his complacency doubles with dread of being found out. Antonia is blanched and superb; conjugal collisions have left her undented. She has a son at Ampleforth, where her fame has absolved her sins; she was recently invited to lecture there on biography. The monks had advised the boys that they should take one drink on their wedding nights, but not two. She is now writing a book about women in sixteenth-century England and affected to be humbled by the amount of work such a theme demanded as compared with biography where you can start at the beginning and go on until the subject drops.

Like a walking warning sign, Harold wears a soured face, skin roughened, teeth crooked: watch out. A master counterfeiter of small change, forever finding new devices for saying as little as possible, he is the sleeve up which the magician himself contrives to vanish. He has a capacious memory for reviews and recalled what I said, flatteringly, about his Proust screenplay. Does he also remember that he misspelled my name when he wrote soliciting a small favour about screenplay credit? *De minimis non curat rex.*

The Queen Elizabeth Hall was galactic with celebrities – Levin and Spender – whose conceit fizzed like dud fireworks, spluttering but never breaking into starry cascade. Isaiah Berlin looked as complacent and discontented as any man who is venerated for having done as little as possible. Afterwards we went to a very poor Italian restaurant. A drunken oik at the next table coughed spaghetti onto my sleeve and then denied ownership, although we had no plates in front of us. His companion, who soon left, admitted the justice of my charge and I was eventually granted a loutish apology. The stain on my sleeve remains.

4.3.83. There are few decisive landmarks in a man's life. The biographer may be able to say precisely when his subject had his last fuck, but the man himself rarely knows when a bracket has closed. I am, however, able to say definitively that I have played my last game of football in the park. When I set off for Holland Park yesterday, I took with me Erasmus' *In Praise of Folly*, a tribute from George Fischer after my radio talks. My injury was comic, agonising, entirely my own fault. I kicked at a ball, missed and, before I could recover my balance, fell heavily on my dangling right leg. It felt as if it had been axed at the knee. The pain was so cruel that I feared I should throw up before I reached the distant bench to which B. Glanville conducted me.

A young Italian from Como said that I should find a doctor who would, he thought, be able to wrench me back into due shape. Brian saw me back to the car and waited to see whether I could drive; while he was there, I had no difficulty; in his absence, the pain increased. A traffic warden was sour when I stopped for directions to a hospital. A policeman to whom I signalled my distress jumped from a bus full of his colleagues. He ordered me to pull around the corner, quite as if he had nicked me with my hand in a jeweller's window. He could then do no more than advise me to drive home carefully. Thanks a lot.

Unable to get across the street to the flat from where I had parked the car, I asked three people to help me. They responded as if it might be a trap. One of them leaned me against the wall like an old ladder and left. I was left to labour the rest of the way to the door of 53. When Beetle saw from the window how suddenly decrepit I was, she rushed out. We went in an ambulance to the Cromwell Hospital where I was X-rayed, found to be substantially intact, strapped up and sent home on crutches. The hospital seems mainly for foreign patients, morose if rich. Doctors talk to them through interpreters. While I was lying on my back, the hard overhead light beat my frown into a headache. I was sufficiently recovered by evening to be able to go to the Cellan Joneses' splendid dinner. I drank Perrier only, but managed to be adequately guest-like in the panelled, candlelit living room, where we sat till 1.10 a.m.

6.3.83. I have rarely read any of Alan Brien's film columns to the end. He displaced Dilys, after holding Harry Evans to a promise made at some cronies' colloquium. The poor man's Ken Tynan, A.B. has been a journalist without any mission but the re-employment of his sparky verbosity. When he left the *Sunday Times* at the turn of the year, I assumed that he was proceeding to another columnar situation. It seems that, in fact, he so resented having his copy cut that he cut his own throat by resigning. Had he engineered a less thumping exit, he might have contrived a gilded goodbye. Impelled by an explosion of affronted dignity, his recklessness has something heroic about it. He has not claimed that an injustice has been done or that a conspiracy of politically-motivated people has driven him to take the fall; he has merely told them that he is not taking any more of their crap. Never popular in the office, his psoriatic countenance will not be missed. A journalist's epitaph is written in spittle. Who now remembers the *News Chronicle*'s once legendary Ian Mackay? He came to Cambridge in my first year with Margaret Stewart, whom he had married (if he had) *en dernières noces*. She was of an old Cambridge family and had dignified connections in the town; they took me to a formal tea-party *chez le gratin* in Sidgwick Avenue. Mackay was a shambling Fleet Street Titan (some read 'tight-'un'): a reformed boozer whose reform was, it seems, far from salutary: he died shortly afterwards. Alan Brien will, I suppose, survive; he has a resale value, or at least a price, and he knows a lot of people. No one's first choice for anything, he has the wit to make the second-best of himself.

9.3.83. Irwin Winkler wants to do a *Darling* of the eighties, with Marty Scorsese. Ron Mardigian was deputed to test my reaction. *Perche no?* When I was supposed to be working with Marty on the Byron project, we scarcely spoke, save across a very crowded room: he was busy with *New York, New York*. An ambitious, inconsistent film-maker, he has not lost the will to be bold. I used to play occasional tennis with Irwin when I first went to LA. The foursome fell apart after its organiser, Bob Shapiro, became head *honcho* at Warner Brothers. Irwin feared that he had offended me over *The Right Stuff*. I had forgotten all about it.

11.3.83. Richard Broke and John Pringle, his producer, took me to Odin's, where the food used to be better. A rich, white Jamaican, with an expensive tailor and a Greek Cypriot chauffeur for his Mercedes 500, Pringle had his heyday in NYC immediately after the war, when he was a young officer among limey-loving ladies. His eyes suggest the calculation of a man whose virility has been at the service of his avarice. Having moved much among the rich, he is himself, I should guess, merely wealthy. He thought that a series about the *richissimes* would enthral the public. He gave an example of whom I had never heard: J.J. Wagner. This figure – so legendary that he figures in no legend I know – was cruising off Jamaica and summoned the young Pringle to a conference on his yacht. Imagine!

'Tiny' Rowland (whom he called 'Rawlings') was another object of Pringle's tale-telling veneration. He said that R. once hired a selection of Madame Claude's prime tarts in order to clinch a deal with some African politicians. He took them on a river boat up the Niger. A party of seductive sumptuousness was proceeding splendidly when the over-excited Minister of the Interior fell overboard and became a snack for the crocodiles. The whole deal fell through with him.

Pringle also much admired Rome's *richissimi*; they had style and content. A member of the Black Nobility once gave a formal dinner and then, when the ladies had retired, demanded that nobody look under the table. A trap door opened and every male member of the company was unbuttoned and given 'the most marvellous blowjob', after which the detumesced men were invited to join the ladies. P. had not been present, but he swore, as people always do, that he knew someone who had. The teaser was that the seated and sated cavaliers had no way of telling whether they had been pleasured by males or females.

In her late forties, Kath is about to qualify as a solicitor. It seemed that, when a febrile young Girtonian, she married the handsome Josh in order to have a stout keel on which to sail through life. After the shrivelling of his career, she came to see that he was financially unreliable. He still has charming, boyish qualities, but is ceasing to be a boy. Kath was loyal and steadfast when things first went wrong, but she then became withdrawn. Neither resentful nor bent on revenge, she set out on the long road to financial security; still at home with Josh, she has also left to train as a solicitor.

Can machines think? The key question is not whether they can provide correct answers but whether they can deliver stimulating incorrect ones. Thought, on Wittgenstein's scheme, has among its criteria not only the capacity to get things right but also the possibility of getting them wrong, perhaps interestingly (as W. considered Otto Weininger had). Is it *conceivable* for a computer to go too far? If proof against 'error', it may assist thought, but it cannot be accused of thinking. Think about it.

If the mathematician has a motive, it is not mathematical.

Wittgenstein's goodish fortune was that he made his mission to the English and that it was Cambridge in which he took refuge. Greeted with tolerance and generosity (the guardians of indifference), he resorted to mantic seclusion. He gave the impression of having imported his wisdom from a source inaccessible to those without his quasi-private language, spoken and gestural. For all Anscombe and Geach's keenness to naturalise (and baptise) him, he was never wrestled by a British angel of sufficient force to make him shuck his '100% Hebraic' legacy.

A new New York magazine called *The Movies* has asked me to write a piece about Julie Christie. Not having spoken to her for fifteen years, I got her number in Wales from John's Caroline (on the understanding that I not reveal its provenance). Still with the same tremor of uncertainty in her detached manner, Julie was quite, not very, friendly. Since she shuns publicity, why should she be seduced by my wish to write about her? I served notice, nicely, that I was going ahead and that was that.

Back in the early 1960s, Julie's beauty was manifest, but not empowering; it embarrassed her. At drama school, she had been mortified, and singled out, by the easy passage her looks procured her at auditions where talent alone was little regarded. Some actors have an immediate, involuntary rapport with the camera. Julie's appearance is never of a woman happy to keep her photogenic promise. Even in so artfully well-lit a piece as *Doctor Zhivago*, beauty falls on her like a shadow. A star who refuses to twinkle, she remains merely unique.

Julie has always sat with her back turned to the direction in which she is travelling. After winning the Oscar, she would accept only modest parts in the theatre, in Bristol. With a perverse sense of destiny, she experienced success as a sort of failure. Her beauty is an affliction which pays a price and a dividend. Pitched between icon and I/con, her only adornment is the celebrity's uneasy halo.

Neither *Shampoo* nor *Heaven Can Wait* offered her more than a supporting role; she is said to have been remarkable in *Petulia*, not least, I suspect, by people who never sat through it. Her private life is a series of retreats, covered by baffles erected by her friends. For years, she had no fancy or even fixed home; in that regard, she chimed with Warren, with whom she lived in a suite at the Beverly Wilshire. He now has a house which, even when he is there, looks as though its owner is away.

Julie has never played the kind of female with whom any prudent or sentimental man would care to spend his life. Promising nothing, she demands the impossible, or at least the improbable. The secret of her durable reputation lies in the position she holds, straddled between fiction and reality (as in the poster with which I had them begin *Darling*). Symbol of a revolt against subordinate femininity, she parades none of the ideological obstreperousness of the 1960s feminist. Before *Darling*, she had a tall, taciturn boyfriend called Don, an art student, I think. Asked what their relationship was, she said, 'I belong to him.' If vulnerable, she refuses to be wounded; if indignant, she is never strident; if contrary, never Vanessa Redgrave. She rehearses the dateless negativity of Antigone, whose 'No!' endures in modern Greece's '*ochi*': a declaration of defiance, never of demand.

Had she been keener for money and acclaim, might she have been a better actress? She seems to echo Mastroianni when he said to Beetle and me (over dinner, with Faye Dunaway, at Carlo's in the Fulham Road), '*Beh, cinema non é gran' cosa!*' If Julie shares Marcello's estimate of the movies' triviality, she cannot match his versatile professionalism. She was distressed, if not panicked, by the *Darling* script's demand that she remove her clothes. John left me to talk her into it. I sought, with sincere duplicity, to justify the scene by maintaining its cardinal place in the plot. She did not challenge my cant; she simply considered herself insufficiently beautiful.* The flaws in Julie's technical competence (Albert Finney said she couldn't do the chat) have kept her unspoilt. At once seductive and embarrassing, her appearances evoke sympathy on account of the beautiful dread she cannot conceal at the prospect of having to perform at all.

13.3.83. Carol came to lunch. It is five years since she visited the flat we had rented in Green Street and there was a *crise* which resulted in her departure in embarrassing circumstances, if only because she could not tell when she was no longer wanted. She has become greyer in the quinquennial gap. The educational cuts have put her casual lectureship at Birkbeck in danger of the axe. She remains bewildered by the animosity with which my old friend Ted persists in treating her. She could not

---

* The scene, in which she marches – in black and white – through her (absent) husband's empty palazzo, shedding clothes as she goes, was imitated, very closely, in a frequently screened golden perfume commercial starring Claudia Schiffer, whose stride suggested no doubt whatever about her charms.

understand the sudden violence of the original breach; she can do no better now. What can he possibly have seen in the uncomely Sybil? Her prime virtue has to have been that she was not Carol. Yet C. is far from unattractive (Josh B. rates her 'Tasty'). Ted promised to let Carol keep the house if she gave him his freedom; once he was free, he went back on his word. It is lucky that sixty percent of the property was in her name. She has quit the Tories to become a member of the SDP, but little else has changed. She still cannot imagine why Ted hates her. Self-criticism is beyond her. She is drowning in the shallowest possible water.

17.3.83. Lunch with Tony Moncrieff at the *Gay Hussar*. He wore a suit the colour of mushroom soup and what could have been a Bodeite tie. With Dickensian *embonpoint* and florid aspect, he has made an adequate career at the BBC and calls half the cabinet by their first names, at least when they are not present. The willingness of the political class to entertain his company doubtless comes of his paying for the provisions, but it has given him *entrée* to the changing rooms of the world's game.

He is just back from Plains, Georgia, where he interviewed Jimmy Carter in his dull habitat. The late President is a man of intelligence, he says, though small wit. He went to Washington, like Mr Deedes, as the honest man's answer to D.C.'s insiders. Having advertised his distrust of the machine he had to drive, he expected loyal responses from the mechanics who serviced it. M. took it as a rare compliment that Carter autographed a copy of his memoirs for him, although the publishers had had him sign a contract to inscribe his name only in volumes in a special, higher-priced run.

M. plans to retire at fifty-five, unless some plum BBC appointment falls free, and then go and teach in the US. Though not malicious, he was quick to recount the senilities of the Chairman, George Howard. He has surrounded himself with young girls whose presence vexes the staff, even though 'he doesn't do anything' with them. When he proposed to take one on a trip to the Western Isles, the Corporation refused to pay for her travel or lodging. Howard has to be rich enough to take on such petty expense, but he was offended and cancelled the expedition. He has grown hugely fat and will shortly be dead or retired.

Moncrieff told a nice story about Clem Attlee. When he was PM, he sent for someone from the FO to brief him on a particular topic. After their official business, Attlee asked if the man's father, with whom he had been at Haileybury, was still alive. On being told, 'Oh, yes, sir', the Prime Minister said please to convey his best wishes to his old school-fellow. 'He may remember me; the name is Attlee.'

I repeated this anecdote to the Provost of Eton, who agreed to smile, at the pre-dinner drinks at Birkbeck, after Sir Harold Acton had given his magic lantern show – about three British ambassadors to Italy – in the Senate House where Beetle once heard Thomas Mann give a lecture. Now antique and duly polished, Acton has taken on an oriental allure: the hairless head of veined ivory, the nodding gravity. He reads only with difficulty; his stately prose was spelt out in enlarged majuscule. In the middle of his sonorous performance, after several crackles of electrical static, the fire alarm went off in a series of blurting raspberries. We were invited to leave the hall, calmly; it was almost certain that it was a false alarm. The enforced interval offered some people a discreet opportunity to depart for good. Finally, the old boy resumed the podium and was rewarded with a fresh round of applause, which I initiated. His mature culture may be genuine; his self-assurance is that of a prodigy who hood-winked his Oxford generation. Despite all his polite concentration on her unfortunate (and unfoolish) cuckold of a husband, the most memorable character in Acton's essay was Lady Hamilton. 'Let me be the last to congratulate you,' I said to him, as we shook hands on the way out of the subsequent dinner.

The Master of Birkbeck was so full of ums and ers that his several speeches were greeted with applause denoting more sympathy than admiration. We walked to Birkbeck and there found John Lehmann and the Charterises. L. is tall and chapped and appeared to be in a stricken daze. I remembered corresponding with him over a play competition in the *London Magazine*, which he used to edit. In 1949, I thought it exor-bitant to demand five shillings for entering a play. I congratulated him on the early volumes of his memoirs and asked urgently for the next one, which quite cheered the old bugger up. Charteris affected to have met me before, though his courtly career hardly makes it likely that our paths, or wooden swords, had crossed. He said that the main duty of the Provost of Eton was the selection of a new headmaster. The post was always advertised, but any outsider who applied was disqualified for want of modesty. Although they went through the motions of judicious appraisal, they always knew whom they were after.

Robert Birley had been a good H.M., though not a popular one; he was lofty and frequently absent. When offered the job, in 1946, he had made bold to ask what they proposed to pay him. There was an awkward pause and then the Provost of the day passed him a slip of paper on which three distinct figures had been inscribed. The two largest sums had been struck out; he was left with the lowest option, which he accepted. Both Charteris and his amiable lady had the air of people who had got away with something they were determined to keep. They hoped I agreed about the necessity of élites, quite as if they feared that I was privy to some new argument against them. The privileged have a clever way of giving an appearance of fragility.

At dinner (not bad, not good), I sat between the John Hales. A tall, whey-faced professor of Italian, he prefers to call himself a historian. She is his well-dressed, white-faced, fair-haired second wife, a Vassar girl, no older than thirty-eight, not quite as thin as her smile. She was much on her dignity, the better to take it off if the evening warmed up. In plain blue suit and white blouse, she made such a show of being unimpressed that I suspected that she took the occasion very seriously. If only to prove that he had stayed awake through Acton's lecture, Hale recalled the Regency rule forbidding three-sided conversations at dinner parties. Sensing jealousy, I proposed that the three of us hold hands like the Hamiltons and Nelson.

Hale founded the history department at Warwick in the early sixties, then moved to UCL, where he is an unadmiring colleague of Karl Miller. When I asked him about the best time to visit Verona, because I wanted to write a novel about Catullus, he scorned so trite an ambition. The denunciatory role quite brought him to life. Perhaps I had been too amiable to his chilly wife. She came, I suspect, from a wealthy family (her school in NYC had been Spence) to whom she no longer speaks, but still speaks *like*. She had met George Steiner once or twice (I suspect once) and had been 'impressed'. She rather hoped, I think, that he would be impressed to hear of it. Hales and farewell.

Stanley Baron told us that he had brought an old school-friend into the firm, in spite of the fact that he had never much liked him, because he knew that he would 'produce'. He hoped that time might have made him more amiable. The man has proved a thorn with a good deal of side, but he has indeed 'produced'. S.'s reputation for shrewd head-hunting has been enhanced, but he would prefer to be accused of having made a terrible mistake. I am not sure why there is such eagerness in the firm for me to write a book about the Seven Wonders of the Ancient World, but S. says that he now knows exactly how it should be done and will be writing to me today. My relationship with Thames and Hudson has been fortified by old Mrs Neurath's declaration to Beetle that she loves her. She will even come to France, though she doesn't like it, to have more of her company. Beetle also made a conquest of Gombrich, who had met George Clare* that very afternoon. Told that we had seen almost nothing of Vienna, he said he would mark our card next time.

* Author of *Last Waltz in Vienna*.

18.3.83. Peter Medawar and his wife were fellow-guests at the Rubinsteins together with Robbyns Landon, the Mozart authority and a power in the classical music business. Landon had been at the T&H dinner the previous night, though I had not noticed him, despite his bulk. He claims to be a 'Back Bay Bostonian' and has the cheerfulness of those who, while secretly grudge-ridden, think it prudent to maintain an amiable front.

Medawar has had two strokes, the second four years ago, and is physically wrecked: distressed face, logs for legs. His brain unimpaired, he gets about under his own steam, with the aid of agile crutches. He goes to work daily at nine, returns to Hampstead for a latish tea. I have always imagined that he had Indian blood; in fact, he originates from the Lebanon, a once tall, now sprawled man with large eyes in a broad, flattish face. One of the eyes, fused by the stroke, glares emptily, but there is an amused vestige of optimism in the stricken body. He and his wife Jean greeted me with the intimacy that comes of encountering a memory: they saw the Footlights in London in 1954 and have never forgotten my performance in 'Joe and The Boys'. I have never done anything less in character, but that was why they thought they knew me.

Jean and Beetle had met at the hairdressers once, when the lady had been rather strange, though flattering, under the dryer. Beetle was sure that she had said at Xavier's that she had only one child. In fact, she has four. One of her two sons is a lone yachtsman who crossed the Atlantic in a twenty-eight-foot ketch. When she flew over the course and saw the size of the waves, she trembled at his courage. She is a grey lady with keen eyes and an alert ear for her husband's call.

Helge had prepared a very nice meal: leek salad (not *quite* sufficiently cooked), excellent *pommes lyonnaises* with garlic, lamb, salad, very good cheese, sorbet with a chocolate *marquise*. How very close we almost are! Helge noticed that Beetle was somehow fragile and asked, tactfully, whether something was wrong. On Wednesday, Beetle saw a young black man kill himself at High Street Kensington Station. She was directly opposite the place he chose to descend, stepping carefully to avoid electrocution. As a train approached, he put his hands up as if to resist its impact, and was then crushed to death. Beetle said she never liked that station and would never use it again. My mother was on her way there when it happened. Her train was delayed by the accident. Beetle visualises the incident again and again. The black man was twenty years old. She can see his face as he looks at his coming death.

The dinner-table conversation was light and anecdotal. It emerged that we were substitutes for Bernard Williams and his tough babe. Robbyns Landon listened to all conversation on non-musical topics with the vacant aspect of a robot unprimed by coin to speak his usual piece. He disclosed only one or two important things, such as who disliked Bernard Levin. As amiable as he was sharp, Medawar agreed with flushed grace to be entertained.

A stark moment came when Helge asked him about the prospects of a sixteen-year-old patient suffering from bone marrow cancer. M. is involved in cancer research and said that headway was being made. Recently, one of his friends had been cured by a black surgeon colleague of M.'s. That the friend abstained from gratitude diverts rather than offends the Nobel laureate. The imminent death of the sixteen-year-old was something he faced, as he does his own, with a good deal of philosophy. If life is unendurable, it is best that it end. The youth of the sufferer makes the onlooker indignant or appalled, but the patient had to make his own reluctant or serene peace with the inevitable. Bone marrow cancers are among the most intractable. The boy had received a transplant from his sister, but it failed to take. The danger is that the transplant material will be attacked by its host or that it will itself become aggressive. Only twins have an almost certain rapport.

Medawar and I were at one in thinking Popper's *The Open Society and its Enemies* as among the most important books in our lives. Popper once said to him, 'Surely you, Peter, would *die* for the truth?' Death seems quite a small matter in certain company. Medawar retires at 11 p.m. When they went to their car, Jean found that she had locked the only set of keys inside. They had been hurried by the presence of Landon on the doorstep and had lost their routine calm. Hilary made to get his car from the garage, but it was low on petrol; he conceded the Galahad role to me.

I drove the Medawars to where they live, near the Downshire Hill church. Its new paint gleamed in the evening light. Peter was fearful lest Jean fall down the cellar steps while going for the spare key to the front door. His sole sign of anxiety about himself is the excess of concern for her. He would, he said, sit in the hall of their nice little house (rather inaccessible with steps from the gate), playing chess on his little electronic device until she returned with the car to which I then ferried her.

Like companions in some larger misadventure, Jean and I achieved a casual intimacy in the few minutes we were alone. M. thinks highly of Jonathan Miller, but Jean found him 'rather talkative'. Jonathan and Rachel were close friends of the Medawars' daughter and her husband (the Garlands). M. called me 'Freddie' easily and at once; either he has spoken about me with others or – the likelier option – he is a friend of Freddie Ayer.

In a second-hand bookshop off Museum Street, where they were playing the budget news on a portable stereo radio, I came on a review copy of William Bartley III's scandalmongering study of Wittgenstein's sex life. It had been vigorously annotated by the owner who had written his name on the front, small but clear: Frank Kermode. The marks ceased about two thirds of the way through, either because K. had lost interest or because he had by then decided what he was going to say, or had already said it. Imagine a woman who finds such a book and is able, by scanning the emphasised passages, to understand why her husband, the reviewer, was impelled suddenly to leave her (a connection here with Carol's experience). The marks – even mere ticks, crosses and exclamation marks – enable her to see what he really thought about her; they grant approval to ideas or appetites she never imagined him to have. She is shaken, oddly grateful that it all 'makes sense'. Then she discovers that the annotations were made by a student to whom the book was lent. She has understood her husband in the light of evidence without authenticity. Her sense of the shape of her case against him is so strong that she cannot rescind the revelation. She has been unblinkered by mistake.

Do not wait for tickets,
Warrants to travel,
Places to explore
Open from now till then;
It is never too early,
Sometimes too late,
So stay at home
And be abroad in that.

Forgetfulness is the step-mother of the Muses. If we could not shed the actuality of things and so be left only with shadows and distortions, there would be no time, no space, and no art.

The William Morris Office boss is married to a rich heiress called Dagmar. She is known around the office as Drag-ma.

Today's writer is like a secret agent who bundles pages together and takes them, under plain cover, to carefully selected 'drops', never guessing that his assiduous paperwork will be taken for negligible trash. Presuming himself to be saving the sum of things, he dedicates his best insights to an extinct cause.

Jo Janni told me of an audition at which a handsome actor looked to be perfect for the lover's role, but the producer feared that he lacked virile ardour. Hence:

'*Ti piaciono le donne?*'
'*Beh, non sono fanatico!*'

1.4.83. The 'egotism' of which the Christian often accuses the Jew is embossed in the selfishness of the Christian with regard to his own soul. No Christian, except a *méchant* paradoxologist such as Graham Greene, in *The Heart of the Matter*, cares to find circumstances in which a man can establish his nobility by laying down his *soul* for his friend. Such an act implies a table of values superior to God's.

If you go high enough in the building, and listen at the key-holes on the upper floors, no matter what tragedy is taking place on the street, no matter how seriously it is taken by those who live and work down below, you will find someone high up laughing.

I should sooner have a crime named after me than a street.

While handsome, he seemed not aware of it, but when his looks began to fade, his hair to disappear, he became a dandy and spent an afternoon each week at the barber's.

What a sweet form of troublemaking to attribute, in somewhat furtive journals, all sorts of *obiter dicta* to people who never said them!

Anthony Burgess appears to live modestly and demand no privilege. His clothes might have come from the liquidation of an expensive shop whose owners misjudged current taste. He cooks his own meals because he is too parsimonious to go to restaurants or hire a cook. He has invested his money in houses, some of which he has never visited. He may even have mislaid their addresses. Wounded by the animus which his secession from England has excited, he is pleased to be a mark grand enough to merit denunciation by the *Daily Mirror*.

One could combine Burgess's story with that of Peter Fairley, the stuffy-seeming member of our TV syndicate who told me that he was at Cambridge with me, though I have no memory of it. He said that he was a member of the Musical Comedy Club and created a waterborne revue on the Cam near Magdalene Bridge. Leslie Bricusse was involved in the plan which called for a finale in which the 'skipper' cast off from shore and the whole cast floated away into the summer night, waving and singing. When they actually *did* cast off, they had forgotten that the power lines serving the stage were all cemented to the land. The Cam became the Styx.

Fairley has one family in London, another in Bury St Edmund's. At once affable and touchy, he has the pursed little mouth and suspicious eyes of a man who has got away with a good deal, but not enough for him to regard his double life with humour or satisfaction. A TV film-maker whose name means something, but not enough to make him a Name, he has the petty brazenness of a man who has never been accused of all the things he has done, yet would have it that he is quite a devil. Since prudence is necessary if he is to get away with it, getting away with it means that only he knows what it is. Forbes Taylor says that Fairley drinks a bottle of Château Latour daily.

The Greeks called having sex with a dead woman 'putting one's bread in a cold oven' (Herodotus V, 95). How odd that they should have a term for it at all!

René Girard, *La Violence et le Sacré*, cites Joseph le Maistre: 'one always chose from the animal kingdom the most *human* sacrificial victims …'

Bernard Frappart, in *Le Monde* 27.9.82.: '*A Beyrouth quand on croise un homme habillé en civil, on se demande à quelle armée correspond son étrange uniforme.*' [In Beirut, when one comes across a man in civilian clothes, one asks oneself to which army his strange uniform belongs.]

The pride we take in the efficient impunity of the SAS resembles Plato's admiration for the Spartan 'night squads' and their place in enforcing social conformity. Because our killers have no names, we cannot betray them. Since their masked missions are enacted only against foreigners and terrorists, there are no inquests.

The bath in the Aeschylus' *Agamemnon* has a little recognised duplicity, a sort of justice as the (unseen) place in which Agamemnon *trouve la mort*. He goes into the house to cleanse himself of the taint of violence, the blood of the Trojans, for which he need not apologise, but also that of the daughter sacrificed to procure the Achaeans' triumph. Laying aside his majestic rig, he bares himself to Klytemnestra's net and blade. The blood he hoped to wash off is not only indelible; it is now mixed with his own. The fates deny him absolution and sanction his death; but guilt is now transferred to his executioner, Klytemnestra. Her death at the hands of Orestes confirms the Erinnyes' power and its limits: implacable by definition, they have no right to excuse anyone.

Why is merit traditionally ascribed to females who do not mourn excessively? The embarrassment caused by prolonged weeping and gnashing of teeth relates to the fear of contagious, uncontrollable indignation against male policies, hence Pericles' recommendation of reticence to bereaved mothers and wives. Leaders fear that women will blame them, not 'the enemy', for the bloodshed which mimics menstruation: in the masculine calculus, killing trumps giving birth, mimicry the vital thing.

'Maternal' similarities of looks are never mentioned or acknowledged among Trobriand islanders; the father is the 'differentiator'. Greeks were held to be tactless if they observed that a child resembled its *mother*.

Arthur Scargill, in his got-up radio lecture with its piss-elegant use of 'albeit', pronounced 'all bite', maintained that the miners (and presumably everyone else) would retain the right to strike even when socialism has been instituted. What he did not say – and was not pressed to answer – is whether they could ever *win* such a strike. Scargill is a king of division calling for unity. If his idea of society were realised, how could the miners remain his foremost concern? No one raised the awkward question. BBC 'impartiality' required that Scargill's inquisitors become his courtiers.

Palmerston: 'There is in the human heart a passion more powerful than the passion for freedom and justice, and that is the passion to inflict injustice and to destroy freedom.'

The banality of Solon's verses, Grote says, 'does not aspire to any higher effect than we are accustomed to associate with an earnest, touching and admonitory prose composition.' Gilbert Murray: 'They possess something of the hardness and dullness of the practical man!' Solon, says C.M. Woodhouse, 'could content himself with bare allusion and side glance, confident that such figures and images... would not fail of sure interpretation'. He claims credit, among his poetic commonplaces, for one great achievement: 'readjustment of the economic conditions in Attika'. Solon's careful character was not, according to Plutarch, immune to a rather coarse (*phortinóteron*) hedonism. The sensualist need not be a bad moralist: he recognises the limits of morals. Solon, the traveller to Egypt (if he ever went), was a man of the world. G.E.M. de Ste. Croix speaks well of his poetry, as he might of Louis Aragon's.

Alan Brien is a member of that class of performer, in print or on the box, who no sooner appears in public than one wonders whom it was that they failed to get.

A long story short. 'She isn't here.' What a man says on the telephone when his wife is with another man.

Ivy Compton-Burnett's novels: when you've read them all, you've certainly read one.*

Jean Brampton. She was auditioning for *Lady at the Wheel* when her dress broke open. She caught her breasts in her hands. 'I nearly showed the lot,' she said. She sang and danced capably, with a sort of smoky aggression, a trouper. A few years later, she committed suicide.

The Jonathan Cape Award for Literature: no prize money, no advertising, but Tom Maschler comes and stays with you for a month.†

Jacques Prévert (1930): '*Il était aussi très douillet: pour une coupure de presse il gardait la chambre pendant huit jours.*' [He was also very thin-skinned; for one bad review (literally, press-cutting) he would stay in his room for a week.]

Scutter and stillness of lizards on Delos, dactyls of nervous sound on the brittle rock.

The Arabic *wasm* is a mark branded on camels. According to Robertson Smith, it was originally a totemic sign placed not only on camels but also on their owners. The word is cognate with *ism*, Arabic for name. How sweet, in the light of the above, was Ike's 1950s remark 'All isms are now wasms'.

30.3.83 G.S. has often boasted about Debbie's participation in the most exclusive seminar in Oxford, Lloyd-Jones's Pindar party. He confessed the other day that she was bored to somnolence after half an hour of

---

* A cheap shot, although *un peu vrai*. When I first began reviewing for the *Sunday Times*, I paid proper tribute to one of Ivy's novels and received a grateful and gracious handwritten letter from her.

† Another cheap shot which ignores Tom Maschler's unmatched patronage of some of the best English writers of his time.

L.-J.'s bitching about the delinquencies of other scholars, *surtout les Français*.

G. was in gleaming good spirits at the Savile on Thursday. He has been having tests and there is no need for the quadruple bypass of which there had been excited rumours. The Courtauld lectureship seems to have assuaged his intimations of exclusion: England has offered a small embrace and he is happy to fall into Britannia's scrawny arms. He even had an amiable word to say about my series of talks which are being repeated on Radio 3. He had to say, however, that I had failed to pay due tribute to an excellent book which Robert Brasillach wrote about Racine.

A lady at the TV centre also spoke well of my talks, which was hardly less pleasing. I spent some hours with Jim Cellan Jones. Overweight, he has parted company decisively with his athletic youth. He was President of Swimming at Cambridge, a modest, enviable eminence, but his timings obliged him to drop himself from his own team. That he left St John's without a high enough grade to go on with his medical exams both humiliated and liberated him. Had he done better, he might well have become a country GP, like his father. Never at the top and rarely in loud demand in the biz, he has done much honourable work (the Sartre trilogy etc). Candid in his dislikes, he has wielded an obtrusive axe among producers in the Drama department. Jonathan Miller is not among his favourites. The latter's saving of the Shakespeare series has not saved it. Jim is doing *The Comedy of Errors* in November, after which he will devote himself wholly to *Oxbridge Blues*. He seems eager and generous in his determination to have me direct a couple of the plays. I do not expect to quarrel, but I await our first easy laugh together.

23.3.83. The Institute of Directors used to be the Senior Officers' Club. I once had lunch there, for a reason I cannot retrieve, with General Wemyss. Now it has been adapted, without charm, for captains of industry. Memorial plaques celebrate forgotten heroes. Functions are held in a variety of rooms. My destination was 'Burton', the name of the ward in *Richard's Things*. I sat and read Wittgenstein in the lobby rather than present myself too promptly.

All Jews, except for Mrs Sofer, the SDP's parliamentary candidate for Hampstead, few of us were comfortable with Israeli policy. George Weidenfeld presided. After a tour of our opinions, he declared that we should recognise that there were times when the luxury of conscience had to yield to the discipline of solidarity. His trumpet was sounded with the air of a patron from whom certain favours might be available. He told me, both before and after I had demurred about the value of mutable values, that he had a specific project in mind for me. He affected to regret that I had not yet yielded to his 'blandishments'. I said, 'Blandish harder.' He reminded me of the important position which Mark Boxer occupied in his firm, as if that should be the clinching seduction.

It is naïve to suppose that a London committee of notables can (or should) make proposals for the conduct of Israeli policy. What coincidence of ambition can there be between an armed state, with a growing measure of religious bigotry at its centre, and the soft heads and consciences of those who live far from its dangerous borders? Only the fear of anti-Semitism, as the ultimate, recurrent evil can continue to unite us. Hence the need to make all anti-Israeli sentiments evidence of a new wave of the old blight. In the name of tolerance, we are urged to be intolerant of anything that might be said, fairly or not, against the 'Jewish' state.

The most aggressive Zionist present was my neighbour at dinner, a woman called Rosalind. She would have been darkly good-looking had she not worn the expression of someone on attachment to the High Command. Ambition and self-denial pedalled a tireless tandem. The smallness of Israel and the unreasonableness of the Arabs made the latter's grievances a provocation. The West should be putting pressure on the Arabs to change their attitude. Her patience was exhausted.

An American called Godson, an *haut journaliste*, with connections with the University of Georgetown, declared that Israel had ceased to incorporate the secular and pluralistic assumptions of western civilisation. We were faced with something increasingly alien and, if the trend towards fundamentalism increased, eventually insupportable. The only answer to this glum prognosis was George Weidenfeld's call for solidarity: Jews are faced with a destiny, never a choice. Begin's policies may be deplorable, his means regrettable, but he has made peace with the Egyptians, destroyed the PLO militarily and faced the Iraqis with the consequences of their hostility. His unblinking obstinacy has gained him the close attention of Israel's enemies, none of whom has chosen an aggressive response. What has this to do with western civilisation or 'traditional Jewish values'?

31.3.83. Godson gave me a lift home in his new Renault 20. Unused to the dimensions of the passenger's seat, I clipped myself quite briskly in the mouth with my briefcase. I listened to him and tried to respond with poised maturity as I assuaged the hurt with the tip of my tongue. After we had mused over the contradictions of enthusiasm, he gave me his card. He had never heard of me, nor I of him. Our solidarity was without substance. He was in his early sixties; his name and person reminded me of Fritz Gotfurt, though he lacked the cynicism of that rusé operator.

Fritz left Germany as soon as Hitler became chancellor. He had the sorry complacency of a Cassandra unable to prevent what he clearly foresaw. I do not know how long Fritz worked for Associated British Pictures but, in his lazy way, he gave them shrewd, disabused, service. As project supremo, he was also able to acquire, among other 'properties', plays written by his wife, for sums small enough not to excite question. Fritz smoked short, slim cigars and wore garter-sleeved shirts with wide blue and white stripes. His keenest interest was in the sexual behaviour of the cast of *Don't Bother to Knock*, Richard Todd in particular. A decorated wartime colonel, then a considerable star, 'Dickie' was a notorious *coureur*, of a discreet 1950s order. He appreciated the decorous *double-entendres* with which I improved the script.

During a lamentable lunch at the Borehamwood studio, I had my only sight of Gary Cooper (twenty years ago, I called a character 'Coop', in *A Wild Surmise*, in tribute). He was very tall and had the glassy look of a man who knew he did not have long to live and had no wish to discuss it. Already all but a ghost, he made nothing of his famous presence. The glazed eyes met no others. In his prime, he was used to the pick of the female bunch. He humiliated the exquisite Patricia Neal when she was in love with him while making *The Fountainhead*. Now, towards the end of the road, the carriage of his body announced that he was not going to throw himself on anyone's mercy; arrogance and reticence were paired in him. I cannot imagine that he ever asked for more lines in any script; fewer perhaps. The world he stood for, in his movies at least, was one of uncomplicated loyalties and monosyllabic decisions. As the hero of *High Noon*, he incarnated an idea of white supremacy that took solitude and superiority for granted. Coop made acting seem easy because he did so little. In temporary exile, he was an idol who had absconded from a distant pedestal. Fritz Gotfurt could not have been less like G.C.: for the exile, everything was *not* to be taken for granted; nothing came to the fugitive pariah save by connivance and contrivance. His survival had been the result of jumping the gun before the gun jumped him.

The director of *Don't Bother to Knock*, for which I supplied dialogue by the yard, for £150 a week (on such activities was a happy family dependent) was called Cyril Frankel. Handsome but not bold enough to be a playboy, he wanted to do an English version of *La Ronde*, an idea that I have peddled like a brazier of old chestnuts, and had a company, so he said, that wanted to commission it, without 'up-front' payment; not my idea of being commissioned. He had little future after the advent of the

Oxford group of Tony Richardson, Lindsay Anderson and Schlesinger who advertised their up-and-coming qualities by making socially-conscious, black and white documentaries. The laurels they won enabled them to graduate to colourful, award-winning and lucrative careers in commercials and feature films.

Two nights ago, Irwin Winkler called from LA to sound me out, again, about working with him and Scorsese on a 1980s version of *Darling*. Marty feared that I held it against him that he had abandoned Burt Weissbord's Byron project. Since I never felt that he was much involved in it, his secession seemed no great treachery; we had only a few meetings, during which his mind was on other things. My only annoyance had been the presence of Marty's temporary wife, who thought her contributions capital. He indulged her because he preferred her to be with Percy Bysshe and his lordship on the terrace of the Villa Diodati rather than alert to contemporary aspects of his life. Marty was deep into preparations for *New York, New York* and deeper into Liza Minelli. I remember only his mimed reprise of a ninety-second student film he made, in the style of a commercial, in which a man applied soap to his beard and rather carefully shaved his face off with a straight razor.

Scouting locations in Israel, Marty and Irwin fell in with a very rich Israeli who was keeping company with a beautiful model who lives in Paris and comes from Minnesota. They wondered where exactly things stood between her and her 'date'. When they were due to fly to Paris, she wanted to come with them (the Israeli tycoon had other business). They did not, in the event, leave on the same plane, but she traced Marty in Paris and pestered him to take her to a party at the Agnellis. She was beautiful and she was lonely. She hounded M., who may have enjoyed the power he had over her rather more than Irwin chooses to see. Neither Irwin nor Marty is now able to forget her, although they had been relieved to be rid of her.

My generous, if slightly vengeful, redemption of Schlesinger from his doldrums led to a commission for which I had no vocation. Frank Pearson, who composes on a word-processor, had already turned in a script so useless that it could not even furnish an apotropaic example. I shall take the money and limp. It seems that John will, after all, soon begin work on *The Falcon and the Snowman* and hence may not have needed to be rescued. His mother has recently undergone serious surgery at the age of eighty-six and has survived, through a show of determination so gallant as to smack of wilfulness: her hold on life has something to do with her hold on others. You feel that John's parents will never let him go. Dutiful and disenchanted all at once, he declares, with accusatory candour that all his awards have been both a tribute to them and a reproach for their early disbelief in his qualities.

Like Bryan Forbes, John ran back to the BBC when the movies turned sour. I am sure that he was more tactful than B.F., who called the unit to a pep talk at which he told them that they were all fine individually but that he thought little of their joint efforts, but John also provoked resentment, by his failure to 'come in' to TV centre. The mechanicals thought his personal set-up at home altogether too grand. Jim Cellan Jones was keen that he and I be seen in the canteen, for democracy's sake. What is more important in today's England than to make a show of loyalty to what you don't believe in? John cannot now avoid giving a Hollywood impression, even though he likes to advertise that he hates them all, dear. He has played the patriotic card by casting Julie and Alan Bates in *Separate Tables*, a wretched piece of rep, and Alan again in the number by Alan Bennett about Guy Burgess and Coral Brown. The latter has cancer and had to have the anguish of her condition concealed by the judicious use of an 'inky'. Her malignant breast was removed after the last day of shooting.

1.4.83. It is some years since our then new neighbours, the Dutch diplomat and his then wife came to call. They drank sherry, especially the lady. Born rich, she could afford to be large, ugly and graceless. When she told us that she was from Frisia, I said, showing knowledge, 'Oh, where the cows come from!' Within quite a short time the marriage broke up. The house which they had renovated, in expensive and banal style, was put on the market for two million francs, but found no buyer. This week we received our first communication from Mr Van Heusde since he visited us a *lustrum* ago. He wrote, from Stockholm, to ask for the use of our tennis court during our absences and his and his new lady's presence. It would, he thought, be 'exaggerated' to build a second tennis court at Lagardelle, which implied that we have prevented him from doing so by having built the second one first. His letter was addressed, undiplomatically, to me alone. I replied that we shall be glad to invite them to play when we are all here at the same time and that, for the rest, the courts at Belvès are excellent. A subtler ambassador might have made it difficult for us to refuse by first returning our petty hospitality. 'In matters of commerce, the fault of the Dutch...'

2.4.83. On the way south we detoured to the village of Saché, in Touraine, where Balzac wrote *Le Père Goriot* amid other volumes in *La*

Comédie Humaine. Its *château* is dignified, not grand. An obligatory guide conducted us, with garrulous pieties, through its grey stone apartments. The garret allotted to Balzac (a favoured visitor, never the owner) is up a spiral staircase reached through a semi-glazed doorway in the little hall connecting the dining room and the *salon*. The novelist's narrow bed was in an alcove in his *cabinet de travail*. He would retire early from his patron's genteel company and sleep for a few hours before being woken, at 2 a.m., to start writing on a board propped on his coverleted knees. He made frequent coffee and ate biscuits and jam to fuel his muse. When he chose to get up, he worked at a plain mahogany table. The mansard window did not quite offer a full view of the valley. His will to work was prodigious, his eye undistracted. When his printing business failed, he pushed his pen and himself, hour after dark hour. Had he been as shrewd as his fictional notaries, he might never have been driven to such torrential invention.

A lover yet to make his amorous dash across Europe, he lived immune to social or passionate distractions. The *salon* downstairs, its *papier peint* now restored in *trompe-l'oeil* swags of two-dimensional curtaining, offered enough company to divert him and enough provincial prattle to impel him up the spiral stairs to seigneurial solitude. Balzac's uncertain social standing (he supplied his own *particule*) was never challenged by the petty aristocracy of his hosts. The peacefulness of Saché allowed him to be the puppet-master of an imaginary Paris: '*A nous deux maintenant!*'

6.4.83 Beautiful Mireille at the St Albert came up to us after our main course to disclose, with relish, that a dissected body, or at least a selection of members, had been discovered by sightseers in a *poubelle* near the *château* of Montfort. She had scanned the paper again and again in search of the gruesome details which had, she said, destroyed her appetite when she first heard them. It did not occur to her that we were eating at the time. She wondered whether the Dordogne had its own *monstre* and seemed to look forward to one of those epidemic *psychoses* which terrorise whole regions. With the beauty and bone structure of a movie star, she wears a different costume every day and regularly, and drastically, alters her hair style. Cheerful and maternal (now superbly pregnant, she has a daughter by an early Vietnamese lover), she conducts an unceasing and warranted romance with herself.

Her husband Michel trained as a pilot in the *armée de l'air*; discovered to be astigmatic, he was disqualified at the last moment. Renouncing flight, he returned to Sarlat to join his father in the hotel business. Garrigou *père* had had a life of his own, and three wives to show for it. He never pressed Michel to become a *hôtelier*, but is happy to have him run the place. The restaurant is the best in our area; the waiters, often young, are as efficient as they are friendly, Georges – with his assiduous '*pardon*' – the best. Michel is habitually generous with asparagus or any other treat he can slip onto our table. When I asked what '*Bretonnaise*' meant on the menu, he said '*Ca se sert avec quelques cailloux*' [It's served with a helping of pebbles]. Even the '*déceptions du socialisme*', although they weigh heavily on employers, evoke a sort of smile. Our neighbour Christiane Barrat, not given to *gros mots*, called Mitterrand a '*salaud*'. She deems him responsible for the low price of walnuts.

9.4.83. Have I made a note anywhere about our visit to Guatemala almost ten years ago? Stee, Beetle and I went first to Belize to observe, from the Fort George Hotel, the last vestiges of empire. Bulging rats ran in the deeply ditched, still British street. You could be sunburned under the cloudy tropical sky. Men of the Royal Welch Fusiliers (Robert Graves's regiment) came to the hotel bar in the evening. Their crudely in-character RSM told us the details of the British defensive plan in case of a Guatemalan incursion: there was one gun for every seventeen miles of jungle frontier.

After three waterless days in the expensive, shabby hotel, we flew from Belize to Guatemala in a plane without air conditioning. I was relieved to hear a red-neck American voice telling us that all would be well, but would remain kinda warm until we made an unscheduled stop in San Salvador. The airstrip was on a high spur, approached over jungle. The plane had to latch its wheels on the very prong of a V-shaped clearing if it was to have space to land. We sat for a short time in the terminal, watched by two heavily-armed militiamen with inscrutable cheek-bones. I wondered what enemy they feared and why, in such a paradise (soon to be riven by a ruthless civil war), they had to be armed at all.

Guatemala was in a state of political excitement. Election posters, row on serried row, covered the sides of the bridges over the motorway, built after a donation by J.F.K. The taxi took us to the American hotel where *mariachis* and banana bread applied local colour to touristic luxury. The city's old covered market, since collapsed by earthquakes, was filled with colours and scents. The incense-rich, saffron air piqued eyes and nostrils with green and purple fruitiness. Dried herbs, as well as custard-apples and other bulbous fruits, were displayed on wide, deep, gently inclined counters. In the corners of the shadowy building, vendors were rotating sausages and kebabs freckled with pimento. Smoke rose to the slatted band of the clerestory, a cloudy blue ribbon under the high hat of the roof.

The travel agents in LA had sold us an excursion to Chichicastenango and Lake Atitlán, which – they claimed – could not be visited except under group auspices. Our coach was supervised by a talkative cicerone who spent the four hours of the outward journey advertising the wonderful Guatemalan people. Each village, and almost every bend in the road, had a stall selling similar polychrome delights. The docile foreigners were encouraged to descend from the bus and acquire mementos. At one such stop, another passenger left a book, face-down, on his Pullman-style seat: *They Fought Alone*, an account of French SOE which I devilled back in 1958. I made bold to tell him that I was its author. 'You are Maurice Buckmaster?' I explained that I had been Buck's ghost; my true name was Raphael. 'Yeah? So's mine. I'm Doctor Raphael from San Diego, California.' He ran a surgical clinic with specialists for every anatomical region from head to toe. If I or my family ever needed surgery, he'd be happy to make me a rate.

Smoky fires, tended by local, straw-hatted Indians, fumed on the wide steps of the blanched church in Chichicastenango. Low smoke gave off an aroma of voodoo. I had taken so keen an aversion from the talkative guide that we ducked out of the escorted tour. We may have been in the remote highlands, but there were many cars and buses. At one of the brightly flagged stalls, we crossed a woman from whom we had bought weavings in Guatemala City; she was embarrassed to be seen replenishing her stock at prices much less fancy than her own.

We were due for lunch at Lake Atitlán at one o'clock, but we were still two hours from there at that hour, our exit from Chichicastenango stalled by a car halted directly in front of where our coach was parked. The car had been coming round the corner into the town when the driver realised that his front wheels has just passed over a large deep, square hole in the roadway. He could be neither encouraged nor intimidated into one more revolution in any direction. Unwillingness to risk breaking an axle some three hundred miles from the nearest replacement made a chicken of him. Planks had to be brought and inserted under his wheels before he consented, with abusive caution, to edge out of our way.

We arrived on the shore of Lake Atitlán at 4 p.m. The coach park was full. In the foyer of the fancy hotel, a *mariachi* band was singing and bonging with rhythmic insistence. There was limited joy to be derived from seeing and hearing men in tassels hammering xylophones with soft spoons. Our group was invited to stand in line to buy tickets for a buffet lunch in advance of seeing what was on offer. I declined, loudly, to pay for food I had yet to see and did not believe was likely to be there. When our guide became insistent, I rounded on him (a literal spin on my heels) and accused his loquaciousness of being the source of our belated misfortune. I shouted so strenuously that the xylophonists ceased their competition.

An American woman, diminutive but rich in self-importance, seconded my accusations: 'We really ought to have a refund, really.' I heard myself say, 'All you think about is money. I don't care about fucking money. I care about getting something to eat for my wife and son.' We were taken as quickly as may be to the dining room, past the all-but-empty platters from which the more gullible customers were seeking to cull their moneysworth. Having been seated in comfort, we were served with good, thick steaks.

Atitlán is a high, wide lake. Even in serene circumstances, who really enjoys looking at lakes for more than a minute or two? There it was, paling to the long ridge of mountains on the far shore. The sky was a blue blazer buttoned to a snowy collar. The locals grace the lake with the secret powers of their gods. There it was and there, no doubt, it is. It has none of the hold on the memory of that little spring halfway up the pass of Thermopylae, where the roasted hillside carries an outburst of green under the shade of a huge tree (chestnut, can it have been?).

On the way back to Guatemala City, two tours were confounded by the disruption of the timetables. Our guide was aboard our bus, but my Philippic had dammed his flow of words. I found an American couple to talk to, both psychiatrists. They had met Jonathan Miller in Hampstead, during a cultural summer. We chatted at length while our coach rumbled, without sanitary or commercial interruption, back to the hotel. Towards the end of the journey, the lady remarked that I had been very angry at the lunch stop. I blamed the circumstances and the height. 'Yes,' she said, 'that could be it. Because nobody ever spoke to me the way you did before in my entire life.'

The tour tickets we had bought in LA included one of Guatemala City. The following morning, neither Beetle nor Stee felt like another guided outing, but I had paid and I went, with five or six others, in a VW minibus. In the rich quarter (with thick walls and gates) near our hotel, the guide knew what each residence cost and how many tiles there were on the widest roof. In the heart of the city, we were shown round the president's palace. Various local woods complicated the floor and walls in marquetry mosaics. The guide was tactful in not dwelling on the history of the manipulated little republic. The fate of Jacobo Árbenz was not then known to me, nor did I have any idea of the degree to which Central America continued to be enthralled by US interests. I presumed that we were in a peaceful, landlocked island, now immune to the machinations of the United Fruit Company.

After visiting the glassed relief map, which gave three-dimensional shape to Guatemala's claim to Belize, we were back in the minibus, on our way to the hotel, when we were witnesses to a band of students running to collect stones from a builder's heap. It seemed like some folk-loric event, until they turned and bombarded a police car and then, as it swarmed into view, a posse of riot police. As if rehearsed, shop shutters fell and were padlocked at the base. Tear gas was fired; local rancour seeped into the VW. Our driver accelerated out of trouble and back to the untroubled tourist quarter. 'He handled himself pretty well,' said my neighbour on the bench seat, a lugubrious man (CIA?) who had taken scant interest in the city's sparse charms. There were more riots that night, and the white pop of tear-gas fire.

17.4.83. 'Is David there?' At Joan Bakewell's fiftieth birthday thrash, Antonia F. told me that, after she and Harold began to live together, Vivien Merchant used to call the house and ask for David, as she had called Pinter ever since they first met. When Harold was trying to get work as a tyro actor, his agent had told him that being called Harold Pinter did not help. 'What would?' 'If you had a name like… say, David Barron.' Antonia's several children were advised to say that no one called David lived in the house. Now that V. is dead, only a few of Harold's friends employ that name. One asked him recently if he liked being called by it; after a pause (what else?), he said that he did not.

Beetle thinks that Harold doesn't like her; it is, I suspect, as if her personality and those unblinking dark eyes accused him of something. As we sat side by side at the tepid Ritz breakfast, Antonia – in the same Jean Muir suede as when we met them at the Queen Elizabeth Hall – was very amiable to me (she said how much she admired *Richard's Things*) but frosty to Beetle, who looked very good. Joan is amazingly unchanged and has scarcely changed her friends. She knows the sort of people you would expect her to know and no one much else.

We are promised that Harold is *accablé* with guilt about Vivien. He gives the impression of a man without heart. The inner room of the temple of Jerusalem is famous for having been devoid of ornament; it was full of emptiness; hence immaculate and immutable. Pinter's supremacy comes of calculated parsimony. Antonia said that in the US, or that part of it where they recently were (Hollywood?), he is best known for his adaptation of *The French Lieutenant's Woman*, of which he was assumed to be the author. She affected amusement at the confusion, rather as if, after his performance at Cana in Galilee, Jesus had been mistaken, on another occasion, for a wine waiter.

Like J. Miller, Harold dislikes the Jewish *religion*; the emphasis is added, a thumb on the scales, to suggest an aesthetic distinction between untenable doctrine and genealogical fact. He looked askance at the young rabbis whom they met in Israel. He was, however, *barmitzvah* and will say *kaddish* at his father's funeral, just as he hopes that Daniel will at his. Is the irrational more marked in Judaism than in Catholicism, to which Harold (said to be intrigued by the character of the Pope) takes no brave exception?

An Israeli academic who came to see me regards Harold as the ultimate instance of the alienated Jew; he was shocked by the morbidity of the symptoms. Harold has made disengagement the essence of his personality, a Proteus whose elusiveness is achieved by never changing. There is something of the spy about him; he can account perfectly for every tick of his watch. To be sure of being unquestioned, he skippers his own side, in life as in cricket. He insists that actors honour the smallest distinction in his punctuation: a comma is an order. He embodies such a perfect marriage of the apparently spontaneous with the wilfully preconceived that you never ask yourself what could possibly ever lead him to be other than Pinteresque. Whole areas of life are, it seems, of no interest to him; he has not even the range of Kafka. If he wrote something not recognisably Pinter, he would not have written it at all. Faultlessness is part of what is wrong with him.

30.4.83. I went up to the Lancaster 'Literary Festival' because they asked me and because I did not know the north-west, or even where Lancaster was. It came after several unappetising options along the M1 and M6. A slab of the Pennines loomed to my right, brownish green shoulders apparently laid open to the snow-white bone. I had stopped for coffee at an excellent motorway café run by Rank: clean floors, bright plastic furniture and girls who called me 'Love', harbingers of the north.

The Lancaster University campus, where *The History Man* is said to have been filmed, adjoined the motorway, neat cubes in the golden evening. The city, built mostly of toffee-dark sandstone, had a one-way system that carried me inescapably to the hotel where I had been booked. The place had Brown Windsor décor. The lift was scarred as if condemned cattle had gored its hard walls. My fifteen-pounds-a-night room, on the top floor, overlooked the car park. It had twin beds at right angles to each other, a clean bathroom and a tea-making machine. The curtains and bedspreads were brown.

I paid a visit to the Priory church and elected not to contribute to its renovation. The castle lacked symmetry. There was an ancient keep, on the southern front, knobs and excrescences all around the glum enceinte dominated by a Victorian mansion, facing north, with sash windows, the formal address of the residence of a provincial governor. My host, Dan Feasey, a grey-bearded man in his late fifties, stopped his car beside me as

I was walking around the precinct. He told me that the place is still used as a prison for some six hundred fairly hard cases.

A psychotherapist of the orthodox Freudian persuasion, he has a little cottage below the prison, looking out towards the pearly horizon where Morecombe lies. Once a great working-class beach-fronted resort, it has languished since northern toilers chose to take wing for Benidorm and Torremolinos. F. has the staid demeanour of a physician who has, alas, cured himself. His wife, a producer at BBC Blackburn, came in while he was making me a cup of tea, her greeting as near as warm can get to cold. She works very hard, he explained. While believing in marriage and stable relations, he clearly relishes the sexual secrets divulged by his analysands. They alleviate his loneliness by paying him to alleviate theirs. Failure doubled with vocation; his smile recurred like a facial stammer.

Feasey offered to be my host at the fancy little restaurant across from the hotel, but I had discovered Dudy Nimmo's number (Yealand Conyers is only seven miles from Lancaster) and had invited her to dinner. She had planned to come to my reading and needed no persuasion. Promptly at the hotel, she declared that she now preferred to be called Dorothy. She wore a hounds-tooth gardener's pork-pie hat, turned down all around her small head, and a Royal Marine's sweater with canvas patches on the shoulders, no evidence of rank. Her face is that of an intelligent Mongol, skin as blanched as a boiled potato, mouth a pursed incision. The eyelids look as if they are unable to close over the beady blue eyes; the clever voice jumps out like a captive urgent to be heard from within an unhappy prison.

Her news was that Nimmo was back; he had bought the house from D.'s mother, Elfrida Vipont, for whom her daughter now feels nothing but scorn, although she has returned to care for her. John has opened an office for D. in Carnforth, so that she can escape from her mother from 9 till 12 every day. The old woman does not have the telephone number. John is away all week. I am not sure whether he still has his other lady with whom, at one time, he was living in Scotland. D. is somewhat pleased that he is adjacent, but she accepts her own hermetic solitude with grim glee. She does not like her children, though she has cared for them devotedly enough; nor do they appear to have time for her. D. belongs to a creative writing circle in Lancaster and sends stories, the latest called 'We've Lost Grandpa', to the local radio station commanded by Mrs Feasey, who rejected it. D.'s terse poems appear in Quaker publications.

I praised and tried not to patronise her as she ate her vegetarian plateful. Once upon a time a nudist, her nakedness is now clothed in idiosyncrasy of an order neither certifiable nor foolish. Her hands were scabbed with the dirt of the farm. Wilfully untouchable, she has become a provincial eccentric who makes apotropaic noises when London is mentioned. Determined on exile without recall, she announced that she had a sort of fit (a miss/fit perhaps) in the Euston Road last time she visited the capital. I hoped that no one in the restaurant would think that I was usually with her.

After my reading, she was unexpectedly fulsome in praising my performance. No, she had not had the smallest wish to be on the stage beside, or instead of, me. Her appetite for parade was gone. Resolutely unattractive, she takes pains that no one should look at her, including herself. She wears her grave clothes as if she will never remove them before she is buried in them. Claire Tomalin claims that she never really knew Dudy at Newnham; she refused to take part in seminars and would never read her neat essays to the cosy company. Her alpha-plus pieces were no longer than a couple of sides in her loopy handwriting. Short, clever measure was and is all her style.

At the centre of the Cambridge stage, she took all the best parts for want of anyone to challenge her. Until beauty became relevant, she was the ADC's actress for all seasons. John alone seems to have sensed, and been moved by, her provincial vulnerability. While everyone else feared her literary armoury, he could only hope that the world would continue to take her for a star. In London, she lost heart and earning power. John sought to comfort her by giving her expensive presents. I remember him as capable of rare, gentle endurance. At a Cambridge party, in Trinity street, I think, above the Post Office, he once yapped at, and discomfited, Mark Boxer who had told Dudy that she should on no account marry 'that ridiculous lamp-post'. There was passion between J. and D. for a while – how their bed creaked with accelerated rhythm above our beds in Montague Road! – but her love was a kind of greed, her desire fear.*

16.5.83. I have enjoyed seeing Schlesinger again. I have hated every minute of the project that brought us together. I should be ashamed to see my name on it. Yet I have promised to rewrite my first draft before it is sent to Paramount. John has aged and mellowed, either with the years or from the failure of *Honkytonk Freeway*, which still taunts him. He asked me, with a trace of malice, whether the Clarks had detected any cooling off in his attitude to them, or whether they had declared

---

* Dorothy Nimmo was posthumously saluted as a poetic genius by Craig Raine.

any lapse of enthusiasm for him.* I indicated that it was not the kind of thing which engaged my attention. Ceaselessly involved in his own arrangements, John combines courtesy with egotism that excludes interest in anyone else. When I asked him his plans for the next little while, intending only to learn of his availability for a fortnight or so, he reeled off a diary distended with engagements for breakfast, lunch and dinner. When not invited out to dine, he often goes out to eat: he knows the merits and locations of all the likeliest restaurants. Torn along an unreliable line between gluttony and self-preservation, his weight seems to fluctuate from day to day. Just as one is about to congratulate him, rolls of gauleiterish fat again rumple the back of his short neck. A day or two later, he will again advertise the gap between trousers and stomach.

He has decided to vest his *sérieux* in the opera. He rehearses his imitation of Solti and of Sir G.'s prissy and officious legate who arranges things to the split second and makes everyone subordinate to his master's Hungarian voice. This allows Solti to pose as more genial than his reputation. John tends to fall easily for the amiability of top people. Clever at observing and mimicking their quirks, he lacks any guile in divining what may go on out of sight. He keeps saying that Paramount are keen on *Desire*, but he never suspects that they may claim to like it, although it scarcely exists except in the sketchiest of outlines, because repeated, if cursory, enthusiasm exempts them from bothering with anything else that he might bring them.

He told me that he never had any sexual connection with a woman until he was over forty. Some of his gay friends were shocked by his deviation. While he saw little comedy in their scandalised reaction, he was warily proud of his ability to consummate the relationship with an actress, which had since been repeated. I did not press for names. Knowing that age will deny him grand-paternal compensations, John has become a keen uncle. He muses, with boyish incredulity, on the fact that he will be sixty-three in 1988, when Placido Domingo wants to work with him. Nothing makes one more dubious of the value of music than the mentality of those who have recourse to it. It is strange to feel affection without trust, admiration without respect. I expect him both to

---

* Known in crises as 'Doctor Clark', Jim Clark was John's frequent editor and salvation. The flop of *Honkytonk Freeway* led to rupture, as failures will. If the breach was healed, it certainly left a scar. Clark was a man of moods. After having been our guests several times, Jim and his wife asked Beetle and me to dinner. He then cancelled the invitation, for no disclosed reason, on the morning of the day when we were due to go to their house. I offered help if anything was wrong. He and I never spoke again.

use me and let me down, not out of malice but because he cannot proceed otherwise.

Clive Sinclair told me that he had been abused by an Arab (he said a 'terrorist') soon after leaving our meeting. The man was in a car behind him and hooted and gesticulated so violently that C.S. thought that his 2CV must be on fire. It turned out that the Arab had been inflamed by the Hebrew slogan on Clive's rear window. His bellicose response was a reaction to the slogan that translates as 'PEACE NOW'.

Did you think it would end?
It will never end.
That is the meaning of the obvious:
World without end.
Expect no originality from God:
His inventing has all been done;
His children are playing
With old toys.

4.6.83. At our Radio 3 mini-symposium with Renford, Scruton's red hair was rustier than I expected from seeing his TV lecture, when he read from the prompter as though he had been warned against being emphatic. Decorum and disdain ride together with him, his chariot harnessed to a hack and a charger. How conservative is it to announce one's own stylistic superiority to all post-war philosophers? Quite the dandy, smooth and barbed, he responds, when you question his advocacy of extreme measures, with a thin smile that is not without humour, or malice. With the soft menace of an egotist who relies on impersonal logic to pasteurise his prejudices, he enjoys the charge of being a provocateur. He showed becoming modesty when he saw that I was reading his volume on aesthetics, but was less gratified when I did not contest his notion that it was dated.

13.6.83. On Friday, after a longish election night, which brought little in the way of amusement, we drove down to Gloucestershire to lunch with Elisabeth Ayrton. We had been to another Thames and Hudson party the night before, at Eva Neurath's house in Highgate. Over salmon and salad, we talked almost exclusively with Bamber Gascoigne and Michael Holroyd. I had never met the former, but we greeted each other like old acquaintances. I said, and meant, that he was the one person who did his public thing so well that even those who satirised him were unable to inject malice into their mimicry.

He had been doing University Challenge for twenty-one years. Since he went up to Cambridge in 1955, he must have been offered the job soon after coming down. He said, almost anxiously, that he did not feel any different from those days and wondered if we did. He did not, I suspect, *look* all that different either; he still has abundant ungreying fair hair, its russet tone perhaps chemically maintained, and the trademark spectacles of the most popular swot in his class. He is quick-witted, but not witty, with an easy attitude to the world which he invigilates and whose sterner tests he elects to sit out. His wife, Christine I think, was slim and sensitive; she seemed inhibited by a reticence that suggested some kind of brave distress. She is a photographer and a sufficiently talented water-colourist to be invited to illustrate children's books. She and Bamber have no children.

The conversation turned to feminism. Holroyd told us of an idea, of G.B. Shaw's, I think, which required all parliamentary candidates to belong to a dyad, one male, one female, so that there would be an automatic balance of the sexes in the House.* This sounds 'fair', but it presumes that the essential 'unfairness' in the state has to do with sexual imbalance. The notion that women have to be promoted, as a class, and that their views can be expressed only by members of their own sex, confirms the prejudice it affects to treat. If women are so naturally and incurably apart that no man can be trusted to have a common interest with them, if every question is to have a male and a female answer, there is small sense in affecting to belong to a common polity.

There was something wholly amiable, if never quite friendly, in our calm controversy. We might be little changed from our university selves but a tincture of maturity threatened. Holroyd made the usual speech explaining why he had not been to university, although offered a place. He did, however, refrain (unlike Jack Lambert) from saying how pleased he was to have been spared the Oxbridge smoothing iron. As we were leaving, the first election result came through, promising great things for the Alliance. I heard Beetle's voice on the landing, never loud or crass, and I recognised how lovely a part of her is that dark vividness of mind and style.

13.6.83. I suspect that Elizabeth Ayrton wants the biography of Michael to be done less for his sake than for hers: once his claim to genius is between hard covers, her investment, emotional and temporal, will not

---

* It seems that Plato's Aristophanic egg (in *The Symposium*) was being laid again, but no account was taken by Holroyd, as it had been two and a half thousand years earlier, of the sub-species of dyadic homosexuals, male or female.

have been wasted. Her response to his infidelities was always implacable fidelity. She insists that Michael and Henry Moore were very close friends, though Steiner insists that 'old Moore' let M. down very badly, especially over the Pisano monograph; he had promised a much more thorough collaboration than is to be seen in the perfunctory introduction.

It would suit Elisabeth if the book she wants me to write promised that M. and H.M. were bracketed in mutual esteem. She holds that in another ten years Michael's reputation would have been unarguably established; he was cheated by the brevity of his life rather than by the limitations of his art. She claims that his bronzes were selling extremely well in the last years, important commissions imminent. I remember that they seemed, in 1975, to be doubtful of the sale value of the bronze castings in which M. said that they had invested some twenty-five thousand pounds. Kenneth Clark was an influential and hostile force; even Marina Vaizey set her sharp face against saying the smallest nice thing about the work.

Elisabeth tried to kill herself after Michael's abrupt death, but rallied as the keeper of his flame. She never went back to Bradfields, but has somewhat reconstituted its vexed tranquillity in The Maze House at Rockhampton. A maze maquette embosses the outside wall; there is a minotaur in the garden and an off-the-peg solarium, of Crittalls' glass, like the one in which Michael, as he waned, cadged heat from the Essex sun. Has E. secreted a fat archive of delicious scandal? If not, what is there for a biographer to discover?

Michael was expelled from school at fourteen or fifteen, after seeking, with the willing complicity of an older girl, to discover whether there could be any truth in the unlikely account of human reproductive processes which he had found in some allegedly reliable source. Michael had had osteomyelitis when he was ten. He became the insatiable reader who, prostrated by undiagnosed diabetes, asked me to bring him something he had not already read. I winkled the most recondite volumes from our shelves; none were virgin to his eyes.

After the abrupt end of his institutional schooling, Michael was 'educated in pubs', under the indulgent, often absentee eye of his father, Gerald Gould, an alcoholic who had been editor of the *Daily Herald* and then literary critic on the *Observer*. M. told me that Gould, who died young, had an accurate eye for the good second-rate, but always failed to spot work of exceptional quality. He wrote novels and light verse and moved in smart bibulous circles. M.'s mother Hertha was an MP and sometime chairman of the Labour Party. There was a comfortable house in Hamilton Place, but both father and mother had responsibilities, and irresponsibilities, elsewhere. Born Ayrton-Gould, Michael amputated his father's name only because he thought it absurd for an artist to be hyphenated (Gaudier-Brzeska notwithstanding).

Michael's French one-time mistress, and mother of his only child, a son to whom he declined to be introduced,* still lives in the Channel Islands. She says that Michael was a prodigy and has early drawings to prove it. In 1940, insulated in wartime England, he was already sufficiently renowned to be asked to design sets for Gielgud's Macbeth. Invalided out of the RAF, after a short and action-free period, he recruited Johnny Minton to assist him. They had shared a studio in Paris just before the war. If 'Johnny' was attracted to Michael, as several homosexuals were, he was 'unable to help him', a way of putting it that makes Michael sound like a shopkeeper temporarily out of stock. Was M. similarly unavailable when it came to Gielgud? If so, Minton was an ideal auxiliary. Michael made no friends among Gielgud's cast. A senior actress asked him why he felt he had to go so far out of his way to make himself detestable.

Exemption from war service allowed him to become the familiar of those older than himself. The precocious age more quickly than the unassuming; he was soon taken to be a man of more years than he actually counted. Elisabeth had no idea, she claims, when they began their affair, that she was going to bed with a man almost ten years younger than herself. She says she would never, probably, have done what she did, had she known. She could hardly conceal the pride in her shameful secret. At the time of their first meeting, Michael was living in a small flat in Langham Place with the woman, Joan, who – such was *l'air du temps* – had changed her name to his. Friends before any females entered the scene, Nigel Balchin and Michael were both members of the Savile Club.

Elisabeth insists that Michael was uninterested in homo-sex, but he did often give primacy to friendships with other men. For a while, his closest male friend was Constant Lambert, who died when he was forty-five. When Michael sang, C.L. deterred him. Was Michael excited by becoming more intimate with Nigel Balchin through the latter's affair with Joan? Before Nigel's waning enthusiasm indicated that she was not worth having, it may already have warranted heat between Michael and Elisabeth. Nigel had little choice but to regard their flirtation with reciprocal indulgence. A successful novelist and screenwriter, of no small

---

* Michael told Beetle and me that, on a visit to Paris, he was in a café having a drink with a friend when a man in his thirties, in a correct suit and carrying a hard-edged briefcase walked in and sat at a table not far away. M's friend said, 'That's your son'. M. looked at the neat, solemn figure and said, 'I don't think I'll go over.'

intelligence, he had a New Man's talent comparable to that of C.P. Snow, though a greater aptitude for plot and observant sympathy with the common run of humanity.

When Joan had been finessed out of the pack, Michael proposed to be the Balchins' instructive companion on a trip to Italy. A left-wing élitist with little zeal for abstraction, he was already an expert on the Renaissance (Barna da Siena his recherché favourite). His articles in the *Spectator* had the *m'as-tu-vu* flash of the self-taught. While going round a gallery, Michael was known to say to his companion, should he or she admire a particular artist, 'I can do you one of those.' If 'three in a bed' was not a conscious ambition, what was wrong with three in a Baedeker?

14.6.83. Once Nigel's complaisance snapped, he returned from Tuscany to London, resigning the future of their marriage to Elisabeth. Michael left her to choose between being wife and mother and being a free woman. Was he more conscious of his mistress's age or of the social shame of betraying his friend? E. and M. returned to England and went to live in Langham Place. The BBC was an easy club; it offered both intellectual stimulus and financial patronage. M. spent time with Dylan Thomas and George Orwell (known as 'gloomy George') and had an occasional seat on the Brains Trust, in which he was the youngest ever participant. He was also an official War Artist. Like 'old Henry', he painted the home front rather than the battlefield. His most famous canvas was of chain-makers.

Michael spent time, but little cash, at the Savile bar. He was, it is said, not quick to buy his round. His early command of a smart critical platform generated more envy than affection. The Grosvenor Gallery took him up. The owner was disagreeable, but there was no more famous place to be ill-used. M. took a romantic view of the artist's place in creation: irresponsible but dominant, he claimed the *droit de maître* and flaunted autodidactic erudition. The wise Englishman used to wear his laurels as if he didn't know where they came from; Michael was too obvious in plucking his own.

In the early 1940s, New York was not yet the central *bourse* of the art world; Paris was closed for the duration. England's brave isolation made whatever happened in London seem both more significant and more durable than it turned out to be. After 1945, the revival of the French and the flourishing of America made London of small artistic consequence. Having ascended a foothill, Michael imagined that he was on top of the world. Inability to gauge his own place was a small example of a general failure, on the part of even the most intelligent of his compatriots, to register the consequences of the peace, aesthetic no less than economic.

The French had been shamed, but the insolence of Parisian intellectuals and the determination of Parisian dealers were part of the reupholstering of the continent. In the world at large, the dollar doubled for the Almighty. Within a few years, Paris and New York were the artistic and intellectual poles. Only Henry Moore, famous for his patriotic pictures of the serried denizens of the London underground, and – to a lesser degree – Graham Sutherland maintained their victorious renown. With a show of tykish simplicity, Old Henry kept the public on side by finding his inspiration in the commonplace. Michael alienated it by recourse to alien and recondite allusion; in the 1970s, his father's old paper, the *Observer*, would put him down as 'a bit of a Borges' (geddit?). He thought, or acted as though he thought, that intelligence should be a pronounced part of the creative process, its presence certified by manifest display. As Hockney proves, if you want your art to be loved in England, it is best to make it seem that you paint by numbers.

16.6.83. Michael's only concession to Jewishness lay in the grafting of Israel Zangwill to his family tree, though never as an explicit blood relation. If he was happier in pursuit of women than in possession of them, might it be because the sex was not uncommonly disappointed by his performance? He was ruefully amused by the response, by one of his casual mistresses, to his suggestion that she kiss his penis. 'Touch that nasty-looking thing with my lips?' M. told me that that wine-addled womaniser Augustus John once glided his hand up his thigh in the Chelsea Arts Club. When Michael objected, John said, 'Sorry, old boy, wasn't thinking'.

Angry ambition must have inclined Michael to be Percy Wyndham Lewis's post-war *amanuensis*. Did he know that, in his pre-war apology for Hitler, Lewis had jeered specifically at 'yiddle Zangwill' (author of *Children of the Ghetto*)? Might it possibly have amused M. (if so, *how*?) that W.L. had no notion of Hertha Ayrton's family connection with Zangwill? Elisabeth said that having W.L. in the house was like 'giving sanctuary to an eagle' (an image borrowed from Aeschylus' *Oresteia*). W.L. never found occasion to be charming; his affectionate nickname for himself was 'The Enemy', yet unlike that draft-dodging drawing-room belligerent 'ole Ez', W.L. had actually fought in the Great War.

Teenage Quixote, the fifteen-year old Michael went off to Spain in 1936 to enrol in a war for which he looked too boyish to be accepted. In the 1950s, he rallied to W.L. out of some sense of comradeship or guilt or louche appetite that no renovated scheme can plausibly resurrect. Was M. seeking the hard, intolerant father whose inheritance he hoped to deserve? W.L.'s Jew-consciousness made him someone to bait, fear, and cherish. By lending him a hand, M. at once disarmed and seconded a sacred monster. M. could not resist the urge to prove himself an English artist. W.L. was a genuine dragon; he sought no after-the-show rapprochement with St George.

Michael may have been too proud to give the public what they wanted; but he longed for them to want him. A socialist who looked to the rich for security, no social system would ever quite suit him. Delighted to be commissioned to build the Arkville maze, he spared little time for his patron. Michael's New England Minos was a Dutch millionaire banker. His new wife became the mistress of the upper New York state property where he had been advised to site his tax-deductible investment in Art. Michael found it cold and lonely. Had he been constructing the maze with his own hands, he might have taken greater joy in it. The workmen deprived him of authorship. He prevailed on the banker also to commission two figures to dramatise the maze. A plan to decorate the gentleman's mausoleum was vetoed by his Artemisia, whose favours Michael failed to secure.

20.6.83. Louise Purslow promises that the series of talks I did for her on the BBC were better regarded 'in house' than the Reith Lectures.

I dined on Wednesday, at Renford's invitation, in the SCR of St John's. He had performed well on the little philosophical programme we did with Roger Scruton, the supposed star, who displayed every attribute of intellectual stardom except the twinkle. The intensity of Renford's frown, lightened irregularly by flashes of almost boyish amusement, hints at anguish he declines to admit. Intimacy is impossible with him because he cannot bring himself to speak personally, even about the death of his dog. Yet he will generalise on the variety of responses that we feel over the mortality of humans as compared with that of animals. He frowns at life like a man who lacks the right spectacles to see it in focus.

After dinner, dons with nowhere better to go sit at tables in a semi-circle at the far end of the SCR, under the long, wide Jacobean ceiling. Its sag promises that one day its figured plaster will prolapse and snow the company with blanched souvenirs. A selection of College silver is set next to an array of glasses ready for a choice of claret or port. On a summer evening, the fireplace was, of course, void of flames; we semi-circled it as if in homage to an absent monarch. All the fellows wore gowns; even the youngest, who circulate the decanters which the butler has supplied after polling the thirsty, relished the opportunity for senior dignity. I wore a PhD number, bobbled on the shoulders, belonging to Peter Stern.

Only one guest, an American, who may have been without academic honours, unless too *désabusé* to give a hoot, refrained from robing. He spoke enthusiastically about word-processing.

I sat next to Hugh Sykes-Davies, whose *fiat* awarded me the Harper Wood Studentship almost thirty years ago. I remembered a florid, gross man, out of humour with the judicious role. He greeted me with condescending courtesy. Steiner, with whom I had lunched, at length, remained scandalised by H. S.-D.'s shamelessness over the Anthony Blunt affair. The arrogance of the Apostles was defined, G. thought, by Hugh's refusal to be censorious: Anthony was still Anthony, he had said, and would always be so. George was exasperated by the Forsterian conceit which made apostolic friendship more considerable that patriotism or moral scruple. I felt no revulsion from my now grey and seemingly androgynous neighbour. Having retreated, or advanced, into monasticism, S.-D. looked decidedly powdered. When I used the word 'primer', it primed him into announcing that there were four distinct meanings of the world in the *OED*, three obvious, the fourth of small interest. He produced this information as if it were casual. Renford indicated that such minutiae were Hugh's speciality. The latter remembered Joe Bain, though he had no idea of what had become of him.* He thought him a 'natural 2.1 who should have stuck to languages'. Hugh, I thought, should have stuck to English; quoting an Egyptian's French, he attached the masculine indefinite article to '*peau*'. Was that the point of the quotation? I doubt it.

Ian Watt told of having reviewed a book on Wordsworth by an American (enough said) who had profited from a stay at St John's by investigating the poet's archive, from which he had culled material he then had the gall to pass off as a 'discovery'. Watt said that professor X. had 'discovered' the stuff just as Columbus had discovered America, something whose existence had long been known to the natives. Renford's face lost its accumulation of frowns; his eyes flashed. He took the opportunity to look, quickly, directly at me. He was graced, for a moment, with the possibility of being, or having been, another sort of person altogether. As it is, he resembles one of those landmarks in a low neighbourhood, tagged with a single Michelin star, which no one goes out of his way to see. Since he has been in my life for over thirty years, he passes for an old friend, but we are perennially on much the same terms. Never offensive (though I could have been spared being asked whether I knew Henry Reed's *Naming of Parts*), nor is he warm or warmer. He recalls his own anniversaries like a minor royalty: he received his fellowship on May the

---

* Joe, who directed me in *Samson Agonistes* in the St John's College chapel in 1952, taught, first at Stowe and then as sixth form master at Winchester.

first 1950 and immediately renounced the research grant for which he had been toiling over Plato. He is about to take a sabbatical at Princeton, where he means to finish the book which his elevation aborted. Such postponements are not rare; the precocious are liable to deliver late.

Renford quoted with some glee the reference to himself in a skittish 'dictionary' which made play with academics' names: to 'bambrough' was to draw attention to the obvious, as if it were not obvious. There was a secondary usage, relating to 'under the bam, under the brough, etc'. He giggled shyly at these and other jejune jests, of which 'to anscombe' was the best. I laughed knowingly at 'he anscombed a collection of Wittgenstein's MSS.' Our collocutor was Peter Geach, a Wittgensteinian whom I had previously met only in footnotes (he still did not wear socks). I did not know that he, now a ranking eccentric, and Miss Anscombe were married. I cannot recall what the satirist said it implied if somebody 'geached', but the large, stammering philosopher took pleasure in declaring that the root meaning of 'to geach' was to steal. He is a Fellow of Balliol, I think, and has been delivering professorial lectures in Cambridge (Carlos, the small Spanish butler, called him 'professor' with the accuracy usual with upper servants). Geach has renounced all prospect of wide fame. Renowned for his aridity, he has become a pompous elder. Fervently RC, he was among those who foisted a priest if not on Wittgenstein's deathbed, certainly on his funeral, as Maurice Drury reports, rather remorsefully. I sat with the dons till about 10 p.m. It was still vaguely light outside. I eased my new Mercedes out of the forecourt as if escaping from antique relatives.

Harriet Sergeant's wedding. We spent most of the evening with the Milsteins, the only people we knew, apart from our very busy hosts. The ceremony had taken place in the morning, at Highgate Church, where the vicar had officiated, after suffering Stephen Cohen to read a psalm in Hebrew. There was a lunch at the Ritz, followed by sleep, before a larger congregation assembled at 1, The Grove, in the evening. Members of the corps of commissionaires stood at the gate, a discreet bouncer or two in case of insistent, uninvited guzzlers. Harriet was encased in a boned white dress and, after weeks of alleged doubt, the air of someone who had made a happy choice. Stephen, who had flirted with Sarah in New York, before taking a moral line over her dropping of Jack Lowenstein, looked rejuvenated, quite as if he had been to the best possible cleaners. Harriet seemed pleased at our present and said that she would hang it over her desk.

The Milsteins were already into the champagne. When I was in his office a few days earlier, M. offered liquor at five o'clock; in the past, he was slow with a cup of tea. Since he was canvassing to borrow our Greek house, he was restrained in his attempts to cut me down to malleable size. He proves himself a close friend by being envious and uncomplimentary. When he told me that I envied John Fowles, I said, 'I might if he were talented'. There is no current giant who seems to me to cast a shorter (or fatter) shadow.

At the wedding, Milstein was pleased to act as host with other people's food and drink. He would have been first to the buffet had Beetle not curbed his enthusiasm. Helping himself is his favourite activity. He is still slim and brown and has allowed his silvering hair to grow long enough to cover the lacunae. Lynn has become very plump; she was wearing a sort of linen tablecloth, cut on the bias. To have become slightly notorious is better than it ever seemed likely to get for her. With greasy curls and the winsome air of a girl up from the suburbs, she impersonates a victorious victim. Assuming that you know how thoroughly she has demolished her once cocky husband, she stands by him if only so that you can measure how much she has outgrown him.

Her tart charm took the form of chiding me for having behaved badly to a waiter when we took them out to Canton Heaven. I have no guilty apprehensions whatever when it comes to my conduct with waiters, which is often more correct than the service. As usual, the critic failed to consider to what degree her presence contributed to the episode. The occasion was so little memorable that I could not recall it, but Beetle was quick to remember that the owner smarmed all over Lynn, who did not trouble to introduce us. The ineptitude of the staff had been an unhappy contrast with the restaurateur's own swagger and the Milsteins' pride in first-naming him.

Milstein can never see a friend without devising some scheme to extract a favour. His delight at having gained access to Ios was so great that he ignored our warnings against taking small children there in August, when the place will swarm with raucous examples of modern European youth. He would not hear, or believe, that the bargain for which he was angling was worth less than what he had not paid for it. I had told him that he was welcome to the house for the last two weeks of August, but he had ignored this stipulation and allowed Lynn to book flights to Mykonos on the 11th, so putting pressure on us to ask Sarah to vacate the *spiti* earlier than we had said or than she wished. Who but Milstein makes a deal out of a favour and then accuses you of not meeting its conditions? You either indulge him or turn your back. He relies on old friends to supply the warmth he cannot obtain by rubbing his hands together.

Steiner is puzzled by the steadfastness with which M. persists with authors whose talents are either minuscule or smaller. The answer is that he treasures the small evidence that he can be decent over something: if he has no conscience, he does have sentiments. Something similar can be seen in Leslie Bricusse: he greets us with the same delight whenever he runs into us. Out come the telephone numbers and the invitations and the smile on the face of the pussy cat. L. makes up to you by giving more than he need, Milstein by taking more than you offered. Lynn saw quickly that they might pay dearly, although not in cash, for staying in a cottage with no basic amenities. M. will, no doubt, blame us for failing to supply what would have justified his belief that he had got something worth having.

Sarah asked me one day, 'Do you really like Stella Richman?' Are there always people in parents' lives whose place no intelligent child can ever quite understand? I remember with what incredulity I regarded the couples whom my parents seemed happy to entertain: why had they been asked, or asked again? My attitude to Stella seemed incomprehensible because Sarah never guessed how her patronage had retrieved our fortunes and, perhaps, our marriage. Sarah sees Stella as a somewhat frantic figure with a son for whom she cannot admit that she has any responsibility except to reproach him. If he complains, she accuses him of not loving her; if he shows signs of independence (after inheriting twenty thousand pounds from his father), then of doing things behind her back. When Sarah offered him her flat as a refuge, Stella threatened to denounce her to the police as being involved in a drugs conspiracy. *Et pourtant*, I regard my benefactress with affection and gratitude.

There is little to commend Milstein to the casual eye, but I cannot sever myself from his prestigious patronage. He asked me, very early on, whether I ever made love to women for the sheer joy of conquest. He knows no better way to command allegiance than to have something on you. At the same time, he assured me that he never slept with his friends' wives. He prefers to turn them into a cross between a family servant and a mother to whom he is not related. Lynn has learnt shamelessness from him, though her purposes and her pleasures are different.

When, at the Sergeants' wedding, we had finished the dance she asked for, she squeezed my hand like a teenage tease. She wants only to be wanted. Could demureness and desire be more sweetly wrapped than in her small-voiced, vanilla-flavoured person? She and M. are alike in their will to rob you of all commonplace faith in yourself or in others. She sniped at Hilary because he had failed to get her more than five hundred pounds for the 'idea' of a chat-programme about what to wear where. She was piqued that she had not been chosen to 'anchor' it. Although her mother's Basildon burr has not been entirely elided, her accent was deemed too Harrodian by the BBC selectors. Hilary's failure to make her even more famous proved that he did not do his best for her, not least because his own wife was also in line to go on the air.

27.6.83. The remarkable, ridiculous minotaur in the little museum in Agen surely has the only functional navel in the history of sculpture. It serves to allow a finger to pull open a metal drawer in the belly of the beast which extends almost the full length of the chest. The monster was built towards the end of the last century and was designed, the curator promised, as a rack for hats and coats. A four-legged minotaur, with skinny limbs and boneless hands, is as rare as it is grotesque. Remote from Michael's perplexed hybrid, the Agen curiosity is an artful amenity fashioned out of an aberration. Also in the museum is a self-portrait of Goya, the plump, never complacent artist's view of himself as he fattens into middle age; he wears a stock but does not yet disclose his need for spectacles. More prudent than self-important, he disguises himself as almost courtly; he might be a physician who comes and goes, but does not entirely belong among those he serves but cannot respect. Giving others what they wanted gave Goya the freedom to look at himself without slyness, though he saw something sly there. The self-portrait allows an artist to visit on himself the uncompromising vision which he can rarely afford when it comes to his patrons. He pleases himself by not pleasing himself. Even a writer can sometimes be noticed to present himself in a worse light than those whom he treats objectively. The self-portrait, however handsome the result, had better be undertaken in a spirit of mercilessness; a look at oneself is a different kind of look from any other.

He desires women, if he does, because he can, if clever or persuasive, get them for nothing. His pleasure comes from the discount, not the merchandise.

Steiner recalls a painful evening when a BBC team came down to Bradfields in order to run the Berlioz film which Michael had scripted, George still winces at the conspicuous scorn with which M. met those whose efforts had been designed to please him. They arrived as discrete acolytes; they left united in hostility. M. seemed not to notice. He must have presumed that he had done the right thing by Hector Berlioz.

At Cambridge, Claire Tomalin wrote poetry of which I cannot recall a single line or topic; can she? Karl Miller accused her, she told me, not too long ago, of no longer being the 'giggling armful' he had once known.

Did she make him laugh or did she achieve the less likely feat of finding him amusing? When she worked for me on *Far from the Madding Crowd*, I took pains to treat her with all the generous courtesy which had been denied me by her Cambridge coterie. She came up with some Wessex folksongs which suited my script, but not a few of her notes were of a technical or literary abstruseness of no cinematic utility.

Like Beetle, Claire was enrolled as a reader for Tom Maschler at Jonathan Cape. When the Chairman, Wren Howard, particularly praised Beetle's reports, Tom called her in and told her he was going to raise her rate to six pounds a day. Beetle told him that that was what she was getting already, upon which he congratulated her and asked her to keep up the good work. Claire called me and Beetle 'lucky, lucky things'. She and Nick came by the Wick once; we had a stilted afternoon with them.

In time, she was appointed what Karl Miller and Nick had both been, in angry succession: literary editor of the *New Statesman*. She asked me to review an occasional book. Meanwhile she was pursued by domestic tragedies and conjugal misfortune. In the wake of Nick's death on the Golan Heights, Harry Evans assuaged his guilt by planting Claire in the literary editor's chair at the *Sunday Times*. When, after long hesitation, Frayn decided to dump his family, Claire asked Jill to 'pray' for her.

After she arrived, from left to right, at the *Sunday Times*, I guessed that I should soon feel the breeze. Those appointed to new commands rarely feel at ease with people who once employed them. For the early part of her reign, I was well enough favoured to abate my apprehensions. How come my current ostracism? My prime error probably lay in attacking Noel Annan, an act termed 'courageous' by John Whitley. I call nothing courage except bravery under the fear of physical assault or annihilation. The attack on Noel A. was ill-advised only if one hopes for academic or social advancement in England, of which I have never had the smallest prospect. Claire did congratulate me on the letter which I sent to Karl Miller, but some congratulations have a valedictory quality. Frayn once wrote me a letter addressed to 'Dear God Raphael', but that was *molti anni fa*. I took him to be somewhat like myself because he read Moral Sciences and came from suburbia. He has assumed the clerkly superiority of those who have moved a hundred yards up the road, but in the right direction. *Noises Off* has given him the cash and the kudos to confirm that his intelligence can turn the world's key. The play is a piece of confectionery with a good second act. It tastes sweet at the time and is flushed away two days later.

Belief in human progress and in the rights of majorities insists that Apartheid is justly doomed. But? But there is comfort of some sadistic kind in observing how injustice can survive. Every privileged person, holding whatever liberal attitude, secretes a pocket of relief at the tenacious pitilessness of the reactionary.

Only on the ancient Greek moon were there creatures who, like the theologians' Jesus Christ, did not excrete.

The ambivalence of Greek gods, especially the mutability of Zeus, exemplifies the oscillation between divine fathers and divine killers. Zeus is both danger and protection from danger. European Christianity is structured on faith; European philosophers wrestle to find a truth independent of it. The singularity of the Jew is that he can be a free thinker who may honour ancestral laws and lore but need not *believe*. Christianity seeks to force human thinking into a unique redemptive scheme. Faith in the Trinity supposedly supplies relief from Judaism's dated and daily obligations, for which there is no dividend except community. The cult of the Virgin sanctifies the irrational, while the cult of Reason implies ambition for unarguable conclusions. The logician rattles no keys and has no cells, but promises to lock us up all the same.

The presumption of privileged clerical readings begins with the augur poring over entrails. His derivative was the ideologue; today, the economist.

It requires modesty as well as intelligence to perceive the world as it really is: puzzlement is an aspect of common decency.*

Had she had a life blessed with conjugal harmony, her schoolmarm prose might have left her unremarked. As it is, the Mother Courage of the bookish cannot be challenged or criticised.

21.7.83. In the young Hannah Arendt's view, to accept that Europe's Jews were heterogeneous was an ill-considered policy. She had to have it that they were a 'nation'. Affectations of diversity were self-deceiving. Zionism entailed consciously taken and united steps. Belief in Jewish innocence could never, in her view, lead dialectically to the next,

---

* Asked when he first suspected that Wittgenstein was a genius, G.E. Moore famously replied, 'When he was the only man who looked puzzled during my lectures.'

necessary stage in Jewish self-consciousness: national revival. Unless at least some politicised Jews took responsibility for what was happening or had happened to the victims of Nazism, Jews in general were doomed to be fossil footnotes to the histories of other nations. They could then be remarkable only for what was done to them, like veal.

Producer of *Roots*, David Wolper sits on his goldmine with the smugness of a man who needs dig no other. He made Warner Brothers rich. Their private jet is at his service. I was promised, when we were making the deal for *Napoleon and Josephine*, that he was both intelligent and interested in quality product. He is a pale man who looks as though he may have been advised to lose weight in order to qualify for a tax concession or a second wife. He has the latter, a tallish woman in her forties called Gloria. She takes the form of an inverted isosceles triangle with a new hair-do. Having taken painting lessons for over a year, she has discovered that she is an artist, rather as one might turn out to belong to a rare blood-group. Thrilled by her talent (she is already selling pictures to department stores), she is mortified to think of all the years she has wasted (not selling pictures to department stores).

A beige man in a beige suit, Wolper says that he knows his audience, but his audience is unlikely to know him. In TV since 1948, when he graduated from USC film school, he has produced two hundred films of one kind (documentary) or another (mini-series). He has an important (what else?) collection of Picasso's sculpture, as well as some Giacomettis, etc. He claims that a remote forbear was one of Napoleon's generals. Like many Americans, he is not good on names, though industrious enough to have made copious notes for our dull meeting. He is also planning a mini-series on Pablo P. and is trading on his reputation as a collector to make useful contacts. The desire to please has bled him of pleasure in his activities. Having done the number one mini-series of all time, he cannot do it again without being his own rival. Warner Brothers look after him so sedulously that he is free to fly around the world collecting cash and kudos; he prefers the former.

He has just been to Russia. When you have enough money, you never have to pay for anything. As a guest of the Soviet government, he had tickets for the Kirov ballet and went to receptions in the Kremlin. He was impressed by the sight of the insignia of Arnold Hammer's Occidental Petroleum on Lenin's desk. Hammer is eighty-six years old and due in Moscow in August, when he will meet Andropov. He never alters his watch and always sleeps on his private jet.

Wolper would not say whether he admired or liked Napoleon. It was enough that N. had been involved in a Great Love Story; that had sold the project to WB. He did say that he thought Reagan a hard man and that hardness was a virtue. Reagan's inflexibility was warrant enough to consider him a good president. Did Wolper regard himself as a hard man too? He did: willingness to fire directors was the proof. He did not mean to be issuing a warning (I had put the question), but he showed no symptom of hospitable consideration. We talked from 9 a.m. till noon and he never proposed a cup of coffee or a glass of juice. Lunch was his first and final offer. He belongs to that tribe of entrepreneurs who do nothing offensive and nothing agreeable.

His favourite reading is about Hollywood, but he rarely attends showbiz functions. I never heard him laugh; I suspect few have. Not even his art collection makes him smile. He passes for a connoisseur because he has been smart enough to corral the best. He maintains with a straight face (he has no other) that Picasso's sculpture will prove more significant than his painting. Yet he sold a picture for two thousand dollars when he was twenty-five, did Pablo, and was able to live for a year on the proceeds. That means, in W.'s notation, that P. was famous from 1903 till 1973, longer than any man who ever lived. I suggested that Aeschylus might have been famous for as long; and, unlike Picasso, Aeschylus actually fought in the legendary battle his *Persae* depicted. P.P. had neither been bombed nor visited Guernica. W.'s most recent reading was a biography of Bill Holden who was not only a star but also a business man: he had interests in Kenya and Canada and all over the place. Did I know he was also an alcoholic who often tried to cure himself? He fell down and bled to death in a hotel bedroom in Beverly Hills. There was almost no blood left in him when they found him, three days later.

L. abhors the flesh; her pale lips are puckered, like beans in soak. She no longer rejoices in the children she was in a hurry to have. She sees them with the baleful clarity that does not deny their dependence on her tight housekeeping. If she has lost her vanity, she has not acquired any polite curiosity. Gossip was never her style. She and Peter did gloat, however, back in 1950s London, over the discovery of pornographic typescripts in their lodger's bottom drawer, where the dirty linen was. Jones too had a First in English. He once told me how, a few years after coming down, he had accosted Frank Leavis on the way into the Gents in Cambridge Market Square and dared to say that that worthy's lectures had changed his life. The consequence was a forty-minute seminar on the steps, an exchange so grave and grateful, on both sides, that it could not excite even the most suspicious copper. Now a successful RSC director, with the pride that comes of calling Sam Spiegel 'Sam', Jones has had the last smirk in several ways, without being anyone of great interest.

23.7.83. For Mausolus. Insecurity begins with the accumulation of riches. The rich man fears impoverishment more than death. The courage of the antique hero has nothing to do with patriotism or possessions; it is the warrant of his status. After Achilles has mutilated Hector's corpse, his only remaining heroic reward lies in extracting gratitude, for its return, from a bereaved father. In *Les origines de la pensée Grecque*, Vernant emphasises the pride implicit in the Mycenaean palace: it both declared that the king had been successful and dared the contender to make his claim. The *megaron*, bastion and strongroom of the Mycenaean palace attracts the assailants whom the *enceinte* is designed to deter. The golden bough was no longer located in a sacred grove; the pillared palace mimics the arbour to which the challenger used to be drawn. Mausolus, a king with no military kudos, feared that he would leave no epic trace. Accumulation was his prophylactic against obscurity. He grew so fat that his ostentation proclaimed its futility: the Mausoleum became a beacon for robbers.

22.7.83. *A Common Pursuit*. Two Newnhamites, call them Alice. and Kay, are rivals for literary fame from day one in Cambridge. Alice becomes an editorial potentate, Kay a reclusive eccentric whose terse poetry seems to pass comment, if only by never doing so, on her contemporary's biographical prolixity. With a new book always imminent, Alice is regularly invited as a guest of honour at literary festivals. How sweet if, at one such, A. were to be accused of having lifted her latest insights on material culled from Kay's thesis!

His wife is a curious creature; she seems always to be the same age, though not always the same sex.

25.7.83. The first house we rented in Jamaica in 1968 was a few miles from Ocho Rios, in a development called Gibraltar Estates. We were shown round by Lord Ronald Graham's assistant. The property was too insignificant for his florid lordship's personal guidance. It was different when he conducted us, later, to the Earl of Mansfield's pad. The Gibraltar Estates villa was small and modern, the usual forelock of bougainvillea over the blanched terrace wall. There was a small kidney-shaped pool outside the living room's screen door. A trio of servants was included in the modest rent. Not far from the sea, we were sufficiently secluded from tripping tourists to believe that we were leading a simple, if pampered, life. The villa's distance from the mains meant that the water was frequently cut off; quite soon, it ceased to come through at all. Stee was still in nappies, which could not be washed. The little pool served to cool us. Sarah and I did a great many underwater handshakes. A drowned worm on the pool floor excited her pity. I said, 'Bugger the dead worm!' The grizzled black gardener later hoovered it to oblivion.

The villa was hot, but not insufferable, the servants likewise; cook cooked. Everything would have been all right, had it not been all wrong. The place belonged to a Doctor Manley, who may or may not have been related to a then powerful Jamaican politician. He had been living there with a white woman whom we met, briefly, in the shopping plaza where she worked in Ocho Rios. She had come from England with her husband, a Scot I think, who was out to make his name as a portrait painter. She had been an innocent bride, he a man of character, much of it weak, but persuasive and domineering. She had assumed that life in the West Indies would be glamorous and easy. There would be commissions for the painter, drinks and parties and fun. Alex promised a life-style which he could not afford, an artistic ambience to which, if it existed, he had no access. He could paint, but he was no artist; he had married her but did not care to be a husband. His sitters were fewer and more demanding than chums had encouraged him to expect.

Alex began to be absent for longish periods, supposedly on commissions around the fancy properties of the North Shore, more often drinking. He did not make much money and spent more. The girl bought a black and white dog to keep her company and deserve her love. She called it Bossy Boots. Her husband became more and more of a bohemian and less and less of an artist. He drank and he abused her. She had seemed well-connected when he met her and he may have presumed that her father would prove more generous than he did. He had, in truth, been unimpressed by her suitor. She now hated to admit that she had made a mistake. Meanwhile, Dr Manley wanted his rent. Bossy Boots alone was happy.

In a desk drawer, I came across several drafts of the letters the girl composed to send to her father. Alex was a write-off, incapable of keeping her or of facing the need to return to the UK or somewhere he might find commissions, or a job. He was a cold and cruel man who maintained that she should find ways of proving that she had faith in him. How many letters did she actually post to her father? At least one *ballon d'essai* was shot down with puncturing paternal accuracy. She had made her bed and was counselled to lie in it. Her response was she had been reduced to 'going down on my knees to a nigger' for a remission of the rent. If she hoped that the appalling image would shock daddy into bailing her out, she was disappointed. With no money for fares, nowhere to run to, she was afraid of Alex, who lacked the strength to pull himself, or their marriage, together.

Dr Manley, the landlord, became the sole reliable element in her life. He wanted his rent, but he was rich and understanding. She hated the idea of him, seeing him through her father's eyes, but she could not hate him, unless her hatred became her only vivid, licensed emotion. Her reproaches became the excuse for Alex's self-pitying binges. He lost interest in her sexually and blamed her for his impotence. The unthinkable became the only thing she had to think about. She paid Dr Manley's rent, and repaid his kindness, in kind. She left the house, from which her husband had absented himself, and went to live with the good doctor.

There was nothing very scandalous or unusual, perhaps, in the Maughamian story which the desk drawer yielded. The predicament of the fair girl, her expressions of disgust and her practical procedure, remain in the mind; so too does the vision of that dry house where Stee took his first steps, seventeen of them. On the third or fourth waterless day, we packed up and left, under the eyes of a bewildered Hilda, who kept saying 'Tings are looking strange today.' Did she say the same when Bossy Boots and her mistress walked out, or were driven away in Dr Manley's car? The move from abhorrence to affectionate dependence on the black man made him white and blackened her father and Alex. She had considerable dignity when we saw her. A rather stately girl, with an apricot complexion, a little older than the schoolgirlish tone of her letters, she had found independence on her knees to a black man. The contrast between her competent exterior and the ungrammatical skimpiness of her inner vocabulary gave her a pitiful attractiveness.

Not long after we had transferred to the Earl of Mansfield's grandiose mansion, Tom Maschler sent me a typescript of Fowles' *The French Lieutenant's Woman*. It contained the author's interpolations and excisions, more of the former. Has there ever been a plumper dandy than Master F.? I had been neither impressed nor excited by *The Collector*, a novel I recall only because it was said, mystifyingly, to be based on the philosophy of Heracleitus. (The *Aristos*, which came much later, was indeed an egotist's rescript of the old Ephesian's aphoristic corpus.) *The French Lieutenant's Woman* was sent to me, of course, in the hope that I should want to make a film of it. The MS was drowned in the flood which engulfed our hire car when we drove to Montego Bay to collect Paul from the VC10 in which he flew, first class, from NYC. Tom asked me several times during the following years to do the script. I had a meeting with him and Dick Lester to explore the possibilities. I suggested a cinematic metaphor – cuts of rehearsals and improvisations in modern dress – which would match Fowles' alternative endings and the footnoted style of his conceit. Tom listened carefully. Lester was either unimpressed or unavailable. When the film did get made, directed by Carel Reisz, scripted by Pinter, they used precisely the scheme which I had proposed. Tom warned me, teasingly, of how clever Harold had been, but he never offered me a ticket. I talk too much while auditioning for jobs,* even when I do not want them or might have had them anyway.

Some professorial theologian has been talking about the surveillance techniques of the Almighty and how His nosiness had put Sartre off the notion of divinity. The professor would have it that the Almighty knows us rather as we know our friends. How heartening is that and why should it be true? And how much would He then know? At the limits of reason, the great banished concepts wait for new, fanciful (or fanatical) re-upholsterers. Only the extension of our vital span is likely to reduce the terror which has, for centuries, patrolled the outer edges of human existence.

The contest for the leadership of the Labour Party is devoid of interesting casting. The Party has taken procedural pains to be sure that no individual of genius should lead it. In avenging itself on the cunning of Wilson and the crassness of Callaghan, who knew enough to pander to the conservatism and narrow-mindedness of the British, the apparat has contrived that mediocrity will be always in charge. Labour will become more and more like the C.P. and dwindle into a mock-serious and impotent enterprise, its numbers never sufficient for the red flag to do more than provoke John Bull. There is no certainty that 'the Left' will never regain power in England but, with luck, it will never achieve, or even advertise, a New Jerusalem.

29.8.83. Nick and Sarah have been here since just before her birthday. We have had many happy days. On his birthday, the first dark and rainy morning since our arrival, Milstein was due to visit Lagardelle, at his own invitation, with his daughter Trudi. As he drove up, in a green 2CV, I consoled myself with the thought that in another twelve hours, at the outside, he would be gone again. I had not seen Trudi since her *petite enfance*. M. was quiet and anxious, not least about the weather. Before lunch we spoke, as usual, of nothing deep or interesting. Never disposed to share what he knows, his tightness is characteristic, even when it would not cost him anything. He was preoccupied with Trudi who, at first,

---

* David Brown, producer of *Jaws* among other multi-million-dollar hits, once said to me at a meeting where I was trying too hard to dazzle with one new idea after another, 'Freddie, as your agent, I advise you not to say another word until you have a deal!'

stayed close to us. He managed to behave pleasantly to Beetle, but he has small memory of the past (he cannot recall anything that happened more than a year or two ago, unless it concerns him intimately) and so is destined to repeat old mistakes.

He had the grace to admire the place and expressed it by a determination to stay the night, or two. I had made it clear, when he called to invite himself over, that we were having no house guests this summer, but he had heard from the Wisemans that they were coming by and so resumed his importunities. Trudi had been stung on the finger by a wasp at the weekend when he called. Given her wounded condition, he did not think that they could make the road journey from Martel and back, all of a hundred kilometres, in one day. When I saw the pettiness of what was left of her symptoms, there was something pathetic in his importunity. It is hard to measure the degree or reality of M.'s distress because there is always something opportunistic even in his least premeditated acts.

His capacity to turn the colour of antique furniture is his principal cosmetic asset. He seems slim, but carries a blubbery corset around his middle; it depends from his ribs and lends him an appearance at once wobbly and emaciated. His body declares the state of his mind. One flinches from intimate contact. The one thing you can be sure that he will share with you is whatever is wrong with him. His loneliness is pitiful; one longs to comfort him, without having to come too close. He said he was disconcerted by the mixture of detachment and sympathy with which I always responded to him, this during a walk after lunch. His guard down, the anguish he bore was displayed, almost vomited, in front of me. The short-term problem was Trudi. He wanted to give her a good time but nothing he proposed was ever agreeable. The humility that was once her apparent badge has become determination not to be deceived or amused or delighted or appeased.

M. and I walked up past the Barrats' house and, all of a sudden, I found myself telling him that things could not continue on their present course; he would be ill if he failed to put an end to it. 'I'M ILL NOW,' he shouted, with terrible resignation. The dread of imminent disaster gave him more dignity than his regular boasts of dealing cleverly with not particularly clever matters. Unable to read his own predicament for the comedy it partly is, he is obliged to a tragic reading. No, he cannot quite be tragic because he lacks the rage, the regret and the language. There is cruel comedy in his flinching from the divorce that I heard myself urging on him. He has, he told me, a refugee complex: he has lived for forty years in a remarkably hospitable society, yet he fears that he will find himself again in the stateless state he knew, with his mother, all those years ago. He made himself at home in a marriage which is now fracturing the security it promised to seal. The family he wanted to have supplies the voices which threaten to bid him adieu.

M.'s distress was so abject that it prompted me to practicalities. I suggested that he not ask Trudi what she wanted to do but should make a timetable and stick to it. As for the future, he had to break away or be broken. He said again that he was so *weak*. All he really wanted to do was to go home; and when he was at home all he wanted to do was to leave.

Tom and Malou came to stay the following Friday. It had been proposed that we all dine with the Littells on Saturday, but one of their many guests, called Sophie, had been involved in an *accident de voiture*. Milstein managed to say few nice things about the Littells, who had agreed to put him up. They had only two bathrooms and kept one of them exclusively to themselves (who wouldn't?). M. craves sympathetic contact like a leech; he laid hands on me and Beetle, who was sufficiently moved by his plight to bake him a birthday cake, though not to return his caresses. She could manage to be kind, never fond. Although we were assumed to be aware of the date of his birthday, he pretended not to know exactly when mine was, two days, as usual, before his own. I had never previously heard him speak of his weakness. I was made the stronger for it. He said that he did not understand how his situation had come about, only that he was powerless to alter it.

Trudi recalled how M. had a lot to drink on the night they landed in Dieppe; he was almost run over, and she had to help him to bed. He did not deny the story, nor tell her to shut up; he contented himself with a soft plea to 'not tell mummy'. He offers her the whip to beat him with.

The Wisemans have been challenged to explain why they lived in France and Malou chided for not having a job, like a real woman. We were cited, on that occasion, as people who did have good reason to live in France, since I was fluent in the language and had a cultural affinity with the country. That Malou is actually French did not exempt the Wisemans from stricture. Beetle and I were advised, back in June, that we should have separate holidays; you never saw anything in tandem.

M. takes what comfort and kudos he can from the office. He cannot make much money from an agency which, in a very good year, generates no more than a quarter of a million profit, but fifty people's salaries depend on him. Because he still dreams of making a killing in the movies, I remain an outer hoop in the target of his hopes. He talks of producing an independent film which would allow us to do what we really wanted etc. I had to repeat the good reasons why quality cannot be procured at bargain rates: one would never get good actors and technicians.

31.8.83. M. asked us again and again if he and Trudi could stay with us. He even suggested finding a hotel nearby so that they could return the next day. He never waits to see what kind of a welcome he will find on the mat. He is so much the wounded party that it is unsporting to recall the bruises he has inflicted. Despite having read my recent short story, 'A Parting Guest', in which I suggested that it was a good idea to bring the pettiest possible present for one's hostess, he had arrived empty-handed, presumably taking it that it was not worth the tax of a flower or two in return for no more than a couple of meals. We might have been less inexorable had he not made a point of deriding the quality of accommodation offered by all the friends he had sponged on so far. M. told us of his stay in an author's house near Cherbourg which was so primitive that Trudi was expected to sleep on a mattress in a dusty loft. There were help-yourself meals on the crumby kitchen table. The following morning, when their hosts were at the market, M. wrote a farewell note and he and Trudi crept away. There are some takers who will not take just anything.

Tom Wiseman recalled how, in the days when he was a top columnist for the *Evening Standard*, his first novel had been savaged by Carl Foreman in the *New Statesman*. Since it proved to the Beaver that Tom excited passions and comment and controversy, Foreman's revenge led to an increase in Tom's salary and the size of his by-line. He also told us (again) of Otto Preminger inviting him to dinner in Hollywood with Francis Albert Sinatra, who was famous for having no time for journalists. The evening went improbably well. If there was an undertone of available menace, Sinatra was accessible and forthcoming. Tom was promised a long interview at whatever time suited him; Frankie's behaviour was so untypical that T. could not but be flattered. Telling the story, he became quite giggly as he recalled the budding romance between himself and the prickly operator. He called Frankie the next morning to clinch the promised interview. It was as if they had never met. Sinatra reminded Tom that he had no time for journalists. T. said that if Mr. S. was not going to honour his promise, the only thing he could do was to write a piece about their conversation with Otto; which he did. Tom seemed rather proud of this humiliating episode and, no doubt, of the skill with which he made a silk purse from the flea in his ear.

Now free of Fleet Street, Tom seems nervous of outspoken views. His speech has something of the fluent foreigner's text-book punctiliousness. Even if he uses no other language, English is his second tongue; better not to make errors than to get anything dangerously right. The pun, playful usage, variant readings, all embarrass him. He pays nostalgic tax to Freud, whom he sees as an undogmatic man of science. Agile as he is, mentally, he avoids his father's fatal error of fencing too cleverly with powerful people. He is not a coward, but he is always aware that he is playing away from home. He likes England (they keep their flat in Hampstead) but he does not find the English particularly interesting. He has no ear for their duplicities. He is drawn to Big Issues as he is to the big market, where England no longer has a stall. His tolerance is a measure of his indifference.

He was most aggressive in the 1950s when the British still had a claim on greatness and London deserved his then vigorous attention. What does he now hope or expect? He cares little for politics and less for gossip. If he is looking for the great clue that will enable him to fathom the nature of the horror, he has no kit to pick its lock. His tone is elevated, occasionally wise, but he does not see it is a matter of imaginative honour to seek out everything that can count against his own convictions. I like him; I am fond of him; I wish him well. He tried once to warn me of the weight of hostility that I face in certain London quarters, because I have been excessively harsh as a critic. I am more ashamed of the few occasions on which I have tempered the wind than of the even fewer when I have been properly ferocious. I do my best to be generous, as Tom conceded with regard to his own *Tsar*. Several showbiz people paid him out when it was published. An earlier collection of articles was slated, he recalls, by Michael Redgrave, whom he had always rather admired.

2.9.83. My mother came by for a couple of nights. She is being driven around Europe by Andrew Rayersbach, who plays bridge with her, Margaret Piesse and Gertie Guest. I heard Andrew give his name as 'Ray' when booking a hotel in Montpellier. He makes a habit of abbreviated incognito, for fear of being taken for German. In fact, his father was born in South Africa, he himself in Kensington. Now in his seventies, he has two grown-up children, the son a chartered accountant, the other a thirty-one year old woman who has been on a camping holiday in the Basque region, where there have been widespread floods. Caravans have been swept into the sea, camping sites wrecked. He consoled himself with the old saw about no news.

He had Keynes' *General Theory* in the car. He had suffered a blow to his private economy after intemperate indulgence in Calvados in Dieppe, where they had been charged an indigestible twenty-six francs each for their *digestif*. A man of careful affluence, he is about to change his BMW for a new one. When stripped to holiday shorts, he revealed a rather feminine body, with a big-nippled, hairless white chest and perhaps shaved *aiselles*.

He announces himself a Philistine, and repeats it lest you fail to question it the first time. He also has the querulous aggressiveness of those who tell you that they know nothing about a subject and then insist on discussing it. He asserted, quite as if it were my fault, that all the plays on the BBC were about people on the dole. He looks back sentimentally on the days when they gave the audience an interval and summoned it back with a bell.

My mother had been looking forward to the tour for many months, and put off visiting John Moss to accommodate it, but she is disappointed by her companion's 'inflexibility' (he makes a fetish of punctuality) and lack of cultural interests apart from music. His favourite reading seems to be maps. Irene's months of working for Paul have brought out the best in her. She now announces herself exhausted by Genius Loci's hot, cramped office. She had nothing more comfortable to sit on than a typist's chair. Two telephone directories served to elevate and, supposedly, cushion her. She has been a good ally to her grandson, but enjoyed the attention of Perry and Charlie, the rejuvenating chatter of the girls and the distant intimacies of telephoning clients. As soon as she got out of the BMW, she announced, with pale promptness, that she had spent the previous night in the lavatory. Her malaise did not prevent her drinking brandy or eating selected dishes. Her abiding appetite is for sympathy.

She insists that the happiness of the family is her paramount concern, if not consolation. In fact, she has often been dismayed by evidence of our well-being, whether in Fuengirola, in Rome or in Los Angeles or here. She cannot ever cede us our autonomy, although she has learnt not to insist on the virtues of a suburban code by which we clearly do not choose to abide. If, as she says, she has never believed herself to be beautiful, she has never been reluctant to draw the dividends of beauty. She has long taken refuge in the myth of her frail health. She hints at severe illness nobly endured, though no grievous symptoms manifest themselves. After I had paid for her to come and holiday with us in Tony Richardson's house in LA, in 1976, she left, by mistake, a note in her bedroom saying that, though her days were numbered, she had been cruelly used by her daughter-in-law.* The threatened cancer failed to mature. My father had been failing for years; she was fractured and fractious; but her tendency to reproachful lamentation and her demands that she be loved in return for her unfailing attention to us have been there for as long as I can remember.

---

* She lived until after her hundredth birthday, in 2010.

3.9.83. The news no longer makes anything of the Day War Broke Out. Who recalls Robb Wilton's catchphrase? We are now much further from 1939 than 1939 was from 1914.

12.9.83. Coming back to London from Langham last night, I saw two men walking towards Kensington High Street with their arms around each other, lovers. They were young; one very fair. The street was deserted; there was no challenge in their display, except to passing cars and to the spirit of the place itself. Their arms were complicatedly entwined. They walked lightly, yet a little awkwardly. Years ago, at Notting Hill Gate, my great-uncle Lionel saw a woman standing at a bus stop wearing a trilby and a man's suit and tie. He clapped her forcibly on the back, and called out, 'Hullo, Jack old man, haven't seen you for ages!' My father told the story less because he relished the woman's embarrassment than in pious memory of Lionel's nerve. In pre-Hitlerian times, an English Jew, of a family long-established in this country, had little apprehension of being invited to go back where he had come from, since he had not come from anywhere. Lionel made sport of the English in a very English way: in court, he is said to have said, 'I deny the allegation and defy the alligator'.

My father was more timid; his wit might sting, it was never venomous. He relied on the regularities of life; he could not have boxed clever in an unroped ring. My mother told me recently that he had been the victim of a homosexual assault, in Eastbourne, when he was sixteen. Was he deeply marked by it? He used the standard club-house vocabulary when it came to 'pansies'. He rarely talked about sex, though he sometimes retailed Stock Exchange jokes. My mother once said that he was 'very sexually demanding'. He liked money and always wished that he had more; yet he never pleaded poverty or denied himself anything he wanted as long as it was nothing excessive. Until the accident, he was neither young nor old; broad-shouldered, he kept slim, clean and well-groomed. He did not look like anyone but himself; only someone in the know would have pronounced him the Jew he never denied being.

25.9.83. I went to Los Angeles last Saturday and came back on Thursday. The solemnity of the trappings and the distance travelled give the impression that something of significance was in train. In fact, I went for a single script conference. Whenever I sit with other people to discuss the plot, characters and ideas for a film, I feel that I am engaged in cheerful drudgery. Massage and message are identical; that's the fun of it. The people I saw were nice enough, serious, amusing and amused enough, to make me feel that I accomplished a mission of worthwhile purpose.

Before the huddles began, I had a whole day of sunshine by the Wilshire pool. I was saluted by a Jerry Lewis, a publicist with whom, he reminded me, I had dinner in Paris almost a decade ago. At the time of *Jaws*, I was recruited, after a chance meeting in the lobby of the Plaza-Athénée, to the suite of Steven Spielberg, suddenly the richest young director in the world.

Some Parisian know-all conducted us to a currently modish restaurant in the Rue de Rennes. The pastry was uncooked, the red velvet décor over-stuffed. For the same money we could have gone to Taillevent or Vivarois. Robert Enrico, a bearded director whose recent hit, *Le Vieux Fusil*, with Philippe Noiret, gave him the *haut du pavé*, was deputed to order the meal. Spielberg deferred to him, with whatever secret condescension. I could not recall that Jerry L. was even at the table. Poolside, I was more amiable than I felt and stood him a pineapple juice. He has been a lifelong sufferer from piles and has recently had cheering treatment. He also lacks a kneecap. *Mon semblable* perhaps, but by no means *mon frère*.

Stanley Donen came to collect me, in the red Porsche, at 12.30. I had been warned that Yvette had left him, but he told me right away, as if confessing a small disease. 'She didn't want to be married,' he said. 'She came up to me about six weeks ago and said, 'I don't want to be married.' Stanley seemed at once stunned and philosophical, rather like Wellington's adjutant at Waterloo when he had his leg blown off. Stanley is cruelly marked, but *Blame It on Rio* is shaping to be a hit;* he is so quietly exhilarated by that prospect that the loss of Yvette seems to have left no more of a dent than some glancing shunt on the freeway. Women can always be replaced, especially if one has a hit. Nothing had seemed sillier or more wonderful than to get married, against all the odds, to a girl much younger than himself who had been many things to many men, but never married. If he had given her a child (if she ever wanted one), might things have been different? 'It's the first time a woman has ever left me,' he said (even Picasso once said the same). Is Stanley a little relieved that the blow has fallen? Damocles ends by being glad that the thread has snapped. Stanley has a new Victor word-processor (a nice imitation of art, since I called him 'Victor' in *California Time*). He showed me its implacable logical procedures with boyish glee. He loves gadgets and here was gadgetry which almost becomes your friend. It dispenses with secretaries and with carbon paper. The writer risks becoming a function of his instrument's versatility, like the cinema organist.

* I wish it had been, but it was not.

In the evening, I drove up Sunset to find Rising Glen Road, missed the concealed sign and drove up onto the roof of Hollywood. The road narrowed and twisted between bungaloid houses. Tall plank fences stand flush to the street. There was no one to give directions; not a bar or store or gas station. Hilltops have been terraced into tight shelves for expensive homes. Calmly desperate, I stopped, stretched out an arm at an oncoming car. I was amazed when the female driver stopped and tried, and failed, to help me. A family standing in the street, waiting for an errant guest, put me right.

I arrived at John's huge front door in rather good time to make an entrance befitting the star of the show. Isherwood and Don Bachardy were already sitting by the pool, everyone close up to them, as if playing cute sardines. I had shaken hands with Michael Childers when we met at the door. John gave me a kiss to which I responded with a hug. He was quick to give me the bad news: Paramount had decided not to proceed with *Desire*. I should, in truth, have been embarrassed by any mild enthusiasm; it would have entailed another set of changes. John seemed disappointed; the cancellation entailed vacating his offices on the lot. He was evicted almost as soon as Shatzenberg, or whatever his name is, had pronounced his decision. John was quick to say that the head honcho had 'come round the table' to prove, I suppose, that he was not personally disaffected. There was something sad in the comfort John drew from so small a mercy.

Isherwood is the oldest boy in the world. At seventy-nine, he has the clean-cut naughtiness that would be quite at home in a school for grown-ups. He gave an odd little bark of appreciation – ha! – if one said anything that amused him. He presumes himself largely forgotten in England. He gives every sign of being happily independent, with no inclination to nostalgia. Bachardy, silvery and smiling, has just starred in a show of his own photographs, drawings and paintings, at a gallery on Hollywood Boulevard. He and Christopher form as married a couple as that landscape is ever likely to foster. The conversation lacked the malicious edge which is one of the usual charms of gay company; there was too much best behaviour. I tried to enliven things by sniping at the British and then I got on to Proust, homosexuals and Jews and finally the similarities – prosily analysed by Hannah Arendt in her Proustian article – between Jews and gays (as I do not find it easy to call them). Garrulity led me to use 'we' to embrace both categories. 'Are you gay then?' Isherwood asked.

It was the first occasion that anyone ever put that question to me. I suppose that the myth of instinctive recognition is as unreliable with queers as with Jews. With small confidence that I can divine who is a Jew and who not, I could certainly deny allegiance to Christopher's sodality. I am unable even to fantasise any appetite for another man, still less a boy. At Charterhouse, in a moment of self-righteous delation, I recall with shame that I considered it my duty to denounce a rumoured romance between two other Lockites to Harry March, who swallowed that prominent Adam's apple a couple of times but, to his credit, took no prim action.

Isherwood seems determined to have done the right thing in finding fulfilment in a life elsewhere (where is more *else* than LA?). He gives self-indulgence the semblance of morality. His attitude derives from the southern California gurus – the first and most influential of them Gerald Heard – to whom a number of exiled intellectuals, including Aldous, turned for guidance. Promising that meditation could pass for a kind of philosophy, Heard became for Isherwood what Charles Williams was for Auden.

Was the dissolution of the Auden/Isherwood dyad due only to the geographical extent of the US? On the east coast, Auden became increasingly Anglican; Isherwood, on the west, oriental. The influence of Kallman and of the opera sealed W.H.A. into the culture from which eastern philosophy detached Christopher. Christianity recruited Auden to a creed which he edited not to embarrass his predilections. As a quasi-married man, the author of *Letter to Lord Byron* lost the urge, unless it was the energy, to go a-roving.

Bachardy has been a happier influence, but then C.I. is more personable than Wystan. There is also something complacent about him, and hard. The inventor of Sally Bowles is without the smugness often found in the author of mythical figures; but he does have the complacency of someone who has observed terrible events and got clean, and richly, away. Like a literary *charcutier*, he trimmed a savage epoch into a set of royalty-rich savouries.

Julie Christie had stayed for what became several weeks in John's house. He showed me the retractable stainless steel ladder by which she ascended to her attic retreat.

31.10.83. *Indecent Exposure.* Slumped in first class, I stayed awake all night reading David McClintick's account of the Begelman affair.* A

---

* David Begelman had been a hot agent before becoming the head honcho at failing Columbia and turning the company around. An incurable gambler, he lifted fifteen thousand dollars from the company account and covered the petty larceny by passing it off as part of Cliff Robertson's residuals. When the IRS

pot pourri of sourced documentary and reconstructed dialogue, the book amounts to an obese non-fictional version of O'Hara's *Appointment in Samarra*: a man breaches the moral code of his society and is eventually driven out and destroyed; in this case Alan Hirschfield, not Begelman: as soon as David was exposed, the former was on the rack. Based in New York, as CEO of a public company, he was obliged to rectitude. As soon as he arrived in California, the West Coast fraternity rated him an intrusive troublemaker. So what if David had raided the corporate till for a few bucks? He had retrieved Columbia's fortunes, big time, and deserved protection not pomposity.

Why did D.B. employ such clumsy means to pick what he himself had put into Robertson's pocket? If he was being leaned on by the bookies, why not go to the colleagues who would have been happy to help him, as they proved *après coup*? The simplest answer is that he knew very well that if he went to his friends and found them all set to bail him out, his last inhibition against recklessness would be swept away. A green light for extravagance would lead to a much, much greater heap of debts. Psycho-talk about self-destruction fails to account for the specific tactics Begelman adopted. How about if he hoped that to be outed as a thief, of a quite small sum, would stop his craziness from going too far? By intimidating himself with fear of the law, he could hope to slow his rush to the precipice. But then why cover the deficit by attributing the fifteen thousand dollars he had lifted to the earnings of Cliff Robertson, who distrusted and disliked him? He was not actually robbing the actor, but the IRS was always likely to pursue the fake payment, since tax should have been due on it.

Was there a mischievous side to David which took pleasure in making it literally thanks to C.R. that he was able to draw the larcenous cash? You bet. Robertson had almost rumbled Begelman cutting corners, several years before. The cheque put two fingers up to the Oscar-winner, behind his back. D.B. found a gambler's answer to a gambler's dilemma. If C.R. was being robbed, it was not of anything he had ever possessed or was owed. What better fun than to use a humourless and honest man's name to conceal a petty fraud?

Jewish solidarity gets almost no mention in McC.'s very fat book. Perhaps the author feared losing the good will of readers and reviewers. But what Matty implied was that Hirschfield should have declined to pillory another Jew in order to pander to the moral scruples of the *goyim*.

---

accused Robertson of not declaring it as income, the actor claimed, with justice, that he had never received it. The subsequent investigation revealed Begelman's fraud.

Hirschfield's eventual eviction from the role of Columbia's CEO and the fact that Robertson never worked again for a major studio gave Begelman the last laugh.*

I went to see Jo Janni before going to the BFI banquet in the Guildhall. Almost every creep in the business had been invited; the producer of *A Kind of Loving* and *Darling* was not. He could not have gone anyway, but is that the point? He sits in a corner of the living room in the same flat in Burton Court where I first met him, in 1955. He has not recovered the use of his stricken left hand and arm. His bulging belly rests on his knees like a pregnant cushion. One evening recently, he went to the kitchen to make himself some *pasta* and heard excited noises from the *au pair's* bedroom; she was in bed with his nurse. Stella insisted that both be sacked. Jo told me, 'Fred, to tell you de truce, all what I wanted was to stay and watch.' In his debility, he has reverted to being Italian: he has been reading *I Promessi Sposi*.

Bob Shapiro came to see Jo in hospital when he was first immobilised and brought him a stack of pornographic magazines, more uplifting, no doubt, than the collected works of W. Shakespeare. Jo's paralysis made it impossible for him either to read or to conceal the things. The nurses were embarrassed by their flagrancy. Bob had the grace to stay in touch throughout his WB presidency. His term of office was abruptly terminated. One day, Jo telephoned and asked to speak to him. He was told that no one of that name had ever worked on the lot. If the phone rings in 36, Burton Court these days, it is more likely to be Michelangelo or Federico than any English-speaker.

Immediately, after leaving William Morris, Bob Shapiro was quick to declare that he was going to produce *Roses, Roses...* without having asked whether I agreed. He recruited Mark Rydell as director and then mismanaged the whole business. Once a power at Warner Bros, he showed no interest in a project which he had treated as a lifeline when he thought he needed it. Bob had a way of calling Beetle 'dear', which

---

* David Begelman did have to leave Columbia, but he had the nerve and the connections, mainly with Texas oil men, to start a new production company which enrolled Stanley Donen and me in another well-paid abortive project. Its expensively decorated new offices overlooked the exclusive Beverly Hills Country Club. David told us that he could look down on the fairway, and rough, of the tenth hole. It amused him to watch the goyim surreptitiously toeing their balls to a more accessible lie. David's old habits were irresistible: in 1995, discovered to have embezzled at least a million dollars of his sponsors' investment, he shot himself in a hotel bedroom in Century City. Rendered notorious, the hotel later changed its name.

she failed to find endearing. At tennis, he would say 'Bob, you're not *stroking!*' Careful dresser, he wore sock-suspenders. His wife Sandy became a high-ranked marathon runner before a stress fracture forced her to fall back on gymnastics. Their young son developed a habit of walking out of the house and walking and walking. They were perfectly nice. One has not the smallest wish ever to see them again.

I had never been to the Guildhall before. The banquet was well organised by lackeys who had welcomed more famous companies than the cine-crowd assembled to hear the Prince of Wales and Sir Attenborough. It was a reunion of a school (too many men, too few women) which I never attended full-time. The nervous eye sought a familiar or friendly face. I talked first to Annie Skinner, continuity girl on *Darling* and recently producer of *The Return of the Soldier*, in which the uncomely Glenda was excellent and everything and everyone else forgettable. Annie was eager to be acknowledged by Dickie, who was red as a saint's day.

Clive Donner embraced me, rather shifty-eyed, as we squeezed into the big room. I like Clive, if only because I have done him several good turns. Perhaps he fears that I expect one from him. He seems ashamed, unless it's proud, of something which he suspects I know about him, even though I do not. I found that I had been well seated, perhaps thanks to Tony Smith, who greeted me very amiably. Roy Shaw was on my left, John Berg opposite me, Peter Plouviez (general secretary of Equity) next to him. I enjoyed my proximity to Shaw. At the party for the Radio 3 Magazine, I had no sooner been introduced to him than he made off. When I challenged him, in a good-humoured way, he claimed to have no memory of the encounter. I almost believed him. Made a little drunk by the formality, I ventured what I hoped were amusing remarks. For example, affecting to confuse the guest speakers and the menu, I read poached salmon with green sauce as '*suprême de Attenborough avec sa sauce habituelle*'.

Shaw is a Yorkshireman, Berg a Jew, Plouviez some kind of a Huguenot. The only adjacent Englishman was called Robert Atkins (no relation of Robert Atkins); he worked for the Commonwealth Institute and had shaved himself raw before the dinner. Berg said he had been at Shirley's when Bill Rodgers showed up and behaved so loutishly. I had no memory of him. He is in charge of the British Council and has the traces of a foreign accent it is nice to hear in the occupant of such a post.

The meal was not bad, the wine quite good, the speeches arch. We were sitting under a statue of Wellington, who might have curtailed Dickie's waffling and that of the Prince of Wales. HRH coped well with the impromptus following Orson's contribution, but became repetitious when he reverted to his script (he mentioned Mountbatten's son, in his role of movie producer, twice). The massive Orson was, like the Abbé de Sieyès, evidence of the capacity to be radical and yet survive. That sonorous voice produced winsome anecdotes about his ancestors and their loyalist allegiance to the Crown. In his eulogy of the great man, Dickie relied on *Kane* to supply the laurels and the millstone. How Welles must hate to be reminded of how early he peaked! Stanley has a similar aversion to hearing any more about *Singing in the Rain*.

Among the other servile heroes of the evening was Marcel Carné, a plump pink person who was less moved by his honour than Dickie was in presenting it. The latter's ability to be moved to tears by almost anything makes one grateful that he is not a Jew, though I am sure that he would weep at the deprivation. His hunger for praise is so insatiable that he speaks well of everyone. Never outstandingly good at anything, he takes care to stand out as quite good at everything. He has done nothing contemptible that begins to be as good as, for scandalous instance, Michael Powell's *Peeping Tom*.* Weeping Dickie craves forgiveness for sins he lacks the talent to commit.

I saw many less than famous faces that should never have displaced Jo (oh how friendly Verity Lambert was!) and, having enjoyed my dinner companions, though not as much as they enjoyed me, I thought it polite to utter a word of welcome to M. Carné. Though I never liked *Les Enfants du Paradis*, I did admire *Quai des Brumes*. So I did my froggy stuff with the round old boy, who attached more importance to his *légion d'honneur*, bright in his button-hole, than to the BFI plaque. I then saw Costa-Gavras and we had a truly enjoyable hour, immune to the profane herd, drinking excellent champagne to help rectify Delors' balance of payments. Costa is a man with whom I should have been, should be, working. It is typical of the silly biz that the only person who ever tried to put us together was that drunken operator Sidney Beckerman.

Later, I saw Jim Cellan Jones, who introduced me to John Mollo, who was in the Remove with me at Charterhouse. He became a historian and is now a sought-after costume designer, expert on military uniforms. He would, he said, love to be involved in *Napoleon and Josephine*. I had to dredge my memory, more of the School List than of faces or persons, before I could believe we had been classmates. Jim had been rehearsing, had no wheels and was wasted. I drove him home to his big, oddly cluttered house in Kew. He has been the most appreciative of producers and

---

* Powell's 1960 film was scandalously ahead of its time and was so savagely denounced by the critics that his career was ruined. In 1981, he was given a British resurrection by being made a Fellow of the British Film Institute.

has often done very good work: *School Play* was so sharp in its satire that it was never repeated.

2.11.83. Izmir is a teeming city; turreted tenements behind the polluted bay. Something is missing: Greeks. Kemal's westernising nationalism was a tribute to Turkey's enemies; his eviction of Asia Minor's Greek population its nastiest evidence. The allied victory seemed to have left his country prostrate before the ambitions of her previous subjects. Woodrow Wilson's pious sloganeering about self-determination and Sykes-Picot's appetite for booty, packaged in new, national costumes, rendered the Ottomans liable to the schismatic disassembly of their empire. The new geography was a jigsawn contrivance of supposedly independent states and kingdoms.

The greatest post-1918 illusion, the Greeks' Big Idea, had the oldest and most valid licence (if one forgets the Jews, as London and Paris were happy to do). The western psyche acquiesced in a neo-crusade to recover Constantinople. The Greeks had never ceased to refer to it as 'The City'. Mythological megalomania (which gives Greeks and Jews their unlikely persistence) dressed Hellenic Zionism as a noble enterprise. Did anyone believe it a feasible military prospect in the long term? The Ottomans had been thoroughly defeated, the Sultan divested of his divan, but did advocates of the recapture of Byzantium truly imagine that the pride of the Turks had been permanently broken? The Greeks were drunk with the good fortune of having opted, under Venezelos' leadership, for the winning side. Among the Europeans there lingered a certain grudge against those who had evicted them from their hold on the Levant. Why else were Arabs sentimentalised, Turks blackened? The lost authority of the latter, and the fear of their resurgence, enhanced the white-robed charm of the former. Their leaders seemed dependable, if only because their thrones were in the gift of the victorious allies.

Kedourie put the case for the Ottomans, in the form of autobiographical *témoignage*. His challenge to the Chatham House Version is a concealed lament for his own Iraqi past, hardly less poignant than Seferis's journals. The crassness of the Greeks, and its savage consequence, was part of a larger European conceit. The Armenians might contest this; they paid with something close to annihilation for the 1915 uprising which Kedourie treats with small sympathy. He maintains that the revolt of the Ottomans' Armenian subjects provoked, if not merited, the pitilessness wreaked upon them. To challenge their lords in a time of war could only be treated as treason. Did the recklessness of the Armenian leaders warrant the slaughter of unarmed men, women and children?

Kedourie deplores the collapse of a *façon de vivre* which had kept the Fertile Crescent in a state of more or less amiable corruption ever since the Persian kings were succeeded by Alexander and his diadochoi. Nations and empires rose and collapsed; greedy benevolence and rapacious *laissez-faire* procured wavering stability. From time to time, excessively grasping rulers pushed their subjects into the arms of their rivals. When a single conqueror embraced a territory too large for efficient control, there was a chance that the lives of its inhabitants could be lived in competitive, if often querulous, peace. Coin was a language more common than *koinê*.

Islam lacks ancient roots in the region it came to dominate. The Jews made disastrous choices, by defying both God and Caesar, and then lost on both sides in the metaphysical shoot-out, but their antiquity cannot be questioned. The Greeks were always able to rely on a measure of European guilt. Byzantium was first weakened by the crusaders and then abandoned to the Turks. The latter's baggy style might charm Byron and other privileged travellers, but the Ottomans have been more commonly regarded as degenerate sodomites. The revolt of Islam and the quasi-equine elegance of the Arabs recommended them to not a few Europeans in flight from bourgeois banality and, said quietly, the curse of Christianity.

After his victorious role at Gallipoli, and his part in the Sultan's eviction, Kemal Ataturk had the charisma to resurrect his country from the early grave to which its Christian conquerors had consigned it. The man from Salonika also showed his contempt for the Mullahs whose calls modern Turks answer more from sentiment than conviction. It would be dangerous to assume that the less privileged populace will never rally to fanaticism; it seems unlikely only so long as the army and/or politicians control the country's affairs. The current regime is repressive and arbitrary, but the NATO connection to the West is undisguised and had probably better be.

In Kusadesi, talking to a Greek shopkeeper, I was touched by the force of his welcome when I spoke in what had been the common language of the whole coast. Caught on the wrong side of history, victim of nothing intolerable, he was camped irretrievably in exile. Greece and Turkey are so close as to be pieces of the same puzzle. It is as if, by some silly decision, they have been divided between children who no longer play together and who deny each other what they could happily compose in common. Their rivalrous rhetoric sharpens antique knives on the whetstone of modernised nationalism.

Today's young Turks deplore the tensions which inhibit tourists, Greeks not least, from coming to be nicely fleeced. An adjacent English couple in our regular *taverna* managed to be shocked by the addition of an extra one thousand lire to their bill. I did not believe there was malice in the waiter's ineptitude. Once I caught the same establishment undercharging us. To tabulate the tourist amenities, ubiquitous yoghurt, magnificent ruins, promises that the absent Greeks are always there. This supposedly marginal area, *mi-figue, mi-raisin*, has surprising beauty, confidence and amplitude. Greece of the fifth century was greener, perhaps more handsomely peopled, than modern Hellas, but Ionia retains a largeness and fecundity that the *stenochoria* of the 'mainland' could never supply.

The hinge of Europe and Asia turned on a mixture of languages and cults. Progress required abstraction, of which money was the economic and philosophy the conceptual projection.

The ancient Ionians faced problems of adjustment and social posture. In accordance with their geography, it suited them to invent a new, quasi-godless theogony. How else were they to accommodate the region's heterogeneous character within a common logic? An impartial creation myth, without proprietorial links, was the only way to stabilise a territory where 'nationality' offered no reliable foundation. The Hellenes themselves were incapable of unity, despite the pantheon whose worship, like their language, was said to define their homogeneity.

Asia Minor, the counter of the ancient world where goods and gods were exchanged.

David Jones, mahoganoid with small success, told me that if I wanted to get the best out of his film of Pinter's *Betrayal*, I should see it twice. 'Tell you what, David,' I said, 'I think I'll just see it the second time.' He remembers his months or years as the Nimmos' lodger with persistent bitterness; he alludes to them every time we meet. He seems to have the idea that Beetle connived at his humiliations. In fact, we were embarrassed by Dudy's loathing for 'Jones'; we never participated in baiting him. I recall that not very long ago, after witnessing the prolonged tedium of Günter Grass's *The Plebeians Rehearse the Uprising* etc., which he had directed, we took D.J. to the Savoy Grill for a poor, expensive meal (the cold consommé was revolting). He had no recollection of our bounty. Do a certain kind of man an extravagant kindness and he will never weigh it against the smallest imagined slight. D.J. is always quite friendly, but he cannot keep his tongue from that petty sore place.

It is generally agreed that Geoffrey Howe no longer has any chance of succeeding Mrs T. He was badly mauled by Dennis Healey over the Grenada affair, although there is nothing much that he could have done, before or *après coup*. It proved only that the Commonwealth is more common than wealthy. Howe's discomfiture was a judgment less on him than on England. What was painful was not so much the humiliation of a sad sack as the pleasure taken in it by the public whose impotence he symbolised. G.H. will never erase the memory of a TV clip in which he was seen trotting from one doorstep to another during the General Election. Hitler remarked on the necessity for a leader never to look like a buffoon. Howe first looked an ass and then proved that he was one.*

Lunch yesterday in a private room at the Garrick hired by a guy called Appel, London bureau chief of the *New York Times*. I put on the suit and the St John's tie. Heather Bradley has been calling me for years. I expected a sort of bridge hostess, angular and antique. She was indeed white-haired, but rather flighty and Irish, if unaccented. She, or someone, had arranged for us to be neighbours. She plied me with assenting glances, urging me to peddle the paper almost anything I happened to have available for the many magazines from which they are making millions. They have, she told me, started to pay real money. This accounts for the fairly *gros bonnets* who had come to consume the offered food (adequate) and wine (excellent): Victor Pritchett, John Mortimer, A.L. Rowse, Adam Nicolson, Bruce Chatwin, Al Alvarez, Rachel (Lady) Billington. When Appel thanked us for coming, I said, 'Listen, the English will do anything for lunch.'

Alvarez sat on my left. He has the brazen furtiveness of a tipster who has not recently recommended a winner. His literary standing derives from an era of earnestness in which his critical evaluations in public prints gave him access to private pleasures that middle age has placed in nostalgia's cabinet. Alvarez is friendly, because diplomatic, and a little woeful. He has made enough enemies to incline him to be ingratiating to neutrals. I asked whether he didn't lose all his friends through playing poker with them. He said, like a rumbled car salesman, that the money 'went round'. There is ruefulness in his address; knowing references to his wives hint at, but do not quite confess, a scarred life. Lack of feeling has been covered with a plethora of serialised dramas. After years of self-promotion, industry, and intellectual hype, he has the small fame, in a

*   In his quiet way, he fatally damaged Mrs Thatcher by his resignation speech in 1989. When I debated with G.H. at the Cambridge Union, he was both pleasant and modest. His lifelong ambition, he told me, was to be a movie director.

small circle, of someone who has had his clever moment. The middle-aged *littérateur* is remembered keenly only by those he has hurt. Al carries the wary smile of the hitman who has neither finished off his victims nor conserved his anonymity.

Victor Pritchett, whose 'V.S.' gave him a certain Cromwellian austerity during his regular days at the *NS*, has a sprightliness at eighty-plus equalled only by Rowse. Both have the *disponibilité* of scribes who are glad still to command a fat dollar and are ready to spring to pieces at the flourish of a commission. Ambulant museum-piece, Rowse has made an exhibition of himself. Having privatised a segment of national history and made a fortune from it, he boasted about the money that 'that lady'* had made for him. Talking about Sherborne and the Raleigh connection, he was unguarded enough to speak of Sir W.'s having owned the place. I remarked that I thought that, if he examined the matter carefully, Rowse would find that W.R. never had a good title to the property owing to the inept wording of a clause in the lease. (The omission of a key phrase invalidated the inheritance which W.R. hoped would secure the fortune of his family after his own disgrace.)

My minute knowledge of the documents in a case which I had not raised myself seemed positively magical to young Nicolson, with whom I then had a long conversation about his grandfather. Adam looked more like his grandmother than like old Sir Harold, whose snobbish person he took to be more a figure of fun than of imposing stature. He recalled a story about H.N. wiping a plate which had been handled by a black waiter. I said that I wiped only *forks*, never mind who had fingered them. Having come down from Magdalene, Cambridge, in 1979, Adam is now writing a book on Frontiers. When I warned him that Steiner was *à ses trousses*, he shuddered with unfrightened deference.

Pritchett endorsed my view that Willie Maugham's cult of the cliché was the consequence of his French upbringing. I recall with new irritation that someone, whose name I cannot dredge from memory's ditch, challenged my propounding of that view. I have taken a great deal of crap from a great many people. Chatwin talked too long about the origins of the Argentinian love/hate of England. He sported the narrow conceit of those who have written a famous book without achieving personal fame. Pride and resentment soften the face and harden the eyes. He expects more of the world than it has quite consented to deliver.

John Mortimer, on the other hand, has the knowing modesty of those who have parlayed a small talent to maximum advantage. In the character

---

* Rowse had excited notoriety and revenue with his boast that he was the first historian to identify the 'dark lady' of Shakespeare's sonnets.

of Rumpole, the abrasive mollities of the QC dramatist are matched by the endearingly repellent Leo McKern. Morty has made effortlessness the mark of all his efforts. He is a sociable troublemaker at whom no one could take serious offence. Regard for his blind father has enabled him to remain the clever heir who cannot pretend to the brilliant eccentricity of the wise old lawyer whose tones he mimics. He resembles a tradesman who is the 'son' of 'X and son'. Having chosen to be amused by the world in which he was unlikely to excel, he has become a better fictional lawyer than he was practical barrister. He acknowledges his good fortune in so marketable a fashion that even his filial sincerities bring in good royalties. Middle-aged for so long that he has become younger than one might expect, his ugliness renders him a landmark. One cannot imagine him being seriously angry nor anyone being seriously angry with him. A talent for easily remembered, never memorable, dialogue and a nice way with entrances and exits have been sufficient to render him uninterestingly irreplaceable.

Appel's name has been Apfel. He has the small nose and large shoulders of an all-American football player. He forecast that Syria would take over Lebanon and he may be right. His sidekick, Michael Leahy was a glad-hander, eager to make a good impression. He succeeded with me by having seen *The Glittering Prizes* again just before he left NYC. He had not realised just how… etc. I accepted the tribute modestly, fearful that his gush would alienate other egos in the room, young Salman Rushdie among them.

13.11.83. Dinner at the Whitleys. They live in a swanky slum, College Cross, Islington, in a house with a pretty early Cubitts fanlight over the front door. They have spent a good deal of time and treasure renovating the interior. A more calculating pair might have preferred to invest in a fancier address. The company included an old man called Waley who had had the next set to John Schlesinger in Balliol. He must have been sixty-five when he went up. His wife is an Italian cookery expert. She had never heard of Paul Bocuse.

David Hughes was accompanied by his recent bride, Elizabeth, a pretty, fair woman in a blue suit. D.H. reviewed *Lindmann* in a solus review in the *ST* twenty years ago. He had forgotten the piece. I had not, even though it was largely laudatory. He was married for many years to Mai Zetterling, who played a delectable *cocotte* in *Trio*, a film of three of W.S.M.'s stories. Since she was older than David, Tom Maschler thought D. absurdly romantic to take her on. The marriage lasted rather longer than Tom's own, but it did finally collapse. D.H. came back to England and re-Britished himself. Handsome, but not as handsome as he once was, he has the carefully groomed greying look of those who believe that a young bride will make them younger. His new love requires him to make a living with the pen as his sole weapon.

He has written several novels (I was tactful enough to have read one of the titles) and he also scripted films for M.Z., though she was too famous and the films too fugitive for him to derive any marketable credit from them. He had just heard that he had been sacked from the job of *Sunday Times* film critic, which he had had only for the few months since the departure of Alan Brien. He seemed uneasy in the company of his host, understandably. John W. either connived at the dismissal or was powerless to prevent it; since he remains Arts Editor, it amounts to the same thing. No one at the table had anything much to say, so I said most of it. The Italian lady knew Jo Janni as vaguely as her husband did J.R.S. Hughes congratulated me bitterly on what he took to be my status in the London game, although I have no sense of it (way to go, perhaps).

On the cold pavement, John said that we must have a 'business lunch' when I get back from LA. The new editor, Andrew Neil, who had been consummately slagged by Paul Foot on *What The Papers Say*, was keen on the video bit, TV gossip etc. John implied that I should soon be appearing in copious print. This morning I received a letter from Claire Tomalin terminating my connection with the *Sunday Times* book section. I have been doing pieces for the paper for twenty-one years.

Jews and Jews. Ruy Lopez; Edwin Montagu; Herbert Samuel; Rufus Isaacs (the guilty, absolved Dreyfus); Namier v. Berlin; Isaac d'Israeli; Lynskey and Sydney Stanley; Keith Joseph and Lord Dannimac; B. Levin and the Appointments Board; Annan, the FO and 'official' anti-S.; Chatham House versions and British vanity; Anglo-Jewish writing; Jew v. Israeli; the non-Jewish Jew (Siegfried Sassoon, Jonathan Miller), the Jewish non-Jew and the bit of a Jew; Cyril Ross, philanthropist: 'I don't much go for the *goyim*.' The remaking of Wittgenstein for the Catholic market and for the British philosophical tradition. Cf. A.J. Ayer, Ryle, Russell and W. English gentleman / American Jew. Influence of Lockean *tabula rasa* 'idealism' and the notion of freedom in a democracy. Cf. Sartre's study of anti-Semitism v. the evasive nullities of Anglo-Saxon 'theories' (Magee). The trim vacuity of Harold Pinter belongs to this cluster, as does Levin's rhetorical Puffery. Arnold (Wesker)'s confusions have a warm humanity, a certain content at least, compared with the posturing of the two sophisticates.

18.11.83. We went to see David Jones's version of *Betrayal*. The barbered conceit of the text and the playing could not conceal the shallowness of the matter, the caution and the lack of daring. Nothing truly dangerous was broached, not even the scandal of desire. There was nothing there but play, pleasure in the obvious deceit of passing off complacency as art, short measure as elegance. Harold's tightness is a kind of fine tailoring; both skimpy and with no give in the pockets, it leaves not an inch of surplus material.

20.11.83. Godfrey Smith called on Sunday and, with the adroit charm of the cadger, dipped for a prize in the small bran of my experience. He is writing a book about the English. Hilary put him onto me for details of local anti-Semitism: Charterhouse and the Appointments Board. While Cambridge people will go to some lengths to do you a disservice, H. cannot resist doing chums a good turn. Even if Oxonians let you down, they do it with a smile. Cambridge people not only stab you in any convenient quarter but have also to announce the justice of their conduct. It is not enough to betray your friends, you must also put them in the wrong. Godfrey has the shape and heartiness of an old pal. If he lets you down, it's with the air of giving you a leg up. He has the facility of the journalist to be everyone's cup of tea, with sugar.

16.11.83. A fellow-traveller on the Courtesy Bus from LAX to the Dollar depot told me that he was in London in 1946. I tried to imagine how the bald and bellied cigar-smoker looked in naval uniform in the years when he was on an admiral's staff, in who knows what capacity, and went to have blackmarket steaks at The Green Parrot, where they operated a speakeasy-type Judas-eye in the stern front door. It was as if this man, fresh from Seattle on his way to San Diego, was the last real person I was to see until I had shaken off the gilded dust of showbiz, which I shall after lunch today with Stanley Donen. I saw Wolper and the Warner Bros linkman, Chuck Maclean, 10 a.m., Monday. Chuck, whom Ron Mardigian suspected of being 'a little minty', wore the gleaming silver tracksuit of the WB baseball outfit. His straight nose was slightly indented by his habitual ingratiating wrinkle. He was the management's vigilante, said to be very nice to work with. In his early thirties, with a modified crew-cut, he has the air of someone more in the service than in the business.

Wolper sold his company to WB eight years ago. He now rejoices in a nicely tailored side pocket of the outfit. Although involved in three mini-series, he can find time to produce the opening and closing ceremonies of the imminent 1984 Olympic games. Pallid and bearded, the lightweight ghost of a bigshot, without flamboyance or manifest flair, he had prepared himself thoroughly for our huddles. His desk is at the head of a very long table with armchairs along its sides. He bobs about on a big orange leather executive chair, which shows how showy he could be if he did showmanship. Enormously rich, neither boastful nor assertive, he settles for smug. He began by climbing down, graciously, over the question of where *Napoleon and Josephine* should start. I was certain that J.'s early years in the West Indies should be included, rather than have us begin with their meeting, as he had proposed.

We proceeded through the story as if we were lawyers, glad to have agreed so promptly on the party of the first part. We had a brisk, frugal lunch in the WB commissary where D.W. always has the same table, right by the kitchen door. Lack of discrimination doubles for modesty. While he is at pains to remind you that his shows have won the loudest awards and the biggest audiences, he is so lacking in ostentation that you wonder just how much power he has. He proposed, with something like docility, that we should go and see Christy Walker over at ABC; they were putting up the money and deserved to be kept in the picture. There was no need for me to see her: my deal had been made without any stipulation that a word or a sentence, let alone our whole 'conception', had to be disclosed to anyone before I delivered the 'bible'.

D.W.'s parade of notes was not markedly impressive, but the lady agreed to be impressed. He had said that she was attractive. Bow-legged, in a black skirt suitable for her kid sister, she had so little knowledge of *Napoleon* that every commonplace element of the story seemed to strike her as thrillingly original. What critic was ever so uncritical? D.W. stumbled ahead of her while she applauded his surefootedness. I had intended to remain silent. Why should I tout for approval when my outline had been for D.W.'s eyes only? Only when he tripped did I step in to lend a steadying hand. The meeting went well, which was good, and quickly, which was better.

Everyone was so pleased that, as we were leaving, the head of the network, a bespectacled kid, stopped by, by chance, to wish us luck and hear Christy's enthusiastic summation. He told us that he had recently been on TV. The journalists had been out to get him, but he had evaded their lances and they ended by congratulating him on his nifty footwork. Slumming in luxury kept me laconic. When we were on the point of getting into the elevator to go down to the garage, D.W. back-pedalled to the reception desk where a black man played the amiable bouncer. David pulled out his parking ticket and had the guy validate it. He had saved himself all of two bucks. Would Darryl have stooped to such bread-and-butter economy? Chuck did the obligatory kiss-kiss routine with Christy. He must be very competent at costing and organisation. Wolper is happy to leave him to it while he deals, quietly, with Olympic hassles. 'Nothing is a problem,' he told me, 'if it gets better when you pour money on it.'

My abiding desire, except in bed, is to get away.

26.11.83. It is clear that the Radio 3 Magazine is not doing well. The wonder is that it is doing at all. I had not met Denys Gueroult when Louise Purslow persuaded me to do him a good turn by being a contributor. He has been reluctant to express his gratitude, perhaps for fear that I ask for more money. He did tell me recently that he had had a letter from a reader who had been about to take out a subscription when he discovered that the October issue lacked a piece by me, which lamed his resolve. He was not a Radio 3 listener and wanted to buy the magazine only if I was in it. I suppose I was flattered; certainly more than I was this week when, in the way of some nice souls, D.G. told me that he had had another letter from a potential subscriber who informed him that he liked everything in the magazine except for F.R.

Gueroult's life was probably defined by the decision to spell his Denys with a *y*. He spent three years in the navy and is expert in dated slang: for example, 'artizifer' for artificer. His homosexuality dates from when that appetite had better be concealed, or at least revealed only to trusted company. I do not put him at his ease, if only because I started by doing him a favour and I am not a member of his équipe. When he failed to run a piece of mine, I told him that, while I was happy to be spared the task, I could not continue unless I was printed regularly. In terms of cash, the monthly piece is very small potatoes: it demands two or three days of concentrated toil; print its only reward. D.G. climbed down upwards by saying that he only hoped that I would not again do a piece about someone taking advantage of me. I told him that if you were the sort of person that other people fed off and whom they were likely to call in order to ask for a favour, it was unsurprising that your liveliest memory should be of friends sinking their teeth in the choicest parts of your talents or possessions.

On Wednesday Beetle and I went to have lunch at *Tante Claire*. I had scarcely sat down before a solitary diner, at the next table, accosted me. His name was Bruce Finlaison. He had the gaunt, used face of a pale man who had loitered too long and too often with baleful eyes on the edge of popularity. We had, he had to tell me, been at the same school, though not in the same period. He treasured considerable animus against Robert Birley, the headmaster who had been his housemaster. He thought Charterhouse as bad a school as I did and confirmed, with no little relish, the depth and width of its endemic anti-Semitism. It was a comfort to discover that my abiding recollections do not stem from paranoia, but I could have done without the loquacity with which my apprehensions were alleviated.

The son of Tim Finlaison, a friend of my father's, Bruce is a doctor in Jersey. He regards his now dead father without sentimentality: 'He was a bit of an alcoholic'. His uncle Jack was a barrister, either very rude or very funny, depending on how you took it. He was married to an exceptionally ugly woman, very rich and epileptic. Bruce did not go to university, but straight to St Thomas's. His father said that he couldn't afford Oxbridge fees, though he clearly could.

Bruce seems to be easily gulled into things he doesn't much like. He has lived for twenty-two years on a tight little island where he first went because he got wind of a good practice in need of a partner. His wife, presently a mature student at Leicester, doing a course in archaeology, seems to like Jersey even less than he does, but they have never been able to dislodge themselves. You sense the disdain for humanity which B.'s own irresolution has fostered. The food in Jersey combines the worst of French and English. Having come to *Tante Claire* to enjoy himself, he had evidently been dismayed to find only himself to enjoy. Had he been a person of old English courtesy, he would have introduced himself at the end of our meal, rather than forced himself on us for its duration.

Odd! I failed to mention my meeting, at the BFI dinner, with Andrew Faulds MP, a bearded and bombastic ex-actor, much exercised in championing the Arab cause. 'Ah,' I said, 'at last I get to meet one of the great Zionists of our time!' He neither protested nor snapped. Seemingly dazed by failure to charm everyone into agreement with him, he said that he was sure that we would find a lot to agree about if we talked the thing through one day. I suspect that I should agree with him more readily than he with me. He may be more dupe than fanatic, but I hope that we shall never be at the mercy of his friends, or even of his confusion.

28.11.83. George McKnelly, once among John Wisdom's favoured pupils, wrote to me some time ago because I had made a silly mistake about the instrument played by Wittgenstein's brother, Paul: it was not, of course, the violin but the piano; hence he was able to continue to play after losing an arm in the Great War. Guessing that my amiable correspondent might have a copy of the photograph of the Moral Sciences club in 1954, in which G.E. Moore figures, I asked him for one. After he provided it, I felt I should ask him to lunch.

I arrived at the Savile rather late, having run up and down Bond Street is search of Wylma Wayne's gallery. I had promised her a painting for her Christmas show of celebrities' daubs. I played the timid card, but she had already set my name on the printed invitation. My guest was said to be in the Morning Room, but before I had the problem of trying to distinguish him, a very large man, in an abundance of business suiting, turned from the notice boards and declared himself. I proposed the dining room; he preferred the bar.

Glass in hand, McKnelly said that the last time we met (under the clock outside Swan and Edgar, where I was waiting for Beetle), I had told him that I was making films for Rank; 1956 then. He has become hugely inflated, red in the face, bushy brows, alcoholic gaze. There is a testy bonhomie about him; he may be modest, but he is not proud of it; he would, you felt, prefer to have something to be loud about. The oddest thing about him is that he was born in Toulouse. His father represented a company that made medicinal tea. Although they left the south-west in 1934 and G. has no French, he swears that he feels at home in France and was able to find his birthplace without instructions when he returned in 1949.

He has worked for ICI since Cambridge and takes pride, if not pleasure, in being a 'one-company man'. He retains great affection for John Wisdom, whose rooms in Whewell's Court he visited soon after going up. The carpet was in holes and there was a new book in the waste-paper basket. The only chair was entirely prolapsed. Wisdom served large quantities of gin in teacups. His daughter insisted that he drink water with it, so he brought in the washing ewer and filled whatever space was left in the cups with the gyp's ablutions water.

McK. still visits W. occasionally and is always welcome. Once he was solicited to stay for a philosophers' get-together to which W.'s contribution to date had been to invite an American academic to dinner. Von Wright was there, although he had already returned to Sweden (was it?); his wife felt unwelcome in Cambridge, so he had kept his chair only briefly. His lectures were said to be very difficult and full of symbolic logic.

George and I talked animatedly and without strain, but I was glad to bid him farewell. He is neither a fool nor very interesting. He said that he had academic ambitions 'until my seventh term'. He married at the end of his third year and became a father on New Year's Day 1954, in which case his wife has to have been pregnant in the spring of '53. He realised that he could not support a family as a PhD student and teaching assistant. He hears that Andor Gomme has become a very trendy dresser: polished boots and couture denim. A.G. was very clever and humourless and has yet to achieve the chair he may well deserve. I once invited him to come to PEN. He toted a stack of flagged books and spoke at great, dull length. His visit put an end to my insolent attempts to get the committee to leaven the intellectual tone of the meetings.

3.12.83. Hilary says that *The Times* would be glad to have me as a reviewer once every three weeks or so. P. Howard's only fear is that I shall prove too expensive. Where does the idea come from that I am financially exigent? The only appetising reward of journalism is instant print. Louise called to say that it is now agreed that we should have six live discussion programmes on the air in April/May/June, an amiable way of inviting me to make myself obnoxious in various quarters.

On Thursday night, we drove to Southampton to see Tom Wiseman's play. We had been prevented by fog from going to the press night. The *Sunday Times* second string, Robert Hewison, coincided with us. He wrote a book about the Footlights in which he quoted my words for Evelyn Waugh and Graham Greene without attribution. He had apologised for this, and another misdemeanour, on the telephone, but I had never met him. In person, he was an average-sized young middle-aged man with stubble and glasses and the professional discretion of the small assassin. Glass in hand, he was a one-man jury in the habit of considering his verdict, ready for any available beer and sandwiches and all set to bite whatever hand might feed him.

Tom's play, about Vienna in 1938, peopled the stage with a selection of appropriate characters. I was uneasy at the appearance of Eichmann in person. For the purposes of the plot, Tom transformed himself into the heroine of the piece, Camilla Bauer, a biting and brilliant journalist. He gave her his character, at once clever and opportunistic, but somehow passive and without the will to survive or to dominate. The dialogue was amusing and polished, but without dramatic edge. The last line alone is memorable, pronounced by Eichmann: 'You never know with Jews.'

8.12.83. I have been asked, as a supposed representative of the 'centre-left', to take part in *Any Questions* on January 6th, with Chalfont and Joan Ruddock, chairperson of CND. What is most peculiar about that organisation is its militants' obsessive determination to ban a weapon which, by comparison with all the other deadly weapons in the nations' armouries, is the most unlikely to be used. Their campaign seems to be at angry odds with that of the government, but it is, in effect, an adjunct to it. If CND did not exist, the West would be obliged to sponsor some body which would remind both the public and the enemy of the iniquity of possessing what such huge amounts of money and ingenuity have supplied. CND appears to be a political pressure group, but its politics are either defective or naïve, since it chooses to credit Communism with good intentions, if only because it wishes it could believe in them.

Although the elders of CND have included atheists and anti-metaphysicals, as well as clerics and fellow travellers, Christianity provides its archetype. The CND gospel reduces resurrection to a mundane matter; it proposes an after-life here on earth; their tract, *The Day After*, panders to the hope of redemption, if only by avoidance: we should place our emphasis on survival, as the Christian does on salvation. We should, however, on no account lay down our lives for our friends. Greater love is not required. Salvation is here below or it is nowhere. The attraction of the doctrine relies on its self-evidence. How can it be wrong to hope that nuclear weapons will not be used? It then becomes incontestable that they should not exist. But they do.

13.12.83. Bruce Finlaison (the family attaches importance to the unusual spelling) was in Saunderites with Simon Raven. He remembered Simon as a forbidding physical presence, glowering and oppressive. Simon has in common with Evelyn Waugh the wish to belong in the world of Etonians and Old Money. He impersonates them with a fawning malice which draws attention to his own cravings, as it did with Waugh. His actual standing with such people is questionable.

Might Simon always have had a residual fear of being taken for a Jew? There are Jewish Ravens. He divides the Chosen into those pretty well indistinguishable from people like himself and 'Jewy Jews', of the kind he has met in showbiz, with their alien vulgarities and two-pairs-of trousers tailors. In fact, Simon was 'saved' by the Maecenaean bounty of Anthony Blond, a bisexual Jewish O.E. of the style most agreeable to Simon's ideal: a messiah with money to spare. Had it not been for Anthony's demanding generosity, with its house rules for locking-up time, Simon would almost certainly have succumbed to Aspinall's poisonous lure. Exile from nocturnal London restored him to the industrious regularity which he might have honoured if he had been admitted the academic *cursus* and become a full-time classicist.*

The bully is likely to have something of Simon's inclination to self-destruction and the Semitic desire to infiltrate society without the buckles

---

* Anthony Blond commissioned the sequence of novels which appeared under the title *Alms for Oblivion* on condition that Simon lived out of London (in fact near Lewes) and left town by 9 p.m. at the latest. Faith unfaithful kept Raven falsely true. Simon told me, many years later, that he did his 'bit' of Greek or Latin every morning.

to be securely at home there. Such a bully is often an unacknowledged auxiliary of the established order, the N.C.O. whose rough justice has never to be endorsed by those whose interests it seconds. The school bully is more effective than any prefect or housemaster in reminding the new boy where he stands, or grovels. Anyone who imagines that tears, charm, wealth or pride can protect him is promptly disabused. The prison into which he has been so expensively pitched is policed, like any other place of incarceration, by its own inmates.

The bully, like the *cacique*, the trusty and the *kapo*,* makes the rules work for him. If his own conduct is illicit so is any appeal to authority to correct it. He enforces the unspoken rule that sneaking ('showing up' in Charterhouse-speak) is the one unforgivable crime. The law of silence, *omertà*, procures the complicity of his victims. The bully becomes the tribune who, they hope, will exempt his acolytes from the cruelty he visits on others. Sartrean serialisation is a common feature of the established order. The novice is reconciled to servility by being made aware of how much worse his condition might be.

The bully's final, typical, service to Authority is delivered by his fall. His punishment is as exemplary as that of the pirate. When Pompey cleared the Mediterranean of privateers, he prepared for its monopolistic exploitation by the Romans. A Flashman's fall is likely to come about because he seriously injures one of his suite or, as in Simon's case, commits an unacceptable sexual offence. By importing sensual gratification into an environment where the exercise of power is the sole licensed pleasure, the transgressor advertises that there can be a world elsewhere, in which the official code is an imposture. Out he goes.

15.12.83. John Whitley's proposal, over lunch, that I become the *Sunday Times* drama critic suggests that he has chosen to confront Claire only by outflanking her. The pleasure of being granted pole position almost persuades me to enter the race. The length of the circuit, however, and the obligation to sit in the driver's seat in such familiar scenery combine to lame my urgency. I should be able to go to America only during the brief weeks when we should also want to repair to Lagardelle. I am in the odd position of being uncertain not only of how the thing will turn out but also of how I want it to. The point is, or should be, would I enjoy it, would I do it well enough, and if I did, so what? How odd this sense of not wishing the final decision to be in my own hands! I am like the consul who, reduced to impotence, elected to spend his year of

---

* Primo Levi recalled that almost the first thing a *kapo* said to him in Auschwitz was 'Hier ist kein *Warum*' (Here there is no *why*).

office consulting the stars. Making inertia decisive, I wait to see what will happen. How shall I manage to honour other obligations, and pleasures? I shall certainly have to renounce my Friday tennis, since I shall be filing copy on that day. I am, however, at last, thanks to Leslie Linder, elected to Queen's and shall be able to play tennis when it suits me. The fact remains that next year, when we shall be tied to London whenever the Lycée is in session, is probably the last stretch of time during which I shall be available to occupy the post which Jack Lambert would have done almost anything to obtain.

How amiable, in retrospect, the period of Jack's presidency over the arts pages! Last night, talking to Ian MacIntyre at the Radio 3 party, I recalled how an unending symposium seemed to be installed in Thomson House in those days. On one occasion, when Cyril Connolly came in, I yielded to his seniority and left the room. J.W.L. called as soon as I was home. Cyril had been greatly fazed by my departure and feared that his stock was slipping with the younger set. I could only declare the true, anachronistic reason for my exit: deference. A few months later, C.C. again came in, while I was correcting a proof. He came over and said fluffily, 'I greatly admired something you wrote recently.' 'Oh,' I said, 'what was that?' 'Something you did recently.' Since I have always enjoyed his high-road erudition, I wish he had condescended more convincingly.

22.12.83. Stanley Price said he was particularly pleased to see Bamber Gascoigne at our very successful little party. When they were both theatre critics, they met in a foyer where S.P. was waiting for Judy. She arrived eight and a half months pregnant. Bamber had patted the protuberance and announced, 'I love pregnant women.' When the resultant Munro was on *University Challenge*, S.P. told him to announce himself to B.G. The young scholar refused. S.P. did not know that Bamber and Christina have had no children.

Our party began prematurely with the twenty-minutes-early arrival of Stanley Baron. He had confused ours with another invitation which he did not propose to honour. I gave him the Arnold Wesker Award for conspicuous bad timing. A.W. came to our 1964 party in Farley Court two *hours* before the due time and stayed through all the preparations. The sitting room in Stanhope Gardens was soon happily loud with multiple conversations. I never saw a single miniature *quiche*, though Beetle had cooked enough for the *Grande Armée*, and never had a bite of smoked salmon, though I had been cutting canapés since lunchtime. The guests drank twenty-six bottles of champagne. Shirley Williams failed either to reply or show up, though Tony Smith promised her advent.

Beating people up is not a method in philosophy. At the Radio 3 party, two days earlier, Renford was, so I was told afterwards, the first non-corporation guest to arrive, one of the last to leave. He has been at Princeton and actually made some headway on the book so long promised to a patient public. The minor success of our broadcast discussion put him in a benign mood. He was quite the giggling young don of thirty years ago. He made bold to say that I had shown little of the aggression of my undergraduate self. 'I know,' I said, 'I didn't mention the Jews within the first five minutes of the programme.'

Scruton was eager to join the more celebrated celebrities. He did not come over to Enoch Powell and Renford and me straightaway; but he was in russet evidence after a glass or two. Enoch thought it prudent not to recall the *Any Questions* on which we clashed, even though I volunteered documentation in the form of remembered dialogue. Doubtless the occasion was more memorable for me than for him, but his forgetfulness smacks of the orator who discounts the effect of his eloquence and allows the past to lapse as soon as may be.

For all his dignified years, Powell has a sports-jacketed youthfulness that owes nothing to sensuality, everything to prodigious propriety. The challenge in those mocking grey eyes invites whoever dares to a bout of mental wrestling. He boasted of renewed attention to an old favourite, Schopenhauer. Used to lording it over second-class company for whom the parade of chapter-headings is as good as accurate quotation or sustained argument, he takes his audience for dullards likely to concede his superiority on the strength of his bibliography. Armed with an unlikely combination of right-wing politics and indifference to social standing, he pays no sentimental obeisance to aristocratic values and alludes to no famous colleagues. He is at once strident and reticent, aggressive and courteous, grand and all but obsequious.

Scruton acts as though he has always kept grand company and has already surpassed Russell in philosophical achievement. He can handle complex ideas with clarity and buzzes waspishly without actually stinging anyone. He advances paradoxical notions ('the state is a person') in an attempt to transfer to an abstract entity the kind of allegiance once due to a sovereign. Now that the divine right of kings has been repudiated, the state is held to be entitled to its dividends. To insist that it therefore makes serious sense to bless the state with personality smacks of humourless posturing.

Scruton said that he was considering giving up his column in *The Times*, not because he had run out of reproaches to level at the follies of the Left, or the centre, but because he was told that he had done his career prospects no good by his regular descents into the arena. Renford said, 'You don't really want to be a professor, do you?' quite as if such an ambition were either ridiculous or excessive in someone of so contentious a character. Scruton, in wire-rimmed glasses so tight to the flat cheeks that the eyes they served might have been buttons, responded with neither a smile nor a scowl. His main concern, he said, was to get more money. He was considering a sortie to America in its pursuit. Enoch then declared, with a heave of emotion, that he intended to stay and fight in this country until the last breath had left his body, though it was not clear what embattled cause deserved such a sacrifice.

Scruton advertises the virtue of virtues he does not invariably honour. I suppose that the US is not as improbable or improper a destination as Belgravia might be, but can an honest English conservative maintain that emigration to Princeton, or points west, is a voyage to the promised land? Colchis perhaps, unless it's Pella. R.S. looks as if he wants to be a bully, but is also looking for someone to make him cry. His lack of charm and wit, if never of intelligence, makes him the kind of advocate for whom his clients feel small gratitude. He arms his partisans neither with clinching arguments nor with the fun of observing the confusion of his opponents. I like him.

23.12.83. At lunch with John Whitley at the Savile, I almost expected a retraction of the offer that I become the drama critic. It almost came: he had not broached the subject to the editor until the previous day when Neil was about to go skiing with the proprietor in Colorado. He could not make a decision until he had been told what it was. Since John is responsible for the Arts pages, he need not, normally, refer every appointment to the editor. The drama critic, however, occupies a cardinal position. I cannot distinguish between hope and dread. All the cheap reasons for jubilation are in place: if installed, I shall be hebdomadally famous, for no famous reason. I shall have the chance to make enemies quail and take pleasure in not taking advantage of my opportunity to play the dominical pontiff. A young critic can make a reputation for himself by cheeking his betters, but I have no career to fashion. To that extent, the position will be wasted on me. Shall I derive more pleasure from it than I did from my recruitment to the radio critics? During those dull three weeks I was prodigiously bored. I do, however, treasure the elaborate after-you courtesies of Christopher Ricks. Nothing that one survives is wasted.

25.12.83. Walking up the lane in the first blue of Christmas Eve, that time of the afternoon when the sky thickens except for the edges where the orchard branches are thin and barbed, a woman came limping towards me. She said, 'Good evening, Freddie,' with deferential familiarity. I recognised Pat Smith, a local who once wrote me a long personal letter, touching and embarrassing. Frustrated and desperate and anxious for an audience, there was something conceited in her address; she had thought herself worthy of attention. I treated her importunity with farewell courtesy. I had not noticed her to be lame, but the small person who came out of the shadows had so distinct a limp that I asked what she had done to herself. She said that she had an arthritic hip and always had. It sounded as if I should have known. She used an intimate tone which suggested that she had thought about me. She wore a peaked cap, a windcheater, trousers and gumboots. The face was pendulous with excess flesh, eyes keen and cheeky. She said that she didn't want to hurt my feelings but she had seen *Richard's Things* and been upset by my treatment of the working class character in the little scene at the hospital where Kate goes to the wrong place and has a small conversation with the charwoman.

Pat comes from a Dedham family of fifteen children, one of whom died recently of cancer. When the girls (ten of them) reached a certain age, members of the local bourgeoisie used to come to her mother and say 'I need a good scrubber'. Pat's suspicion that I treat working class characters without due respect may not be vain. What do I really know about such people? Pat works in an old people's home. She said that she recently said to one old boy, 'I'm taking you to bed.' 'All right,' he said, 'but I should warn you, I haven't done it for quite a long while.' She said, suddenly, that she herself had been 'celibate' for five years. 'I was tired of being a sex-symbol,' she said, a lame woman in drab clothes, on her way to feed her donkeys.

28.12.83. What Tom Wiseman remembers, above all, of the *Anschluss* is how the Viennese changed overnight from amiability to malice. The concierge who had been so friendly became an instant Nazi, cruel and vindictive. The most telling moment in Tom's play was when the waiter in the café metamorphosed into a brown-shirted lout.

30.12.83. I spent yesterday at TV Centre, trying to persuade myself that I had found the right girl for *He'll See You Now*. Had Jim Cellan Jones not been present, I might have settled for Barbara Rosenblat. She read the script with intelligent attention; she looked better than I expected; and she is disposed to love me, in the professionally useful way that would make it easy for me to direct her. She made nervous jokes as if to prove that she could be the girl I was after. Jim fears that she will be monotonous or insufficiently attractive. I am grateful for actors who are at least possible; he seeks perfection. Barry Dennen, a neat American actor who might well do for Dr Stein, suggested I send the piece to Bette Midler, whom I have never enjoyed but whose cabaret act is commandingly funny. It turns out that she is available and we have sent her the script.

The general mood at Wood Lane seems glum. I have met Terry Coles several times in the loo. He had a lugubrious manner and confessed that, for the first time in a long while, he is not actually engaged in a production.* Keith Williams, forever caressing his whitening prong of a beard, looked in to congratulate Jim on *The Comedy of Errors*. Jim has often shouted at the little man, but he took his compliments on the chin. Among those who came to see us was a bearded, thickset actor and his wife, Thelma Ruby. Beetle and I used to see T.R. in 'intimate revue' in the Fifties. Fleshy and slightly pop-eyed, never a beauty, she acted being attractive well enough, but without the brazen self-promotion that made Fenella Fielding into the veriest instance of a north London vamp. Fenella became a character through will power and big breasts. Her flesh was ivory white; her wanton huskiness promised erotic aptitude. She qualified as a *demi-mondaine* while being a nice Jewish girl who knew very well that she was overdoing it. Thelma never went in for sultry nonsense. She could sing and dance and she was presentable, but never a turn. When Revue vanished from the West End, I assumed that she had betaken herself to family life, but she never, in fact, had a child.

Her husband was professor of drama in Tel Aviv for many years. He was fluent in Hebrew; she was not. She gave the impression of determined fidelity to a man who had always been happier than his wife. They have retired to England, somewhat defeated. Had they been really happy in Israel, would they not have stayed there? They were friends with Meyer Levin, a Chicagoan who became a fervent Zionist. He not only wrote *Compulsion* but also discovered the diary of Anne Frank. He acquired the dramatic rights and wrote an excellent play based on the diary. When it went into rehearsal, the producers deemed it unsuitable for an American audience. The father, Otto Frank, was a party to bringing in the Hacketts and Lillian Hellman. Levin became obsessed with the injustice of his treatment and took them all to court. He was awarded considerable damages, since it was decided that his script had indeed been the foundation of the Broadway hit, but part of the settlement stipulated that, by taking the damages, he forfeited the rights in his own original work, so far as the professional stage was concerned.

---

* Terry Coles was scheduled to produce *Oxbridge Blues*, but when he was shocked by the script of *Private Views*, I decided that I could not work with him. *Private Views* was not, in fact, included in the series and has yet to be filmed. I wrote a novella of the same name which was published in 2014.

Levin continued to dream of staging his own version. Thelma's husband enabled him to do so by mounting an amateur production in Tel Aviv. A general in the Israeli Air Force came with some of his officers. The evening was a triumph. '*Nu?*' said the professor. '*Nu,*' replied the general, in manly tears. It was agreed that the production should tour military bases. It was, everyone said, ten times better than the saccharine Broadway show. Otto Frank heard what was going on and prevailed on the Israeli authorities to scotch the project. Levin, having written so famously about compulsion, was unable to abate his own compulsive rage. He was inhibited from ever writing anything else and died broken by an injustice which deprived him of his own personality. The professor said he had been very close to Levin. Thelma seemed more reserved. Perhaps she had loved him.

Sidney Gampell, head of Reuters' London bureau, was a name my father used to conjure with. His self-esteem earned C.M.R.'s amused affection. S.G.'s son, Michael, was at Charterhouse with me, a year my junior; a prematurely middle-aged schoolboy, bespectacled and hirsute. Like a rare and intelligent monkey, he was clever but not exceptional. I doubt that we ever spoke. His younger brother was killed in an accident when he was sixteen. Michael became an extremely capable solicitor and the protector of the family trust. He married and had three children. Not long ago, he was discovered to have embezzled half a million from his clients as well as the entire family trust fund. He was indicted and sent for trial.

His children were all adolescent. A daughter was about to enter UCH as a physiotherapy student; a son was at Charterhouse, a younger daughter at St Paul's. UCH arranged for a grant; Charterhouse gave the boy a double scholarship. When the trial was due, the boy asked for leave to go and see his father. His housemaster agreed and took him to the place himself and stayed all day and brought him back afterwards. St Paul's refused to help in any way. The wife, who was forty-eight, had had no inkling of the trouble to come. She had never had to work. They had lived a sumptuous life in west Sussex. After Michael was convicted, she found a job, but has no hope of a pension or of any financial support in old age. Sidney is unable to lift his head. Bluster gone, he is waiting for oblivion.

Billy Wilder: 'You can always tell when you are on the skids in this town: nobody asks you to be a pallbearer any more.' While trying to pull the cork of a bottle he was opening for us and Stanley Donen, Billy said: 'See that? Forty years of masturbation and I still don't have a muscle in my hand.' He told us that when stuck on how to proceed, he asks himself 'What would Lubitsch have done?'

2.1.84. The Summerskills elected to spend New Year's Eve with us. We have a relationship of distant intimacy. They became our neighbours on Ios by chance. Mimi is admirable and absurd; in her indefatigable snobbery, she drops names as a mad housewife drops plates. Vanity leads her to comb the world for La Follette relics; she will cross the Atlantic to salute the latest achievement of her clan. There is co-opting generosity in her embrace, undeniable appeal in the large, slightly crazed eyes. She loves to give, and receive, hospitality.

The Greek Left has been bemused by the failure of the Pasok government to fulfil expectations. After thought, the solution has been found: the CIA is responsible for the imposition of Andreas Papandreou on an unsuspecting populace. The absurdity is rendered plausible by the undoubted interference of the American embassy during the Colonels' regime. The Greeks have been duped and manipulated for so long that paranoia is a national condition. The Summerskills get their information mainly from the rich parents of students at Athens College, on whose benefactions it and John's salary as president depend. He remains alien to Greek (and European) culture, like some highly intelligent hick.

Levin and Pinter supply the two poles of English Jewish alienation. The former renders his utterances non-kosher by a protracted parody of Augustan mandarin; Pinter's brevity inhabits a solipsist's ghetto in which no one else has any standing. He disqualifies variant readings, even of what is not said. Levin, on the other hand, delivers a *sostenuto* flow, with so little prospect of a full stop, that interruption becomes Philistine. Pinter's collage assimilates all dialogue to slogans and cuttings. His art seems to be based on overhearing the crossed lines of other people, but it is a conceited confection which demands invariable presentation.

Levin appears to belong to the public world. Where is the journalist without his readers? Bernard is reticent about sex, not only because he is strikingly unstriking, but also because it is an activity, like sport, that demands non-verbal competence. He resembles a defendant who has been asked, by a captious court, whether he has anything to say before sentence is passed. He then talks for the rest of his life. There is superb servility in Levin's archaic tone, with its invocation of 'my masters'. His first public persona was the loudly clownish Taper; his *Spectator* column was surmounted with cap and bells. Recently he has been attacked both by Russell Davies, not unkindly, and by Julian (*né* Alphonse) Symons. The latter makes no overt play with Bernard's Semitic origins, but his attack concentrates on style and vocabulary (cf. Karl Kraus on *mauscheln*).

An outsider of unattractive appearance, Levin is Catullus's 'little bugger who certainly knows how to talk'. He was the first post-war journalist to mock the parliamentary grandees whose lictors rendered them all but inviolate. His derision lacked caution, but it was never reckless; his prose stood taller than he did; its ironies had a parodic gravity not often evident in the House. He was an arriviste who had travelled a long way to be disappointed by the quality of the party he has chosen to crash. Verbosity and humour furnished a one-man double act; the commentator usurped the stage. The freedom crucial to him is that of hearing the sound of his own voice. He has substituted *loquor* for *cogito* in Descartes' proof that he exists.

In the centuries when man believed that God knew our every action, no one felt inconvenienced by His ubiquity. Now that other men are able to keep one eye on our activities, we are less easy. Having reorganised the system of surveillance, we have replaced theology with secular programmes. The Iranians are right: the US and Russia are the enemies of God; they have nationalised Him.

Pristine Christianity asserted the paramount significance of the individual's play for salvation. The traces of its anti-social origins can be seen in the egotism which placed belief above allegiance. However unified and communitarian Christians may have chosen to appear, they were always a band of individuals seeking to save their own souls in the hope of eternal bliss. The Moslem is pitched halfway between Jew and Christian in this regard. If Christians claimed to be a band of brothers, there was a limit to their fraternity: each individual was responsible for his or her salvation. There was always the promise of appeal from earthly decisions to a higher court. The outcast could be nearer to God than the Pope. The elimination of individual ambition, in the socialist ethos, aims to return humanity to the world in which community is the prime unit. Man without God becomes irretrievably political.

5.1.84. I guessed that I was going to London for no good reason and I was right. The actress who was supposed to have an excellent New York accent did not even have an excellent London accent. She had been in *Widows*, the feminist answer to the underworld and had the unwashed allure of a slightly fresher Verity Lambert. We are now waiting for a reaction from Bette Midler whose nod will supposedly turn my little play into an event, though I am not sure it will still be a play. The fee is equivalent, for her, of what she would get for a month in the salt mines; but she might care to leave NY for a week or two. Since I shall be handling TV cameras as well as a difficult lady for the first time, I shall quake and try not to show it. I am so far from being a capable schemer that I know neither what will happen nor what I should like to happen. It is likely that I shall become the *Sunday Times* drama critic and that Ms Midler will not do my piece. The reverse is also likely.

Jim C.J. took against Barbara Rosenblat. Trying to amuse and audition at the same time, she was full of Jewish quips that did not greatly amuse. I still thought she came through the reading remarkably well. She is the only one of the many females who have sat in the little office whose delivery of my lines suggested that she understood them. No other actress so far has come within a mile of passable. Jim has a breadth of experience to which I defer. He worked for a whole season with Judi Dench, whose physical propinquity would put me off the food at Bocuse. I suspect that negotiations with Midler will break down and I shall be committed to Ms Rosenblat. For the rest, I prevailed on Don Hongray to rethink the set for the restaurant scene. Now we have some light and shade and variety of height and colouring. He is keen but knows nothing of the nuances of American city life.

The Gag Reel. When I was in LA Gene Taft showed me a cache of footage in Bob Evans's screening room. Bob's house was off Benedict Canyon. With brown awnings over the windows and front door, it had the look of the kind of disreputable and expensive restaurant where they choose not to display a menu outside. The interior was full of expensive gear that failed to alleviate the impression that it had been gutted by removals men who left behind only those items without any trace of personality. The furniture is grouped as if chairs and couches had been invited to chat among themselves. In this hotel for one, there is no residue of dialogue, no patina of lived life. The strewn, unopened magazines are there because the studio which Bob left many months ago is probably still supplying the literature which replaces books. Bob was out of town, setting up the film which he was supposed to direct but which is, in fact, to be shot by Francis Coppola, the writer commissioned at the last moment. Evans presumes himself capable of all the creative activities, but neither his script nor his directorial ideas excited investors. He is one of the many executives who have assumed the mantle of Thalberg without having the build for it.

Gene Taft and I sat through the two shot-for-shot similar versions of *An Affair to Remember* for which I had undertaken to furnish a modern triplet. Gene then had the 'projjie' (Stanley Donen's term for projectionist) screen the gag reel shot by J.R.S. on the set of *Marathon Man*, the shocker with which Bob Evans claimed to have re-established John's commercial credibility after the *échec d'estime* of *The Day of the Locust*, which could never be called 'the day of the low-cost'. While shooting *Marathon Man*, Dustin and Schles reached the point of not speaking except when necessity demanded. John had forbidden Dustin to see the rushes and was paid out with every possible truculence. The gag reel made Bob the scapegoat. Dustin's imitation was merciless: shifty energy, facile slyness, it was all there. He also mimicked the scene in the movie in which the mad dentist (Larry Olivier) drills him to agony in order to extract some forgettable secret. In the gag reel, it is his false penis – the kind of plastic dildo with which John would like to believe that all middle-aged ladies amuse themselves before saying their prayers – which the demon castrator attacks. The whole movie is parodied mercilessly by its highly paid actors and by John, as though they had been obliged by some artistic accountant to admit that they had invested their talent with scandalous lack of scruple. It is typical of Bob's charm (and vanity) that the footage making a fool of him was in a privileged place in his screening room. Since Bob is obsessed with his sun-tan, Dustin portrayed him as a toasted, twitching neurotic. In reality, Bob suffers from a chronic infection of the gums and opens his mouth carefully, to avoid having his teeth too visible.

7.1.84. I had intended to spend another day on the script of *Love Life*, but the whole morning was trivial with the telephone. Doll complained at the non-arrival of the post, quite as if she had been panting to type on a day when, to my annoyance, she had arranged to take her grand-daughters to the pantomime. She has worked for me, loyally and efficiently, for sixteen years and I have never felt that she liked any of the work she so neatly reproduces.

After that came the police. They had already called to inform me that a stolen Mercedes in Hastings carried the same number plate as our red 280SL. Thieves use plates that match the genuine article so that if a computer check is run on a stolen vehicle it seems to establish that the plates are appropriate to it. I guessed that the car's sojourn at the Crawley garage, where it was treated for the serious injuries incurred on our way to Glyndebourne, had given Sussex copyists their opportunity. The sergeant implied that there might be some sinister connection, if not conspiracy. Self-importance and curiosity are the badges of the CID. Had he really suspected that we were implicated, he would have arrived without warning.

Steve Kenis had asked me the previous evening whether Susan

Sarandon was a good idea for Natty. I could not get hold of Jim and took it on myself to say yes. Susan was in London until the weekend and could read the script and decide right away. Steve called after the cops to say that Susan wanted to do it. Jim was unreproachful and we have agreed to cast her, an excellent bird in the hand.

We met at the William Morris office. She was an unassuming lady who could not possibly be the Susan Sarandon I had admired in *Atlantic City*. Could this be the woman for whom Louis Malle left Alexandra? She told us that she had recently been robbed of all her latest fortune as a result of trusting an investment adviser who put her into oil, supermarkets and trouble. As soon as you get swindled of all your money, the IRS puts in a demand for all the tax on the money you no longer have. She is not Jewish and she is not a comedienne, although she has done song and dance. Getting her a work permit from British Equity is the sole remaining problem. She had one before and should get one again. It is a mildly exciting prospect to direct a real talent, if not quite a manifest star. I liked her; she is confident, nervous, self-assured, attractive and a little plain. She will have to *act* rather than just be Natalie C.

I went from our happy encounter to Victoria to entrain for Westgate-on-Sea to take part in *Any Questions?* in a rest-home for the blind. I sat for an hour and a half as the train went through unfamiliar places where thousands of commuters live. I alighted at the empty station. No taxis waited. I went into the local Social Club, a large bar in a hall where men smoked and would later play snooker and tug one-armed bandits, and was directed to the Ivyside Hotel, on sea road, a ten-minute walk past boarding houses and a private school where, behind beaded curtains, two shadows were playing, or sparring, with sparklers.

The hotel wore a dented AA sign, like a previous conviction. It was faced with a great deal of sea-viewing glass. I followed Jean Rook with a blind man into the bar where Carole Stone, returned to Bristol duties, gave me a kiss. She has frizzed her hair and cinched her waist. The previous producer had been a militant feminist, a left-winger and very ugly. Carole was Venus *rediviva* by comparison. Joan Ruddock appeared candid, fresh-faced and liable to be competent. She had no fear of speaking, but she did have a fear of not speaking. Her earnestness was untempered by humour or modesty. She had to unfold all her ideas, on every topic, with unmeasured profligacy. She had as much to say about the mouse as about the mountain.

Chalfont was in his element: shallow water. Having become a personality by virtue of being a defence and disarmament expert (he told us that there are no cruise missiles at Greenham Common), Alun Gwynne-Jones was taken into government by Wilson and made a Lord so that he could bring peace to the nations to whom the Tories had denied it. He showed his gratitude by blackguarding the party that gave him his petty eminence. He has the quick literacy of those who have read many authors and met more. It pleased him to parade that he had served in the same regiment as Anthony Powell, the least elegant of elegant writers, and that he recognised most of the characters in his novels, although they had been transmuted by Powell's small art. He put his sentences together with the facility of a journalist making sure that his copy was palatable. Like many converts, he has made turning his coat into a particularly chic kind of tailoring. Having spent his journalistic life assessing forces over which he exercises no control, he conducts himself like a big wheel when, in fact, he is a fifth one. He conveys smug resentment; he has achieved eminence but, in his own view, deserves to be much more important. Likeable and civil, you sensed the shortness of his fuse.

12.1.84. Richard Gregson is a new father and an older man. His face is thicker and ruddier, the white hair, once paradoxical, now looks appropriate. His sense of humour, alive in the pouched eyes, like a merry fire in a landlady's grate, promises that he will always have a kind of naughty independence. His affection depends on his capacity to be irresponsible. He brought a bottle of champagne and some good stories. He has been in LA, seeing R.J. about a thriller pilot which he has written and R.J. is to produce. R.J. is number one in the *Cue* ratings, although he confesses, and few will challenge, that he is not really an actor at all; he is a salesman. In this he has something in common with Warren. Each is a narcissist to whom his own reflection is not quite a sufficient, though certainly a favourite, companion. Without Warren's appetite for artistic recognition, R.J. has derived fame and fortune from a show which no one except anonymous millions ever admit to watching. *Hart to Hart* concerns a millionaire and his wife who are so bored by affluence that they operate as private investigators; complacency needs the spice of danger.

R.J. is now very rich, on account both of his personal earnings and of his and Natalie's angelic investments. Members of the Hollywood inner-group for many years, they put their money in copper-bottomed shows, without taking any interest in more elegant, but risky ventures. They were square and they squared their cash. R.J. stands to make five million dollars on each new series of *Hart to Hart*. He supervises the production with unblinking care. When he discovered that the producers had cheated him of $1.8m, he not only secured immediate payment, he also made sure that an extra $100,000 was added to the budget of each new show in order to maintain the quality of the product. It usually deteriorates when a proven success reaches its latter days.

Richard and Natalie's daughter Natasha now lives with R.J. Richard asked her why he continues to work so hard, even on marginal things, neither commerce nor art, such as Clive Donner's *To Catch a King*.* 'He does it', she said, 'because when he is working, everyone has to look after him, and when he's at home he has to look after everyone else.'

In her London heyday, Georgia shared a Mews house with Peter O'Toole, Gareth and Stanley Mann. The last-named might be the twin of one of those lacquered suit-stands which used to be supplied by fancy hotels. O'Toole was more lively, even when drunk. R.G. recalls an occasion when Peter vomited all over the carpet. Georgia ordered him out of the house, even though it was pelting with rain, and out he went. There was a dustbin by the front door which became animated when they opened it some time later. O'T. had been huddled in it during the whole period since his exit and now craved return.

Not long ago Gareth took Paula Weinstein to the Dome for dinner, the in-place at the time. *Le tout* Beverly Hills was mirrored in the fancy décor. When G. and Paula entered, he saw Georgia at a table with Marty Feldman, near the door. He asked for a table at the very back of the restaurant. He was about to start his soup when Georgia appeared suddenly and loudly at his table. 'You homosexual prick! Who's this Lesbian bitch?' These civilities were the prelude to further endearments. The in-crowd ceased their separate confabulations in order to enjoy the diatribe. It culminated in Georgia tipping Gareth's hot soup into his lap before retreating to her swivel-eyed companion. Waiters administered first aid and a second dose of soup to Gareth and everyone tried to resume suitable gourmet conversations.

Gareth had reached his second course when Georgia returned for another take. It was less attractive to tilt *vitello tonnato* into Gareth's hot lap so – after another cascade of epithets – she poured his wine over his carefully coiffed blonde and balding head. His hair descended in lank streaks, dripping Chianti tears on his gaunt cheeks. Gareth leapt to his feet and said that he would kill the fucking bitch. Georgia gathered that she might have gone too far. She fled, pursued by the man who had entered on marriage, at the same time as their celebration of Jonathan's

---

* About a Nazi plot to kidnap the Duke of Windsor, played by John Standing. In fact, they would have had only to send him an invitation to be treated like a king.

seventh birthday, with a declaration of the maturity of their connection. He cornered her behind Feldman and told them that they had better get out of the restaurant *at once*. The vocal italics were effective; off they went. Gareth turned to go back to his place, in the large silence, and realised that he had to parade through the fancy diners with a huge red crotch and liberally irrigated head and shoulders. He squelched to his table and set about the delicate task of selecting a dessert from the trolley.

16.1.84. The Cape party is the occasion on which Tom Maschler likes to think that he repays, at a single throw, all the hospitality he has received or solicited during the previous year. On that particular November or December evening, he is open-handed and eager to have pleased. He believes the party to be a great event for which celebrities cancel their holidays and postpone their elopements. The building is crammed with hard-boiled egos. Since there is no agency for introductions, the company fractures into exclusive segments. I had one casual chat, with Bel Mooney, who had been my nearish neighbour at the Society of Bookmen dinner at which Steiner electrified the troops and leavened the droops. She is married to Jonathan Dimbleby. She told me that he was so struck by my story *The Day Franco Came* that he had copies made from its printing in *The Fiction Magazine* and distributed them to all the people involved in making a documentary about fascist Spain. I was flattered by this unglamorous tribute, but would it have hurt Master D. to buy his people a copy each of the struggling magazine?

At Anne Becher's on Thursday, I heard why Susie Kennaway had not been at the Cape thrash. *The Kennaway Papers* were never intended to be a book. Susie compiled the dossier in the hope that a film might be made of it. A friend happened to show it to Tom Maschler, who spotted the possibility of a scandalous success. He persuaded Susie, with no great difficulty I imagine, to add more revelations and swept her misgivings aside with the routine operator's slogan, 'Trust me.' She trusted him; and all seemed to go well. Godfrey Smith, an old Oxford pal of both Susie and James, was easily persuaded to serialise the book in the *Sunday Times*. Susie was invited to be in on the editing of text and pictures. In depicting her triangular conjugal drama, she had taken trouble to conceal the identity of her lover, except from the knowing.

When Godders failed to call her, as he had promised, in order to supervise the set-up, she called him. He seemed surprised to hear from her. 'You're too busy to come in,' he said, 'Tom told me.' She said that she was *not* too busy, but G. Smith insisted that she was. When her presence proved that she had nothing better to do, she found that the extracts had been arranged under photographs of Le Carré, whose name was not mentioned in her manuscript. Why was she so eager to protect him? *The Naïve and Sentimental Lover* infuriated her with its inept vulgarity, though Cornwell may have meant it as an abject tribute. She injuncted the *ST* from publication of her book. Tom has not spoken to her since.

Susie has dyed her hair Naples yellow. Now married to an accountant, she carries something of the allure of the *aventurière*. She keeps James's flame remarkably alive. She maintains that she had nothing to do with the recent biography, but read it closely and failed to see him in it. I remember most clearly from her book that six-second orgasm when James finally returned to her bed. It has the shameful conviction of absolute honesty. There is something discontinuous between sexual pleasure and all other pleasures that makes its memory as vivid as a crime. Some women are amazed by desire and its satisfaction.

Even as Susie tells all, there is becoming reticence in her. Yet everyone is made aware that she is a widow, and whose. Having run a restaurant for a while, she came to prepare curries for the Weech Road guests. Anne was wearing a pinkish dress that had belonged to Tony's mother in India, a spray of sequinned flowers over the left breast. Her friends rallied with unforced gallantry to drink her gin. I sat forever talking to the clergyman husband of Jean Storey, a briefly famous Cambridge actress. They live in St Alban's and he may well be a bishop one day. Why else did he tell me that he had no desire to be one?

28.1.84. I am sitting in LHR at half past nine on a Saturday night, doing something I have never done before, waiting for a woman who is not Beetle to come off an aeroplane. I was certain last week that I was to be deprived of Susan Sarandon because of the dog-in-the-manger exclusivity of Equity, with whose larky General Secretary I sat at dinner in the Guildhall. Jim Cellan Jones' combative determination took him where no man often goes, over the union's heads to the DOE. They promised a quick decision, found that everyone had gone for the weekend and were embarrassed into giving us a winking OK. Her deal was confirmed on the last day allowed by the William Morris agency, which just happens to represent all the interested parties.

I have disappointed Barbara Rosenblat, who seemed to me rather good. Jim thought otherwise. She took it in weary good part. Now she has changed her style to match her more compact self. She sings at *thés dansants* and at the Ritz. I suppose that Sarandon will be in a different class; for the sake of the show and my conscience, I hope so. I am not used to making decisions that wound other people. As a director, hiring and firing is part of a game in which, one has to believe, people are used to taking knocks.

On Wednesday I had a meeting with John Peter, Robert Hewison and John Whitley to settle the arrangements whereby I should take over as the *ST* drama critic. I have yet to advise them that I cannot take the job. I have realised, at the last minute, that I do not really want to sit in the theatre five nights a week in order to earn six hundred pounds and the opportunity to thumb my nose at Claire Tomalin. Last night, at the Cambridge Union, I proposed the motion 'That this house rejects the Glittering Prizes'. I did not announce that I was about to reject one of them, but I am.

Louise will never allow Michael Holroyd to take part in one of her programmes again. He once agreed to appear and then, during a live broadcast, did not say a single word.

8.3.84. Weeks have passed without an entry here. Ms Sarandon did indeed arrive and my devotion to her purloined all my time. She came on like an intelligent woman who happened to be an actress, establishing that she was very politically involved. Even though it had cost her the opportunity of being escorted by Calvin Klein, she could imagine no greater honour than to be unwelcome at the Reagan White House. She has had to wear spectacles ever since appearing in *Extremities*, a play in which she was handcuffed to a bed, raped and also very ill-used. Now in her mid-thirties, she went to Catholic college in DC. The oldest of nine children, she is amused and a little bemused by the recent parting of her prolific parents. Her youngest brother is sixteen. She has been into just about everything; she has given up drugs because they make her sick, not because they do you harm. She doesn't drink either; but she does take all kinds of medication and produces new symptoms daily.

Probably jet-lagged, she seemed scarcely ever to emerge from some critical condition or other. She was afraid that she did not look her best and I am afraid that she was right. There was, however, a lot of cleverness in her performance. She worked quite hard, but not quite hard enough. I am not sure whether I handled her skilfully, since we had no outbursts of temper or temperament, or whether she played me skilfully and so avoided being pressed to do better. Making no effort to be agreeable, she talked too much about all the offers she was getting to appear naked in unsuitable films or in a space suit in unappetising TV series. When someone asked her why she was so butch, she replied that if she was masculine, she was also gay. Even when she is getting what she wants, she is not sure that she really wants it. If she thanks you for something, a meal or a book, you suspect you have made a mistake giving it to her. I felt that I alone was pedalling our tandem uphill. Yet she showed no signs of awareness of my lack of directorial experience.

Susan was staying in the Bywater street house of Rupert Everett, a young actor who recently made a name for himself in *Another Country*, the Julian Mitchell play of which I greatly enjoyed the first act and did not stay through the second. Everett opened in *The White Devil* at Greenwich during our rehearsal period and was cruelly mauled by James Fenton, whom I am delighted not to be replacing in the *Sunday Times*. Directing is all-consuming but rarely all-demanding. The director has all the responsibility and often claims most of the credit, but he depends greatly on others. He manages events, but he cannot control them. He rarely takes decisions of consequence without consulting others. The job is more diplomatic than artistic. Bill Goldman was astonished by my silly ambition when I confessed it to him many years ago.

It has been a great pleasure, nonetheless, to be the master of how a scene plays. Susan may have been in regular need of hot drinks and vitamin C (I was prudent enough to buy her four tubes of Redoxon after the first day of rehearsal), but she was always on time, except when her taxi failed to circumvent an accident. She was willing to entertain whatever suggestions were made. A star without ever having been an ordinary actress, she began her career by standing in at an audition, reading for her ex-husband, and was taken on at the same time.

Fantasies of closeness were soon dissipated. She had no wish to be friends. She had liked the script but she had no free time for its author or his family. None of our invitations was accepted. She was excited at having spent an evening with 'Marilyn', the latest transvestite from the video world. She was especially enchanted by the wisp of beard on 'her' chin. Physically, Susan is a svelte wreck; she suffers from sciatica and neuralgia. Her shoulders slope as if pulled down by two heavy buckets. She has very little humour; all my jokes became lemons. Even Jo Janni did not amuse her. Yet she liked to give the impression of being a lively young person, rebellious, unpredictable, not to be relied on for decorum. She was toying maturely with going to Nicaragua, probably with Julie Christie, to draw attention, with humanitarian gestures, to the iniquity of US foreign policy. Her invasion of Central America made sense only if she was a star of sufficient twinkle to make the horoscopes alter their courses. She needed, and did not wish to need, reassurance on that score. There was always something truculent about her.

She had been married at twenty by her own decision. Her mother would not speak to her for three years afterwards, although she had been very close to her and her main helper in raising the family. When the marriage broke up, Susan played the wounded party, though she may well have fired her share of shots. Christopher brought his new lady to the apartment to select what they wanted. Madam failed to covet anything, even among the smallest and rarest articles. Susan found herself forcing precious belongings onto the indifferent visitors in order to prove that her taste was not as bad as all that.

If there is something clownish about the lady, she prevents one from laughing by her inability to be at ease with herself. What might amuse turns out to be disquieting. Her pride in her independence was stained with misgivings. She imitates the prowl of the cat, but when she walks by herself, you fear she will turn her ankle. If she was never grand, she never bought anyone a drink or even a cup of coffee. Did I not like her? I did not dislike her. She did a good, quick job. She never thought it worth the trouble to unpack her bags; she was more concerned with the ones under her eyes. She has an unlikely physique for a movie star: pop eyes, bodiless red hair, disjointed body, smileless brow. Yet she plays beautiful, successfully. The mouth is very pretty, mobile, sensual and articulate; and she has those big breasts. She may have little humour, but she can deliver a line very cleverly, in a way that seems to lack guile; she came out with my jokes as if she has just thought them up and was not trying in the least to be funny. What could have been a sketch became something of pathetic delicacy. She never patronised or condescended to the work, even though she could have been making a thousand times as much per week. When the piece was done, she did not stay for the party. She took hypochondriac's licence to go home to bed. I inscribed a copy of *Richard's Things* to her and mentioned what a disappointing job Liv Ullman had done. Susan said that we could do a remake, set in the US. I never heard from her again.*

Barry Dennen, the best of second fiddles, told me how someone asked of a certain actor (perhaps himself) 'Is he possibly a home-owner?'†

Angela's happiest memories are of working for Keith Waterhouse and Willis Hall; 'Keese and Villis', Jo Janni called them. On one occasion, in the early sixties, mortified by an excess of cash, the northern duo

---

* She received the annual (Cable TV) Ace Award for Best Actress for her performance in *He'll See You Now*. My script won the award for Best Screenplay. It got lost in the mail.

† As a young man, Barry Dennen lived for a year with Barbra Streisand. He later came out as gay.

collected £1000 in pound notes from the bank and flung them into Bond Street from their fifth-floor window. They had been very poor in their childhood, the only two pupils in their school who had to apply for the special 'shoe grant'. The mortification was so enduring that Willis used to send Angela to buy his shoes. He associated fittings with the shame of having to hand in a chit to the shopkeeper. She would take the outline of his feet to Dolcis and they supplied approximate sizes. Willis accepted whatever she brought back. While he and Keith were distributing cash to the toilers of Bond Street, A. realised that she was being paid eight pounds a week and might as well profit from the shower of largess. She went down and gathered some of the fruit where it had fallen. Most people ignored the notes, either imagining them false or thinking singles not worth bending down for.

Although Willis now lives in the North and Keith in London, they write alternate episodes of *Wurzel Gummidge*. Angela smiles as she confesses that she came from Golder's Green. Her father was protective, if not possessive. One night, when he discovered that she had been seeing B.M., still technically a married man, he slapped her. She ran out of the house and took herself to the office. Where else could she go? She let herself in and was startled by a voice asking who was there. Albert Finney had just parted from Jane Wenham and had sought shelter *chez* fellow working-class northerners. A. and Albie talked all night and had fun making breakfast.

7.3.84. Wengen. We stayed in a hotel rather remote from the slopes but of efficient luxury for the fairly very rich. When we skied on the first morning, we lost our way and ended at Grund, whence we took a train to return to Wengen. At Kleine Scheidegg we found that Sarah's skis were not in the little tender where we had stowed them. After a mere two hours' exercise, she had been robbed, it seemed. We returned, disgruntled, for outdoor lunch at the hotel. A party of English-speakers were waiting for their ordered food in the sunshine. They spoke in the rather loud, cultivated tones of those with money in their accents. One man was particularly noticeable, rather red-faced, unlined, with staring brown eyes, a Harpo mop of greying curly hair, argent in the dazzle of snow and ice. He spoke clearly and resonantly; he was used to being listened to. He looked at us with undisguised but not patronising assurance. When our food came before theirs, I made a deprecating speech, hoping that we had not purloined their dishes.

After Stee and I had gone off to ski (Sarah could not do so until the following day, when her skis were returned to her), Beetle told us that the noticeable man said, in a voice meant for export, 'He wrote rather a good novel when he was younger.' He then looked at Beetle with a look that might have been insolent, unless it was inquiring. Was he talking about me? Probably, but not certainly. I saw the same people at the swimming pool that evening. They had locked themselves out of the sauna. We exchanged courtesies.

Last night we went to Bryan Marber's fiftieth birthday dinner; fifty-four guests at the Santa Croce restaurant where Sarah and I had a lousy meal with Denys Gueroult. Bryan's brother Stanley made the obligatory speech. He told the story about the new rabbi at the funeral prayers of a man he had not known personally. He calls on one of the mourners to say something in praise of the departed. Although he repeats the appeal every night of the *shiveh*, no one volunteers. On the final night, the rabbi insists that there has to be something to be said in favour of the dead man. A reluctant figure rises at the back of the room, shuffles his feet and announces, 'His brother... was *worse*' (pronounce 'voice').

11.3.84. Roy Yglesias was once ranked tenth in British squash and still plays agile tennis at the age of sixty-nine. Despite his Hispanic style, he is egregiously English, a nice man who seems to love his wife (whom he often mentions) and for whom life is an enjoyable, unfinished journey. He was made chairman of Longman's, apparently to his surprise, and has written a number of textbooks which keep him comfortable with royalties. Although he twits Social Democrats on their 'treachery', he is a member of the Labour party more out of benevolence than ideological fervour. A socialist much possessed by the loss of his family fortune, he often mentions his great-grandmother who unwisely married a man much younger than herself. He absconded to South Africa with all her money. In the days before the Married Woman's Property Act, there was nothing to be done. His grandfather persuaded the scoundrel to give his wife an annuity. Roy owns a cottage in Sussex which he lets for the summer. It was rented recently, through an advertisement, to some people from Pretoria. They turned out to be direct descendants of the fortune-hunter who ruined Roy's family.

15.3.84. Dinner at Tom Maschler's with Philip Roth. He has become elongated and leathery in appearance; high sloping forehead above a pronged, haughty but plebeian nose. The fingers are long but scarcely 'sensitive', more appropriate to a mechanic or a dentist than to an artist. He is torn between clownishness and downishness. He can indeed be funny, but he would not have you forget that he is clever. He may not strut, but he alludes to his rivals with a certain disdain. He showed us how Norman Mailer took the chief reviewer of the *New York Times* in a headlock and asked him how he was, as if there was a good chance that he might not be 'just fine' for all that long. Mailer has an intemperate insolence which escapes the taint of Jewish self-doubt with which P.R. is so preoccupied. Philip has the novelist's rare and important capacity to seem to be experiencing everything for the first time, yet he is also heavy with the sense of being prevented from being himself by the claims of a clan which he can neither embrace nor renounce. He is an alienated Jew who keeps going back – cannot ever really leave – where he came from: Newark, N.J., a Bethlehem with room at its Ramada Inn. He seeks constantly to disqualify himself from being its favourite son and is vexed by its greedy familiarities: instead of ticker-tape, they pelt him with affectionate abuse. Zeal for being a pariah makes him an outcast, though he would like to be taken for a regular American with serious artistic credentials and political savvy.

Sex dominates his consciousness; images of scandal and outrage keep intruding. He dreamed recently of visiting a man in hospital who had had his genitals transplanted so that they emerged from the centre of his breastbone. Did he announce this grotesquerie because it was just the sort of thing Philip Roth would produce? When he sought an explanation, there was no Tiresias on hand. I suggested that the author of *The Breast* had made an analogy which Susan Sontag advanced when she claimed, in the French style, that a woman's breasts (nipples?) were a kind of (guess!) penis. Philip was not interested. He preferred to be amazed and abashed by the cryptic shamelessness of his own creative mechanism.

He was labouring under the lash of a cruel review by Martin Amis, who has been savaging his work for several years. He was particularly and naively pained by the fact that he had met and got on well with the little chap. He did not accept that it might just be that M.A. didn't like the new work (I cannot say that I do). Philip's success has crowned him with uneasy hauteur. Can it merit a trilogy to itemise the anguish which follows pissing on your own doorstep? The body appals, affronts and fascinates him. He itches with voluptuous solicitations. We discussed dreams in which the subject is either naked or half-naked and everyone else dressed. He denied having such dreams any more but was conscious that they were not erotic. My easy suggestion was that they came from childhood when the only naked person in the world seemed to be oneself. The odd status of the first person has something to do with an inescapable sense of one's own vulnerability; everybody else, discreetly armoured, is immune to nudity's embarrassments.

Roth said that he did not keep a notebook, although he has tried from time to time. He could never be sure for what audience he was writing it. There is aggrieved bafflement in his posture to the world. He hardly knows to what constituency he is addressing his life. The writing of books gives him membership in Literature, but the autobiographical mode makes self-revelation his principal subject. He is too busy re-inventing himself to have time for larger creations. He seems to fear that if he loses sight of himself he may not find himself again in the crowd. Isn't 'Our Crowd' one of his derisive titles? He wants to be the exception; but he is subject to the rule: who can be exceptional without it? Less rebel than *nebbish*, P. is decked with graduate school and lecturing credentials; yet despair is his abiding condition, unless it's his consolation.

Claire, who is amiable but not all that bright, neither sighed nor laughed at Philip's revelations. She has too long a personal knowledge of male sexuality to be distressed or diverted by its extravagance. Relaxed and poised, she is his mistress, never his keeper. A Persephone who does not relish the New England Hades, she does not accompany him to Connecticut for his six months there. He treats her with the not quite possessive presumption of the celebrity who can take a beauty for granted. Emancipated from responsibility, he can scoff the fruit but need not cherish the tree.

Fay cooked a deceptively classy meal. One had the impression of being in the hands of an expert and then realised that the potatoes were not cooked, the salad not washed, dessert non-existent. It was a meal more presented than prepared. Fay was a ghost at her own table; having made a bold declaration of independence, she did her duty, with inexpensive ingredients; so there. She writes a pertinacious column in the *Evening Standard*, bubbling with culinary sauce, but when she talks at table she delivers no verbal seasoning whatever. She speaks in the thin, resigned tones of a woman whom no one addresses because she is worth listening to. Courtesy, never appetite, impels one to turn to her.

16.3.84. To get everything wrong is a kind of inverted omniscience.

We had the idea, based on her air of Peter Panic youthfulness, that Miranda Pinto must live her own life and have had several affairs, not least with Jimmy Jenks, Frank Pinto's best friend. In truth, she is no free-ranging chick. She has neither a joint bank-account with her rich husband nor even a credit card or a single charge account at any store. She had one thousand pounds when she married F., twenty-one years ago, and she now has four hundred pounds. When she said that there had to be 'something wrong somewhere', he said only, it had 'worked'. By keeping her a slave, he had made sure that she could never leave him. Why would a pretty women endure such indignities? Can she derive some kind of pleasure from them? The experience she has most enjoyed is, she said, breast-feeding. Her loins may have let her down, but her nipples have not. She looks good at forty-three or forty-four, if one does not look closely; she has been advised to smile, though her heart be breaking.

Frank Pinto is Narcissus with a puddle before him. He seems to be able to laugh at himself, but despair is always there. If he is without his pills for twenty-four hours, he becomes lachrymose. Miranda is the victim who must succour and shore up her persecutor. The self-righteous paranoid has no sense of what he might be doing wrong. F. goes on holiday only one week in the year; he has to be within range of a telex and available to his clients. With no happy use for money, he cannot endure a moment of not making it.

A little while ago, Miranda had a serious road accident, through no fault of her own. She suffered painful neck injuries; she cannot jump and has no feeling in the outsides of her hands. On the morning after the accident, she woke, semi-paralysed and in pain, to find that F.P. had gone off for a day's golf. He denied her the services of a good lawyer. She received only one thousand pounds' compensation and inadequate treatment. Something in her misfortunes causes her to smile at them. She suspects that F. is waiting to go mad, like his mother; his ruthlessness promises that the dreaded moment has not yet arrived when there is nothing he can do to her.

At the table of the likeliest devils the spoons are short, and nobody counts them.

Never trust a man whose library contains not a single unworthy book. He will deny that he has an arse-hole.

I dreamt that I had concealed the body of Mr Wood, the quondam restaurateur of Manor Field, in my luggage in a hotel room. Why ever should I dream such a thing? I have not seen the man in thirty years and recall only that he had a persistent, husky laugh.

19.3.84. How much does it matter who or what your subject is? Concentrated attention on any life can yield the kind of exotic fruit for which Graham Greene, never deeply interested in people, chugs up the Paraná to harvest. Philip Larkin's wilful provincialism is the clearest antithesis to G.G.'s globetrotting appetite for foreign dishes and bills of intellectual fare. I have been reading Larkin's modestly smug pieces with irritated deference. As if pandering to Amis, he deplores a poet who dabbles in foreign cultures. If Larkin lacks imperialism's English-speaking vanity, he is suspicious of the polyglot; he cannot imagine that other tongues can say anything he could care to learn. The resolution to settle for where he has settled leaves him perched on a firm, narrow base. Yet intimations of anguish hang around the shining brow; he would be unhappy if deprived of unhappiness. Perhaps he wishes he had more to hide. A plain cook who prides himself on his sauce, he seems on several counts to be right: he insists, in an old-fashioned, sensible way, on the need for literature to be about something.

He crimes Auden for having turned from experience of life to experience of books. W.H.A. took to heart, before others had it in their heads, the structuralist notion that the poet is the mouthpiece of the language, a writing instrument or corporeal ballpoint through which its impersonal genius is relayed. Larkin attributes Auden's resignation from specific observation to his recourse to the US. It is proper, we gather, to accuse a man of having ratted on his native connection, uncomely to mention the then illicit homosexuality which disposed him to take ship. It could as well be said of A. that he had succumbed to the bind of a homosexual 'marriage' as that he has been deracinated by the purchase of a one-way ticket. Larkin's prosaic machinery is too decorous, in public, and too monotonous in style to confront psychosocial complexities. He is cursed, unless he is blessed, with courteous caution; it arms his criticism with dated chivalry.

Larkin's admiration for James Bond echoes that of Amis; it is difficult for an outsider to be sure which of the two is more eager to defer to the other. What both envy in Bond is the facility of his seductions; he manages with grace the social fluency for which their parents failed to equip them. Bond finds the high wire of metropolitan life as easy to tread as the pavement on Bond street (is the choice of that expensive thoroughfare as his homonym entirely coincidental?). Bond's violence is excused, for Larkin and Amis, by the patriotism he displays in its exercise. Nostalgia for good and brave causes passes for common sense; hence the tendency to look back in complacency to the days of National Service. The naming of parts and the liberation – 'smoke if you want to' – that came under licence from bastard corporals fill the Amis-Larkin connection with virtuous recollections, skiving a part of them.

The old lower ranks' cry 'What's the big idea?' is echoed in the suspicion of all ideology except, of course, the one that seems so natural than none dare call it ideology. Somewhere along the well-turned line, we get the impression that the Oxford chums are not really as happy in their high-horseplay as they would have us believe. Larkin has abstained from wedlock, thus acquiring a brief, unlikely fellow-feeling for Henry de Montherlant. He discounts the homosexuality which renders

Montherlant's wariness of commitment to the ladies a form of covert preference for *les garçons*. As for marriage, Amis has indulged in disjunctive fantasy, and then practice, while seeming to embody honest-John Bullishness. What Kingsley really admires in Bond is that he honours the higher narcissism. When it comes to the ladies, the happy logic of James's profession demands that he love them and leave them. Amis affects to esteem a man who saves the sum of things for pay, but what he really relishes is the trumping domination of a Higher Authority.

Amis and Larkin would have us believe that they would prefer to be pistol-whipped than pussy-whipped, at least until the choice became practical. Both down-to-earthlings are, in fact, prisoners of the theoretical; they peddle snake-oil so banal that it seems like First Aid, but they have small experience of the cruelties of the big world; the cases they treat have rarely been marked by anything more painful than spilled ink. There is comedy, of a typically bookish order, in Amis's reproach of Nabokov, on account of what he got down to, on the page, with young Lo. Yet Amis's own conjugal conduct was more reprehensible than V.N.'s ever was. Nabokov's capacity for feline vengeance was second to none, but would he ever have descended to unsubtle malice? N.'s idea of the novel precluded its use as a blunt instrument; his thuggee was slyer than that. Both Amis and Larkin affect to rely on British cookery, with local ingredients, and to have no taste for extra-territorial showiness. Their smug small-mindedness underwrites an attitude to other literatures and crises that is the quasi-academic correlative of football supporters' loyalty to their silly colours. What do I care? I shall never belong to any specific literary stable or race under communal colours.

I received a letter from some demanding toady addressed to 'Sir Frederick'.

In *Carnets de la drôle de guerre*, Sartre tells of the outrage of Alsatian peasants (and others, no doubt) when evacuated from their farms, often built round a courtyard in elegant style, to the backward regions of the Limousin and the Périgord. Disliked as 'Boches', they reciprocated by describing the natives as '*sauvages*'. Some five years later, it was a detachment of the SS, to which Alsatians furnished a substantial contingent, that was responsible for the massacre at Oradour-sur-Glane. After the war, when it was demanded that the murderous Alsatian SS stand trial, the Parisian authorities preferred, for *raisons d'état*, to grant them an amnesty. The fear was that, if the accusations grew too loud, Alsace might vote not to re-join France, but opt for independence from the savages. The amnesty avoided embarrassment, but created a grievance against those who voted for it from which François Mitterrand is not exempt. Sartre himself is unguardedly contemptuous of the Limousin population. He writes harshly of Thiviers, his father's birthplace. His mother was from Alsace.

R.G. told me some years ago of the melancholy comedy of Stanley Mann, the rewrite man *par excellence*, and his wife's affair with Mordecai Richler. S.M. returned early from London to the south of France and found them asleep in bed together. He left the house silently and returned at the expected hour, when all resumed, for a time at least, as if nothing had happened.*

King Kong is a compendium of routine paradoxes and prim vulgarity. K.K. is a black animal without sexual parts; a gigantic teddy bear of cuddly menace, his buttocks show no division. Peaceable by nature, even when he puts human beings between his jaws, it is without any obvious appetite; it appears more that he is filing them in order to keep his hands free. He is never seen eating and his U birth-certificate promises that he will never be seen to excrete. He resembles the Greek philosopher's idea of a creature on the moon: fifteen times larger than life and, precisely, a stranger to excretion (so too was Jesus Christ, according to some theologians). In some respects, King Kong is the noblest savage, childlike in his amazement at (white) flesh, tender in his devotion to his love-toy, the explorer's wife, whom he himself explores out of pure curiosity. The movie has much the same plot as Styron's *Confessions of Nat Turner*: K.K. is cornered and beaten by the white man's technology, but there is something contemptible, as the film acknowledges, in the cruelty visited on his baited person. The Manhattan socialites would have him captured alive, but the inadequacy of their shackles stands for the futility of repression in the sexual and social sense. Neither money nor power can hobble the beast. Finally, the civilised (white) world can do no more than slaughter the bewildered 'monster' and then crowd around its corpse with maudlin curiosity.

20.3.81. I met Will Boyd at the London Library as I was taking out a copy of *Oxbridge Blues* after discovering that I do not have a copy in London. I needed the text to do the TV script of *The Muse*. There is a rule, frequently honoured by chance, that if an author goes shopping for his own work he will be surprised by another. Brian Glanville once caught B.S. Johnson asking for one of his own novels in a bookshop.

---

* Over ten years later, I wrote a short story based on this note, entitled 'Shared Credit'.

Will has just finished his third novel, *Stars and Bars*, and had the same emancipated air, on a Monday morning, as I did; we went for coffee at Fortnum's. He shares my unimpressed view of Larkin. What seems like modesty is self-effacing pride: L. will not appear on television because he has become freakishly fat. He drinks several pints of beer before lunch and has the jowls to prove it. Will is about to do an eight-parter on Cecil Rhodes, in longhand which another will transcribe. He looks always as though he has just had a shower after an early game of squash; the beefy result of Gordonstoun perhaps. Now a very industrious novelist, he has abandoned the journalism which once kept his name before the London audience. He thought me quite right to have turned down the *ST* drama critic job.

One night about ten days ago I kept an appointment at the Adolphe Tuck Hall where I had agreed, months before, to deliver a talk on Anglo-Jewish Attitudes. Prompted by old Sonntag, a lady pestered me until I capitulated; the petty celebrity carries a white flag as the hay fever victim his Kleenex. From the moment of my acquiescence until my arrival in the crowded hall, I heard nothing from the organisers. They neither confirmed the date nor invited me to dine, before or after. No one was there to greet me and when I had finished, there was no offer of a drink or a lift home. I had taken considerable trouble to prepare my speech. Not a single question alluded to it. There was less truculence in the inquirers' tone than on other occasions, but a hint of reproach, common to those who complain of being misunderstood but insist on misunderstanding all explanations of their condition. These days, when you refer to 'the Jewish religion', you are told that you have hit a wrong note. Years ago, it was only those who alluded to the Jewish *race* who were suspect. I was introduced in a perfunctory way and the vote of thanks was taken as an opportunity to drum up business for the admirable AJEX.* *Une occasion à ne jamais répéter.*

24.3.84. I have spent an anxious week wondering what Tom Maschler will think, or say, about *Heaven and Earth*. Meanwhile, I have all but finished the TV adaptation of *The Muse* and should have managed it had I not had to go to Wood Lane to a little piece of sound recording for *He'll See You Now*. The shooting of *That Was Tory* has been rescheduled for August. I should have had to miss the *grandes vacances*. Jim said, 'You don't really want to direct it, do you?' and I was off the mild hook. I think I did a pretty good job with Ms Sarandon, though I should have insisted

---

* The organisation devoted to Jewish ex-servicemen and women.

that she be a little more accurate at times. Had there been any rapport between us, I might have got more juice from the orange, but I gave it a pretty good squeeze.

Directing has more to do with managing people than with creative activity. Nearly all of one's time is taken by making decisions, few of them as inventive as choosing an epithet. The director is offered an endless succession of alternatives; his forte has to be prompt selection. The worst thing about the procedure is that he is never able to work at his own speed. Frustrated by the laggard machinery, he spends his day encouraging others to get on with it. Television is more like journalism than film: it offers prompt exposure in the place of considered effort. The TV director is a short order cook, always hot, almost never creating a memorable banquet. His life is all first nights that are also last nights.

A.L. Barker, a writer of decorated distinction, contributes a short story to the latest issue of PEN news, sponsored by the Arts Council. The first paragraph offers the following: 'He had never before witnessed such an exhibition – if he could call such an essentially private in-fight that – and was sufficiently distracted by it to neglect to change down in time for a corner. Having to do so in the act of bringing the car off the straight was a piece of bad driving which crystallised his displeasure.' There are enough ineptitudes to prime a dozen master-classes. Not the smallest hint of originality, or even accuracy, atones for the cluttered vacuousness of the prose. When were crystals ever precipitated by tardy gear change? The metaphor is weary and inappropriate. The author has nothing to say and says it badly. There is something pettily remarkable in seeing a promoted name touted above a piece bereft of the smallest personality. A.L. Barker may be on the list of the saved, but it will be a dull heaven in which she has an archangelic role. A literary number has only to be commissioned by some lofty body to ensure that it will be cautious, dated or deliberately daring, which is a form of datedness. Quality cannot be procured by the fiat of a committee; the committee itself is something to which any good writer will refuse to subject himself. The publisher of pornography is more likely to provoke something amusing and unusual than the dispenser of official bursaries.

George Steiner's latest fascination is with Stalin. He gleamed excitedly as he evoked the images of Radek, Kamenev, Bukharin and 'all the most brilliant Jews of their time' in conference with the Georgian. They were arguing that the Soviet Union would have to devote itself to improving the standard of living of the people, both to avert discontent and to present a happy face to the world. Light industry had surely to be given priority. Stalin – 'the uneducated Georgian of whom we still know almost *nothing*' – quietly asserted that the future of the USSR depended on heavy industry. How did he prevail? And how did he *know*? Power, especially vindictive power, attracts G.S. to the point of impersonation. We shall yet see him puffing a pipe under a sagacious moustache. Having briskly disparaged *Tom and Viv*, as soon as he heard we were going to see it, G. has just (22.3.84) recommended *Masterclass*. He told me excitedly that Pinter had decided henceforth he would write only committed plays with a political purpose. It sounded as though G. had access to the minutes of some tight cabal; in fact, he had got his information from that common gush of gossip the *TLS*.

Heaven and Earth. Prepared to be angry or conciliatory, grand or humble with Tom and his young female helper, I was all of them. They were wary and sapping, all at once, and I was testy and amiable. When they complained about the cleverness of the text, I said that they resembled people telling a conjuror that they like his rabbit but did it have to come out of a hat? Having spent so many careful months on the text, I did not take kindly to the commercialising tutelage of sensitive salespersons. What was lacking was something I scarcely miss, any recognition that the book is a recension of themes in *Middlemarch* and *Daniel Deronda*, as well as an attempt to revise or examine (ah examine!) the nature of motive, in life and in fiction. No one in the book knows why he or she is driven to do what is done. How different was the meeting? It would never have taken place if my earlier books with Cape had sold well enough for Tom to be apprehensive of losing my allegiance. The occasion served to vindicate his role as benefactor rather than salesman, his happier function. Tom is all right, and all wrong.

In the evening, when we played tennis at Lloyd's with Adam Raphael (a Carthusian!), Tom actually produced five pounds as a contribution, only a little less than his fair share. How much do I admire his ability to keep a great literary house alive by generating best sellers and gimmicks such as J. Miller's pop-up book, complete with erectile penis? I fear that my fidelity owes more to cowardice than to honour.

I had played with Adam only once before, in the late 1960s I suppose, when we happened both to be at the old Slazenger court in Hall Road, NW8. No one else had managed to turn up. It was extremely cold. The night's snow had mantled the skylights above the court. Pearly light came through the wired icing. Adam is a considerably better player than I am, but I played well enough that morning for him to remark that I must have been taking lessons. I was flattered by his good opinion, as if it confirmed my promotion to the circus of which P. Sergeant was the ringmaster. Adam rarely played with us; I suspect he did not relish either the company or the standard of play.

That cold morning remains in my mind for the strangeness and remoteness of the court, isolated by glassy roads. Nervous loyalty to the occasion made me keep the faith. I then found, to my amusement and annoyance, that Patrick and the other player had failed our feast. Adam and I did not play for long, but our rallies proved unforgettable. When, over drinks at Lloyd's, I mentioned that distant day, Adam was entirely unreminded of it. He had no trace of it in his head; even my description of the opaque skylight had no Proustian effect. 'Ah well,' I said, 'that just shows the difference between a novelist and a journalist.' He agreed.

29.3.84. Last week, early one morning, between the alarm and the orange juice, the telephone rang. It was a man called Whitty, calling from the British Council in Athens. There was some difficulty in obtaining a copy of the Byron film from BBC enterprises. He wondered if I could procure a copy quickly and directly and bring it with me. I said I would do my best and we exchanged banalities about the weather in Greece (it was cold and rainy) and what would happen at the airport when/if I was denied entry with the negative. He said that he would be there to meet me and look after us; all would be easy and well. Since then, the Queen has gone to Jordan, despite the inauspicious bomb. This morning, between the alarm and the orange juice, Beetle came back to check the name of the man who had called from Athens. Whitty, was it? It was. He had been assassinated in the street in Athens by an Arab motorcyclist, apparently because some group deplored Her Majesty's trip to Amman.

I suspect that Dudy (now Dorothy) Nimmo's self-absorption is so constant that she will never understand anything that happens to anyone else; in the midst of any drama, she was aware only of when it would be her turn to say a line. She remains locked in the plainness from which stardom was expected to spring her. Did she fear all along that there was nothing for her higher up the ladder except the likelihood of an even heavier fall? When she seemed exaggerated and embarrassing, with those hectic appeals for love and endless recitations of family activities, all the time she was Stevie Smithing; and now has become sardonic smithereens.

The Gordons are coming to London. Years ago, they tell me, I announced that it will be a pleasure and a privilege to take them on a tour of Cambridge. I tend to credit all Americans with qualities of wit and alertness, more a tribute to my mother's quickness than the fruit of frequent experience. Just as I invest Stanley Baron with the quick humour of Stanley Donen, so I bless the Gordons, in their absence, with Algonquin verve. Desire to ingratiate myself with those I fear (and whom do I not?) has always stood in the way of honest assessment of my own desires and preferences.

Harry was a great pleasure to me during the first visit to Fuengirola. I was excited to hear the opinions and be privy to the artistic adventures, in the advertising business, of someone who lived in the city of my childhood. With none of the affectations of Cambridge people, Harry seemed to have had easy access, despite his Philadelphian provenance, to the famous world of 'Andy (Warhol) and co' in arty NYC. Since 1938, I had been back only once, briefly, in 1949. Americans seemed, in the 1950s, to be possessed of a go-getting spontaneity I could only envy.

After university, Beetle wanted to go to the States to work; she might have done so had she not met me. I was wearing Kansas City zip-fronted, no turn-up pants at the time. In Fuengirola, the Gordons had an aggressive confidence. Charlotte had been art editor of *Seventeen*, a magazine for the puberty belt. She had been 'let go', due to a 'clash of personalities'. She had a character with which it was difficult not to clash, no matter what colours one sported. Her CV carried her, on a high horse, through closed doors. We endured, never welcomed, her irruptions. She was always telling us what we should really do. In a time of yielding women, she was militantly forward. I remember being attracted to her only once, when she came across the sand to where I was sitting on the Fuengirola beach in front of the Massons' house. She had a swimsuit under her dress. She stood close and peeled off the top layer to show her legs and hips.

Harry wrote to me regularly when we had gone back to England and were living in Bergholt. His regular and elegant script, on the thin paper he favoured, had something of the tone of the even-tempered, older brother I never had. I replied promptly, and at length, hoping for more. Although I now look back on Sarah's birthplace sentimentally, I did not greatly like living in The Old Mill House,* partly because I missed that easy walk, from the Calle Tostón, along the *carretera* and then along the Calle Jose Antonio (I doubt if it is still called that) to Harry's studio for a *copita* of *anis seco* and a look at the new work. The smell of paint fused with the sound of evening movement in the *pueblo*. We talked, I cannot recall what about, until I could imagine that Salvadora had our supper ready.

Beetle, I think, could happily have stayed in Bergholt, but Anne Moore would neither give us a long lease nor sell us the house, although

---

* John Constable's father's house.

she did later dispose of it. I was not sorry to stamp my foot, shake off English dust, and return to Andalucia. We had more money by then, though it did not last long. I had brought a new car, a Standard Ensign, grey and more powerful than the Ford Anglia in which I had rolled lopsidedly home from Gibraltar a few months earlier. Stella Richman's commissions furnished most of the funds, although the sale of *The Limits of Love* to Lippincott had been the turning point of our fortunes: $2,500!

The Gordons found us the Villa Antoñita. It had a tower room in which I wrote *The Graduate Wife*. Nuala C. came with us, to look after the children. In theory, we were freer than we had been a year before; in practice, the help soon proved to be pregnant, though she denied that it was even possible, until stretched button-holes proved more convincing than disclaimers. I rarely went back to Harry's studio in those early months of 1961. The Villa Antoñita was in the suburbs, on the road to Los Boliches (Lo' Boliche' in toothless Salvadora-speak). On Tuesdays we walked there, with Paul in his pushchair, to buy the two-day old *Sunday Times* or whatever the Canadian guy had on offer.

Charlotte would often drive up to the house, in a rather proprietorial way, usually as we were about to eat lunch. Since we were in her debt, for finding us the place, we hardly knew how to deter her. She liked to load the local children into her Simca and give them a ride along the *carretera*. In those days, Spanish kids seldom had a chance to go in a *coche*. Char would swagger to our door, that long cigarette-holder between her large teeth, like some official inspector. She knew the natives better than we did and was working in clay with Pepe, who owned a kiln. Having been out of Spain for so long, we had lost our tenure on local parity. The Gordons had a feeling for the place, the language and the culture. Thanks to H., we had access to the tiled tennis court in a villa a few hundred yards away, on the far side of the *carretera* from the Villa Antoñita. Owned by absent Germans, it was guarded by high walls and tight gates. We went frequently to play and then swim in the pretty pool. When I took off all my sweaty clothes and jumped in, after a hot set, H. followed my example with a certain timidity.

Harry's birthday was in June. By way of a thank you for the service they had rendered us, I invited them to come to Granada with us in the new car to hear the concert Segovia was to give in the Court of the Lions. We left Paul and Sarah with Nuala and Beetle's always willing mother. Nothing disagreeable happened on the trip. The concert was very nice; so was the Alhambra Palace Hotel. We drank gin fizzes on the long narrow terrace overlooking the plain of Granada. Not yet thirty, and very young, I was rather pleased when waiters actually brought what I had asked for.

We were all rather old-fashioned in playing at grown-ups. There was easier intimacy between us and the Gordons than we had had with the Nimmos, but the surroundings were happier than Shepherd's Bush.

I recall Char keeping us waiting long enough for H. to become irritable (having sensed our irritation) while she patronised a potter in a back street, but nothing else of the weekend remains in my mind. The children had survived, Sarah with nappy rash, and we received no marked thanks from H. and C. for the long trip. Neither Beetle nor I was happy, each separately, that summer. My parents came to stay *chez Henriqueta* (the only modest hotel on the Costa del Sol which offered non-rancid butter). Two or three days into their visit, we had a loud scene at the Villa Antoñita. My mother burst into tears at the sight of Paul leaning to kiss Beetle's hand at the dinner table. It ended with my yelling at my parents that they should 'fuck off out of my life'. Their demanding intrusiveness was beyond endurance. I was wrong only to have been craven for so long.

My father was the same age as the century. At that time, he seemed in fair health. He had recently retired from Shell, after long years of vexation at the hands of Trevor Powell. I do not remember what my parents did in Fuengirola. I have a feeling that I paid for the hotel (it was a comfort not to have them staying in the house); we certainly entertained them to regular meals, though we were far from flush. Cedric was never mean, but he had no compunction when it came to freeloading. He never had as much money as his tastes required. He looked to me to supplement his income and regarded me somewhat as an enterprise in which he had invested, as indeed he had. Perhaps he was aware that my mother would not have a royal income after his death. Since he was eleven years older than Irene, the thought may have weighed on him; but I doubt it. His attitude to Beetle and me was chiding and expectant. He insisted that Irene's virtues be recognised, despite the bad light in which she was liable to display them. Their visit left us rancorous and exhausted. I do not blame it for anything that happened later, but it certainly made me unwilling to return to England, where Cedric liked us to be: 'He does like to have you on the island,' my mother used to say.

The Villa Antoñita was not available for the summer season. We managed to rent the Villa Sol, at the other end of Fuengirola, near the Somio, a café where we came to drink gin fizzes and talk and talk, cheerlessly, about our marriage. The Villa Sol was small and had mean windows. We had an excellent new cook called Maria. Salvadora subbed during her weekend absences. All should have been well, but proved not to be. Tom Maschler's visit was no more agreeable than it had been the previous year. He too had some call on our indulgence; it was thanks to him that we had been able to rent Anna Freeman-Saunders' house in the Calle Tostón.

Late that summer, when I was quite broke, I had a talk with Harry in the narrow Garden of Remembrance, just down from the Somio. He was pleased to tell me that he had been offered a job in New York at six thousand a year, six thousand *quid* that was. It was a fortune I never dreamed of commanding. A few weeks later, Beetle's father died. We had to return to London for the funeral. Jonty Smulian, a friend of Charlie Reiter's, whom I scarcely knew, lent me the money for the tickets to fly from Gibraltar. We did not have two certain seats, but managed to take the last pair on the plane just as the original purchasers came panting through the door. Desire to prove myself to Beetle made me ruthless. I remember repeating Baron Moss's tiresome slogan, 'I'll see you all right, girl.'

By the time we returned, I was able to repay Jonty's loan, but when I requested the Midland Bank to send me £250, Mr Webb replied that he would do so as soon as that sum appeared in my account. Selwyn Lloyd had become the squeezing Chancellor. I was shocked to find that the possession of a chequebook did not entitle a man to draw cash whenever he needed it. Stella Richman came to my help with a new contract to write plays for ATV. We left Fuengirola in September and drove to Ste Maxime where she and Victor were waiting for us.

On our arrival there was a message to call Gareth Wigan. David Deutsch wanted to buy the film rights of *The Best of Everything* and commission me to write the screenplay. Our bacon was saved. I was never again worried that I should be unable to make six thousand pounds a year. It seems now that nothing was ever going to stop me. It had not seemed so in August 1961, when I had the sorriest birthday of my spoiled life.

Sarah does not mean to spend long on Ios this summer. She may not go at all. Yet last summer she was very happy there, until towards the end. Then Stelio Drakos's little son was drowned. The whole family loved him. Stelio was already ambitious for him and wanted him to go to Athens College. Old Giorgios, now old indeed and resigned to elderly pottering, adored the pretty child. On that terrible day, the whole family was busy with work in the taverna. The little boy was left to play on the quay. We have watched children playing there all the years we have been to the island. It was assumed that nothing would happen, and nothing ever did, until the little boy slipped off the deck and drowned in silence. The Drakoi have become rich from the tourists. Now Stelio says that he will never go back to the island. He has a daughter and soon he will have another child. At the funeral there were terrible scenes, accusation and agony. The heart has gone out of old Giorgios. He sits by the water and looks at the tranquil killer bay.*

10.4.84. Peter Gethers, whom I never much liked, though I welcomed his overtures as a publisher, sent me a copy of *Eleni*, by Nicholas Gage, who is Greek by birth. P. said he was very proud of the book, quite as if it would never have been written without him. It tells of the Americanised author's search for his origins and especially for the murderers of his mother during the Greek civil war. It is labelled a novel, but there is little or no fiction in it. Gage validates his story by insisting on its truth. The language in which he clothes the search is either banal or hyperbolic. The whole enterprise is punctured with contradictions. Of course, it has happened over and over again that novelists use their experiences ('How not?' as the grand Sibylle Bedford put it, in *The Legacy*), but the modern 'industrial' habit of making the prospects of a novel depend on the promise that it recycles famous events or scandals reduces the place of imagination in fiction to that of the couturier. When the donnée is publicly touted, the producer/publisher (enter Gethers) becomes the commander of the enterprise. The words can be cut or dyed or cut again, since they are not organic to the text. The true novelist grafts real incidents onto his narrative only if it suits the secret thrust of the whole piece. His responsibility is to be true, not truthful. The awarding of the Booker Prize to *Schindler's Ark* is the promotion *ad absurdum* of a destructive trend. The 'creative' editor becomes the arbiter of when a book is finished, the author a proud figurehead at the service of the means of production and distribution.

A sheaf of unopened *TLS*s lies on a shelf in my room in Lagardelle. Should I die or disappear, a diligent debunker might find them there and announce my hypocritical pretentiousness. In fact, the unopened numbers were sent here during the autumn, when we were in London, despite my request that they be sent to Stanhope Gardens. They then sent me the back numbers; hence I have duplicates here and there. How many false inferences are drawn by biographical researchers? What fun a man might have in creating a well-documented archive, apparently the very opposite of the respectable legacy he is presumed to have wished for! The fabrication of false facts can supply a kind of 'verifiable' fiction. It would have something in common with the dossiers assembled, back

---

* Sarah would never forget watching the drowned child being driven along the beach in a truck while his mother ran keening in its traces.

in the 1940s, by Dennis Wheatley and J.G. Links, a collection of bric-à-brac which would certify a wholly false 'truth'. A collection of 'papers' rather than a continuous narrative could supply a wealth of lines for the ingenious to read between. There could also be a deck of photographs, like those found in the cottage on Iskios by Daniel Meyer, in *April, June and November*, susceptible of arrangement in happy or unhappy sequence, according to the more or less scrupulous ingenuity of the editor.

How much more evocative *The Kennaway Papers* would have been, had they been composed of scraps of paper, notes, letters, mostly undated, the detritus of a remembered, authentic crux! Susie K. told Anne Becher (so the latter told me) that I had been wonderfully comforting when we spoke at A.'s party. S. had cooked the rather heavy Indian meal and acted as Anne's vigorous legate.

Susie is famous, once and for all, for having been the woman in two famous lives. James's fame is less reliable than Cornwell's or whoever he is when he isn't Le Carré, an Achilles who appears, in Susie's book, to be all heel. James was the love of her life, although he twice deserted her, in the first place for other ladies, in the second by dying. She is determined that his books stay in print. *Tunes of Glory* was his first and remains his best book. He lived a self-destructive myth in which wine and women were the principal pursuits. He went over the top in his assault on the world of letters and success (in film).

Re-reading *Tunes Of Glory*, you are moved by sympathy for the dead colonel, but there is something not quite satisfying (ah satisfaction!) in the elisions which became habitual in K.'s fiction. They seem to imply something outside the text itself as the *real* story. In his later fiction, the implicit object of the young author's unblinking pity seems to have been himself; observed from the angle of vigorous youth, James was already exhausted and rejected. Courageously fearful of what was coming, he made his fiction only apparently a lament for the past. His conservatism was less political than apprehensive: he dreaded the future in which he would become senescent. Eagerness for the future is an appetite for the time when we shall have less time to live. Nostalgia has less to do with the virtues of the golden past than with dread of a looming, steel-grey dawn. James wrote as if composing a series of dirges; it was Kennaway he mourned for.

There are things here which are all but unspeakable, less the essence of the truth than its sour fumes, the farts of the human digestion of facts, fancies and fears. So? The passion to recover Susie, after he discovered that he might have lost her, was that not due, in part at least, to the style of regret that made him seem always to be lamenting the fugacious nature of life and its pleasures? Susie was not so much his one true love as the notched talisman of his youth. To lose her was not merely to be a cuckolded loser, it was also to be undeniably older.

Consider the tunes of jealousy to be played on the triangle: the assault on the ego (and the ago), the thrill of betrayal (and of being betrayed?), envy of the fame that would come to Cornwell, the *peggior fabbro*. Susie, the socialite, the mother, the reliable target of macho assault had to be transformed into someone inaccessible, elusive, pains-giving, cruel hence desirable. The novelist rigged his own plot and his own rack. He may have craved freedom, the louche life that tarts and liquor (and that black leathery Soho pad) had symbolised; but his craving was for a scheme more elaborate than accidental pleasure could provide. How else could he be a figure of sufficient stature to merit a book about himself? He went to writing as his soldiers went to war. The film business was his rich and frightful battleground: in it he saw the degradation of his own talent, but also an opportunity for fame and fortune, escape from the banalities of domestic grammar. He liked it when things got rough beyond the scope or (he imagined) appetite of a nice wife. The great betrayal reconciled him to the domestic scene, by making it a war zone. He could then devote all his enraged subtlety to the reconquest of what had been too easily acquired in the first place.

The cloying conceit of Le Carré's *The Naïve and Sentimental Lover* is, alas, the only piece of 'art' to emerge from the clash. Did James ever confront the jumble of his own contradictions? He could not make his kind of comedy out of his own predicament because it hurt too much. In a sense, he died of wounds, albeit by accident. Susie may have no reason to feel guilt, but her diligence in tending the flame has something of apology in it. Is she also preserving the prize of her finest hour, when she was the rib of contention between two brilliant competitors? Does she also belong so irretrievably to the conjugal matrix of the fifties that she feels that she let James down, however richly he deserved it? She has courage and energy. If she has ended up, in reduced circumstances and the unglamorous company of a very nice accountant, she had the pride and the guts to pull the plug decisively on Tom Maschler's little ruse.

Whom was Susie protecting from the spotlight? Her book stripped James of most of his armour. He was enough of a man not to require concealment, but Susie did nothing to hide his weaknesses. You may sympathise with his rabid bewilderment, when she broke out, but it is difficult not to find him at once comic and embarrassing. Since James was dead, Susie can only have been protecting David C.; from whom or what? The publication of her book made it certain that everyone in the knowing world would see through the camouflage. Among gossips and literati, Le Carré would be out of the closet with a bang. Only total reticence could have spared him. We are left with the likelihood that Susie wanted to have things both ways. Who but a moralist could chide her? By publishing the text before the *Sunday Times* supplied the pictures that blew the gaff, she gave James's name the dominant place. He is seen to regard her as the centre of his life and to insist that she remain there. Her decision to stay with him was made 'correct' by the energetic potency of the man. Her lover, concealed or not, appears as rather a wimp. Their passion was charged by James's wayward history. Without him to hurt, would she and her lover ever have reached such heights of ecstasy? The unnamed shadow was never the same kind of lover as James, who generated the others' sense of their own importance. Susie and David were not only taking pleasure in each other, they were also daring the whirlwind to huff and puff and blow their straw house down. It happened, as it will on such occasions, before anyone was quite ready for it. The agony was greater than the pleasure which, all the same, had its cruel delights.

Hence the answer to the riddle of why Susie pulled the plug on the *Sunday Times* is not far to seek. So long as Le Carré's name was not paraded, his life compromised, by giving the *hoi polloi* access to his romantic secret, Susie's dutiful, if scandalous, tribute to her husband could serve equally well as a declaration of her abiding love for D.C. As long as she did not actually embarrass him (he has new domestic relations of his own) by bringing the gutter press (i.e. the press) to his door, her book would have something of the effect of Caro Lamb's 'Remember me!', in a tactful register.

Was Susie's panic, when she discovered that the *S.T.* was about to disclose what she had kept wrapped, induced solely by *pudeur*? She is as likely to have feared that Le Carré would regard her as the deliberate wrecker of his current conjugal felicity. He could scarcely complain that the book was being published, since he had cast the first pebble in his own à clef number (everyone knew that the Kennaways were in his sights). Susie gave as good as she got, and behaved no less honourably, by giving the pseudonymous Le C. a pseudonym. She had no need to reproach herself as long as the mask remained in place. Refusal to make a killing (as Tom wished) by bringing Le Carré in from the cold might well be expected to commend her to her ex-lover. At the same time, her book can be read as a loving resurrection of James. Could the duplicity of the loyally disloyal wife be better commemorated than by a double-headed coinage?

It is curious that J.K. was drawn, in spite of himself, to the cinema, perhaps because of the prompt purchase of the film rights of *Tunes of Glory* and its subsequent screen success (some said that the film, with

Alec Guinness, was better than the book). Subsequently, when he tried to write directly for the screen, he failed to achieve anything comparable. There is something feminine, in the old-fashioned sense, about a writer's relationship with the movies: to get top dollar, he must be seduced rather than make the first move.

I have always been a bad loser, but last week my tendencies, after losing to Stee at Scrabble, became grotesque. Today, while apologising, I mentioned at lunch that de Gaulle had contrived to give up smoking by announcing 'De Gaulle *ne fume pas*'. He was then obliged to verify his own public declaration. I am hoping I can show as much resolution as *Le Grand Charles*. Meanwhile, the silly gods arranged that I beat Stee at tennis for the first time this holiday.

11.4.84. The morning is *apsophios*, full of life, not to say *amolevtos*, which proves that I have been conning my Greek vocabulary, again, preparatory to our excursion to Greece in May. It will be haunted by the fragment of conversation I had with Kenneth Whitty, who seems to have been a genuine friend of the arts. His tone was both businesslike and amiable. The unfairness of his death is appalling and argues for the justice of Beetle's objection to the remark, in my new novel, that nothing is not pleasing to someone. Yet the doomy observation carries a tincture of truth. The decency of Mr Whitty did not prevent someone in the Foreign Office suggesting to the Press that his murder, by a masked motorcyclist, might have been the consequence of a domestic quarrel. The reason declared by whatever terrorist group claimed 'responsibility' was, quite plausibly, that the assassination was in protest against the Queen's trip to Jordan.

Last night the French news caught a 'moment of emotion' when the brother of a young soldier recently blown up in Tchad attempted, during the obsequies, to ram the Minister of Defence, Charles Hernu, with his car. Was this too to be attributed to some domestic vendetta? The driver was shot in the *cuisse* and his mother, fearing that she was losing another son, ran to him across the parade ground.

The Queen has been in the news here, since the French have been gloating over the alleged *froideur* between her and Mrs Thatcher. Her Majesty (the Queen, I mean) is becoming more and more demanding in her later years and less reticent. Her comments from Jordan were both understandable and, we have to hope, dictated by Foreign Office ghosts who required her to find the sight and sound of Israeli jets on patrol more 'terrifying' than the unremarked malice of the Arabs. The kingdom of Jordan resembles one of those shops in Beverly Hills which proclaim that they have been in business for all of ten minutes and advertise their tradition of service. It has no ancient boundaries and was founded to suit the policies of a waning empire. I have no wish to see Hussein evicted and admire his pertinacity, but for the Queen of England to be 'depressed' at the sight of Jewish settlements, on a map, is not very different, *mutatis mutandis*, from de Gaulle's comments on, and in, Quebec. No Jew has to be an unconditional supporter of what has turned out to be a foolish policy, as I always thought Begin's was, but the Queen's apparent willingness (at the Foreign Office's instigation) to join the Arab legion, after the conspicuous indifference of the British, when it came to the murder of millions of Jews and the degradation of whoever survived, suggests that Her Majesty's capacity to be saddened sits on uneven springs.

Meanwhile, in the Périgord, the cherry blossom is pouting and the birds are making long distance calls (cheep hours?) in the hazel tree. Only M. Brault is vile. His *pompe à chaleur* is not working; no amount of cajolery can elicit his contracted help. Beetle thought him a scoundrel *dès le début*, but I did not see it. The danger with foreigners, for me, is that if I can make myself understood, and have them smile, I am tempted to assume that they are excellent fellows. It was much the same with the scoundrelly Giorgos on Ios when he borrowed money from me and repaid us in honey filled with plump dead flies. He now owns a café-restaurant in what used to be his sad shop. Back in 1962, he wanted me to be his partner in a chicken business. We were going to buy some land between the edge of the village and what is now the post office. I might have become the part owner of a valuable property. I had almost no cash at the time. What I had we invested in the two plots on Mylopota, the first house we ever owned. I have often wished that we had stayed there and turned the *spiti* into something more – what? – *hermetic*. I should like to have a wall around the place, more terraces, a white corner out of the wind where I could work and read. The house is difficult to keep nice: dust blows up from the concrete floor; the work that has been done is often shoddy. I am a poor supervisor, easily gulled, impatient to be through with and utilise whatever I have commissioned.

12.4.84. Jack Lambert was a war hero. He came to the *ST*, or at least to Kemsley's, as a result, I believe, of his acquaintance with Denis 'major Major' Hamilton. He had all the qualifications, DSO, DSC, and the precocious editorship of *The Grocer's Weekly* or some such. He had been shaken if not quite shattered by his naval experiences. Jack could hardly bring himself to speak; when he did, he stammered painfully. He was treated by Catharine (Read), whose speciality was vocal rehabilitation. She succeeded in restoring his confidence and he asked her to marry him. She had wanted to be an actress, but decided to devote her life to Jack instead. He seemed to be well set in the race for editorial preferment, but something lamed his enthusiasm for the *cursus*. He was, he told me, too happy at home to be willing to invest himself wholly in the office.

He had perhaps seen too much of real battle to have much stomach for the merciless infighting of office life. If he had lost the will to scramble for editorial power, he was eager to be influential. He is one of those satraps who ducks the dangers of regal ambition. He deferred with seditious fidelity both to Hamilton and to the untrustworthy Leonard Russell. When the latter retired (or died?), Jack was given control of the arts pages. He was a lazy eclectic who liked what he liked and relished the free access to cultural shrines which his episcopate sanctioned. We might jeer at his lack of rigour, but he collected, mollified and stabled a rare herd of contributors whose loudest complaint was likely to be that their pieces had been truncated or held over.

Harry Evans and Jack should have had a good rapport. Neither had been to university; both claimed to be the better for it. Harry was provincial and plain, Jack a Londoner and a public schoolboy, an officer and a bit of a gentleman, with the profile of a matinée idol *manqué*. Jack was also a member of the *Sunday Times* old guard, a Phanariote faced with a Young Turk. Scrawny and clerkly, Harry owed his promotion only to services rendered to the *Northern Echo*, never to his heroic personality. He used to greet me with effusive shyness when we crossed in the arts department or in the corridor. I could never recognise the fellow, probably because he changed opticians so often on the ascent to contact lenses. The editorial chair added a cubit to his stature; he grew taller sitting down.

The *stasis* within the paper hardly touched me. I never thought to make a career there. I like to have new books and I like writing pieces about them, *ecco tutto*. As J.W.L. moved, slowly, towards retirement, he became more and more anxious. His fears that he would be evicted before his time were at once boring and well-founded. After his upward descent from the north, Harry Evans was for some time under the aegis, and the hammer, of D. Hamilton. Having experienced much the same subjection as Jack had, did Harry feel a measure of contempt for a man who had crawled without having the top prize in his abject sights? Once sovereign, after Hamilton's assumption of overlordly remoteness, H.E. was able to exercise muscles previously employed mainly in genuflection. Who was more contemptible or embarrassing a witness than Jack, whose dissimilarities were a reproach and whose similarities provided an obsequious mirror?

Jack slumped into paranoia. Soon the facts came to match his fears. The death of Nick Tomalin was the primer of his eviction. Nick had not wanted to report the Arab-Israeli war. He had enough in Vietnam, however brief his stay. Harry persuaded him to go to the Middle East, even though he had no appetite for Bathsheba. When Nick was killed, on account of his excellent bladder (he did not get out of the vehicle when the others went to piss and so was still in it when the Syrian heat-seeking missile found the warm engine), Claire was entitled to compensation for the loss of a husband.

At Cambridge, Nick had been both president of the Union and editor of *Granta*. Yet he had the fugitive air of someone whose bail was about to expire. It is as if he became an investigative journalist to avoid being investigated. Nick's father was an Old Carthusian, a communist, a drinker and a womaniser. Locked in a double-bind of admiration and reproach, N.O.T. admired and disapproved. He knew that there was always likely to be something furtive behind most things, not least, perhaps, because he himself was ill-at-ease over his purposes. He thought he could remain a boy by refusing administrative and domestic responsibilities. He told Stanley Price that he had not aged because he had never craved power. His speciality was righteous revelations.

H.E. chose to replace J.W.L. with John Whitley, a one-time colleague of Harry's, I think, in the North, and to make Claire literary editor. Jack muttered and sulked for a long while before accepting mothballed elevation. He was made 'Chief Reviewer' and given a desk in a remote cubicle, whence he descended to play a vocal Banquo in the Arts Department.

In *Technics and Civilisation*, Mumford remarks (his italics): '*The army is in fact the ideal form towards which a purely mechanical system of industry must tend*'. Atomic warfare is the epitome of automation. Salvation and perdition are available from the same merchants. Science has replaced God, a consequence of the distinct academic community established in Alexandria. Press-button warfare is the apotheosis of the OTC's TEWT (technical exercise without troops), the activity of a specialised caste, unconcerned with the welfare of other ranks. The wholesale disqualification of the working class is implicit in the theoretical future, civil and military alike; *very* alike.

The last laugh, does one really want to wait that long?

The irrelevance of the (brief) controversy about the Hitler diaries can be summarised by Wittgenstein's remark 'What one writes about oneself cannot be more truthful than one is'. The hopes of the public and the publicists could never be met by the diaries, whether forged or authentic. The ivy cannot rise higher than the tree.

How decisive they would all like the great Alexander to be! Historians seek to divine his real motives as augurs did the future by examining entrails. Who can ever know his paramount purpose when he set out to empress the world into his service? His father Philip had been murdered at a ceremony in which he was to be inducted into the company of the twelve gods. Philip's death was Alexander's opportunity. There was duplicity at the heart of the succession: Philip had divorced Olympias, who might have been the model, if only the dates fitted, of Euripides' Medea. The king had been far from reliably partial to Alexander. Philip's death enlivened his son; gratitude and guilt were beyond distinction. The remorse which Alexander displayed after he killed 'Black' Cleitus can be read as a reprise of what he felt on the death of Philip. Did he not call Cleitus 'father'?

Every general embodies duplicity. He must care for his men as if they were his children; yet if he is to succeed, he must order a good number of them to their deaths. He may call on the enemy to avoid bloodshed, by seeing reason, but his idea of reason, like the Spartan Aphrodite, wears battle-dress. George Scott's Patton laid it on the line when he admitted, among the battlefield's corpses that he did 'love it so'. Alexander needed to transcend his one-eyed father, whom he had reason to hate, in order to redeem himself in the eyes of the king who left him the inheritance without which he could never eclipse him. To claim that Alexander went into battle as early as the Issus with a plan to unite Persian and Hellene is fanciful. Yet the synthesising, syncretistic ambition may always have been there, implicit in 'Medism', for Greeks both a criminal charge and an abiding temptation. If Alexander wished, above all, to be the incarnation of Hellenism, the Hellenes were reluctant to accept a Macedonian intruder as their champion. Freud wondered what women want. Alexander wanted, I think, to be remembered.* If all those Alexandrias were not enough, his adventure itself was his loudest mausoleum. Alexander's mutability makes the city of Proteus the emblem of his many-facedness. His duplicity presaged that of all sorts of European

---

* Some dispassionate shit has written somewhere of a beautiful, blonde, naked eighteen-year-old Jewish girl whom Himmler tried, a little, to exempt from the fate of her people. As she was hustled to her death, she called out, 'Remember me, remember me!'

empire-builders, with all their affectations of concern for the welfare of their subjects and a certain appetite for the colourful panache (and cuisine) of the natives.

How well Larry Durrell can write, and how cheaply! Cf. the reference to Shop Stewards at the beginning of *Constance*.

Seferis, 'Days of June 1941', written in Crete between May and September '41:

'The new moon is out in Alexandria
Overcoming the old in its embrace,
And we are passing through the Gate of the Sun,
In the heart of darkness, three friends.'

The old gate to Alexandria, so Keeley and Co. tell us, was once called the Rosetta Gate, which accounts for the naming of the stone which Napoleon's savants discovered and were later obliged to relinquish to the English, after Nelson destroyed most of the transports which had carried the Army of the Nile. William St Clair says that Lord Elgin supervised the negotiations which allowed the French to go home, without much of their booty but free to fight again another day. Seferis' image of the new moon with the old in her arms evokes the interlocking of past and present in the Mediterranean.

Madness is mental nudism. It refuses to leave the soul mantled in decorum. The nudist may not mean to embarrass, but there is a kind of aggression in him or her. The vegetarian is similarly self-assertive in his mildness. Reluctance to participate in the common meal is as self-righteous as it is humane. Their dietetic perversities (as Caligula and others have seen them) contribute to the suspicion attached to the segregated conclaves of the Jews. Shylocks with separate seating plans are taken to be concocting spells against those at other tables. All modesties have their immodest aspect.* Who pronounced himself more entitled to the crown than Julius Caesar when he refused it?

13.4.84. P. seized an opportunity available to cleverer men, who missed it. He saw that financial publications could be priced at almost any sum, provided bosses and business schools found them indispensable. Siting his Pergamon in Switzerland afforded opportunities for continental

---

* Solicited to write a review of C.E.M. Joad's latest philosophical work, Bertrand Russell famously replied 'Modesty forbids.'

indulgences for which none of HM's revenue men could crime him. Meanwhile, his London office was the capital of a satrapy on which the Great King Rothermere could rely for lavish tribute. *Money Mail* became one of his empire's nice little money-makers.

Journalism in the 1940s and even into the fifties, had its working class complement. When I devilled in the *Sunday Express* newsroom in 1949, reporters, sub-editors, even feature and news editors, resembled non-commissioned officers, of various stripes. They maintained discipline on behalf of a class to which they rarely belonged and whose members were rarely in evidence. Pre-war, of all the lonely souls in England, none was less likely to escape his origins than the pleased-to-meet-you petty bourgeois. The war needed more officers than the traditional officer class could supply. The wardroom had its clannish ways, but a personable young man, apt for instruction, could make his way more easily there than in an old regimental mess. The nautical parvenu was fortunate to be conscripted to transcend his social range as a service to the nation. Training and imposture were all but the same thing. Patriotic duplicity made an officer and almost a gentleman of him.

P. has proved an alert and amusing observer of the City's quarter-decks. He had the wit and experience to see how things actually work among those for whom work is a *façon de parler*. With no call to challenge the practices of those who passed for his masters, he enjoyed being wise to them. He has occasionally blown the whistle on conspicuous chancers, such as Jim Slater. Idols are made to fall. Behind the hale and the heartiness is a small cupboard with skeletons inside and trophies of vanity on top. He has, I imagine, had no call to deny that he was a Jew; those blue eyes and the fair complexion have the sort of handsomeness which reflects well on him in the pool of Narcissus. He dresses in the fashion of the businessman who – in a pin-stripe suit with the right things in his inside pocket – loses his trousers in a Ben Travers farce and is revealed to be wearing sock-suspenders and silk drawers. There is something of the secret agent in his tailored flamboyance; he trails no trace of his origins. His best camouflage lies in drawing attention to himself.

Having been a friend and speechwriter for Margaret, he has resigned himself to seeing less of her now. With no illusions about the depth or durability of political and politic friendships, he is untroubled in a world where reciprocation rules. He has kept himself afloat by clinging to the top deck rather than the wreckage. He has the charm – by no means contemptible – to be both superficial and disabused. He is veneer through and through; tap him and you can be confident that he will sound hollow all round. That sonorous consistency promises that he will never embarrass you with confessions, unless they are boasts. There is something personable about a hedonist who does not belabour you with his realisation of the futility of pleasure. The repentant sinner may be welcomed by God; he offers small entertainment to man. We can endure being told how luxurious a life someone enjoys, but it is too much to be asked to sympathise with his discovery of its emptiness. If P. exults over his money, he does not vaunt it as evidence of virtue. He is shrewd enough to observe that nearly everyone who passes for a golden boy carries a percentage of tin. That the business world is fraught with fraudulence and imposture makes it a succulent pasture for grazing journalists. Life has taught him that very little in this world is well deserved.

After the young Martin Amis had delivered the first draft screenplay of *Saturn III*, Stanley Donen, who had been misguided enough to produce a turkey, rang me and said 'Freddie, you're talking to a drowning man.' Out of friendship I agreed, with unfeigned reluctance, to do two weeks' work on the script, as long my name was not mentioned on the screen. Martin had been happy to take the money, but denied all responsibility for the fiasco.

The 'sordid little secrets' of which Edmund Leach spoke with trendy scorn, these can be the stuff of happiness; the abiding secret of the happy family is the matriarchy which make its members feel at home.

The comedy of revelations is that the confessor ceases to be the thing he was before he declared himself. The spy who admits his duplicity is no longer a dangerous player. Reduced to singularity, he takes on a sad dignity. We cannot wholly hate the man who has been found out; discovery takes from him the potency which rendered him literally intriguing.

The dark glass is language; it reveals and clouds the issue in a phrase.

Did we ever really drive through a burg called 'Nowhere, Arkansas'?

When a girl blundered into his room in Méribel on New Year's Eve, imagining that it belonged to another man, B. pleasured her as well as he could in the circumstances. Logged with champagne, he made rather a hash of it. Neither embarrassed nor mortified, he suggested she stay until the morning when he would be more up to it.

Levin supplies the garrulous heads to Pinter's tails. The one is reticent in order to conserve his standing as the suffering servant of his art; the other conceals his uncertainties under a swagger of elongated euphony. Harold is a master of collage; he finds his pieces of colour in what he overhears, not in what he sees. His patchwork is a verbal quilt that he throws over the names (those of Yorkshire cricketers for example) which he allots to the various puppets of his fancy. As a polemicist, Levin goes into every battle or skirmish with the same calibre of armament, the same ration of ammunition, the same verve. Like Prince Rupert, his first charge so exhilarates him that he assumes it to have won the day (or at least the day's attention). Intellectually, he bolts his food; he is having his coffee before more cautious people have broached their main course. Pyrotechnic energy is available for the anatomisation of nuts. Since he has to think quickly to honour frequent deadlines, he attacks big issues with much the same artillery as the petty. His copy has to conform with the style which his constituency of readers finds 'typically Bernard'.

Levin is, above all, complacent; having started out as an uncomely suburban you-know-who, he has risen, via the LSE, to metropolitan eminence which, in his eyes, speaks well for the good taste, no less than the tolerance, of British society. Nothing can be very wrong with a country than has had the good sense to applaud his promotion. As a *parvenu* Jewnius, Bernard has a parodist's eye for the integuments of bourgeois society; he knows and confesses himself to be an outsider, but he is also a fan of common decency, notably impatient with those incapable of civility. He has embraced many causes and teased the zealots of more than one can well count, but what he holds dear above all is the occasion to be eloquent about them.

On Jewish topics he has been singularly cautious in his outspokenness. The article on Jeremy Isaacs'* 'gospel' is a typical text; it attacks Isaacs' critics by deriding their excessive indignation, thus seeming to align itself with the rational faction, but – and this is a typical British trope – he then less deplores Channel 4's assault on Christian credulities than the intemperate style in which it has been couched. The tone in which he sneers at Isaacs' show is that reserved by classy Jews for manifest kikes. He defends Christianity on behalf of Christians too reticent to say aloud what one Jew is rarely afraid to say to another.

Bernard's regular parade of his own stylish literacy is comically cousin to that of John Simon, another 'foreigner' who makes particular play of the inelegances and solecisms of prosaic native sons, especially academics. This careful audacity relies on the civility of the cultivated:

---

* At that time, Isaacs was the chief executive of the recently formed Channel 4.

they must accept reproach for their faults without violent response or lose their claim to be cultured. Anyone who tries literally to swat the gadfly announces himself to be no gentleman. Bernard likes to put people in their places and they are often the places from which he accuses them of originating; hence he once called Charlie Clore 'a Polish Jew'; although C.C. was, in fact, born in England, of parents from Lithuania.

B.L. has been persistent and Philippic in denouncing Communist inhumanity, but there is something in the ostentation of his rhetoric which, in Ronnie Harwood's phrase, 'lets them know he is there'. We come to admire the writer's nerve more than we sympathise with the victims; what remains of his charges is the echo of righteous hooves. One has the feeling that the paramount purpose of his galloping cadences is that readers should miss him if he fails to appear in regular print (he once told me that he found it easier to be eloquent three times a week than merely once). The jaundiced Jeremiah makes himself as indispensable as the little patch of yellow in Proust's Vermeer without which, like Turner's touch of red, the whole picture would lose focus. His disappearance would cause a commotion, not because we love his person but because we have become addicted to his rococo verbosity. His shadow is more substantial than the man.

In *The Journalists*, Arnold Wesker was clever in one cardinal phrase: what all journalists have in common is the question, 'Who does he think he is?' He was right to depict the crawling vanity of those critics of the world who are themselves subject to the capricious tyranny of their employers. Sadly, Wesker lacked the wit with which to Levin his pie. He failed to observe the journalists' essential dilemma: none but a very few dare show initiative likely to displease their editors. The hack may know everything, but has small use for it unless it gets the editor's nod.

Nick Tomalin was probably justified in claiming (to Stanley Price) that he had kept his youth by refusing to canvass for executive office. Certainly he wrote one of the most memorable articles in modern journalism: 'The General goes Zapping Charlie Cong' alerted us for the first time, in 1966, to the altered nature of post-war war. It proclaimed the big-gaming brutality of a campaign that many, including Levin and Kingsley Amis, wanted to us to believe was a necessary and righteous commitment. What we remember from Nick's piece (written when he was in his mid-thirties) is the ignoble nature of uneven combat, without a vestige of the wary respect for enemies to be seen, sometimes, in conventional warfare: there was no way in which Hector could meet Achilles in SE Asia. Because unpoetic, journalism is the only style apt to describe an exercise in callousness of the kind that turned quondam doughboys into whooping killers. The American heli-gunships were like airborne trucks full of Nazi SA men, bullying the streets in search of defenceless prey.

The training received by GIs may not have enabled them to beat the Vietcong, but it has certainly removed their civilian scruples. Governments in the past have been conscious – the Romans conspicuously the first – of the need to resettle disbanded legions. The menace of mass unemployment makes it very dangerous to instruct men in the use of arms, break down their reluctance to kill, and then return them to the streets of their own cities. The American way made it unlikely that any general effort would be made to accommodate those who had fought, unsuccessfully, in a losing and loudly undeclared war. Since most of the rank and file soldiers were peacetime candidates for unemployment, the war seemed temporarily to alleviate the social situation, not least by generating a boom in a good number of industries.

The cunning which enabled L.B.J. to prosecute the hostilities, without any formal declaration licensed by congress, sanctioned the public never to admit the war to consciousness as an act of common patriotic policy. It became the loudest surreptitious operation in the history of democracy. As those who wanted to nuke Hanoi complained, it was never waged with all available force. By refusing officially to admit the source and pathology of the violence which came home to spot whole swathes of the US population, America failed to take the chance to grow up. It is foolish, however, to suppose that anti-bodies have not been formed. By the use of predominantly mechanical means, the US is likely to avoid any further conscription. The Russians may not have better morale, or higher efficiency; unsupervised by a critical press, their soldiers can be driven with immeasurably greater callousness and indifference to casualties. Without a popular creed, enforced either by fantasy, as is the case with the Iranians, or by a totalitarian *apparat* like the Russian and Chinese, what democratic state can keep men in the field, unless they are specialists and paid accordingly? Any willing *levée en masse* depends on a conviction that the motherland is in peril. The alternative is recourse to specialised machine-minding mercenaries to save the sum of things.

Mumford: '*The army is in fact the ideal form towards which a purely mechanical system of industry must tend*'. Nuclear warfare is the epitome of automation. Salvation and perdition are available from the same merchants. Science makes God superfluous. Automation, civil or military, will procure the wholesale irrelevance of the working class as fighting men.

Was the Alexandrian *Pharos* always kept alight or only on gala occasions? It smacks more of an advertisement than a safety precaution. McLeish thinks it was lit by woodfires; is oil not more likely?

The Roman republic was doomed to dwindle triumphantly into a tyranny as soon as the legions began to be rewardingly successful. What first enriched the state soon came to subvert it: the rewards of war, under a winning general, were immeasurable greater than the dividends of peace. Returning legions had to be accommodated with land and favours lest they turn trained swords against the institutions for which they were supposedly fighting. Victories can be as menacing to social stability as defeat. Cannae united Romans of all classes; Zama never did. The booty of the 'patriotic' Punic Wars was negligible compared to that distributed among the legions after the eastern, loot-laden campaigns of Sulla and Pompey.

The emperors who came to be acclaimed by their victorious troops were obliged to lead them to the treasury which their spears, never their votes, could open. Nuclear weapons seem to make that sort of thing impossible. There is never likely to be another Ike, a general so popular that he was graced with civil laurels. No individual will be responsible for triumph in an atomic war; if such a thing were to happen, only the sorry plaudits of the well-bunkered will live to greet it. There can, fortunately perhaps, be no heroes in a nuclear conflict, only survivors who are likely to revert to scavenging savagery.

Gene Taft, poor guy, told me that Mick Jagger was my fan, though he did so more to remind me that he knew Mick than because Jagger supposedly knew me. I cannot believe that he has ever heard of me. Gene talked with anxious admiration about M.J. and was glad to declare that he was a shrewd stock exchange analyst and a regular reader – as everyone knows but I had to be told – of the *Wall Street Journal*. Gene had had a project with M.J., about an entertainer who fathers an illegitimate child and gets to know him years later, et cetera. Taft bounced back with the idea of adapting the plot to fit Baryshnikov and canvassed the notion of my doing the necessary tailoring. Gene was often let down by alleged friends. Very sore and broke, he took us to La Scala and ordered half a pound of caviar.

Although physically ill-favoured, he was obsessed with *bella figura*. He drove his sister's tacky Japanese car, but could not resist fancy gear. Having bought that $900 fur coat, he suffocated in his extravagance. He seemed so confident of setting up *Love Affair* or whatever he proposed to call it that he behaved with reckless insolence in response to Orion's comments. He was such a bold advocate of what I had written with a leaden heart and a light touch that I assumed him to have Plan B. I left California after that visit to Warren in his warren with confidence that the picture would be set up within a matter of months. Since then I have heard nothing.

Gene has been directing a picture for Tri-Star, the outfit master-minded by Sydney Pollack. Gene had never directed before and was nearly fired, but he has hung in there and is now editing and all that. The likelihood is that I shall never hear from him again, but he did swear to me that he had a quarter of a million in the property. Perhaps he will rise again and, God help us, direct the thing himself. The sound of his voice will send me into mild shock. I am not proud of finding him so distasteful; he has always been patient, courteous and appreciative. He compares rather well with certain old friends in the Biz who let you down with comic predictability.

Once Bob Shapiro, for now eminent instance, was let go by the William Morris Office, he announced instantly that his first project as producer would be *Roses, Roses...* I do not recall being given any choice in the matter. He was promptly rejected as superfluous by his old buddy 'Laddie' (Alan Ladd jr) whose bumpy ride at Fox had been eased by Shapiro's massage. Laddie had very recently become a potent potentate as a result of the success of *Star Wars*, which he and Gareth Wigan had wanted to cancel halfway through shooting; it was way over budget and had no stars. The troika headed by Laddie, which been on the point of ignominious ejection, found themselves sitting on a gold mine.* It did nothing to enhance the prospects of *Roses, Roses...* or Master Shapiro: once empowered, Laddie had no wish for the company of someone who had been the witness of his distress. Gareth relieved Bob of his claim to my script and sent it to Bob Altman, who liked it very much until, some months later, uninvigorated by the proposed budget, the great Hollywood maverick ceased, like any canting creep, to have any time for it at all.

When Shapiro was appointed Head of Production at Warner Brothers, then President, before becoming abruptly ex-President, he neither promoted *Roses, Roses...* nor he did he propose any new subject to me. Once, in London, when I was treating Paul and Sarah to dinner at *The White Elephant*, Bob had the bill sent to WB.

---

* The trio had previously been so ill-regarded that Frank Yablons, whom they had displaced as head honcho, is said to have put it about that 'when you call the studio and ask for an ass-hole, three guys rush to pick up the phone'.

Robin Jordan has slippery possibilities as the maquette for a fictional character of singular mutability. When he called me last August with that air of tracking down an unsuspecting mark, he had pretty well abandoned the American accent he sported when living, on Staten Island, with the 'great wife' whom he no longer knows. He is now making lots of money, he told me, quietly, and lives in Chelsea with his Argentinian lady. He introduced me to her during that rather odd Romantic Festival at the QE Hall after posing larkily as an anonymous autograph collector.

I was always easily deceived by him; so were others: Hugh Trevor-Roper was markedly galled at having selected him for the Christchurch scholarship open only to a selected squad of Carthusians. George Turner, who denied me access to their number, had made Robin a school monitor, apparently as the result of a Freudian error: the current housemaster of Lockites told me that my name had been submitted by Harry March, but Robin was, at the time, a Christian (he sang in the choir). R. was a seducer with the lineaments of an ascetic. At once aloof and ingratiating, he stood apart (detesting the JTC, for instance), but he was eager for a certain kind of recognition. Of all my contemporaries, he was the likeliest recruit for the secret service of almost any nation or ideology. He loved the intimacy of the shared, almost imperceptible, glance more than the shared bed. He laid hands on you – he often assessed people's biceps – with sympathetic complicity: he did not want you so much as to be you.

Trevor-Roper spoke of Robin's 'falling into bad company'. Clever enough not quite to have faith in his own excellence, he relied on his looks rather than his brains, the mark of the uneasy dandy. He derived his self-esteem from comely winsomeness. His reluctances resembled those of Jonathan Miller, who avoided the limelight till the house was full. One of Robin's heroes was Roy Farran, a cut-price Lawrence of Arabia, who combined publicity and secrecy. Robin's disappearances and resurrections parodied those of that long-forgotten rogue celebrity. He wanted to be a hero in a battle where his opponent in particular thought well of him. In the boxing ring, he sported a regard of insinuating, if bloody, intimacy with his adversary. He was fascinated by the great heavyweights of whom he would never be one and knew in which round Joe Louis floored Max Schmeling.

His glance made allusion to some secret he had guessed about you and was too tactful to mention aloud. He alone realised how deeply I was scarred by my petty persecution in Lockites, which he had done nothing, at the time, to alleviate. Was he perhaps *envious*? His pleasure was in the close attention which amounts, almost, to impersonation. His half-brother was a fugitive criminal, a Heathcliffean figure to whom Robin's schoolboy propriety can be seen as a masked tribute. After Oxford, Robin went to South America and, he gave me to understand, became a bodyguard to a dictator. Robert Carn, in *A Wild Surmise*, is closely modelled on him.

Going to the US in the sixties turned him on to whisky and women. When I met him again, in 1968, he was married to a nurse and earnestly involved in Biafran relief. Now a zealot for humanitarianism, he was working in advertising. He was amused, if not embarrassed, to hear that I was still married to the same woman. He once wrote a novel, of which he sent me some uninspired pages. His best fiction was himself. *What's Become of Robin (since he gave us all the slip)?*

There is an incongruous similarity between Chares (who took ten years to build the Colossus of Rhodes) and Fabergé: the exaggerator and the miniaturist have a common insolence in their incommensurate meticulousness.

The bad loser is the solipsist refuted.

John Erickson writing, in *The Road to Stalingrad*, about Stalin's Terror: Corps commander Gorbatov, after a brief appearance 'before grinning judges' was sentenced to fifteen years imprisonment.

A woman in the Chelsea deli dropped several pound notes to the floor. 'Lady,' an American said, 'you're shedding your leaves.'

Bad Books, a story about the rupture between Amis and Wain. W.W. Robson, c. 1963: 'One thing you can say for them, they do have a good sense of humour; except for Wain.'

Things that we shall never, never know: did Chirac vote for Mitterrand against Giscard? My bet is yes.

Au bout de longues années, ce ne sont que les anciens ennemis qui s'embrassent.

27.4.84. We went to George's lecture at King's College in the Strand. G. introduced me to a man from the *Observer* who had escaped from the poisonous atmosphere of the office for a whiff of the real dust. He said he was a good writer, but a better sub. Trelford has the support of all the journalists; they regard proprietor 'Tiny' Rowlands as mad, mainly because incapable of a sustained argument. The capacity for sticking to the point is typical of those who solicit judgment, rarely of those who deliver it. Men of wealth and power are not disposed to be trapped in inconsistency. For them, language is a cudgel. The *Observer* man said that Trelford, some fifteen years younger than he, chose him as a friend when he came from editing a paper in Africa. I was startled by the element of calculation. Do people regularly go about deciding whom it would be a good career move to like?

George was introduced by Professor Stewart Sutherland, to be distinguished from Stuart, a psychologist who suffered a breakdown and has been the same ever since. The lectures were to commemorate F.D. Maurice, a Victorian theologian evicted from professorial chairs with impressive frequency. George made a wry comparison between himself and the bold pariah who dared to suggest that the damned may not, after all, suffer eternal torment. G.'s affectations of unworthiness were belied by flawless performance. He read from a text, but made it seem like the polite score set before a blind musician; even when it seemed that he had mis-sorted the sheets, one had the feeling that it was a tease. His method is incantatory; enunciating the English language with emphatic courtesy, he refuses to avail himself of colloquial facilities. The journey from the thought to its expression is indicated by the little smile on that moony face.

How far did G.'s happy lamentation over the unruliness of language go beyond the Pauline observation about the looseness of the tongue? He gloated over the boundless *disponibilité* of speech, which issues in 'Anything can be said about anything'. Does the scandal amount to much more than the insolence of negation, the hookiness of adjectives etc.? 'Whereof one cannot speak' is the topic G. is most tempted to broach. He contrasted the limits imposed by the physical – the 'certainty' that terrestrial man will never do a one-minute mile or leap fifteen feet upwards, unaided – with the limitlessness of the conceivable in speech. He sees something perhaps lethal, certainly delicious, in man's verbosity. Who but a rhetorical spellbinder is so conscious of where words can lead, might lead, should not lead, are bound to lead? All the possibilities of education and its perversion thrill George to minatory eloquence. The preacher and the demagogue, the builder and the wrecker, the king and his shadow (the assassin) conspire in the same language, announce and denounce, corrupt and edify. The revulsion which excited Swift's 'Celia, Celia, Celia shits' impels G. to revel in the golden ordure in the dark shaft of discourse.

Man can never be conclusively happy because he can never have the last word, which is G-d's. The immortal offers no evidence of its existence;

it has nothing to prove. The eternal is distinct from the unending; it has no extension.

28.4.84. Imagine the discreet pleasure of the director of the Irrigation Service whose longevity kept Cavafy from succeeding him. Did the poet have any ambition to reach the top of that short ladder before falling into retirement? Who can resist a pang of envy (the silly luxury of the comfortable) at the solitude of the clerkly genius with his narrow cosmopolitanism? For the outsider at the heart of the matter, deprivation doubled for election, solitude for liberty. The consolations that petty cash could buy, in café and brothel, were a guiltless aspect of the Levantine world.

Cavafy had no interest in mainland Greece, no sense of exile from alternative presents; he looked forward to the yesterdays that he drew so immediately to him. Believing that this facility was evidence of unrealised gifts as a historian, he aimed his perception along the steady sight of a remembered dream, or fact. The bumboy becomes remarkable, beautiful, because chosen, like an epithet or the shirt in that window. The opulence of C.'s imagery makes no distinction between glass bead and precious jewel. Mutability is the symptom less of the futility of human ambitions than of their mystery.

Everything can be said of anything, but only by certain people.

If there were permanence and certitude, there could be only mathematics.

If there were no time, what kind of a place could there possibly be?

His father could not tolerate scoundrels. He often ate in the Oak Room at the Plaza. One day a man came and sat at an adjacent table. G. said, 'That man is a gunman.' His father reproached him for being a fantasist. The man soon left and another came and replaced him. It was Lucky Luciano, for whom the earlier man had been a scout. G.'s father called the waiter and demanded that the gangster be evicted. On being denied, he refused ever again to set foot in the Oak Room. Please, did he have another globe?

Israel is a rhetorical rather than a political or religious *topos*. It commands admiration or rage, the passionate involvement of so many people because it is a turn of speech made into reality. The drama and the misfortune of Israel is her transfiguration in the world's grammar; she fails to be a country like any other because she – is that the right pronoun, is there one? – cannot be pronounced in the same bland, territorial tone.

If Christianity had spread eastwards, how weird and improbable it would now seem to the polytheistic and tolerant West!

We are quicker to forgive Guy Burgess than Anthony Blunt; the latter behaved no worse but the former is more fun. Who chooses to impersonate a lugubrious prig who knows all about Poussin but had nothing amusing to say? Guy B. is a folk-hero because camp strikes us as entertaining. Box office has replaced morals. Nixon may have been a better president than Jack Kennedy, but JFK belongs in the pantheon, tricky Dick in the bestiary; JFK was a pretty fellow, Richard Nixon a five o'clock shadowy operator.

The play will last as long as possible; there will be no intermission.

Israelis cannot live quietly among their neighbours, never draw easy curtains, belonging as the others belong, localised as they are local. The Jewish state, whatever its courage and ingenuity, will never live with gates open, doors unlocked, its edifice unchallenged and unresented, never. The Jew has a mundane distinction that supplants metaphysical election. He may no longer imagine or believe himself chosen (though some do) but he is never foursquare with his fellows. Uniquely placed in the estimate of others, he rides on unlikely odds, cheered and jeered in the same alien breath. There is something inescapably anti-democratic in the persistence of the Jews. If votes were all that mattered, they would have been counted out of existence long ago.

30.4.84. Something keeps me from tackling the little radio piece I promised the mini-boss more than a year ago. I am not a stranger to such petty procrastination. My lifelong resentment of gardening, which I should like to like, can be put down to my failure, in my first term at Charterhouse, Oration Quarter 1945, to send for my ration book. Why was it not sent with me, or after me, and why did my mother never guess that it might be needed? Today a telephone call would rectify the omission. Back then I was haunted by the knowledge that I should write for the damned thing and by the certainty that failure would lead to a humiliation I could easily avoid, save that it was inevitable. When my postponements became chronic, HAM sentenced me to work for many hours in the house garden. I hated the authorised leer of the baize-aproned gardener. Sullen rage was a liberation from the dutifulness that had made me the polite creature of my elders. No longer willing to endure the blameless-ness of pre-adolescence, I found my sin in omission, the dullest access to damnation. There is still almost always one small thing that I have not done, some promise whose consummation I delay. So now I am faced with a pleasant task and an uncensorious taskmaster and I dither, even on a Monday morning, impatient for Porlockian pretexts for another postponement. I suppose I await the reproaches of the patron whose impatience will give me that gritty incentive without which the swine can never have their pearls.

The fantasy of being a film director has lost its glamour in the usage of time. I once imagined divine powers of ordinance and ordnance, the artil-lery that would enable me to force my world on the world, make craters in the smooth surface of mundane indifference. I have learnt that autocracy is a dubious dream. The director waits for others as often as he imposes his authority on them. He is an artist, if he is, whose art is compro-mised by contingency. Everything is too mechanically conditioned for the dream to be realised without explanations and compromises. Fancy becomes drudgery, spontaneity laggard. The director is an artist after the work has been done and before it begins; while it is in progress, he is cheerleader and sergeant-major, cadger and Ali Baba, sovereign and pretender. He dreads the tantrums not only of the stars but also of the sparks, even the extras, the hairdresser, the driver. The target for endless ambitions and resentments, he can never look to anyone else for reassur-ance. His greatest virtue the capacity to keep his own counsel, to excite no suspicion of inadequacy or disapproval, he must give the impression that he knows exactly what he is doing, while at the same time being open to suggestions which he can make his own, by agreeing to them. The fear that possesses the writer, that his script will be mutilated or mispronounced, means nothing to the director; when it comes to allaying his dread that the thing is not good enough, or might be better, nothing is sacred. The director may claim that he is concerned only with quality; his paramount concern is to finish before his magic and the producer's treasure are spent. His credibility depends on appearing tireless. His closest associates will do their angelic best to supply him with comforts that will please or reassure, gossip that amuses, flattery that sustains, in order that his potency be bolstered. He must be tireless, beneficent and, if jovial, thunderous: better ridiculous than pedestrian or, lamest of all, sorry. Familiar with solitude, indifferent to unpopularity, aware of the endless ways in which his work can be frustrated or sabotaged, he may, like Bismarck, cry but never on anyone's shoulder. His ability to intimidate makes disliking him into the flip side of fidelity; he will then continue to be served by those who wish him no good. All malice must be converted into pitiless efficiency. He is there to supply the last word. If he never said 'cut', nothing would ever end; without 'action', nothing would ever begin. Approval and disapproval are his cardinal business. He can be all kinds of a bastard, but he must appear to know what he wants or as much as he needs. Other people will help to win him fame, without his being markedly creative, so long as he can lure or bully actors, technicians, writers, into contributions which they will later applaud him for having accepted. His aura must convince them that they could never have done it without him.

5.5.84. We rarely disagree about films; but I liked *Un Amour de Swann*; Beetle was unconvinced by the playing, bored by the *longueurs*. I was undisturbed by the ineptitude of Delon, the piggy plumpness of Odette (nothing like the fine courtesan of the original's original, Laure Hayman), the inelegant silliness of Forcheville, who should have been a threateningly virile rival, not an unhorsed chevalier in hired pink. There was a commanding authenticity at the heart of the thing, a love story and a story about love, even though it concerned only desire and scarcely touched on the pleasures of affection, trust and common purpose. The film concentrated on possession, the sexual correlative of money. Cash was in evidence only with Swann, who actually produced notes; the others relied on credit.

Charlus, inadequately charming and falsely slim, depended on his prodigious personality and insolent attributes. Master of ceremonies, private and public, he made appreciation into an erotic transaction: he would advance a man's career if the man accepted his own advances. Disdain for trade made sexual transactions a deliciously perverse business. Charlus was more exquisite than Swann; aristocracy, however gross, excuses activities which the mere gentleman, who must rely on a code to sustain his status, can never permit himself. The warning Bazin gives Swann, that he and Oriane will not be able to receive him with his wife, if he marries Odette, could/need never have been given to an equal. No marriage, if solemnised by the Church, however ill-considered, could ever disqualify am authentic grandee from the society into which he was born. Swann may have been a member of the Jockey Club (not mentioned in the film), but he was never among those who granted membership. Exquisite manners made him eligible for the highest circles; their tailored confection declared that he was at a tangent to them.

The great quality of the film, despite the limitations of the boudoir atmosphere, is that it understands and depicts, understands by depicting, the discrete nature of male sexuality. It sees the female, through Swann's greedy, polite gaze, as a distinct, distressing species. Excitement and dismay are the same thing as Swann realises that love is pitiless, tasteless even. The curiosity excited in him by the thought of Odette's lesbian *passades* is part of a desire to know things which have nothing to do with knowledge in the common sense: her provenance is as fascinating as that of an *objet d'art*. The drawing of the Rhodian coin which Swann brings to Oriane is an enlargement of an artefact from an island renowned for realistic images, votive offerings, of which the story we are seeing is a modern counterpart, tribute to the demanding heartlessness of Aphrodite. Oriane *aime bien* Swann and yet she remains callously calm when advised of his imminent death. Immortals cannot lament, or alter, the mortality of their admirers, nor witness its end.

The film's erotic skill lies in its close-up of the male condition, at once magisterial and powerless. Swann's hope of a cure, his belief that he may be recovering from the improper, undeserved passion he feels for a woman not of his *genre* makes him pathetic in a way that his cancer, about which he has no illusions, fails to match. He has a stoic endurance, even humour, in his last days, something the affliction of love never evoked. In love, he is desperate; in the face of death, ironic, almost *delivered*. As every essayist who has been to Dieppe will not fail to mention, *l'amour* and *la mort* have continental affinities, lost in translation. Swann's visit to the brothel is done as well as it could be; the *pissoir* and the bordello are declared, without prurience, to double for the *bistrot* and the *Grand Vefour*, serving adjacent appetites. When selfish, sex is a form of excretion, though top of the range.

Jeremy Irons has an inventive insouciance which deserves the recognition it disdains to solicit. The direction is not always as happy, but the scene in which Swann seeks the third party who is in Odette's house when they are about to make love and who is seen for a moment at the front door, fighting to escape, before we realise that it is Swann himself whose image we are observing, is perfectly presented; not least because it seems that there is something accidental in the eagerness with which we are pitched into imagining that the fugitive third person is before our eyes. The counterpoint between Swann's pursuit of Odette and his appalled pursuit of her past, and the insolent appetites of Charlus, whose references are so grand that others are deemed lucky to come within his condescending scope, is somewhat misguided; the vitality of the heterosexual obligation seems so much more demanding, necessary at least in the explanation of Gilberte's very existence, that Swann looks to be caught in the web of being; by contrast, the perversities of Charlus are a celebration of the negative, a refusal of the great and ruinous connection. Selfishness, however grand the self, ducks the drama into which Swann finds himself pitched. Manners give the outsider a way of adhering perfectly to the surface of things; their perfection makes him aware of the alien in him: who but an outsider takes such pains to avoid the smallest solecism? He speaks the *boulevardier*'s language with due propriety; he lacks the *argot* to be at home in the gutter.

6.5.84. The readthrough of *Sleeps Six*. There was a traffic jam in the Cromwell Road. I feared I should be late. A private hotel had had its top two floors burned out. A propped fire-engine had its ladder to the blackened place. Five people were said to be missing, though they might not have been in their rooms. I reached the church hall, not very late, and was introduced to Ben Kingsley and Diane Keen and was matey with (Sir) Jeremy Child. Kingsley has brilliant eyes and a humour that their glitter announces and almost excuses. He read well, with that capacity for hinting at possibilities which marks actors who will prosper in rehearsal. Diane was reported to be beautiful but wore the unassuming mien of a working woman, tracksuit trousers, in some kind of velour, sun-lamplit face, dark, confident not very large eyes. She played ordinary without trying. Jim spoke rather lengthily, paying over-kind attention to the text while salting the sugar with slightly sarcastic allusions to my presence. I have nothing but gratitude for his enthusiasm; but we do have a history.

Do television people understand the place of glamour in the cinematic representation of desire. Jim is afraid of facing beauty and stammers in its presence. He treats everybody with loud camaraderie, but flinches from intimacy. His genialities promise melancholy. He wants to be an artist as well as a tradesman, but makes it clear how like journalism television is: the best work is briefly saluted and then all but forgotten. He has refused big money for small, unworthy jobs ($100,000 for six weeks recently) and Maggie thinks him a fool for his fastidiousness. They have lived meagrely, and survived; the threat of affluence opens a gap.

Lunch with G.S. at the Savile with a candidate he wants me to sponsor. Tom Rosenthal joined us for coffee. He was happy to tell us how long one has to wait to join the Garrick. I said that I did not care to serve four years of *attente* in order to join Jack Lambert in the gents. T.R. is held to be very pompous; he seemed more swollen than grand. Although he went to Pembroke, he was wearing a St John's college summer shirt. I suspected he had acquired it at the Harvie and Hudson sale. He said he had seen me in *Epicene*, in 1952, in the college gardens. That he was then a schoolboy advertised that I was older than he, though his bald, bellied and bearded person looked otherwise. He was a loyal friend of Michael Ayrton, not even flinching from publishing *The Midas Consequence*. We agreed (having been joined by Michael Le Marchant, once Michael's dealer) that M.A. was top of the second class. With rare gifts as a draughtsman, he lacked a colourman's instinct; there was always something wished for, perhaps too considered, about his choice of pigment. The paintings at Agnew's were almost all extremely nice. One sensed the influence of forgotten peers such as Rex Whistler. A biography of M., which would neither proclaim a genius nor decorate a reputation, excites and alarms G. Can Elisabeth be expected to relish a cocksman's progress? I have no tenacious desire to remain on close terms with E. or her progeny. Her tone after Michael's death assumed that she was very close to us, whether it was true or not. I liked and enjoyed M., because of similar interests and attitudes and because of the access he offered, by proxy, to a world never open to me. Yet his sense of exclusion, or eviction, was keener, and more rueful, than mine. G.'s candidate, Gordon Whattles, is doing research at New College and will doubtless be given a fellowship shortly. He is handsome, a member of Leander and altogether a coming man, though so burdened with abilities that he lacks any spontaneity. He is researching into the conversion of atheism into deism in the last years of the *ancien régime.*

21.5.84. My Byron evening at Athens College brought a good turn-out of Greek dignitaries and diplomatic stringers. The British ambassador, Perry Rhodes, limped in with his nice wife; he had injured his knee playing tennis. The Finnish ambassador was with a couple of Baltic female friends. Athens is still a village, at least for senior residents. They were there because it was one of the things people were going to; another was taking place in Kolonaki square, where the ex-foreign minister was billed to attack the government. The Greek orator is still an entertainer capable of theatrical panache. Supporters of Athens College are rabidly hostile to the Papandreou government, which has advertised disapproval of the privileged status of the private schools of which A.C. is the most conspicuous. The college's charitable status has been challenged even in Mrs Vlachou's paper: an article deplored the recruitment of the musical prodigy Dimitri Sgouros in order to attract funds. John Summerskill was in a state of apprehensive rage. He called Elena V. on the Saturday morning and was little gratified by her response. Despite the gibes of the socialists, the college is over-subscribed; many ministers and members of their entourages are graduates. Few leading figures in finance or government have failed to pass through its gates.

The college was founded by exiles from Cairo and Istanbul. Mainland Hellas had a poor standard of education. Its apathy appalled the sophisticated diaspora. Recently Athens had a golden opportunity to enrich itself by becoming the financial centre of the Middle East. Refugees from Beirut poured in and raised real estate prices spectacularly. The Greeks failed to draw the dividends of their neighbours' calamities. They lacked the flexibility, or opportunism, to elasticise their economic laws in order to admit the flow of capital which could have benefited them greatly. The Pasok government, so the businessmen say, is too full of ideologues and academics (many summoned from abroad by the ex-professor Andreas) to be prepared to pot the sitting ducks available to it. The Socialists have been hampered by their scruples on one hand, their greed on the other: determined to tax the rich as vigorously as they can, they know that Greek millionaires have always been resourceful in evading whatever nets have been spread to trawl their wealth. The means adopted have succeeded only in punishing the guileless. The charges on ostentatious wealth, such as yachts, have driven the shipping magnates to foreign harbours. The descendants of those who devoted their fortunes to the war of independence now summer in Turkish ports and enjoy their courtesies.

The Roumanian-born Greek next to me on the flight home said that Pasok had closed down the country. A gourmet of fiercely anti-socialist purpose and passion, he regarded the Greeks with exasperated affection. In the video business, duplicating, dubbing and packaging material for the Middle Eastern market, he would not have them anywhere near his plant. He disliked Arabs and would work for them only so long as they kept out of his way. He respected the Israelis for their demanding competence. He had seen a good deal of suffering and cruelty; it had left him hostile to all ideologies. With no wish to trade on the infirmities of the destitute, he could not abide being in India, where his partners had seen the chance to make millions from the cheap labour in Bombay. The beggars had turned his stomach; although he had no large plans for their redemption, he could not live among them without seeing them, as some entrepreneurs did. He did not propose to stay in Greece after the business was sold (he hoped to make a million within a year or two), nor did he fancy the US. He favoured London where, he said, one ate extremely well.

While homegrown rich Greeks have less open disdain for their compatriots, their cosmopolitanism announces a need for more admiration than their small country can offer. They are wary of the *laos* whose welfare Andreas is eager to cherish and whose votes are his confidence. The Greeks are divided, undisciplined, obtuse, and unreliable, qualities mirrored in their leaders. They will always find a way to survive, if sometimes at the expense of others. The Greek is a fiercely loyal family man, as well as tyrannical, selfish and unfaithful. Even someone like A., who does not speak the language, is marked by the social grammar which lends priority to the first person.

The Summerskills are dominated by the rich men and calculating women on whose beneficence their standing is based; there is no bread on Greek waters without strings, or hooks, attached. They must command financial support in order to merit the respect of the governors; to hold their heads up, they grovel for funds. John has no administrative assistant; he writes his letters like a student, with someone on hand to translate. The Summerskills have been in Greece for half a dozen years, but they have no facility with the language. I suspect that they are regularly misunderstood: we found no room reserved in the hotel in Rhodes where they promised us an obsequious reception; nor were their tickets waiting for them, as some *armateur* was said to have arranged, at the Flying Dolphin. They claim famous, well-heeled acquaintance in all parts of the world without enjoying any reliable favours. Melina Mercouri is the latest to seek to exert her influence on behalf of some friend's child; and she is not used to rejection. John has to be absent at the weekend or he is forever answering the telephone. Since taking up the presidency, he has become a steady drinker.

As he drove us across town to Tourkolimani, where he had lunch before taking the boat to Hydra, he drank beer from a can stowed by the gear-shift. He had the dexterity that comes of long recourse to one-handed steering. The strain of his position has carved cracks in the corners of his mouth. There is no easy time in his day, no reliable laurels on which to repose. His dismissal by governor Reagan from the presidency of San Francisco State was anything but dishonourable; none whose opinions mattered to him failed to respect his endurance; but now his enemy is President of the United States. John wishes resources of moral and political strength on Mondale, whom he met on a recent tour. Do they hope for an ambassadorship if Mondale is elected? Mimi may be a La Follette (if repetition is any proof, she is *certainly* a La Follette), but she is too antique and insufficiently rich for diplomatic preferment. There is something warm and impressive about her, but her vanity is pretentious and absurd. She gave us a nice room in the presidential lodge, but she had to be pressed for something to eat, although we had flown a long way at their invitation and had no transport.

In the restaurant *El Pescador*, on the Avenida Ortega y Gasset, a man sat waiting nervously, but with dignity. He looked at his watch and waited afresh. At last, a plain woman, a good deal younger than himself, came and sat down. She had a narrow face and a manly haircut. Something in her charmless despair spoke of desertion and betrayal. She was inconsolable and immune to pity. The man took her hand from time to time and stroked the flesh adjacent to the thumb. He made no speech of sympathy or distraction. He sat with her as though she were a sentient corpse, beyond retrieval but deeply loved and regretted. It seemed that knowledge of the woman's state passed between them without any call for speech. The father, if that is what he was, became more and more tender as the meal continued, without ever seeking to encourage or cheer the woman whose dry anguish appeared to be sealed into her character, not the consequence of any specific misfortune.

Why has Arnold Wesker been largely rejected by a cultural establishment which, for a while, seemed eager to embrace him? The fall of individuals is an aspect of an unconscious social scheme for dealing with the kind of criticism which, taken seriously, might lead to self-doubt. There is a limit to the kind of things a society will allow, and even encourage, in the way of reproach. In their vanity, Raleigh and Byron dared to wager themselves against antagonists who outnumbered and outgunned them. The careers of illustrious scapegoats indicate the limits of insolence. Society becomes particularly resentful when its critics claim to have a world (or even happiness) elsewhere. Any establishment is frustrated by being unable to reach its critics. One may do most anything one pleases in England, but it had better be in England that he does it.

'Fat? She was like bring a friend, you know?'

Philby: the deceiver's abiding pleasure is the conviction that he is in charge.

The clever liar has sole custody of the truth.

He opened his lifelong rival's memoirs with trepidation. By the end, his worst fears had been confirmed: he was never mentioned.

Frederic Raphael
© Volatic Ltd 2018

Index